P9-AZU-354

WITHDRAWN

Protecting
Our Children on
the Internet

Jens Waltermann,
Marcel Machill (eds.)

Protecting
Our Children on
the Internet

Towards a New Culture
of Responsibility

Bertelsmann Foundation Publishers
Gütersloh 2000

Die Deutsche Bibliothek – CIP-Einheitsaufnahme

A data set for this title is available
at Die Deutsche Bibliothek.

© 2000 Bertelsmann Foundation Publishers, Gütersloh
Responsible: Dr. Marcel Machill, Jens Waltermann
Copy editor: Sabine Stadtfeld
Production editor: Christiane Raffel
Cover design: Tammen Werbeagentur, Osnabrück
Cover photos: Tony Stone / Zefa
Typesetting: digitron GmbH, Bielefeld
Print: Hans Kock Buch- und Offsetdruck GmbH, Bielefeld
ISBN 3-89204-474-0

Contents

Introduction

Jens Waltermann, Marcel Machill

"Think Big" is the slogan rightly used by those involved in developing a global approach to self-regulation. The finer points are crucial in the implementation of a self-regulatory system, counter to those involved in designing concrete systems. Whoever wishes to develop an internationally accepted system designed to ensure both the protection of minors and freedom of expression on the Internet must not regard these contrary statements as being incompatible.

The global Internet transcends borders and national authority. It requires a new approach to media policy based on self-regulatory initiatives, international cooperation and the integration of the multiplicity of interests found in politics, supervisory authorities, the Internet industry, civil liberties groups, child-protection organizations and criminal prosecution. Media policy must assign an entirely new role to the individual user. The Internet environment places control over which information and content the user sees into his own hands. The new medium does not depend on mediators such as publishing houses, television or radio stations, newspapers or the music industry. The Internet permits "mass communication" one to one. However, across the globe we are not prepared for such a fundamental shift of control. We must develop new regulatory mechanisms. We must call into question traditional regulation, frequently dispense with regulation altogether and, instead, put protection and selection mechanisms in the hands of the individual user. The new mechanisms must be designed with great precision, and they require a broad consensus of the players involved.

How can a filter system for problematic content on the Internet take account of the justified interests of civil liberties activists and representatives of groups calling for freedom of information at the same time as considering the equally justified fears of parents and teachers who do not wish to expose children to all types of content? How can such a system be conceived to enable intercultural use? These are key questions explored in this volume which ranges from fundamental aspects of self-regulation to detailed consideration on how a system is to be set up.

The new approach to media policy developed here is based on a new culture of responsibility in dealing with the media. At the center of this new culture are media users themselves. They are free to select from a rapidly growing number of informational, educational and entertainment-oriented offerings. To an ever increasing extent, they are forced to make choices.

"User empowerment" signifies a mixture of conveying the competence to choose and providing the technical instruments, such as Internet filters, that enable choice for the purpose of avoiding certain content. Few are so naive as to believe that the problems associated with the development of digital media may be solved through technical means alone. Filters are by no means a substitute for the supervision of children by their parents. And more important still: all users need education enabling them to deal confidently and critically with content in both the new and the "old" media.

10

The protection of minors and the safeguarding of the right to free expression have always been two primary aims of media policy. They remain at the top of the agenda even though new approaches must be developed to meet the special challenges of this medium. No single player, whether a media supervisory authority, a government or a large industrial company – can "manage" the Internet.

What is required is an intelligent combination of approaches – some established, some new – at various levels: the Internet industry must provide itself with rules ("codes of conduct") that are both flexible enough to deal with constant technological change and robust enough to ensure responsible conduct. It must place technical means such as filters at the disposal of users. It must provide hotlines to advise users and take up problems that have been identified. Through the prosecution of illegal content and its central role in education, the State provides fundamental pillars of the system. However, a key role is played by the individual citizen.

The challenge

In the Bertelsmann Foundation's "Memorandum on Self-regulation of Internet content" (chapter I of this volume) it is stated: The Internet will change the way people live. It offers extraordinary opportunities for enhancing creativity and learning, for trading and relating across borders, for safeguarding human rights, for realizing democratic values and for strengthening pluralism and cultural diversity.

In Germany, there is generally much less awareness of the opportunities offered by the Internet than in, for example, the USA or Australia. In the United Kingdom and Sweden, the Internet is a permanent feature of the school curriculum. Relatively speaking, Germany is a "developing country" on the Internet. However, the growth rates for Internet use are enormous in Germany as in many other countries. Any statistics relating to this area can only be a snapshot of a rapidly moving target. In the foreseeable future, a clear majority of the population will be "online."

Attitudes among the public at large with regard to problematic Internet content are clearly discernible even now. In Germany, as in the USA and Australia, a large majority of the population is convinced that "the Internet has attendant risks."[1] This basic skepticism is even more marked among people with Internet access (in Germany 90 percent of the respondents with Internet access compared to 81 percent of the general public; in the USA 86 percent to 85 percent; in Australia 78 percent to 76 percent). An important part of the skepticism is due to pornographic content. Conversely, problematic content or safety concerns are by no means the only reasons why people steer clear of the Internet. At 81 percent, the most common reason for not using the Internet was "I don't need it either professionally or privately."[2]

Protection against problematic content

Even if focusing on problematic content, the intention of this volume is by no means to promote a moralizing debate about restricting pornography in general. Adults have a fundamental right to decide on the content they wish to see. After all, pornography is for the most part, legal. And it should remain so. At the same time, parents

---

1   The results originate from a survey performed by the Allensbach Opinion Research Institute on behalf of the Bertelsmann Foundation. In June 1999, in each case, a representative cross-section of the population in Australia, Germany and the USA was asked for its opinion about Internet contents and possible safety mechanisms (cf. in this regard the contribution by Renate Köcher in the present volume).

2   ARD/ZDF-Arbeitsgruppe Multimedia: Nichtnutzer von Online: Einstellungen und Zugangsbarrieren. Media Perspektiven 8/1999, pp. 415–422.

should have the possibility of protecting their children from content they consider problematic. Internet content that is clearly illegal in most countries such as, for example, child pornography, is only a secondary concern here. In view of the vile crimes associated with the dissemination of child pornography via the Internet, the issue has rightly been at the center of attention of politics, law enforcement and the media. However, child pornography on the Internet is not a mass phenomenon. Law enforcement authorities must be put in a position to effectively track down child pornography on the Internet and to bring the perpetrators to trial. Within the "new culture of responsibility," the State and the police and their cooperation with the Internet industry play an important part (cf. in this regard Ulrich Sieber's contribution in this volume).

In respect of the much greater challenge – the creation of a new culture of responsibility vis-à-vis legal, but harmful content – state regulation can only play a secondary role. A picture of ambivalence emerges from opinion polls asking who is best placed to provide solutions to dealing with harmful content. In Germany as compared to the USA, the level of trust in the judicial system and law enforcement authorities – the classical "representatives" of regulation and enforcement – is still high. 32 percent of Germans name the judicial system and law enforcement as the appropriate bodies for assuming responsibility with regard to the Internet, 28 percent cite the political system. By contract, only 6 percent of Americans see the judicial system in a key role and only 2 percent place primary responsibility with the political system. In the USA, the assumption of responsibility is mainly considered to be the task of Internet users themselves (48 percent). In Germany, only 19 percent express this opinion. However, there is broad agreement among respondents in all three countries as regards their support for individually adaptable filter systems: 76 percent of the German population and 80 percent of the US population are of the opinion that filtering should be performed autonomously by users.

When we talk about Internet filters, we are well aware of the insufficient reliability of most filter systems presently used. A wealth of literature in the US provides critical appraisal of filter products. A study commissioned by the German Federal Ministry of Economics comes to the conclusion that "up to now, technical solutions for filtering content do not offer adequate protection" and that "a rating system tailored to the needs of the German or European cultural area does not exist."[3]

The opinion polls carried out in Australia, Germany and the USA revealed that striking cultural differences exist with regard to Internet content to be filtered. 43 percent of US respondents would, for example, wish to filter out images of nudity whereas these are only seen as problematic by 13 percent of Germans. Conversely, 61 percent of the Germans polled were in favor of blocking out scenes of violence. These are considered to be a problem by only 39 percent of Americans. A filter system must take into account differing needs in different cultural spheres and, ultimately, the needs of every individual user.

The proposal presented in this volume is for a filter architecture designed to include various adaptable elements rather than a single filter. The international initiative of leading Internet industry players ICRA (Internet Content Rating Association) has set itself the task of developing such a system.[4] What might such an architecture look like? The model outlined relies on both self-classification by content providers and active decision-making on the part of parents and guardians:

1. The providers of Internet pages (i.e. content providers) classify their offerings themselves (in the same way as a food manufacture

---

3 Protection of Minors and Filter Technologies on the Internet. A study undertaken by Secorvo Security Consulting GmbH on behalf of the Federal Ministry of Economics and Technology (December 1999).

4 www.icra.org

indicates on the packaging the ingredients in his product). The result of this classification is "poured" into an electronic label which can be read by commonly used browsers.

2. Users or socially relevant groups such as, for example, churches or trade unions then produce so-called filter templates. These templates reflect the ethical and moral beliefs of the particular group with regard to what a child should be allowed to see on the Internet and which content should be blocked. A differentiated approach according to age is possible here.

3. Parents or guardians select on their home computer (or at school) a filter template they trust.

4. The selected template can be combined with further positive or negative lists of websites.

5. While surfing on the Internet, the activated filter template read the labels produced under point 1 and only allow content to appear if the label corresponds to the filter template and the site is not included in an activated negative list.

6. A blacklist might include, for example, a list of websites containing Nazi propaganda. Since it will hardly be possible to encourage the providers of such pages to classify the content themselves, such content is filtered out separately if parents have activated the relevant list.

7. A positive list includes websites of which parents "definitely" approve (e.g. serious news magazines), even in cases where they would be filtered by the selected template.

A system to ensure the protection of minors and freedom of expression

Internet filters only represent one element within an overall system for ensuring the protection of minors and freedom of expression. In such a system – if it is to be effective internationally – there needs to be close cooperation between the Internet industry, users and the State extending beyond national borders (see figure below).

Figure 1

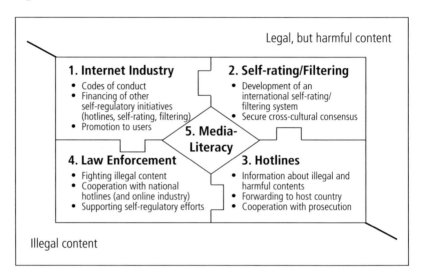

The Internet industry can improve the protection of minors by developing codes of conduct. These are intended to ensure that the providers of content and services on the Internet act in accordance with their social responsibility. Ultimately, the creation of such codes is in the interest of the industry itself since they reinforce trust of consumers in the Internet as a medium which is a prerequisite for the broad development of the Internet business. As a matter of principle, the State should not hinder self-regulatory mechanisms. Instead, legislators should create a legal framework that allows self-regulation to develop.

Self-regulation has its limits. Without support from the State, there is, for example, no guarantee that the providers of child pornography will be caught and punished. However, self-regulatory mechanisms might themselves make a contribution towards ensuring that criminals do not go unpunished for using the Internet for their own purposes. In the final analysis, self-regulation properly conceived reduces the need for state-determined standards which lack effectiveness and flexibility in dealing with a fast-changing Internet environment.

The use of hotlines can establish new routes of communication between users, in particular, parents, media-industry initiatives, and law enforcement authorities. A hotline enables users to respond to illegal Internet content by drawing attention to where it is to be found. The hotline receives the report and, if necessary, sets in motion a process of response. The response includes processing the report, providing the user with feedback and a decision about whether to forward the report to law enforcement or a self-regulatory authority.

Finally, the creation of suitable structures for criminal prosecution is the fourth level at which an integrated solution must be developed. These structures are necessary in order to combat computer crime and illegal Internet content, as in the case of child pornography, as well as to pursue instances of invasion of personal privacy, software and data piracy and, for example, money laundering via the Internet. Achieving this requires the establishment of central bodies or finely tuned coordination between existing authorities. An essential prerequisite here is that prosecutors have at their disposal adequate technical equipment and that they receive training on an on-going basis.

Users are the central element of the system. The instruments presented here confer greater responsibility on the users. Awareness campaigns and support are needed for hotlines and rating and filtering mechanisms to reach a broad audience. Particular responsibility falls to state education, and training should not only impart technical competence in dealing with computers and the Internet but, above all, the ability to handle media content critically.

About this volume

The reports and contributions as well as the Memorandum reflect a 15-month process of consultation and research on the basis of which the Bertelsmann Foundation developed a catalogue of recommendations for ensuring the protection of minors and freedom of speech on the Internet. The Foundation was supported in this efforts by a network of 36 experts. The members of this group come from Europe, North America, Asia and Australia as well as from an extremely wide range of interest groups: regulatory authorities, the Internet industry, politics, civil liberties associations, Internet initiatives, and academia. In September 1999, within the framework of the Internet Content Summit in Munich, the Memorandum was handed over to the German Federal Minister of the Interior, Otto Schily, in lieu of governmental authorities around the globe and presented to the general public.[5] An updated version of the Memorandum, which takes account of the considerable public debate on this issue, is provided in section I of the present volume.

In section II, the recommendations summarized in the Memorandum are commented on from perspectives which could hardly be more diverse. The contributions by the German Minister of the Interior, Otto Schily, Bill Clinton's former adviser on questions relating to the Internet, Ira Magaziner, by the EU Commissioner Erkki Liikanen, the German State Secretary at the Federal Ministry of Economics, Siegmar Mosdorf, the President of the *American Civil Liberties Union*, Nadine Strossen, the Deputy Chairman of the *Australian Broadcasting Authority*, Gareth Grainger, the Chairman of the *Singapore Broadcasting Authority*, Niam Chiang Meng, as well as the American Internet expert Esther Dyson and the Califor-

---

5   For a survey of the international press reports on the Internet Content Summit and the Memorandum, see *http://www.bertelsmann-stiftung.de/internetcontent*

nian media scientist, Jeffrey Cole. The commentaries reflect the richness of debate at the Summit.

As the contributions show, the Memorandum meets with approval in countries, such as Singapore, which has traditionally advocated state-oriented regulation of the media; countries, such as Germany, which find themselves in a transitional phase on the way to increased self-regulation as well as in the USA where – in the words of Ira Magaziner – politics tends to "show restraint," and to "take account of the decentralized character of the Internet," "observing and learning" about "the developments resulting from the interaction of so many creative forces from the private sector."

The contributions also reflect voices of concern – again coming from very different directions: whereas, for example, Nadine Strossen sees a danger of state censorship even in *voluntary* self-classification, Otto Schily stresses that he sees self-regulation alone as insufficient in dealing with harmful content and that the State, with its monopoly on the use of force, must intervene to ensure safety on the Internet. This conflict exemplifies the challenge to the development of a new culture of responsibility on the Internet. Although a global approach is required in response to this global medium, the traditions of responsibility that exist throughout the world are highly diverse. All must be taken into account when undertaking an initiative such as the present one.

Castigated by some as representing a preliminary stage on the way to censorship, and thought by others not to go far enough, with its recommendations to industry, users and politicians, the Memorandum sets out goals without merely describing the lowest common denominators. The scientific basis for the Memorandum is provided by four reports on self-regulation and codes of conduct for the Internet industry (Monroe Price, Stefaan Verhulst), on a filter architecture (Jack Balkin, Beth Noveck, Kermit Roosevelt), on Internet hotlines (Herbert Burkert) and on the duties of the State and the prosecuting authorities (Ulrich Sieber). These are supplemented by the detailed final report on the representative opinion survey concerning attitudes to the Internet and its regulation in Germany, the USA and Australia (Renate Köcher). With their analysis of self-regulatory, co-regulatory and regulatory processes, Price/Verhulst (Oxford University) lay the foundation for a self-regulatory system for Internet contents. Balkin/Noveck/Roosevelt (Yale University) subsequently concentrate on the criticism of existing self-classification and filter systems for Internet content and develop a new, intercultural, filter architecture. Burkert (St. Gallen University) examines the role hotlines play within this system. In the course of this, he develops minimum standards for hotlines and discusses various models, ranging from hotlines organized along purely private lines through to state-operated hotlines. From an international comparative perspective, Sieber (Würzburg University) analyses the statutory framework as well as the relationship between the Internet industry and the criminal prosecution service. He develops recommendations for further legislation and for practical cooperation between service providers and the police.

This volume also contains a service section. Aimed primarily at academics, it includes a selected bibliography relating to the topics of Internet policy and self-regulation as of the summer of 1999. We owe a great debt of gratitude to all those – the authors of the reports and the members of the network of experts[6] – who have participated in the international discussion process on self-regulation and the protection of minors on the Internet which the Bertelsmann Foundation initiated. We also wish to extend our thanks to our partners at the organization of the Internet Content Summit 1999, David Kerr (coordinator of the INCORE[7] process), Hansjörg Kuch (Bavarian State Chancellery), and all those who have contributed to the event's success.

6   List of names in the appendix.
7   www.incore.org

Our wish is that the present volume might make a contribution towards the international search for a balance between the protection of minors and freedom of expression, between North America and other regions as they make their way onto the Internet. In the spirit of this new medium, let us put the users first.

Chapter I

Memorandum on Self-Regulation
of Internet Content

Responsibility on the Internet – Self-Regulation and Youth Protection

Key recommendations

1. The Internet: changing the way people live

As an international community of users and providers of information, we are at a dramatic turning point. The Internet will change the way people live: it offers extraordinary opportunities for enhancing creativity and learning, for trading and relating across borders, for safeguarding human rights, for realizing democratic values and for strengthening pluralism and cultural diversity. The change holds promise and it holds challenges. Although a limited phenomenon within the overall amount of Internet content, racist and discriminatory web sites, child pornography exchanged in certain newsgroups and chatrooms and "how to" guides for terrorist activities are too disturbing to ignore. Mechanisms have to be developed to deal with illegal content, to protect children online as well as guarantee free speech.

2. Self-regulation of Internet content: towards a systematic, integrated and international approach

No single approach, relying on one form or one set of actors, can provide a solution to content concerns in the changing and shifting environment that is the Internet. For a public response to be effective, it must be integrated, systematic and dynamic, sensitive to public needs and national differences within a framework that encourages robust communication. Only such a systematic approach – bringing technological potential together with the energies and capacities of government, the Internet industry and the citizenry – has the promise of success in meeting what often seem to be competing goals. Given the global and borderless architecture of the Internet, such a systematic approach requires not only coordination at a national and regional level, but its scope must be international.

3. Internet industry: developing and implementing codes of conduct

Codes of conduct should be adopted to ensure that Internet content and service providers act in accord with principles of social responsibility. These codes should meet community concerns and operate as an accountability system that guarantees a high level of credibility and quality. As part of the codes of conduct, Internet providers hosting content have an obligation to remove illegal content when put on notice that such content exists. They have no obligation to monitor content and they should not take down or block legal content considered harmful for children since filtering should take place at the user level.* The procedure for notice and take-down – while laid down by regulation – should be reflected in codes of conduct and

---

* Added after the Internet Content Summit 1999 for purposes of clarification.

26

should specify the requirements for proper notification of service providers. The service provider may include in its contracts with users and content providers terms which allow it to comply with its legal obligations and protect it from liability. It is in the best interest of industry to take on such responsibility regarding illegal content since it enhances consumer confidence and is ultimately good for business.

4. Sharing responsibility: self-regulatory agencies enforcing codes of conduct

To be effective, codes of conduct must be the product of and be enforced by self-regulatory agencies. Such agencies relieve individual service providers from passing judgement on their customers' content and ensure adequate processes in dealing with complaints.* Self-regulatory agencies must be broadly representative and accessible to all relevant parties. Subject to a process of acquiescence by public authorities they should enjoy certain legal privileges enhancing their functions. Effective self-regulation requires active consumer and citizen consultation by such agencies. Without user involvement, a self-regulatory mechanism will not accurately reflect user needs, will not be effective in delivering the standards it promotes, and will fail to create confidence.

5. Governments: supporting and reinforcing self-regulation

Self-regulation cannot function without the support of public authorities, be it that they simply do not interfere with the self-regulatory process, be it that they endorse or ratify self-regulatory codes and

---

* Added after the Internet Content Summit 1999 for purposes of clarification.

give support through enforcement. There are clearly limits to what can be achieved by self-regulation. The process cannot alone guarantee that child pornographers are caught and punished, although self-regulatory mechanisms can help ensure that criminals cannot use the Internet with impunity. Governments should, through education and public information, raise awareness among users about self-regulatory mechanisms such as the means to filter and block content and to communicate complaints about Internet content through hotlines.

6. Self-rating and filtering systems: empowering user choice

Filtering technology can empower users by allowing them to select the kinds of content they and their children are exposed to. Used wisely, this technology can help shift control of and responsibility for harmful content from governments, regulatory agencies, and supervisory bodies to individuals. Thus, at the core of the recommendations for an integrated system of self-regulation and end-user autonomy must be an improved architecture for the rating and filtering of Internet content. There should be an independent organization to provide a basic vocabulary for rating and to oversee updates to the system at periodic intervals. Content providers worldwide must be mobilized to label their content voluntarily and filters must be available to parents and guardians of children and all users of the Internet.

7. Internet filtering: ensuring youth protection and freedom of speech

A good filtering system realizes several important values: end-user autonomy; respect for freedom of expression; ideological diversity;

transparency; respect for privacy; interoperability and compatibility. The system should be designed to place filtering decisions in the hands of the end-user and to discourage or prevent upstream filtering by governments. Equally important, the system must feature a user-friendly interface that encourages actual use of its features and makes choice a real possibility for the vast majority of end-users. Third parties should be encouraged to develop and provide free filters. Industry should promote the availability and use of filtering systems, educating consumers about how to filter and making it easy for parents, teachers, and other concerned adults to choose filters, install and adapt them to their set of values. Regulatory requirements on service providers to screen or filter content should be avoided. Government or regulatory agencies may supply filters but should *not* mandate their use.

8. Hotlines: communicating and evaluating content concerns

We need technical and organizational *communication* devices to ensure that users can respond to content on the Internet that they find of substantial concern. These "hotlines" ensure that – where necessary and appropriate – effective action can be taken to remedy such concerns. The task of evaluating the legality or illegality of specific data is difficult for Internet providers and should, therefore, be integrated into the work of hotlines as self-regulatory agencies. In order to function, hotlines need an environment and operational rules that honor their specific task of handling illegal content. Legislators should formulate minimum requirements on the organizational setup and procedures of hotlines and, in turn, shield them from criminal or civil liability incurred in the proper conduct of their business ("safe harbor"). While the primary role of hotlines is in determining and communicating illegal content to law enforcement authorities and industry, they should also raise awareness to deal with legal material considered harmful to children.*

9. International cooperation: acting against content where it is located

There should be an international network of hotlines governed by a framework agreement containing minimum standards on the handling of content concerns and stipulating mutual notification between hotlines. The hotline in the country where the content is located is asked to evaluate it and to take action. This mechanism results in content providers being acted against only if the material is illegal in the host country. The mechanism also overcomes difficulties in the complex diplomatic procedures necessary for cross-border cooperation of law enforcement authorities.

10. The legal framework: limitations on liability

There should be no criminal responsibility of mere access and network providers for third parties' illegal content transmissions taking place in real-time through their networks. Host service providers merely storing third party content should be held liable only if they have actual knowledge of illegal content, and if a removal of such content is technically possible and can reasonably be expected. Providers party to an enforceable and broadly representative self-regulatory regime, recognized by public authorities, should not be liable for third party content when complying with the requirements of that regime and the decisions of the relevant self-regulatory body.

* Amended after the Internet Content Summit 1999 for purposes of clarification.

11. Law enforcement: cooperation and continuous training

It should be a priority to create adequate law enforcement bodies to combat computer crime and illegal content like child pornography on the Internet. This requires the development of centralized units and/or a robust coordination of existing competent bodies. Such units must have adequate technical know-how and on-going training. The Internet industry should cooperate in training. Law enforcement and the Internet industry should develop cooperative structures to exchange views on common points of concern.

12. A "learning system": education and constant evaluation

No self-regulatory mechanism can work independently of an education and awareness campaign. The Internet industry should develop a continuous online and off-line effort to provide general awareness of self-regulatory mechanisms such as filtering systems and hotlines. Schools should provide the necessary skills for children to understand the benefits and limitations of online information and to exercise self-control over problematic Internet content. The Internet is, itself, a process, an enormous system for change and response, feedback and transformation. Like the Internet, the legal system and self-regulatory mechanisms around it must incorporate similar practices of learning and changing. The integrated system recommended here depends on continuous (re-)evaluation.

1 Introduction

Everywhere, citizens, governments and industry are seeking to maximize the potential of the great new information technology that is the Internet. More than any medium that has come before it, this interactive tool empowers its users with the freedom to communicate, to distribute, to seek and gather information, to develop and disseminate opinions. Extraordinary opportunities for enhancing creativity and learning, for trading and relating across borders, for safeguarding human rights, for realizing democratic values and for strengthening pluralism and cultural diversity are clearly inherent in the new world heralded by the Internet. The new information technology will improve openness, transparency and efficiency at all levels in public as well as private domains. The Internet will change the way people live. Such change holds promise and it holds challenges.

An important challenge comes from illegal and harmful content. Although a limited phenomenon within the broad range and staggering volume of all Internet content, racist and discriminatory websites, child pornography exchanged in certain newsgroups and chatrooms and "how to" guides on terrorist activities are too disturbing to be ignored. Such illegal material is a topic of broad debate. It leads to uncertainty about the capacity of existing legal approaches to effectively curb Internet misuse.

Another challenge is posed by content harmful to children yet legal when consumed by adults. While there are legal and cultural differences between countries in what is considered harmful to children, most countries have restricted the distribution of, for example, sex-related and violent material in traditional broadcast media. Governments have, however, hesitated to apply the same rules to the Internet because of the different nature of the medium. They would simply not work in a medium that is available anywhere around the world at any time of day or night. The significance of harmful content will become even more politically sensitive as access to the Internet through television and telephones becomes ever broader and more pervasive.

Mechanisms have to be developed to deal with illegal content and to protect children online. But they also have to protect free speech.

Even if not targeted directly, browsing, surfing, or following suggestions from search engines may lead to material containing unwanted, troubling, offensive as well as surprising or amusing material. This mixture of the deliberately sought for and the unexpected may well be one of the attractions of the medium. To be able to profit from this opportunity, to make such encounters possible, while still allowing for the protection of children and for selective approaches to information gathering and communication, is perhaps one of the most important tasks in further developing the Internet. The power of self-regulation must be harnessed to take up this task, to increase citizen confidence and to reach the full economic, cultural and social potential of the new technologies. The private sector had an important role in the creation of these technologies and in their development and use. Partnership between the public and private sector is now needed to maximize the benefit of these technologies and to minimize their risks.

The Bertelsmann Foundation has, over the last nine months, brought together a global network of representatives from government, industry, law enforcement, non-government organizations as well as scholars and experts to make recommendations concerning these questions and to advise on the structure and implementation of an internationally coordinated approach.[1] The group examined best practices, a variety of legal approaches and was asked to focus particularly on the contribution self-regulation can make to the current keen anxiety with regard to illegal and harmful Internet content. The Foundation's aim was to expand awareness among the key stakeholders of the role self-regulation can play and to do so with the geographical, professional and disciplinary variety necessary for so expansive and complex a task.

The memorandum that follows undertakes the difficult task of summarizing the results of the rich and complex interchange within

1   Appendix I and II

the network of expert professionals, industry and non-profit representatives, officials and academics. The memorandum is addressed to governments, the Internet industry and users, to regulatory and law enforcement authorities, to self-regulatory initiatives, to children's advocates and user-representatives. All will have to take on responsibility for Internet content. Cooperation among all will be needed to put these recommendations into practice.

2 Towards a systematic approach

As an international community of users and providers of information, we are at a dramatic turning point. The architecture of speech, with all its implications for political life and democracy, is being radically altered. Societies are coping with the consequences of harmful and offensive content at a moment of rapidly changing information technologies. Entire structures for the delivery and reception of speech are being transformed. Habits, patterns, laws designed to protect against specific harms are potentially challenged by global, interactive and decentralized services.

We have not only learned how *to deal with* content concerns in the more traditional media, we also have culturally learned *to live with* varying degrees of insecurity, with communication risks; we have learnt how to decide which risk levels to accept and which to refuse, which "back-up" mechanisms to use.

No single approach, relying on one form or one set of actors, can provide a solution in such a changing and shifting environment. For a public response to be effective, it must be integrated, systematic and dynamic, sensitive to public needs and national differences within a framework that encourages robust communication. Only such a systematic approach – bringing technological potential together with the energies and capacities of government, industry and citizenry – has the promise of success in meeting what often seem to be competing goals. Given the global and borderless architecture of the Internet, such a systematic approach requires not only coordination at a national and regional level, but its scope must be international.

A systematic, self-regulation-based approach is especially desirable because the alternative – reliance on overbroad, highly intrusive regulation, with laws differing across national borders – yields short-term, often crisis-driven, mostly ineffective solutions. And these responses cannot meld together the complicated political and social objectives in a successful way. The illusion of action is no substitute for a considered and comprehensive, flexible and dynamic approach.

Content concern response systems are necessary to manage the disturbances the Internet can hold. Processes and institutions have to be developed, tested and implemented, and learning processes have to be initiated that help to create trust and to empower users.

3 Self-regulation as a foundation

Meaningful and effective self-regulation provides the opportunity to adapt rapidly to the quickening technical progress globally and, when properly encased in collaboration with government, is preferable to mandatory governmental regulation. The general benefits of self-regulation include efficiency, increased flexibility, increased incentives for compliance, and reduced cost. A carefully structured program emphasizing self-regulation is especially harmonious with an Internet setting because it mirrors the Internet itself, as a global, essentially private and decentralized network of communication.

Effective self-regulation requires active consumer and citizen consultation based upon shared responsibility at all stages of development and implementation. Without user involvement, a self-regulatory mechanism will not accurately reflect user needs, will not be effective in delivering the standards it promotes, and will fail to create confidence.

The development of a self-regulatory regime for the Internet must comprise several complementary actions, tools and mechanisms. Moreover, self-regulation cannot function without the support of public authorities, be it that they simply do not interfere with the self-regulatory process, be it that they endorse or ratify self-regulatory codes and give support through enforcement. There are clearly limits to what can be achieved by self-regulation. It cannot, for example, by itself ensure that child pornographers are caught and punished, although self-regulatory mechanisms can be of assistance in ensuring that criminals cannot use the Internet with impunity.

The creation of self-regulatory mechanisms should, to the extent possible, be the product of cooperation or collaboration between state bodies and the Internet Service Providers (ISPs) or self-regulatory bodies. Self and legal regulation should each complement the other in relevant areas. Developing an ideal synthesis involves interweaving their specific instruments, not merely adding both together – a process best achieved through dialogue among all the parties concerned.

Another major challenge in self-regulation is the prevention of a "free-rider phenomenon" where some actors expend significant resources on the development, monitoring and implementation of codes and standards, while others simply profit from their existence or ignore them altogether. The effectiveness of self-regulation will depend largely on full collaboration and commitment among all industry players such as content providers, service providers, and relevant software and technology industry.

It is in the best interest of industry to develop self-regulatory mechanisms as they enhance consumer confidence and are ultimately supportive of business objectives. More people will migrate online when they are confident that their families will not be exposed to harmful content. With regard to the implementation of an effective self-regulatory system, the following points are of crucial importance.

First, codes of conduct should be adopted to ensure that Internet content and service providers act in accord with the law and with principles of social responsibility. These codes should meet community concerns and industry needs and operate as an accountability system that guarantees a high level of credibility and quality.

Second, to be effective, these codes of conduct must be the product of and be enforced by self-regulatory agencies.

Third, because of the transnational nature of Internet communications, coordinated activity among such agencies in different jurisdictions is an essential element of self-regulation.

Fourth, effective self-regulation is not possible without the support of law making and regulation including legislation that embraces and empowers the self-regulatory process.

Fifth, there should be widespread use of rating and filtering technology. To this end, content providers worldwide must be mobilized to label their content voluntarily, and filters must be made available to empower guardians and all users of the Internet to make more effective choices about the content they wish to have enter their homes.

Sixth, a comprehensive self-regulatory system also requires content response and complaints systems for users, such as hotlines.

Seventh, awareness among users of the means to filter and block content, to redress complaints and of the level of conduct that is promised by the industry is crucial to the success of any self-regulatory framework. Education by public and information distribution by private entities must work hand in hand to raise this awareness.

Finally, techniques must be found to measure the effectiveness of self-regulatory mechanisms and to determine what national and transnational measures – if any – are necessary to compensate for their deficiencies.

With respect to these recommendations and the discussion of

codes of conduct that follows, it is important to recognize and allow for national/cultural differences. The implementation and practical expression of these recommendations is likely to vary from country to country and this needs to be respected in order to avoid perceptions of the Internet as furthering monocultural imperialism.

As to codes of conduct, they should be endorsed as a front-line mechanism for addressing content issues and be based upon industry's social responsibility. In particular, they should distinguish between illegal content and the protection of minors from potentially harmful content. They should delineate the mechanisms through which self-regulation will occur, including provisions for cooperation with end-users as well as public authorities.

Industry-wide codes may be more useful instruments of protection than those developed by small groupings of companies within sectors. They are more comprehensive and transparent which prevents confusion among users.

Internet Service Providers provide a technical service (access to the Internet, hosting content or both). They are not in the business of telling their customers what they should or should not access, nor should they be expected to exercise control over what content is published. On the other hand, they have an obligation to take steps to remove illegal content when put on notice that such content exists. The procedure for such notice and take-down, while laid down by law, should be reflected in codes of conduct and provide for the interests of all involved to be respected. An ISP may include in its contracts with users and content providers terms which allow it to comply with its legal obligations and protect it from liability. In this process of cooperation, self-regulation must not become an engine for greater control than would occur if the state itself established all standards.

Recommendations for governments

- Government bodies should encourage and incentivize self-regulatory initiatives by industry as an efficient, flexible and cost-effective mechanism to address Internet content concerns that can secure a high degree of compliance.
- Governments should consider a process of acquiescence or ratification of codes of conduct developed by industry and may want to consider supporting their enforcement.
- In carefully specified instances, governments should protect the capacity of self-regulatory agencies to handle and disclose information on illegal content to law enforcement authorities ("safe harbor"). Also, ISPs must have the protected capacity to remove potentially illegal content from their servers.
- Governments should, through education and public information, raise awareness among users of self-regulatory mechanisms such as the means to filter and block content and to communicate complaints about Internet content through hotlines.

Recommendations for the Internet industry

- The Internet industry should develop codes of conduct as a front-line mechanism. Self-regulation of Internet content will enhance user confidence and will increase overall demand for Internet services and e-commerce.
- These codes must be clear and transparent about their policy objectives. In particular, they should delineate the mechanisms through which self-regulation will occur, including provisions for cooperation with end-users as well as public authorities.
- Self-regulatory agencies (SRAs) should be created by industry both nationally and internationally to foster the creation and implementation of codes and standards. Such agencies should

include a range of content providers as well as service providers.

- SRAs should have a legal structure assuring independence. Important criteria are: institutional stability, composition of the board, links to government, and financial and organizational autonomy.
- An easily accessible, impartial and independent body or agency to hear complaints and adjudicate on breaches of the code should be created by the industry.
- The Internet industry should raise user awareness with regard to self-regulatory content concern mechanisms through appropriate means of information dissemination (at the time of hardware purchase, conclusion of service contracts, and through public campaigns).

Recommendations for joint action

- A mechanism of quality assurance should be provided to assess different self-regulatory consumer empowerment mechanisms and to act as a proxy for insufficiently informed consumers.

4 Rating and filtering

Filtering technology can empower users by allowing them to select the kinds of content they and their children are exposed to. Used wisely, this technology can help shift control of and responsibility for harmful content from governments, regulatory agencies, and supervisory bodies to individuals. Thus, at the core of the recommendations for an integrated system of self-regulation and end-user autonomy must be an improved architecture for the rating and filtering of Internet content.

A flexible filtering system can help individuals choose what kinds of content they wish to view and what kinds of content they wish to allow their children to see.

A good filtering system realizes several important values: (1) end-user autonomy; (2) respect for freedom of expression; (3) a diversity of beliefs and values; (4) transparency; (5) respect for privacy; and (6) interoperability and compatibility.

First, the filtering system should respect end-user autonomy, allowing end-users the right to choose whether or not they want to filter, and it should provide end-users with meaningful choices that reflect different cultural values and ideologies. The system should be designed to discourage or prevent upstream filtering by governments in order to ensure that all filtering decisions are made by the end-users. Equally important, the system must feature a user-friendly interface that encourages actual use of its features and makes choice a real possibility for the vast majority of end-users.

Second, the system should be sensitive to freedom of thought and expression. It should not block pages whose content is unrelated to the criteria used for filtering, and it should not attempt to block pages because they are critical of the filtering system being employed. As a default rule, the system should not block unrated sites unless the end-user specifically requests this option.

Third, the system must be sufficiently versatile to be compatible with a wide diversity of cultures and ideologies, and it must be flexible enough to change over time as values change.

Fourth, the system should be transparent for end-users, raters, and programmers. End-users should know when access has been blocked and why. Raters must be able to understand the substantive meaning of different ratings and easily apply them. Finally, information about all aspects of the ratings system should be public so that programmers can create new implementations of the ratings system, and others can easily build on their work.

Fifth, a good filtering system will respect privacy. It will not facilitate collection of data about the filters a particular person is using when they surf the Internet.

Sixth, and finally, filtering software should allow different ratings systems to "talk to each other" and be applied seriatim or in combination. End-users who can use different systems together have the greatest degree of freedom in constructing a filter to suit their particular needs.

To achieve these goals, we recommend a "layer cake" model[2]. Our model consists of three layers placed over a software specification. The "plate" on which the system rests is the PICS[3] software specification, including PICSRules, and (eventually) the RDF[4] specification.

Our solution relies on a division of labor between first and third parties. We ask first parties (content providers) to describe their content with a standard set of vocabulary descriptors, using terms that are likely to lead to convergent practices. We are less concerned with whether the vocabulary descriptions are value-free (an impossible goal in any case) than with whether most first parties will apply them in roughly the same way. The goal is not ideological neutrality but predictable convergence in behavior. One might call these descriptions "objective" but a more accurate term would be "intersubjectively convergent." This basic vocabulary constitutes Layer One of the system.

We then ask third parties to produce "templates" that combine and rank combinations of these content descriptors in ways that match their particular set of values and beliefs. A template takes the raw materials of content description and then combines them into different categories and decides which combinations are better and

---

2 Illustration as Appendix III
3 PICS = Platform for Internet Content Selection (labeling protocol developed by the Word Wide Web Consortium)
4 RDF = Resource Description Framework

worse with respect to a given value system. We do not ask third parties to be ideologically neutral – indeed, we specifically ask them to rank certain types of content based on their values about what is good and bad, and what is more or less harmful to children. The goal of third parties in the system is to set up basic standards of evaluation that will be applied to the convergent descriptions of first parties. Because the basic task of third parties is to set up ratings templates, they do not have to rate sites individually. These ratings templates created by third parties form Layer Two of the system. An end-user's browser will read the vocabulary elements in Layer One and filter them according to the templates in Layer Two.

Because ratings templates will be relatively simple and easy to set up, we expect many different organizations will be willing to create them. Moreover, because the templates will be publicly available, organizations can model their efforts on previous templates, making the costs of template creation even smaller. Finally, because all templates will be based on a common language, end-users (or other organizations) can mix and match them to produce custom templates suitable to their ideological tastes.

The third layer of the cake consists of ratings of individual sites that can be added to the results of Layers One and Two. Such ratings might include a "white list" of acceptable sites (for example a list of news organizations) provided by third party raters. Layer Three can also contain blacklists of forbidden sites, and, indeed, any other PICS compatible rating system. The purpose of Layer Three is to allow third parties to offer more contextual judgments of individual sites to fine tune the system. While we think that Layers One and Two offer more diversity than any previous rating system, the addition of Layer Three should greatly enhance the system's flexibility.

End-users can install (or have others install) any combination of templates in their browsers. They can also add any combination of PICS compatible filters and whitelists. As a result, even though web site operators use a single Layer One vocabulary, end-users can choose from many different and powerful filtering systems.

This proposal features several different layers and many possible options for innovation. But ease of use is not inconsistent with a system that is both flexible and powerful. It is important to distinguish between the complexity of the *filtering system* and the complexity of the *user interface*. A car is an extremely complex piece of machinery under the hood, but its user interface is designed to make it easy to drive. Software companies spend millions of dollars a year to make their user interfaces easy to use despite the complexity of the underlying software engines. We see no reason why this expertise cannot be adapted to filtering, which, in many ways, involves a much less complicated piece of software.

Users should be able to have templates and white lists installed when they first purchase their home computer. They should also be able to click a button on their browser and be taken automatically to places on the Internet where they can download new templates and whitelist updates with a few clicks of a mouse. All of these operations can be made easy and efficient with good software design.

Recommendations for governments

- Governments should recognize that privately created and privately maintained filtering systems can promote individual autonomy, and respect freedom of thought and expression while protecting children. Governments should encourage the use of these filtering systems as part of any scheme of self-regulation.
- Governments can encourage the creation of filters through, for example, tax incentives. However, governments should not impose criminal sanctions for failure to rate websites, and they should not filter content upstream.

44

Recommendations for the Internet industry

– Content providers worldwide should be mobilized to self-rate and label their content on a voluntary basis.*
– Members of the computer and telecommunications industries should promote the adoption of a flexible filtering system along the lines of the layer cake model described in our report. Such a system should be incorporated into browsers, search engines, and web authoring tools. The system should also include encrypted ratings or other technological devices to defeat upstream filtering by governments.
– Industry should promote the availability and use of filtering systems, educating consumers about how to filter and making it easy for parents, teachers, and other concerned adults to choose filters, install, run, and alter them.
– Software design should promote ease of use for end-users. Software designers should create easy-to-use interfaces and "wizards" so that end-users can quickly and simply install filters and revise filtering choices.
– End-users should also be able to quickly and easily add particular web sites to lists of approved or disapproved sites. The ability to install filters or alter filtering choices should be prominently displayed on the browser toolbar and not hidden several layers deep in browser menus.

* Amended after the Internet Content Summit 1999 for purposes of clarification.

Recommendations for a non-profit rating organization

A *The advisory board*

– There should be an independent organization to create the initial basic (Layer One) vocabulary elements for the system and to oversee updates to the system at periodic intervals. This organization should be nonprofit and not under the auspices or control of any particular business organization.

– The advisory board should comprise a broad range of expertise on rating and filtering issues. Responsible for creating the initial Layer One vocabulary, it should also create easy-to-use questionnaires to facilitate self-rating by first parties, and easy-to-understand guides for the creation of templates by third parties.

B *Other organizations*

– Other organizations should be encouraged to create ratings templates for Layer Two that reflect their values and concerns and to create Layer Three blacklists.

– Other organizations should be encouraged to pool their resources to create Layer Three whitelists. These whitelists would include sites that are permissible for children to view (e.g., news sites) even though they might otherwise be filtered (for example, because they contain descriptions of violence). Whitelists create better incentives for cooperation and synergy between non-profit organizations than blacklists, because groups have incentives to spread and share information about sites that they believe are acceptable for children. Blacklists, on the other hand, help end-users block harmful content that is not otherwise labeled.*

---

* Amended after the Internet Content Summit 1999.

Recommendations for end-users

– End-users should demand easy-to-use filtering from software and hardware manufacturers that puts choice in their hands rather than in the hands of others.
– End-users should take whatever steps they can to learn about filtering options available to them.

5 Hotlines as content concern mechanisms

The term "hotline" characterizes organizations ensuring communication from users about Internet content they find of significant concern. Such communication can take place by phone, fax or e-mail. The connection is usually qualified by easy accessibility, high availability and an assured response. We know of hotlines in the private sector where enterprises offer direct access to "help desks" or related services dealing with consumer and client requests.

Hotlines also ensure that an evaluation of content concerns takes place and that effective action can be taken to remedy such concerns In this context, hotlines are the organizationally supported link between users, content providers, self-regulatory bodies, organizations providing rating and filtering services, and law enforcement. "Content concerns" may range from a merely passing personal irritation to confronting illegal content. Hotlines have to be open and *not* restricted to criminal law issues like child pornography. On the other hand, they certainly must not exclude these issues.

Mechanisms maintaining and enhancing the communication function of the Internet can be a very effective way to respond to content concerns not sufficiently addressed through filtering mechanisms. In order to function, communication channels need an environment and operational rules that honor procedural and substantive values.

Hotlines have to be perceived as integral parts of content concern response systems and should be implemented and operated accordingly. In particular any procedures developed for their operation should not only take into account the legal obligations of handling sensitive material but the basic rules of substantive and procedural due process, as well as data protection and freedom of expression rules. Hotlines have to fulfill three basic requirements: they must be available, transparent and reliable.

Recommendations for hotline operators

- Hotlines have to be available. The general public must be made aware of their existence. Their availability has to be widely publicized on the Internet as well as in traditional mass media. Therefore, points of mass entry on the Internet (portals, content providers) should contain links to such systems. It should be ensured that linguistic barriers of access to hotlines are either minimized or compensated for. There should be several media available to access hotlines (e-mail, physical mail address, telephone/fax). There should be a first response to users within 24 hours. If operated automatically, an organizational backup should be maintained to ensure human response.
- Hotlines have to be transparent. Users should be aware – at the point of entry – of the persons/organizations responsible for running the hotline system and those persons and organizations on whose behalf hotlines are operated. Transparency also means that the rules and procedures according to which concerns are being processed are explained at the point of entry: e.g. which concerns will not be processed; which concerns will be handed over, when, under what criteria and to which public authorities. The system should be explained in sufficient detail and additional help should be available.

Users should have the ability to track their concern throughout the process and they should be informed of the final outcome of the process. To this end, hotline operators should be informed accordingly by public authorities so that they can provide this information. Organizations running hotline systems should, at regular intervals, make publicly available reports on the basic statistics and experiences with their systems.

– Hotlines have to be reliable. Hotlines have to be part of a technically and organizationally reliable and sustainable infrastructure. Organizations should be aware that they have to dedicate appropriate resources to such systems. Processes should be designed and applied in a manner that ensures that the legitimate interests of the parties concerned in these processes are adequately recognized. The availability and processes of hotlines should be monitored independently. Systems of evaluation, "consumer information," and quality certification should be encouraged. Hotline systems should have appropriate measures implemented to ensure privacy and data security for their users, including systems by which points of entry to hotline systems can be verified.

– The typical procedure[5] (provided there are no compelling rules that demand a handover to law enforcement authorities) should run as follows:

(1) The input by the user would be confirmed (information to the user).

(2) The hotline organization would check the input as to whether the formal point of entry criteria it has set in its policy are met. It would also verify the input as to whether the claimed content concern can be found as described by the user.

(3) If the (formal) entry criteria are met and verification has been successful, there will be an internal evaluation procedure as to the qualitative criteria with the purpose to determine

---

5   Illustration as Appendix IV

whether further action is needed (evaluation). This decision-making process will have to follow the criteria prescribed in a policy placed at the entry point of the hotline.

(4) If this evaluation leads to a decision that no further action is needed, there should be – for reasons of transparency – an information to the user of the outcome.

If there is a decision on further action the third party has to be addressed. Such a third party may or may not have subjected itself to such an action (within a self-regulative organization). In the latter case the contact merely has the character of a notification. Where illegal content is concerned, a handover to law enforcement may be required.

If the third party has subjected itself to the self-regulatory procedure, it is necessary – for reasons of due process – to give that party a hearing, or the third party may simply decide to take the action requested. A handover to public authorities, as indicated above, might also be necessary – even if the third party responds positively – if there are compelling legal reasons. However, providers subject to a self-regulatory regime that take action according to the requirements should be privileged in a legal proceeding.

(5) Finally, a record of the procedure should be kept and, depending on the transparency policy that has been decided, the user should be informed of the outcome.

– There should be an international network of hotlines governed by a framework agreement containing minimum standards on the handling of content concerns and stipulating mutual notification between hotlines. The hotline in the country where the content is located should be the entity to evaluate it and to take action. This mechanism results in content providers being acted against only if the material is illegal in the host country. The approach also overcomes difficulties in the complex diplomatic procedures necessary for cross-border cooperation of law enforcement authorities. It is an essential component of an international approach to dealing with content concerns.

– Whether national or international, user complaints may also relate to misrating of first parties in the context of self-rating systems. Hotlines, therefore, serve as backup mechanisms for the important self-regulation pillar which is self-rating and filtering.

Recommendations for hotlines operated by public authorities

– Public authorities should not hesitate to show presence on the net. Where hotlines are operated by public authorities, they should unequivocally be made recognizable as such, and the legal procedural rules that are followed in their operation should be explained clearly to users.

Recommendations for hotlines operated as cooperative efforts between public authorities and the private sector

– In cases where hotlines are operated in private-public cooperation or under rules of cooperation, such rules should be publicized at the point of entry, and whatever consequences such cooperation might have should be explained clearly. In particular possible ambiguities arising from margins of discretion in the handling of notices should be avoided.

Recommendations for governments

– Regulation should formulate minimum requirements on the organizational setup and procedure of hotlines the fulfillment of which should shield hotlines from criminal or civil liability incurred in the proper conduct of their business ("safe harbor").

6 Government involvement and the interrelationship between legal regulation and self-regulatory mechanisms

Law enforcement is the basic mechanism employed within any country to prevent, detect, investigate and prosecute illegal and harmful content on the Internet. This state reaction is essential for various reasons: It guarantees the state monopoly on power and public order, it is democratically legitimized and directly enforceable and it secures justice, equality and legal certainty. However, a mere system of legal regulation armed with law enforcement would be ineffective because of the technical, fast-changing and global nature of the Internet. In a coordinated approach, self-regulatory mechanisms have to be combined with law enforcement as a necessary backup.

Recommendations for governments

– There should be no criminal responsibility of mere access and network providers for third parties' illegal content transmissions taking place in real-time through their networks.
– Host service providers merely storing third party content should be held liable only if they have actual knowledge of illegal content, and if a removal of such content is technically possible and can reasonably be expected. The regulation of "notice and take

down" procedures should specify the requirements for a proper notification of the service provider.

- Providers party to an enforceable and broadly representative self-regulatory regime, recognized by public authorities, should not be liable for third party content when complying with the requirements of that regime and the decisions of the relevant self-regulatory body.

- Laws should recognize (self-)rating and filtering mechanisms as well as age verification systems to exclude responsibility of providers for content harmful to children.

- It is essential to have adequate legislative powers with respect to computer-based investigations, in particular, adequate powers for search and seizure. It would be helpful to make available a preservation order, which could "freeze" evidence in a fast procedure and thus leave the decision about its delivery to a court judgment. In addition, legislation should be clearer on the obligations of Internet providers with respect to the collection, storage and transfer to law enforcement of data relevant to investigations.

- The power of law enforcement agencies to patrol the net and to act undercover as well as to actively participate in dialogues (chat) with potential perpetrators should be clearly defined and duly limited to ensure effective law enforcement and to protect the privacy of citizens online.

- It should be a top priority to create adequate law enforcement bodies to combat computer crime and illegal content like child pornography on the Internet. This requires attention to all levels of law enforcement, including prevention, detection, investigation and prosecution, and can be achieved by developing centralized units and/or a better coordination of existing competent bodies.

Recommendations to law enforcement

– Law enforcement agencies dealing with computer crime must possess adequate technical know-how in a highly technical and fast-changing environment. Training must be comprehensive and on-going.

– When prosecuting illegal content, law enforcement agencies should concentrate their efforts on tracking down and prosecuting the content providers producing or publishing illegal content. Internet service providers and self-regulatory bodies (such as hotlines) should be seen as natural allies in the pursuit of this goal.

– The process of detecting crime and gathering evidence should rely on all legal means and sources available. This should include complaints from users, input from industry and notifications from hotlines. The development of efficient trace-back procedures on the Internet should be encouraged.

– Official diplomatic procedures for formal legal assistance should be replaced by more direct cooperation of competent authorities. This could be achieved for example, by developing better communication channels, "focal points" and common databases within law enforcement agencies. International training forums would foster cooperation below the official level and help standardize practices.

Recommendations for the Internet industry

– In order to make codes of conduct enforceable and to move towards internationally consistent minimum rules, codes of conduct should be incorporated into the contracts between Internet providers and their clients as well as into agreements between providers.

- When taking down illegal content, Internet providers should not be over-reactive and instead respect both criminal law and the civil liberties and information rights of their users in order to avoid private censorship and breach of contract. Self-regulatory agencies should provide independent evaluation mechanisms for content concerns, relieving providers of such evaluation.

Recommendations for cooperation between law enforcement and the Internet industry

- In many countries, both law enforcement and the Internet industry can contribute to better cooperation. Law enforcement should treat Internet providers as potential allies in the fight against illegal content on the Internet. There should be an appreciation on the part of law enforcement of the technical difficulties providers may face in combating illegal content. Law enforcement agencies should ensure organizational transparency to facilitate cooperation with service providers. Service providers should understand that appropriate cooperation with law enforcement is in their interest by facilitating a safe Internet environment for everyone. Internet providers should have a clear understanding of their obligations under existing law.
- There should be a regular exchange of views and mutual training between Internet providers and law enforcement agencies in order to discuss common points of concern, exchange law enforcement know-how with technical know-how, ensure transparency in the relationship and build mutual understanding.
- The Internet industry should consider logistical support to law enforcement. This could include:
  (1) creation of contact points within the Internet industry, accessible 24 hours for law enforcement agencies and the provision of technical support in appropriate cases

(2) taking all commercially reasonable steps to verify the identity of subscribers, while protecting subscribers' privacy

(3) the freezing of evidence in urgent cases in accordance with data protection law

(4) advice to users that any posting, transmission, access to and storage of illegal content may result in removal, termination of service and notification of law enforcement.

– As long as there are no clear legal regulations for self-initiated notifications with respect to serious crimes such as child pornography, Internet providers should consider transferring illegal data to the police without transferring personal data, thus giving law enforcement agencies the option to obtain a judicial delivery order. Self-regulatory agencies like hotlines can evaluate content on behalf of providers before data transfer takes place.

7 Awareness mechanism: media literacy and education

No self-regulatory mechanism can work independently of an education and awareness campaign. The Internet industry working in conjunction with government agencies, where appropriate, should agree to the development of a continuous online and off-line effort to provide general awareness of self-regulatory systems such as filtering systems and hotlines. Such a campaign should be directed at children and parents as well as a general campaign involving society at large. Child-safe sites or so called "fenced gardens" can make an important contribution to introducing young children to the Internet. The culture of self-rating and pluralism in filtering underscores the need for increased media and IT literacy for all ages and a greater role for third party groups involved in self-regulation. Schools should provide the necessary skills for children to understand the benefits and limitations of online information and to encourage greater self-control over problematic Internet content.

8 A learning system

Technological innovation is a determinative aspect of evolving forms of self-regulation. Therefore, industry and joint industry-government research, nationally and internationally, on the relationship between technology and self-regulation should be intensified. In addition, public debate about the opportunities and hazards of technological approaches to content-oriented self-regulation should be encouraged. Evolving patterns of self-regulation should allow for adjustment to technological innovation.

The Internet is, itself, a process, an enormous system for change and response, feedback and transformation. Like the Internet, the legal system and self-regulatory mechanisms around it must incorporate similar practices of learning and changing. The integrated system recommended here depends on continuous (re-)evaluation.

Chapter II

Two Perspectives –
Internet Content Summit 1999

The Role Governments Should Play in Internet Policy[1]

Ira Magaziner

The one thing that we know for sure – and it is the only thing that we know for sure about what our policies should be for the Internet – is that we do not know for sure what they should be! The Internet is new, it is moving very rapidly. It is bringing very profound changes and none of us understands where it is all going. And that is why we in the U.S. Government took a very cautious position towards any type of intervention in the development of this new medium. Because the chances of government's doing harm by mistake, not intentionally, but doing harm nevertheless to the development of the Internet are very great.

We are now approaching a new millennium. We spent over a thousand millennia as a human species living in tribal organizations, hunting or gathering our food from trees and bushes and living in

---

1   Speech delivered at the Internet Content Summit 1999 in Munich, Germany.

very rudimentary social organizations. It was only really about 15 millennia ago that we saw the emergence of agrarian societies which were based upon changes in our understanding about how to grow food, about how to husband animals, and how to use different implements and different materials that we found in our environment. Then about one quarter of one millennium ago, we had the Industrial Revolution where the coming together of two very significant inventions, one the invention of the steam engine and the other the harnessing of electricity, allowed us to reform the nature of our economies and change profoundly the societies that we lived in.

And now beginning just a few decades ago, less than one tenth of one millennium, we now have the Information Revolution. Again, the coming together of two technologies – the ability to process information very rapidly using miniature circuits, and the ability to communicate by light – allows us to transmit very large amounts of information in very small periods of time very cheaply.

You are all familiar with the micro-processing revolution that has occurred, perhaps less familiar with what has happened in communication by light. But today we can take a fibre as thin as a human hair – and because we can send multiple wavelengths of light across that one fibre, we can put 180 different messages at the speed of light across that fibre at once. This means that we can send all of the information in the United States Library of Congress which includes all of the books ever published in the United States and send it from one end of the United States to the other in 14 seconds across one fibre.

Now each of these stages in the progress of human history had very profound economic, social and political implications. What we could see as each transformation took place was a complete upheaval in human society. And that upheaval generally produced positive benefits for the human race. It produced greater economic benefit, greater social interaction, an increase in individual human freedom. It is perhaps useful to consider the industrial revolution when

62

thinking about the major transformation we are facing today. It took about 150 years for the harnessing of electricity to work its way through the developed world. And during the course of that time, there were fundamental changes in commercial, legal, economic and social paradigms. Over all, there was a great freeing up of people's capabilities. The ability to use our minds to a greater extent. The ability to have more time free from struggling for subsistence. The ability to have much greater economic and social comfort. But it required fundamental changes in our legal and commercial systems. And some countries moved quickly to embrace those changes and they were the ones who moved ahead. Others tried to hold on to their old ways of doing things, ways that characterized the agrarian organization and they fell backwards.

We can also see that in the Industrial Revolution there were some very serious negative side effects that were created for society – problems of child labour, of industrial pollution and other types of safety problems. And societies were too slow in dealing with those problems. We are still trying to deal with them today.

The Internet as a driving force for economic performance

When we look ahead to the Internet Revolution, we can already begin to see the economic, social and political benefits. The US has had a very good economic performance over the past 8 years. The Internet Revolution, only about 7 or 8 years old now, has driven the growth. About 40 percent of the real growth of the US economy is due to the physical building out of the Internet. And if you add the effect of electronic commerce, the figure is well over half of the growth in our economy.

We in the government had the sense to see that this revolution was occurring and tried to think about how to best foster it. But most of what has created the revolution economically in the United

States happened independent of government. There were four factors that came together to enable this good economic performance:

1. The invention of the major enabling technologies for the Internet,
2. The freeing up of significant amounts of money for private investment. As we turned our federal budget deficits into surpluses, hundreds of billions of dollars were freed up for private sector investing in these new technologies.
3. The existence of a tradition and institutions for venture capital allowed a great deal of this money to flow into the small companies and new ventures that are building the Internet economy.
4. The early adoption of a coordinated market driven strategy by the U.S. Government to enable the Internet economy to grow in a predictable legal environment and free from over-regulation, taxation and censorship.

The combination of those things – the technology, the availability of money, the tradition of venture capital, and the market driven government policies – have allowed the Internet Revolution to take off in the United States and have propelled our economy. We now have the lowest unemployment rate that we've had in over 40 years. We have the longest peacetime expansion of our economy in our history and yet we still also have a low inflation rate. And that has continued and looks like it will continue into the future because we are riding the wave of this new transformation, this Information Revolution.

We also see other benefits in this revolution besides economic ones. For one, political democracy and the ability of individuals to control their own destinies politically, has been and will continue to be enhanced by this Internet Revolution. Dictatorship depends upon control of information. The Internet means that it becomes impossible for dictators to control information. Information becomes available to everybody via the Internet. And the Internet allows people to exercise their opinions and judgements outside of the organized power elites of societies.

Internet policy: an open approach

We have begun to use this effectively in the U.S. Government. When we first developed our Internet strategy, we took a step that had not been done before by posting the first draft of our Internet strategy on the Internet for comment. We took the step of posting the first draft up on the Internet for comment and then all of the proceedings of our meetings related to Internet issues were also posted on the Internet and all the comments that came back were also posted. And initially many of my communications colleagues in the White House were afraid to do this. They were afraid of what the reaction would be to posting policies that are just in draft form. And of course we did receive some comments back as you might expect from the Internet like "The best thing you and the government could do is die." But most of what we received was quite positive and quite good commentary. We went through 18 virtual drafts of our policy where we got in hundreds of comments, took many of the comments, revised the draft, posted the new draft, revised again as we got more comments and so on and the result was a very open process that produced a much better set of documents and a much better consensus quicker than could be gained by traditional means. So the Internet is also a tremendous force for political democracy.

It is also a force that can help contribute to social well-being. We are already beginning to see this with education and with healthcare. People no longer have to flock to the cities in order to gain their work. They can work from remote locations. People who live in areas that perhaps do not have as robust a healthcare environment now can have access through tele-medicine to the best healthcare advice in the world. People can have access to educational information from their homes from the best experts around the world. All of these things improve social life as well.

And finally we believe that the Internet can contribute to better international understanding. It is still the case in the United States that about one quarter of our people never travel outside the United States during their lifetimes. And the ability to communicate by the Internet internationally we think can only help international relations by allowing people who do not travel to have direct exposure to people from other countries.

Now we also recognize as we look at these benefits that there were going to be certain negative side effects of this revolution that have to be dealt with because it could otherwise have a negative effect on society. Potential violations of privacy can occur in a much greater way in the Internet world than before. Problems that parents will have in raising their children because the children will have access to pornography and speech that parents may not wish them to see. We also have new types of crimes that create new problems for law enforcement.

The real challenge that we have is to try to set rules of the road for the Internet which allow its tremendous positive potential – this transformation – to take place and to get the economic, social and political benefits while at the same time setting rules of the road that deal with the negative side effects.

Key principles of U.S. Internet policy

In the U.S. Government, we developed a few key principles that we felt should guide Internet policy-making. I'll give you a couple of highlights of these principles and then a couple of their applications.

The first principle is that the private sector should lead in the development of Internet policies. For those of you who are not from the United States, the Democratic party in the United States of which President Clinton is leader is traditionally viewed as the party of government, a party that recognizes that government has useful roles to play in society. And if we were talking about other issues like healthcare, I would be advocating a much more active government

66

role in the United States than we have today to provide healthcare for our citizens. But with respect to the Internet, we came to the conclusion that because the Internet moves so quickly, and because change and flexibility are so necessary, and because it is inherently a decentralised medium, private collective action is preferable to government action in setting Internet rules. It would be a mistake for government to take too heavy-handed a role in trying to coordinate the rules for the Internet or to try to protect against some of the negative side effects of the Internet. To do this would slow down the tremendous economic and social engine of the Internet.

Private stake-holders should lead

And so as a first principle we came to the conclusion that the private stakeholders should lead in the development of the Internet and that even where collective action was necessary, it was better for that to be private collective action where possible and not government-led regulation. Because the government-led regulation would take too long to develop and it would be too inflexible once it was developed and put into law. When you put something into law and you establish the agencies to monitor and regulate something, it becomes a very difficult process to change, a very difficult process to keep flexible.

Also when you have many governments as in the U.S. and Germany, federal, state, municipal, each passing their own laws with respect to the Internet, you also run into problems of jurisdictional conflict which can take years and years to resolve.

The slow processes of one government can be made even slower and more bureaucratic when international coordination is carried out through large inter-governmental organizations. The Internet grew up with nonprofit, private stakeholder-based groups providing coordination. The setting of protocols and the architecture for the

Internet occurred not top-down through groups like the International Telecommunications Union. In fact, the International Telecommunications Union rejected the Internet for many, many years, rejected packet switching, rejected the protocols of the Internet. But instead coordination has occurred through the Internet Engineering Task Force and Internet Architecture Boards which are stakeholder-based groups of people using the Internet around the world who come together according to a set of democratic rules that they developed and carried out. Now we recognize that that type of style, the traditional Internet style of organization, had to change as the Internet became bigger and more interests became involved and it became more complex. But we still feel that that formula of having stakeholder-based private non-profit international groups set up to try to solve individual problems is the best way to develop rules and co-ordination for the Internet rather than starting with the proposition that governments have to come together to negotiate those rules.

The model the U.S. Government seeks is one where you do not have one big private organization governing the Internet because the Internet can't be governed in that way. But rather where you have specific, special-purpose organizations brought together to solve specific problems. These organizations would be based in the stakeholders of the Internet: the producers, the consumers of the Internet. So there would be the Internet Engineering Task Force dealing with protocol issues, we have a new group ICANN (Internet Corporation for Assigned Names and Numbers) trying to deal with technical management related to the domain and addressing system of the Internet, organizations like the Internet Content Rating Association (ICRA) that has started to form with the help of the Bertelsmann Foundation to deal with questions of content, perhaps other organizations like one we have started in the United States in the private sector called the Online Privacy Alliance to try to deal with coordination of privacy protection and so on. Different special-purpose organizations formed of stakeholders to try to set rules and solve problems.

Governments should refrain from acting

Now obviously governments do not disappear. They should not disappear and governments will be in the background trying to help promote the development of these organizations. There will develop cases where government action is necessary. But because this is such a fast-moving and uncertain area, I believe that governments should do something that is very difficult for governments to do, which is to refrain from acting. Governments should watch, learn, see what is happening, what is developing through the many creative forces in the private sector and among the stakeholders and users. There will be certain areas where consensus develops that government action is necessary and then government will act in very precise ways that help support the private sector collective leadership.

That is the basic model that the U.S. Government has followed. So, for example, in areas like digital signatures and electronic contracts, the United States Government has not passed a law specifying how to form a contract electronically and under what circumstances and who is allowed to authenticate signatures electronically and so on. Instead, the government let the market develop and the government just passed a law recognizing electronic contracts and electronic signatures. But the law gives freedom to the private sector to allow a market to develop in digital signatures and authentication. So again the government role is to stand back and allow private collective action to occur and to intervene only when it becomes clear that it would be useful.

The Internet – a market driven medium

The second principle is that the Internet should be a market driven arena. There are two different models that one could think about for the growth of the Internet economy. One model – and this was the one that we started on in the United States as did other countries – was to consider the Internet as an extension of the telecommunications industry. The Internet is really a communications medium and in every country in the world, telecommunications and broadcasting are regulated. In some cases, they used to be government-owned but always regulated. And so it was natural in many countries to start thinking of the Internet as a regulated medium.

The other model though is to say that this should be a market-driven medium; that buyers and sellers should be able to come together freely and do business. The role of government is not regulating, not setting prices, not saying under what conditions the buyers and sellers can come together but rather the role of government is simply to help in the establishment of a uniform commercial code for the conclusion of contracts so that if the buyer and seller wish, they can enter into a contract that has legal protection from governments. A very different role. It is not a regulatory role. It is a role essentially enabling private interactions and giving legal protection to them.

The U.S. Government decided that that market-driven model is the right model for the Internet economy, not the regulated model of the telecommunications industry.

The reason why we first regulated telecommunication was because when the infrastructure was built for telecommunication, the size of investment necessary relative to the size of companies that existed was huge and so governments licensed monopolies in order to build the infrastructure because it was the only way they could get the infrastructure built. Because they were setting up the monopolies they either owned them or regulated them.

70

But with the Internet economy, we're not going to have that type of situation. In fact, we're going to have the greatest competition ever seen in the history of free enterprise. Telecommunications companies, computer companies, software companies, television and cable companies, satellite companies, wireless companies, electric utilities, consumer electronics companies – all are competing to build out the Internet. And if we allow that competition to occur instead of trying to regulate it, it will produce great efficiencies and great consumer choice. So it is a very different situation than we faced with the dawn of the telecommunication age.

With broadcast television, we had a limited amount of spectrum to allocate. And so governments became involved in allocating that spectrum and because there was a limited amount of spectrum, it became a public duty to regulate what information and what type of programming went over that spectrum. With the Internet, there will be almost unlimited bandwidth so the government no longer has to play the role of allocating spectrum and conferring that kind of advantage.

Now what is most difficult for the U.S. Government, and I suspect it will be true in all governments, is how to deal with the convergence of these different media that will occur in the next few years. You'll access the Internet and make telephone calls from your television set; you'll have broadcast television and make telephone calls from your computer. It will all come to your home either by television cable or telephone line or satellite or wireless technology, but it will be one converged environment.

The U.S. Government believes as a matter of principle that the converged environment should be deregulated, that competition should be allowed.

Now this does not mean there is not a government role. For example, we think that the government has a role and we've actively put it forward in the United States to ensure that the Internet is available to everybody. It should not just be available to rich people or to middle-class people, it should be available to poor people as well. Because the Internet has the ability to narrow income distribution gaps if it is available to everybody. Or it will widen income distribution gaps if it is only available to the wealthy. So we do think there is a role for government to play both in spreading the Internet throughout society and also in spreading it to developing countries through aid programmes so that we can encourage economic and social development for everybody. But we do not think the government has a role to play in regulating or micro-managing the way in which the Internet is built out or the way in which business is conducted.

Respect the decentralized nature of the Internet

The third principle is that we need to respect the nature of the Internet in whatever kind of policies we do have to set. For example, technologies change very rapidly on the Internet and, therefore, any policy that is tied to a specific technology will be useless before it is enacted. So everything that government does has to be technology-neutral. Similarly – and this is perhaps the most difficult thing for people to understand – it is inherently a decentralised medium. So any attempt to centrally control the Internet, even if it is desirable – which it is not – but even if it were desirable, is impossible, and life is too short to spend too much time doing things that are impossible.

If you want to censor the Internet as a government, I do not think it is a good idea but it does not matter if it is a good idea or a bad idea – you can't do it. It won't succeed. You can't even keep the Internet out of your country unless you shoot satellites down from the sky and confiscate every television set and every telephone in your society. There may be some dictators in this world that try to do that but they won't last for very long.

Similarly you can't enact centralised rules on privacy and then enforce them. As I'll say in a minute, privacy protection is extremely important and it is a value that we in the United States hold to be very important. The real question as a government is how to do it effectively? You can pass a law and you can make the law as detailed as you want and you can make the penalties as strong as you want, but if you can't enforce the law, what have you done? You've made a false promise to your people. You've said do not worry, the government passed a law, we're protecting your privacy and then the government can't do it.

There are 20,000 commercial websites forming every week now, and they are all over the world. No government agency can monitor all those Websites and know when there is a violation of privacy. And even if it could monitor them all, more than half of them would be outside of one's own country and the servers could move from one place to another from week to week. The legal processes involved in making such a prosecution get very, very difficult. Sure, we could catch some people who are violating a privacy law. But not the majority. And so what happens? We've set up a false promise for our people. We've said we're protecting your privacy and we're not. So what do you do instead on questions of undesirable content where you can't censor and questions of privacy protection where the government can't guarantee that it is protecting it is citizen's privacy? I will come back to this later.

A final principle that I'll talk about is that the Internet is the first medium that is being born global. So the traditional way in which industries grew up within countries and then countries negotiated how to make them work together does not work with the Internet. From the very beginning, it is a global medium and, therefore, it needs global co-operation. The Internet should be a seamless global marketplace. And that is why when we released our strategy on the Internet in July of 1997, Bill Daley, our Secretary of Commerce, and I then made a tour. Actually, Germany was the first country to which we came. We discussed with other governments and with private sector groups around the world how to co-ordinate our approaches on the Internet. This is a global marketplace from the very beginning.

So these principles of private sector leadership, a market-driven environment, respecting the nature of the medium in what we do and seeking a global solution from the beginning are the key principles that we felt in the U.S. Government should govern the way the Internet developed.

Empower people to protect themselves

Now I want to return my remarks specifically to these questions about self-regulation and about respecting the nature of the Internet when setting policies on privacy and undesirable content. Ultimately, the best solution is to empower people to protect themselves. The idea that the government can protect people in the Internet Age does not work the way it could in the Industrial Age. The government needs to play a role but it can't play a role that is outside of its competence or capability. You need to give tools to people and information to people to be able to protect themselves. As a government you need to incent the private parties to come together and try to get them to set rules of the road that can be flexible and effective.

In the case of privacy, there is broad agreement by governments and the private sector on a set of privacy principles developed by the OECD. The principles say that somebody who is operating a website should notify visitors to the site when they are collecting information, and what they're going to do with the information. And the consumer who is visiting the website should have the ability to opt out, to say no, I do not want you to collect that information.

The U.S. Government believes there should be private membership organizations to audit this. If I have a complaint, if I feel I have visited a website where they told me they were only going to collect a certain kind of information but I think they did more, I have some easy way to complain and get it resolved. And this organization should also monitor the websites to ensure that they are conforming to these principles. And there should be some visible means such as a seal or a symbol that these self-regulating organizations can confer on websites that are following the principles.

Under this system, when I visit a website, if I see a privacy symbol, I know that it is a site that is following these privacy principles. If I come to a website that does not have a symbol, then I know it is not a site that protects privacy and I may leave the site right away if I want to. A consumer is not going to read five pages of a privacy policy and understand the legal niceties but if there is an established set of principles, those principles are carried out through self-regulatory organizations and they're reflected in a common symbol or seal on a website, then any consumer can know when they are privacy-protected or not. And so in the United States we have a group called the *Online Privacy Alliance*. It is made up of companies that represent a high proportion of the Internet traffic in the United States and it has established these principles for companies to follow. There are a few organizations – one called the *Better Business Bureau* and another one called *Trust e* and there is now also another group forming from our accounting firms – that actually carry out these seal-based programmes and do the monitoring for the companies that join.

The company joins, the company has to submit that it is doing certain things to protect privacy that correspond to these principles and the organization – *Better Business Bureau* or *Trust e* – monitors that and awards the seal which is then posted on the website. And if you as a consumer have a complaint, you can click on the seal and that organization will hear and arbitrate your complaint.

The advantage of this system is it is flexible and it is something that can evolve with time. What it also allows is the government and industry to go to consumers and say "the Internet is a free place, we do not pretend that we can control the whole Internet. You can do what you want and go where you want. But be careful, if you go to a website that does not have one of these privacy seals, your privacy may not be protected. It is your choice." Some people may not care if their privacy is protected and some may. It is their choice. But you have given people the information and the tools to limit themselves to privacy-protected places on the Internet if they wish and you've also created an incentive for companies wanting to do business on the Internet to join a seal-based organization. If they do not they are going to limit the number of people who visit their website. A lot of people won't come if it is not privacy-protected. And finally you've got around some of the problems of jurisdiction. Instead of every government having its own privacy board and every government having its own slightly different privacy rules and every time a new government is elected, they review those rules and change them, you now have an international system where the symbols are the same and they roughly mean the same thing.

You may have different organizations in every country enforcing them, but it is a universal system. That is the model that we are moving towards with the Internet. A private self-regulating mechanism.

Similarly, the U. S. Government believes that private sector self regulation of undesirable content is the right solution rather than government censorship.

The U. S. Government vision is consistent with the Memorandum

I'd like to commend the Bertelsmann Foundation for the convening of this conference, the convening of the panel that produced the Memorandum being discussed and also for the Memorandum itself that was produced for this conference. I think it is an excellent start on considering questions of self-regulation of undesirable content.

The general vision that we hold in the U.S. Government which I think is consistent with the Memorandum is that what you want to do is empower parents to be able to protect their own households and their own children. Self-regulation means giving tools to people to regulate for themselves what comes into their homes. The government shouldn't be involved in censoring. When you sign up with your Internet service-provider, you should have many choices of filtering systems associated with many organizations. You as a parent should be able to choose which filtering package you might want to have for your home. In the United States, you may have religious groups – the *Christian Coalition* – sponsoring a filtering package or a children's group like the Children's Television Network or other groups. And according to your own values as a parent, as a family, you choose what filtering package you want to have from among many choices. And if you're the type of parent that mistakenly believes you understand the Internet better than your children and you want to let everything come through, then you can do that. And in your browser and your search engine should be the ability to make specific filterings if you want. So if you love violence and you hate sex, then you can filter out the sex and keep the violence or the opposite. It should be your choice as a parent or as an adult to decide what you want to do to protect your own household. One of the great things about the Internet is that it has the technology to do that pretty well – not perfectly – but pretty well. When I was growing up, magazines had content that our parents did not want us to see. Sometimes, we found ways to see them anyway! So you never have had perfect protection of children but you can have very good protection with the Internet using filtering.

It is a more workable system than censorship. And most important, it empowers people. It says to people, look we can't as a government fully protect you but we can encourage the private sector to give you tools that can go a long way. You need to exercise responsibility to use those tools.

In these areas like content and privacy and also in the technical coordination of the Internet, it is something very difficult that we're trying to do. We're trying to find our way towards new forms of international organization and new forms of rule-setting. My good friend Esther Dyson who is somewhere in the audience today is understanding the nature of this difficulty with *ICANN* and the technical co-ordination issues. Whenever you try to blaze new ground, you're going to make mistakes, you're going to take two steps forward and one step back as you move ahead. This is a new area, it moves very quickly – we do not understand where it is headed. So we will make mistakes – collectively as a world set of users of the Internet and as governments as we try to move ahead.

But it is important that we not just fall back on old ways that are not going to work, that we keep trying to explore these new ways of doing things, that we overcome the difficulties and that we develop the kinds of organizations internationally which will really enable the positive benefits of this revolution to occur for all of our people as soon as possible.

We have a great challenge ahead of us. It is very exciting. There have been only three or four times in human history when these kinds of transformations have taken place. We have the honour to be living through one of those periods of transformation. We must make sure that we use the opportunity well.

Worldwide Communication –
A New Culture of Common Responsibility[1]

Otto Schily

We have been experiencing an ever accelerating development in the field of information and communication technology over the past few years, which is characterised by a fascinating increase in the performance of IT-systems and by ever shorter intervals in which innovations occur. This results in major new tasks in the political, economic, organizational, cultural and social field. We are faced with a multitude of new problems, not least in the field of IT-security.

Encryption, electronic signatures, error-free software technologies and the protection of our children and youth from harmful content on the Internet are some of the major subjects of the current discussion about security strategies on our way to the information society. Terms such as data highway and multimedia are characteristic of a

1   Speech delivered at the Internet Content Summit 1999 in Munich, Germany.

thorough-going structural change in the economic, governmental and cultural field.

Internet technology – driving force and motor of economic development

The driving force of the development is Internet technology. In the years to come it will change almost all fields of society. "Nothing will remain unchanged" is Roland Berger's assessment of the perspectives of the information society in an expertise commissioned by the 13th German Parliament's Study Commission on the future of the media in the economic sector and society.

The dimensions which the most recent developments have taken on are especially striking if we trace their origins back in the intellectual history of Europe as Arno Borst describes so impressively in his essay "Computus, time and figure in the history of Europe" which is really worth reading. He writes how the Latin term *computus* leads to certain progress in the Roman culture of late classical antiquity. In Latin, the verb *computare* meant to add up, to count on the fingers, and at the same time illustrates that the Roman figures imitated the fingers of a human hand. According to Arno Borst, computare supplemented the term *numerare*, i.e. to allot, to count. Later on, there was a new word for reckoning by means of pebble stones, namely *calculare*, i.e. to calculate with the help of symbols for figures. The substantivised form, *numeratio*, was restricted to the process of cash payment, continues Borst. But *computatio*, then *calculatio* later on stood for a wide mathematical summation and economic estimation up to social assessment and moral rating. Arno Borst's book contains many more interesting historical discoveries. But I will not go into detail now and come back to the present.

The development of the Internet and IT-technology offers great opportunities. Knowledge is the most important economic asset of

80

the new century. More knowledge and education stand for more quality of life. This quality is further enhanced by the fact that information technology allows increased efficiency in all fields of life. Information technology is the prime mover of economic growth and the basis of many new highly qualified jobs.

The Internet does not only help to overcome the usual restriction to linguistic or cultural areas as we know them from the traditional media, but also fundamentally changes the relationship between the media producer and the media consumer according to the slogan "A website for everybody." The new technologies in principle allow everybody to become emancipated from the role of the mere passive recipient and to present himself as an active provider of contents.

The Internet and the new information and communication technologies exert an influence on how we learn, how we work, how we see ourselves and the world. The handling of the Internet is a fundamental new cultural skill, and it is the task of all those in responsible positions in the government, society and the economic sector to provide the opportunity to acquire this knowledge.

Creation of the best possible framework conditions in Germany – the most important future policy task

The development of a modern and globally competitive information economy to ensure Germany's attractiveness for business and the provision of the best possible legal framework conditions and infrastructure is a high priority for the Federal Government in the field of economic, research, education and media policy. In late September the Federal Government will present a programme of action for "Innovation and employment in the information society of the 21st century" which re-defines the objectives for shaping the information society and outlines a variety of initiatives and activities.

The large scope and the comprehensive approach of the programme of action can already be seen from the headings of the chapters listed in the section "Strategic priorities of the programme of action." These read:

- Promote wider access to the new media
- Include multimedia in education
- Enhance the confidence of providers and users through a reliable legal framework
- Promote innovative jobs and new uses
- Push ahead the technological basis and development of the infrastructure
- Make the State a trailblazer in implementation
- Promote European and international cooperation.

In order to advance the use of modern information and communication technology, it is important in particular to learn to handle and manage the flood of data and the information and communication technologies in a competent way.

Competence in handling modern information and communication technology, means more than the merely technical capability to work a computer. It also includes intelligent navigation through the wealth of information offered, the ability to seek – and find – information in a targeted way, to assess it and to make use of it to increase one's own knowledge. Equally important is the ability to ignore undesirable or harmful information.

Man must be at the centre of the enormous innovation process ahead of us. Technology must serve man, not vice versa.

Crime on the Internet

However, the almost precipitous technical development also involves risks and dangers. These include the increasing misuse of the new technical possibilities by criminals and extremists. The spectrum of criminal activities, which has developed on the Internet, is alarming. It ranges from gambling and violations of copyright, the supply of stolen goods, drugs and firearms to instructions on how to build explosive devices and the dissemination of extremist ideas, the glorification of violence and child pornography. It is true that, in this respect, there is no fundamental difference compared with the traditional media. But there is a difference in so far as such contents in the new media often evade criminal investigation and prosecution. The fact that digital information can be easily reproduced and that the world-wide interlink of information systems facilitates the evasion of penal or other sanctions by the State reduces the effectiveness of traditional control methods. According to experts it has to be expected that the use of the new information and communication technologies will promote certain crimes, especially offences in the field of economic crime such as fraud and money laundering, but also economic espionage and sabotage.

We have to expect that crimes will be committed in new ways and that criminals will develop new strategies.

Limited possibilities of governmental action and interference

Beyond the specific issue of combating crime, we will have to examine whether and to what extent there can still be effective governmental intervention and action is effective in view of the global nature of the Internet and the speed of technical developments and, in addition, what this means for closer global co-operation of states.

The question as to which conclusions have to be drawn from globalisation and increasing social differentiation has for some time been at the centre of the current debate on the need to reform governmental institutions in Germany and in Europe, but also in other parts of the world.

Many consider the concentration of governmental activity to a core of governmental tasks to be at the top of the current agenda. This is reflected in terms such as "deregulation," "lean administration" and "strengthening of social self-responsibility."

Whether these terms are always used in the right context remains in doubt.

As can already be clearly recognized today, the multi-faceted and complex relationship between the State and the economic and cultural sectors in a democratic body public will undergo radical changes under the influence of the new information and communication technologies. Anyhow, we have come to recognize that the State almost inevitably develops in the wrong direction if it assumes an all-out responsibility for all sectors of society. On the one hand, the State can not de facto fulfil the demand for being responsible for each and every aspect of public life, and on the other hand, this demand is in contradiction to the citizens' desire for freedom. More importantly, the State would paralyse self-responsibility and creativity if it assured such all-out responsibility and attempted to force legal norms and other regulations upon all social processes. In a statement which was published two days ago recalling the election of the first Federal President Theodor Heuss on 12 September 1949, Federal President Rau and the former Presidents Herzog, Weizsäcker and Scheel discribed this interrelation as follows:

"Only a multitude of responsibilities and initiatives keeps a community together. In addition to governmental action which promotes equal opportunities for all, we need the commitment of as many citizens as possible to social, humanitarian, cultural and ecological tasks. We have to provide for a multitude of opportunities and open new avenues for engagement." Therefore, we will presumably have to consider something like a re-naturalisation of the creative processes in society.

The new communication and information technologies provide unthought-of new possibilities, also with respect to a broad-based modernisation of governmental structures and the administration.

84

However, such a modernisation process must not be reduced to a task of the State, but should be understood as a common responsibility which must involve the State, the cultural sector and industry. This is the concept of a dialogue-oriented policy as it is advocated by the new Federal Government. This was made very clear by Federal Chancellor Gerhard Schröder when he declared dialogue, co-ordination and co-operation to be the basic principles of his policy. This dialogue is of particular importance in the field of media and communications policy. It will be successful if all players strive to achieve agreed targets.

The initiative "Germany 21 – Getting ready for the information age," an example of co-operation between the State and industry

I particularly welcome the initiative "Germany 21 – Getting ready for the information age." This initiative launched by industry is designed to find and implement a joint strategy of the government and the economic sector for development towards an information society in Germany. The spectrum of subjects ranges from framework conditions provided by the State and technical infrastructure to basic and further training, the establishment of new companies and the promotion of women in IT jobs. It should also be mentioned that the initiative is supported by companies from almost all branches of industry, which means that the emphasis is on a common overall target.

Federal Chancellor Schröder has assumed the patronage of the initiative Germany 21. There can be no clearer indication of the importance which the Federal Government attaches to this initiative for enhancing co-operative action. Several Federal Ministries, among them the Federal Ministry of the Interior, participate in the initiative. For the time being, several working groups are working on a concrete definition of the objectives of a joint strategy and the related measures.

I am convinced that the Memorandum published at this conference on "Responsibility on the Internet" will meet with great interest in the initiative Germany 21 and that it will help in setting common targets. Hence the co-operation of the State and the economic sector has to be based on the principle of self-responsibility of the various parts of society and on the concrete implementation of this principle.

Self-regulation of the Internet allows a high degree of flexibility in new regulatory issues

Self-control and self-regulation of the Internet and the new media services – as demanded in the Memorandum – offer the opportunity to realise objectives that serve the interest of the general public, which can not be attained by sovereign regulatory action. Self-regulation in the field of the new media allows a high degree of flexibility as regards new regulatory issues. In contrast to government agencies that are bound to comply with strict formal rules, self-regulation bodies are in a position to respond to changes in the media landscape in a comparatively swift and unbureaucratic way. Self-regulation thus takes a burden from the legislative and executive bodies. It avoids interference with the freedom of the press, broadcasting, information and opinion, which are protected by the *Grundgesetz* (Constitution), and fully corresponds to the principle of subsidiarity of governmental action.

The Internet – no legal vacuum

Self-regulation in the field of the new media, however, cannot completely substitute legal regulation. It is the State that has the ultimate responsibility for the protection of the legal system built on democratic values, the concrete shape of which is dependent on the various legal traditions. The State is obliged to intervene by regulatory action where compelling considerations of the common good and public security are not, or only insufficiently, taken into account. Therefore the Internet cannot be a domain in which no legislation exists as is sometimes demanded in the discussion on the necessity and possibilities of regulating the Internet. Some dispute the State's legitimation to exert influence on the world-wide computer network. In this context they forget that the Internet could only develop at all because government-funded institutions, i.e. universities and research institutes, made servers available throughout the world. Also against the background of the further development of the Internet, the State is now as before obliged to protect the rights of its citizens from those who misuse this system. Therefore legal vacuums are not acceptable. Protected legal assets, values and cultural standards that are generally acknowledged by society must not be abandoned in an increasingly interlinked world. We must not allow technical progress to cause damage to the established order and the legal basis of people's living together.

The Information and Communication Services Act (IuKDG) determines the legal framework for the new information and communication technologies in Germany

In 1997, the legal, technological and organizational framework for the development of new media and telecommunication services in Germany was determined by adopting the Information and Communication Services Act (IuKDG) and the State Treaty on Media Services signed by the heads of the Länder Governments.

In this context, the voluntary self-regulation of the new telecommunication and media service providers was assigned a key function, in particular in the field of the protection of minors. Accordingly, these providers are obliged to ensure effective protection of minors (§ 7a of the Act Concerning the Distribution of Publications Harmful to Minors and § 8, sec. 4 of the State Treaty on Media Services). Anyone who commercially offers electronic information and communication services has to appoint a Commissioner for the Protection of Minors. These regulations do not only have a high symbolic value; by providing for appropriate organizational measures concerning the service providers in Germany, they also ensure that children and young people will be shielded to a large extent from harmful contents.

As an incentive to service providers to create a structure for voluntary self-regulation which ensures the protection of minors, we have offered them the opportunity to delegate the responsibilities of the Commissioner for the Protection of Minors to a voluntary self-regulation body. This option is of particular interest to smaller and medium-size service providers with regard to keeping their costs low.

Recognition of the independent role of voluntary self-regulation in German law

This provision emphasises the independent role and importance of voluntary self-regulation supplementing governmental activities in order to abolish illegal and harmful Internet contents.

Taking this as a basis, the association "Freiwillige Selbstkontrolle Multimedia Diensteanbieter e.V. (FSM)" [Voluntary Self-Regulation of Multimedia Service Providers] was constituted to attract new service providers as members and to encourage them to adhere to a common Code of Conduct or otherwise to punish any violation thereof.

The Code obliges service providers to take appropriate steps so as to ban illegal and harmful contents, particularly those harmful to young persons. It shall be ensured that information offers comply with the accepted journalistic principles. In addition, it stipulates that the competent authorities must be informed if a danger for a person's moral or physical welfare or freedom is suspected.

The activity of this German self-regulatory body has shown a promising development: within a single year the FSM received 832 notifications, 212 of which were objections. 42 complaints affected the offers of German content providers. More than half of the remaining contents that users disapproved of originated from the United States of America. However, the majority of complaints about foreign contents could not be pursued any further because no contact person was available.

International initiatives to combat illegal and harmful Internet contents

In the context of international co-operation, youth protection and the fight against illegal and harmful contents are vital issues, too. Proposals for solutions and initiatives are being discussed in the European Union and other international bodies within their scope of responsibility (OECD, G8 States, Council of Europe, UNESCO).

Taking into account the transnational character of the new services, the Federal Government has always prioritised this kind of international co-operation for combating illegal and harmful Internet contents, because it is the only means to protect public interest effectively. Therefore, it will continue with its successful activities within the competent international organizations.

EU Action Plan for the Promotion
of the Safer Use of the Internet

Worth mentioning in this context are the guiding activities of the
European Union, in particular the "Action Plan for the Promotion of
the Safer Use of the Internet" and the "Council Memorandum on
the Development of the Competitiveness of the European Audiovisual and Information Services Industry by Promoting National
Frameworks Aimed at Achieving a Comparable and Effective Level
of Protection of Minors and Human Dignity" (98/569/EC). Both
the Action Plan and the Recommendation serve to fight illegal and
harmful contents, especially Internet contents, throughout the
Community. The documents address the EU Member States as well
as service providers and user organizations.

Minimise state intervention and limit coercive
measures to an indispensable level

Thus, coercive measures shall be limited to a necessary minimum so
as not to impede the social and economic progress which itself is
closely related to technological and economic development. Accordingly, one objective is to promote the development of common
guidelines and methods that allow for a Europe-wide harmonisation
of the national frameworks for the voluntary self-regulation of service providers.

In addition, the Memorandum encourages all parties concerned
to carry out joint initiatives which should particularly aim at facilitating Internet access for children and young persons, promoting
high-quality contents appropriate for this age group, banning all
Internet contents that disregard human dignity, and at testing new
technologies for parental control. The EU Commission will submit a
report about the results of this Community-wide co-operation to the

90

Council of the European Union and the European Parliament in the fall of 2000.

The Memorandum on voluntary self-regulation of the Internet – a welcome initiative

The initiative of the Bertelsmann Foundation for shared responsibility in the Internet demonstrates the willingness to contribute to the common good. What is laid out here in an exemplary way is the necessary new interpretation of and attitude towards a sense of solidarity between the State and society, and in this particular case between the Internet industry, the new telecommunication and media service providers on the one hand and the Internet users on the other.

The offer of co-operation contained in the Memorandum is to be welcomed. As regards the approach and the concept of the proposed self-regulation system, it points in the right direction.

Lasting success of self-regulation systems – a question of effectiveness and feasibility

However, a lasting success of self-regulation initiatives and systems as well as their acceptance is very much a function of their effectiveness and feasibility.

As has been pointed out in the Memorandum, an essential prerequisite for a self-regulation system is the development of codes of conduct.

When it comes to content-related self-regulation activities, transparency is the main criterion. In order to adequately support such transparency, the self-regulatory bodies should be accountable (on a regular basis) for their activity. Public debates might also have a positive effect.

Curiosity and open-mindedness of young people towards the Internet – fears of parents

Today, young people are well prepared for the multimedia future. Quickly and easily they acquire a high media competence. To search the Internet is for them far less difficult than for their own parents. Or as 14-year-olds put it: "If my dad is searching for something in the Internet, he will ask me for help." The traditional distribution of competence within families has seen some changes recently.

Youngsters hardly know the difficulties their parents have in mentally processing and learning how to handle the wave of media and Internet technologies that has broken over them.

Dealing with new telecommunication and media services often places excessive demands on many adults. Therefore, they should be given support in understanding media technologies and their contents, for instance through simpler information.

Filtering systems – solutions that make sense

Technologies such as filtering systems which enable parents to block certain contents harmful to young people generally present an appropriate solution. However, it must be ensured that this technology-based security does not give service providers an alibi to delegate their responsibility to parents. Particular problems are to be expected in socially underprivileged families where parents will hardly know how to apply such technologies responsibly. At risk are mainly those families where violence is an accepted means to push through one's own interests and to solve conflicts. Because these parents lack the necessary sensitivity towards the presentation of violence, it is unlikely that they will filter out the relevant contents. What follows from this is that technological tools can help content providers to meet certain requirements, but they will not substitute personal responsibility. Therefore we must avoid a situation where the use of technology-based Internet filters gives content providers the possibility to get away from their share of responsibility.

As far as the legislator and the Government are concerned, the Memorandum provides for a supportive function. In my capacity as the Federal Minister of the Interior, I can assure you that generally this function will be carried out. Of course, details will have to be discussed; this conference, and in particular the workshops, offer a forum for just this. In the same way as the Internet is constantly changing and progressing, the recommended integrated system should also be subject to permanent re-evaluation.

The Federal Criminal Police Office "on patrol" in the Internet

Useful measures in the fight against child pornography to be taken by law enforcement authorities include random checks in the Internet, i.e. "patrolling in the Internet."

On 19 to 20 November 1998, the Standing Conference of the Ministers and Senators of the Interior (IMK) commissioned the Federal Criminal Police Office (BKA) to assume a central function for Germany in carrying out such independent investigations of the Internet and online services. In addition, a co-ordination office on child pornography was set up at the Federal Criminal Police Office, whose task is to collect and evaluate the reported results.

The German Information Security Agency (BSI) creates an Internet search engine

In order to make these investigations even more efficient, the German Information Security Agency was asked to develop an Internet search engine in co-ordination with the Federal Criminal Police Office. This search engine will facilitate the detection of contents relevant under criminal law, the preservation of evidence, and the establishing of the identity of the sender and the addressee. Thus, we hope to control the dissemination of contents and images containing child pornography or extremist and racist propaganda via the Internet.

We know that the great majority of end-users would prefer the Internet to be free of objectionable and harmful or illegal contents. This is also demonstrated by the growing number of online and off-line reports to the police. Internet providers, too, receive a great number of such reports and inquiries. Therefore, Internet providers and the hotlines operated by them could function as an important connecting element between the Internet community and public authorities. They could inform and train end-users on Internet-related matters. As far as risks and dangers of the Internet are concerned, information should be given primarily by the contract partners of end-users.

Encryption – a contribution to security and confidence on the Internet

If we want to guarantee more security and confidence in the Internet, new encryption systems will be indispensable. With the "Guidelines of the German cryptography policy" which were adopted by the Cabinet on 2 June 1999, the Federal Government has reformulated its position towards the encryption of electronic data in the private and business sectors. It was pointed out that the Government does not intend to limit the free availability of encryption products in Germany. The use of secure encryption technologies is considered a decisive prerequisite for the protection of the data of citizens and of trade secrets as well as for the evolution of electronic commerce.

The Federal Government will actively support the distribution of secure encryption technologies in Germany.

Voluntary self-regulation – a special form of enhanced responsibility of each member of our society

We must not respond with fear or mutual mistrust to the grand perspectives opened to us by these new information and communications technologies. Instead, we should get ready to use and to optimise these technologies for the citizens' benefit. However, it is not a sign of timidness or even hostility towards technology in general when we retain a clear view of the risks resulting from technological developments. I hope for understanding and confident co-operation between industry, cultural institutions and the State in order to keep these risks as small as possible. With this conference and the Memorandum on "Responsibility in the Internet" we set an example for shared responsibility which reflects the contributions of all three players.

Before I conclude my remarks I would like to come back to Arno Borst's book which I mentioned earlier:

"If we cared not only for the interdependency between man and nature, between nature and society, but also for the relationships within our community, that is between ourselves, we would be able to open up better perspectives as well as greater challenges. Having specialised in humanities, it is my task to remind people that the computer is just predictable, but not accountable. There stands a clear fact behind this: There is more to carrying out measuring and calculation functions than just handling numbers, as soon as the time granted and allocated to humans comes into play. Because then certain criteria have to be determined in advance; during the process promises must be made and schedules must be met; in the aftermath accounts are to be rendered. Since the time of Plato and Aristotle the human history of numbers and time not only moves around momentum and quantity – as this essay wanted to show – but also around duration and quality. Each era saw its inhabitants asking the same old question, whether they should rise above the moment or rather arrange themselves with it or finally loose against it. Each era had many controversial answers to give which reflected the conflicting aspects of time.

Which of these answers would become history did in the end neither depend upon the environment or the tools people had in this particular period, nor upon the era's orientation either towards the past or the future, nor even upon the symbol which was created to manage its present times. What it actually did depend on was the sincerity and prudence of those who were responsible for setting certain standards and who were accountable for them, in a way that they also had to account for things which they could not predict."

As I see it, Arno Borst is right when he emphasizes that every technology must always retain its tool character in as much as man should not go in quest of his origins or his final target outside but rather inside himself, and that this quest can be successful.

Chapter III

Comments on the Memorandum

The Bertelsmann Foundation has asked seven distinguished experts from four continents to comment on the Memorandum. Their different perspectives – policy making, media supervision, civil liberties – are intended to reflect on the recommendations of the Memorandum and to spark further discussion. The editors want to thank all commentators for their contribution.

Siegmar Mosdorf

Parliamentary Undersecretary, Federal Ministry of Commerce and Technology, Berlin, Germany

The Internet presents new challenges to politics, the legal system and society. It is a new medium offering users previously undreamt-of possibilities for communication and information. However, the decentralized structure and global character of the Internet require the creation of new instruments as a means of ensuring responsible use. This is particularly true with regard to the need to effectively protect children and minors from undesirable contents in the new media.

The Bertelsmann Foundation has been considering important questions related to the new media for some time now. Again and again the innovative proposals formulated by the Foundation have pointed the way ahead. The Bertelsmann Foundation's memorandum on self-regulation of Internet content is no exception. Produced in cooperation with international experts, it provides specific recommendations for decision-makers in politics, economics, law and the social sphere. "Self-Regulation on the Internet," the project presented by the Bertelsmann Foundation within the framework of the memorandum, aims to improve the protection of minors on the Internet. Central to the project is the belief that, in the case of the global medium known as the Internet, no government, no company and no state institution can protect young persons from illegal and harmful contents on its own. In recognition of this fact, the project pursues a coordinated approach at four levels of responsibility:
- self-regulation of the Internet industry
- self-classification and filter systems as technical aids
- hotlines for users
- criminal prosecution in addition to self-regulation.

Protecting the young from illegal and harmful contents in the media is a matter of particular concern to the German government. An essential prerequisite for the development of the information society in Germany and elsewhere is the confidence of all participants (providers, users, state supervisory bodies, data-protection control institutions) in the safety of the technical systems as well as in the system of protection against their misuse through illegal and harmful acts.

98

The Federal Information and Communication Services Act and the State Treaty on Media Services concluded between the *Länder* have introduced important provisions relating to the protection of minors from illegal and harmful contents in the new media. These provisions expressly include the establishment of voluntary systems of self-regulation and self-protection by technical means. The statutory measures on the protection of minors consist of a three-tier system which both corresponds to the degree of danger posed by the contents and takes due account of the right to freely form and express opinions. These rules have received great attention within the EU and beyond.

The Federal Information and Communication Services Act has recently been evaluated by the German government. Its findings confirm that – along with statutory rules – voluntary self-regulation represents an effective means of control, above all in the case of contents in the new services which have been produced in Germany. However, against the background of the global nature of the new media, national rules alone are shown to have only a limited effect. Ensuring the effective protection of minors against harmful media contents requires the creation of an international network of voluntary self-regulation extending beyond European and international agreements as well as improvements in self-protection by technical means through the provision of suitable filter and assessment systems.

The German government attaches particular importance to international cooperation in combating illegal and harmful contents on the networks. It therefore vigorously supports the EU action plan entitled "Promoting the safe use of the Internet by combating illegal and harmful contents on global networks" as a necessary further step in developing the protection of minors at an international level. The plan focuses on four main areas of action: the development of voluntary self-regulation by the service providers, a comprehensive exchange of information underpinned, for example, by a European "hotline" network, the creation of filter and assessment systems which take account of the cultural and linguistic diversity within Europe as well as the promotion of measures designed to sensitize parents, teachers, children and young persons during instruction on how to use the Internet in accordance with the principles of the protection of minors. Within the framework of the action plan, the EU Commission will provide financial support to two hotlines (IN-HOPE, BELHOT) in order to create a European hotline network and four projects concerned with demonstrating filter and assessment systems as well as measures aimed at sensitizing people with regard to protection issues. The industry is working in close cooperation with the EU Commission.

Experience gained during the evaluation of the Federal Information and Communication Services Act shows, as do the discussions at the international level, that, in the multimedia age, increasing importance is attached to technical self-protection. With regard to the protection of minors, a large number of technical possibilities for filtering relevant Internet offerings already exist. However, above all with regard to differences in culture and law, according to current knowledge, none of them provides sufficient protection of minors in every respect. This finding accords with the results of a study "The protection of minors and filter technology on the Internet" which was commissioned by the Federal Ministry for Economics and Technology within the framework of the evaluation of the Federal Information and Communication Services Act. Due out soon, this study takes the form of a stocktaking exercise. It reports on the technologies already available for implementing measures related to the protection of minors during accessing of the Internet, determines the need for improvement and further development, and assesses each technology in the context of the need to protect minors. The study proposes, as a self-protection measure, the voluntary labeling of unproblematical contents by the producer and, at the same time, a broad-based public information campaign. The Bertelsmann Foundation's project is heading in a similar direction. The task of this summit will be to answer, from a variety of angles and with international cooperation, questions connected with such a self-help procedure, for example, questions about assessment standards.

It is the German government's view that, in addition to statutory rules, voluntary self-regulation or co-regulation measures and international agreements, effective protection of minors in the context of the media depends in particular on improving the media competence of the users. On the basis of the action plan "Innovation and jobs in the information society of the 21st century," presented in the fall of 1999, the German government will take specific measures designed both to enable, in particular, young persons to assume personal responsibility when using the new media and help them maintain a critical distance vis-à-vis problematical contents.

Erkki Liikanen

Commissioner, European Commission, Brussels, Belgium

It is noteworthy that a European approach to the difficult and controversial area of illegal and harmful content on the Internet has been in place since October 1996, when the Commission adopted the Communication to illegal and harmful content on the Internet and the Green paper on the protection of minors and human dignity. This can fairly claim to have been a world première. The European Parliament and the Council both endorsed the Commission's approach.

These have been followed up by a number of important policy documents, including the Bonn Conference Ministerial Declaration signed by ministers from 29 European countries, the Recommendation on Protection of Minors and Human Dignity and the Action plan on promoting safer use of the Internet.

Within the framework of the Action Plan, particular attention is drawn to creating a network of hotlines and encouraging self-regulation to developing filtering and rating systems and encouraging awareness actions.

The Commission believes that a combination of these actions will be an effective way to fight illegal content on the Internet and to protect minors from harmful content, while respecting the right of free expression.

A European network of hotlines

Community co-funding will support a network of hotlines, which allow users to report alleged illegal content and use of the Internet and have effective, transparent, procedures for dealing with complaints. International cooperation will also be encouraged.

The role of self-regulation

Following the seminar held in Saarbrücken, in its Council conclusions of 27 September 1999, the Council recognizes the contribution that self-regulation can make to safeguarding public interests in accordance with national cultural and legal traditions, with the support of national legal systems ("co-regulation").

Under the Recommendation on Protection of Minors and Human Dignity and the Internet Action Plan, it is stressed that coordination of different national initiatives is essential. Guidelines are given for the codes of conduct to be developed, which will be supported by the Commission.

Rating and filtering

It is important that there is a variety of such tools and that the responsible end-user (parent or teacher) has a choice between different systems available, and the choice whether or not to use them at all. There should be transparency as to how ratings are arrived at including the criteria used to rate content or to include it in a stop-list (black or red list) or a go-list (white or green list). Such systems should as far as possible be configurable to individual users' requirements and preferences.

The systems should be able to cope with different languages and cultures and different types of concerns.

Filtering software should be adjustable and parents and teachers should be empowered to deal with unwanted content according to their preferences.

The Commission fully supports efforts to propose a system whereby parents and teachers have the technical means to filter content according to their value judgements. In a Union of 15 different member states this means that considerable national differences may occur. It is therefore important to take account of cultural and linguistic differences.

To ensure a high level of protection, a critical mass of sites has to be rated. The memorandum rightly refers to the need for self-rating. There is still a great deal of work to be done to encourage content providers to label their content in order to make it easier to find. A common rating vocabulary has to be found which filtering software recognizes and account has to be taken of national differences.

Awareness

Under the Internet Action Plan a considerable part of resources is dedicated to awareness-raising measures.

This means informing parents, teachers and children about ways of dealing with potentially harmful content. Work already under way on media awareness should include an Internet package.

The Bertelsmann Foundation Memorandum

The Bertelsmann Foundation are to be congratulated on the imaginative way in which they have gone about drawing up the memorandum. They have invested considerable effort in associating a range of well-qualified experts and have as a result ensured that the final result is a valuable contribution to a lively and informed public discussion.

The Commission is naturally pleased that the principles set out in the memorandum are completely in accordance with the lines of the policy which it proposed.

As pointed out in the memorandum and in several Commission documents, one single approach will not be successful. The Commission recognizes the need for close international cooperation of both public services and private content and service providers.

All these parties have a stake in a responsible use of the Internet. Trust and confidence are one of the prerequisites for the further take-off of the Internet, so that everybody can use the vast amount of information available in a responsible way and reach the benefits of the Internet. Empowering parents and teachers to chose the content children are allowed to view of, is one of the main means establishing trust.

In this context, this memorandum has made a very important contribution which will help further to raise awareness concerning illegal and potentially harmful content on the Internet and to pro-pose solutions.

Gareth Grainger

*Deputy Chairman, Australian Broadcasting Authority (ABA),
Sydney, Australia*

The Internet is a marvellous opportunity for the whole of human-kind. It enables extraordinary scope for instantaneous communica-tion of information, ideas and even gossip between people in the most far-flung corners of the globe. For us to take full advantage of its potential there are a number of issues which have to be ad-dressed. One of those is to confront ways in which to spread access to the Internet so that the whole world can benefit, rather than creating gaping gulfs between the information rich and information poor. Another major challenge, and the one which this Memoran-dum on Self-Regulation of the Internet vitally relates to, is how to deal with public and parental concerns about problematic content on the Internet. Wherever these concerns exist there will be an ongoing reluctance by people to take the Internet into their homes, schools and workplaces. If the Internet is genuinely to become a true global tool for information, education and communication then those concerns must be addressed in a satisfactory manner. National parliaments face considerable pressures from their electors to take action to deal with the problem of illegal and harmful Internet content. The internationally distributed and interactive nature of the Internet means that any attempt to deal with the Internet in isolation from other countries will be very difficult to accomplish. National actions must fit into a pattern of international understanding on the best ways in which to deal with Internet content issues.

The Bertelsmann Foundation is to be congratulated and thanked for having the wisdom, vision and foresight to understand that a forum was needed to advance debate on the best ways to deal with Internet content issues at the international level. It has sponsored a process, including the conduct of valuable research in USA, Germany and Australia, which has laid the groundwork for a major world summit on Internet Content issues held in Munich from 9 to 11 September 1999.

The Memorandum on Self-Regulation of the Internet, written by the Bertelsmann Foundation, has emerged from the consultative processes of a wide range of experts from industry, Academe, and national and international policy makers. Very rightly, I believe this process has raised serious issues about inappropriate restrictions on freedom of expression and highlighted the importance of self-regulation to any national or international scheme for dealing with Internet content. The Internet is too diffuse to be easily amenable to narrow or exclusively government-based regulation. Effective dealing with the challenges of Internet content requires an active coalition of industry, the community, governments and law-enforcement agencies to develop sensible and appropriate schemes for dealing with illegal and harmful content at a national and international level. Industry must accept the responsibility for self-governance under codes of conduct. Parents, teachers and the wider community must accept their responsibility to provide appropriate supervision and education, especially for young people, in the use of the Internet. Citizens must have the right to complain and express concerns about problematic content to complaints hotlines. Governments and law enforcement agencies must actively work with industry and the community to ensure appropriate underpinning for such self-regulatory arrangements. Both industry and the community must be given the necessary tools to deal with content issues, especially through content labelling and rating schemes.

All of these matters have been addressed in admirable detail in

106

this Memorandum. I believe this document contains all the ingredients necessary for this process to move forward. Every country will find its own best and most appropriate method for dealing with these issues to meet their own specific national and cultural circumstances. There will be differences from country to country in the specific detail. However, the ingredients are presented in this Memorandum for the ways in which any country might appropriately respond both to the challenge and to the splendid opportunities of the online world.

Esther Dyson

Chairman, EDventure Holding, New York, USA

This response is my personal reaction to the Bertelsmann Foundation Memorandum on "Self-Regulation on the Internet." I applaud the Foundation's attempts to deal with a tough issue, and this response is intended helpfully, not destructively. Like it or not, many forces want to "regulate the Net," whatever that means, and "self" regulation is probably better than regulation by some "non-self" authority. However, it is not clear who the "self" is to be in this case.

Overall, the document leaves me feeling distinctly queasy. So much of it defers details for implementation later. Such and such must be done: Who will do it? Illegal content: Sure, we're all against illegal content, but who decides what is illegal? There are too many questions left open to be answered by some legitimate authority later on.

The basic problem is that the group is attempting to come up with a global solution, topdown. But the nature of the world is that it is a collection of sometimes interacting communities, not a single global administration to be governed top-down. In some spheres there is need for coordination and collaboration, but it does not necessarily need to be governed globally.

Of course, the idea is that the system for Net content regulation would be run by well-meaning, enlightened individuals who know what is best for everyone. But what happened to the notion that people know what is best for themselves and their children? What happened to regulation by citizens themselves of the content they choose for themselves or their children, rather than regulation by a "self" of industry entities beholden to their governments?

The document proposes the creation of a full, broadly integrated set of institutions that can "protect" us all from the problem of illegal content. I fear that we will end up with a worldwide bureaucracy always forced to take the "safe" route, calling for the removal of questionable content.

ISPs are properly relieved of responsibility for actions against their customers; let the worldwide content-rating system take the heat. It *will* take the heat, and dismiss it, because after all it is protecting the public, and a few mistakes here and there are inevitable.

Now let me consider some details.

Illegal content

What *is* illegal content? Throughout the document, the writers refer to "illlegal content such as child pornography." If there is any content other than child pornography that they think should be illegal, the authors should have the courage to specify what they mean. They make one broader reference: "... racist and discriminatory websites, child pornography material exchanged in certain newsgroups and chatrooms and 'how to'-guides on terrorist activity are too disturbing to ignore. Mechanisms have to be developed to deal with illegal content, to protect children online as well as free speech." But that is all.

Later, there is some expectation that "illegality" of content will be determined in the home territory of the publishing website, and will be taken down in accordance with that territory's laws – and presumably by its law-enforcement officials. But in the world of the Internet, with mirror sites, anonymous e-mail and the like, this may not be feasible – fortunately!

The proposed rating system

The proposed rating system, with its three layers, is nicely designed. The idea is to encourage sites to rate themselves, using some common vocabulary, and then to encourage second parties to create rating "templates" with combinations of various metrics and that vocabulary to reflect their values. Finally, a third set of raters should make specific whitelists of acceptable sites – acceptable to children, mostly – beyond the more abstract criteria of the second layer. In theory, that neatly eliminates the value issue from self-rating.

However: First, in the more detailed rating section, the authors propose that the vocabulary be created by an international group of experts of high integrity: "In addition to experts on civil liberties and Internet policy, the board should include social scientists who can advise about what kinds of content are more and less harmful to children." What are these social scientists doing defining a value-free vocabulary? Surely they belong only in the second layer.

Second, a global vocabulary is inherently limiting and too constrained. It is a matter of emphasis, but the value is in the third layer, where people make editorial choices. Otherwise, where's the appreciation of quality, of a sense of humor, respect for the truth? Surely children need to be protected from bland junk as well as from trashy or harmful junk.

Moreover, the focus on protecting children seems excessive. Perhaps it is this focus that makes the idea of almost universal filtering politically palatable. Surely people will have other motivations for filtering, but they might not want to use a filtering system as blunt as this one. Personally, I'd like to see a rating system for truthfulness, for disclosure of advertising relationships, for bias, for political leaning, for assumed audience. (Is the site for techies or for consumers?)

At least there's a provision that unrated sites would not automatically be excluded by most filters.

Child pornography vs. children viewing pornography

The report seems to gloss over the distinction between child pornography, a legal term that connotes the use of children in pornography, which is (almost) universally illegal. This generally involves abuse of actual children, and content on the Net is evidence of the actual abuse of children. This is quite different from the viewing of pornography (on or off the Net) by children, which is almost certainly harmful in excess (like almost anything in excess) but is quite a different matter.

Privacy issues

I also have some concerns over the report's attitude to privacy protection – and implicitly, to anonymity. It is important to catch criminals, but we need to maintain a balance among society's various needs. There is a suggestion that the Internet industry (broadly defined) should "tak[e] all commercially reasonable steps to verify the identity of subscribers, while protecting subscribers' privacy." That does not seem to be necessary: Abusers can be shut off without their identities being known; persistent abusers will eventually become identifiable.

Constructive criticism

So what are alternative, positive approaches? First of all, private groups such as the Bertelsmann Foundation are doing the right thing by getting involved in this debate. They should raise people's awareness of the issues and encourage them to think for themselves – and to pick content for themselves and to offer content-rating services or choices to others. The Bertelsmann Foundation should encourage private groups and companies to develop and promote rating services, not just for porn or violence, but for quality, advertising disclosure, data-collection-and-use practices, and the like. These services, like many services designed to "solve problems," are a huge business opportunity.

The Bertelsmann Foundation should also encourage widespread consumer-education campaigns, led not just by foundations and governments, but also by companies (known as "advertising"). Just as consumers look for price, nutritional information, fabric content, care instructions, warranties and other information on products, so should they be encouraged to look for similar meta-information on websites.

In short, let's look at the role that informed, empowered citizens can play in keeping the Net a place they want to live in.

Nadine Strossen

President, American Civil Liberties Union (ACLU),
New York, USA

Thank you for the opportunity to comment on the "Memorandum on Self-Regulation of the Internet." As a member of the "Expert Network," who worked with the Bertelsmann Foundation, I appreciate the dedicated efforts of the many persons who contributed to this project.

First I will offer several general comments about the Memorandum overall, and then I will focus on the two specific aspects of the document that I find most disturbing: the call for universal self-rating and the discussion of hotlines.

General comments

1. First, I would like to correct some misleading press accounts that have come to my attention, which were apparently based on an unauthorized receipt of a preliminary draft version of the Memorandum. As Appendix II to the Memorandum clearly states: "Not every expert agreed with all the Memorandum."

   While many members of the "expert network" discussed the topics addressed in the Memorandum, many of us, as individuals, disagree with at least some aspects of the Memorandum.

   I must stress that I, for one, disagree with many of the Memorandum. I realize that representatives of the Bertelsmann Foundation understood this, which is, I assume, why they specifically took the initiative to invite me to submit these comments, and to have them integrated in this volume; I appreciate this opportunity.

2. I do enthusiastically endorse the thrust of portion of Recommen-

dation 12, insofar as it calls for "an education and awareness campaign" on the part of Internet users, including children, and urges schools to "provide the necessary skills for children to understand the benefits and limitations of online information and to exercise self-control" over Internet content that they might deem "problematic." I agree that there should be a strong emphasis on schools providing young people and their parents with the "necessary skills to understand the benefits and limitations of online information." Indeed, to underscore the importance of this recommendation, I would place it first, rather than last.

I am in complete agreement with the "Global Internet Liberty Campaign ['GILC'] Member Statement Submitted to the Internet Content Summit" that:

"Approaches that emphasize education and parental supervision should receive far more attention than they have to date, as they alone possess the potential to effectively direct young people toward beneficial and appropriate uses of the Internet. Ultimately, the issue is one of values, which can only be addressed properly within a particular family or cultural environment. Neither punitive laws nor blocking technologies can ensure that a child will only access online content deemed appropriate by that child's family or community."

3. I also want to associate myself with the thrust of Recommendation 10 insofar as it states: "There should be no criminal responsibility of mere access and network providers for third parties' illegal content transmissions taking place in real-time through their networks. There should be *no* regulatory requirements on service providers to screen or filter content." I fully concur that access and network providers should be understood as conduits or carriers for speech, not publishers who bear the legal responsibility for the content of communications.

Comments about specific aspects of the recommendations universal self-rating

Recommendation 6 states; "[A]t the core of the recommendations for an integrated system of self-regulation and end-user autonomy must be an improved architecture for the rating and filtering of Internet content. Content providers worldwide must be mobilized to label their content and filters must be made available to guardians and all users of the Internet to make more effective choices about the content they wish to have enter their homes."

In other words, the "core" recommendation is for a system of universal self-rating to be combined in a "layer cake" of filtering. I strongly dissent from this recommendation and view it as a significant threat to the principles of free expression enshrined in the Universal Declaration of Human Rights, the International Covenant on Civil and Political Rights, the European Convention on Human Rights, and analogous national guarantees, such as the First Amendment to the U.S. Constitution.

Many of my concerns are detailed in the GILC Statement, to which the ACLU is a signatory. But I want to elaborate on the issue of self-rating, which receives little or no critical examination in the Memorandum.

The ACLU initially examined the self-rating issue more than two years ago, in our White Paper, *Fahrenheit 451.2: Is Cyberspace Burning? How Rating and Blocking Proposals May Torch Free Speech on the Internet* (see <http://www.aclu.org/issues/cyber/burning.html>). Unfortunately, the concerns we raised then have only become more pressing in the intervening period. As our White Paper noted, calling upon Internet content providers and speakers to "self-rate" their expression is no less contrary to the basic principles of free expression than a proposal that publishers of books and magazines "self-rate" their publications, including all stories and articles, or a proposal that participants in street corner conversations rate their oral statements.

To illustrate the very practical adverse impact that self-rating schemes would necessarily have upon freedom of expression, we described five specific reasons why they would have such negative consequences, providing particular examples. Since universal self-rating is at the "core" of the Bertelsmann proposal, I will now excerpt from the White Paper the pertinent discussion of the five reasons that are most relevant to an international audience.

Reason #1: Self-rating schemes will cause
controversial speech to be censored.

Kiyoshi Kuromiya, founder and sole operator of Critical Path Aids Project, has a website that includes safer sex information written in street language with explicit diagrams, in order to reach the widest possible audience. Kuromiya does not want to apply the rating "crude" or "explicit" to his speech, but if he does not, his site will likely be blocked by many as an unrated site. If he does honestly rate, his speech will be lumped in with "pornography" and blocked from view. Under either choice, Kuromiya has been effectively blocked from reaching a large portion of his intended audience – teenage Internet users – as well as adults.

As this example shows, the consequences of rating are far from neutral. The ratings themselves are all pejorative by definition, and they result in certain speech being blocked.

Some have compared Internet ratings to "food labels" – but that analogy is simply wrong. Food labels provide objective, scientifically verifiable information to help the consumer make choices about what to buy, e. g. the percentage of fat in a food product like milk. Internet ratings are subjective value judgments that result in certain speech being blocked to many viewers.

Reason #2: Self-rating is burdensome, unwieldy, and costly.

Art on the Net is a large, non-profit website that hosts online "studios" where hundreds of artists display their work. The vast majority of the artwork has no sexual content, although there's an occasional Rubenesque painting. The ratings systems don not make sense when applied to art. Yet Art on the Net would still have to review and apply a rating to the more than 26,000 pages on its site, which would require time and staff that they just don not have. Or, they would have to require the artists themselves to self-rate, an option they find objectionable. If they decline to rate, they will be blocked as an unrated site, even though most Internet users would hardly object to the art reaching minors, let alone adults.

As the United States Supreme Court noted in *Reno v. ACLU*, one of the virtues of the Internet is that it provides "relatively unlimited, low-cost capacity for communication of all kinds." In striking down the Communications Decency Act (CDA), the Court held that imposing age-verification costs on Internet speakers would be "prohibitively expensive for noncommercial – as well as some commercial – speakers." Similarly, the burdensome requirement of self-rating thousands of pages of information would effectively shut most non-commercial speakers out of the Internet marketplace.

In addition, the ratings systems are simply unequipped to deal with the diversity of content now available on the Internet. There is perhaps nothing as subjective as a viewer's reaction to art. As history has shown again and again, one woman's masterpiece is another woman's pornography. How can ratings such as "explicit" or "crude" be used to categorize art? Even ratings systems that try to take artistic value into account will be inherently subjective, especially when applied by artists themselves, who will naturally consider their own work to have merit.

The variety of news-related sites on the Web will be equally difficult to rate. Should explicit war footage be labeled "violent" and

116

blocked from view to teenagers? If a long news article has one curse word, is the curse word rated individually, or is the entire story rated and then blocked?

Even those who propose that "legitimate" news organizations should not be required to rate their sites stumble over the question of who will decide what is legitimate news.

Reason #3: Conversation can't be rated.

You are in a chat room or a discussion group – one of the thousands of conversational areas of the Net. A victim of sexual abuse has posted a plea for help, and you want to respond. You've heard about a variety of ratings systems, but you've never used one. You read the self-rating web page, but you can't figure out how to rate the discussion of sex and violence in your response. Aware of the penalties for mislabeling, you decide not to send your message after all.

The burdens of self-rating really hit home when applied to the vibrant, conversational areas of the Internet. Most Internet users don not run web pages, but millions of people around the world send messages, short and long, every day, to chat rooms, news groups and mailing lists. A rating requirement for these areas of the Internet would be analogous to requiring all of us to rate our telephone or street corner conversations.

Reason #4: Self-ratings will only encourage,
not prevent, government regulation.

The webmaster of a site that sells sexually explicit photos learns that many people won't get to his site if he either rates his site "sexually explicit" or fails to rate at all. He rates his entire website "okay for minors." Powerful government officials learn that the site is now available to minors. They are outraged, and quickly introduce a bill imposing criminal penalties for misrated sites.

This example is not hypothetical. Australia has already enacted a similar measure and it is inevitable that governments in both democratic and totalitarian nations will decide to take advantage of these ready made tools for censorship. As odious as I find the Australian law, I shudder to think of how these tools could be put to use by governments in nations such as China.

Reason #5: Self-ratings schemes will turn the internet into a homogenized medium dominated by commercial speakers.

Large media companies will be able to consult their platoons of lawyers who will advise them that their websites must be rated to reach the widest possible audience. They then hire and train staff to rate all of their web pages and third-party filters will routinely permit access to their sites. Everybody in the world will have access to their speech.

There is no question that there may be some speakers on the Internet for whom the ratings systems will impose only minimal burdens: the large, powerful corporate speakers. But so far the democratic nature of the Internet has put commercial speakers on equal footing with all of the other non-commercial and individual speakers.

Today, it is just as easy to find the Critical Path AIDS website as it is to find the Disney site. Both speakers are able to reach a worldwide audience. But mandatory Internet self-rating could easily turn what one judge hailed as "the most participatory communications medium the world has yet seen" into a bland, homogenized medium dominated by primarily American corporate speakers.

The problems of self-rating are not cured by the "layer cake" approach endorsed in the Memorandum, with its reliance on third-party filters to decide what is actually blocked. First, most of these filters would inevitably block unrated sites. In some countries, they will be required to do so by law. Moreover, and equally important, the third-party filters add another layer of subjective judgment to the entire scheme and will undermine any value in allowing users to self-rate by overriding the speakers' own characterizations of their speech.

Despite the claims of their publishers, filtering software programs have proven to be – and will inevitably continue to be – both under- and over-inclusive. On the one hand, they permit some sexually explicit or other speech that the end-user might well choose and expect would be blocked based on the publishers' claims. On the other hand, whether by mistake or by design, they block some valuable speech that the end-user might well choose and expect to see, again relying on the publishers' claims. The well-documented and widely-known examples of these problems are too numerous to detail here.

Many of the problems of under- and over – inclusive filtering and blocking software are due to the sheer volume of content on the Net. Those problems will only worsen as Internet content and use continue to grow geometrically. The potentially infinite content of the Internet will also ensure that only a few third parties will even attempt to create sophisticated filters, and, as is already the case today, most of those filtering programs will reflect similar points of view and/or will be crude and mechanical.

Hotlines

In my view, the Memorandum's discussion of hotlines does not adequately address questions of due process. Recommendation 8 concludes: "The task of evaluating the legality or illegality of specific data is difficult for Internet providers and should, therefore, be integrated into the work of hotlines." The Memorandum encourages a system where Internet service providers and content hosts would take down "illegal content" based on the legal conclusions of hotline operators.

Consistent with fundamental due process principles, matters of legality should be decided by courts of law, not by private or quasi-public hotline operators. While the Memorandum's discussion of the powers of the hotlines is not fully detailed, the Memorandum seems to vest the hotlines with, essentially, judicial power. Hotline operators, though, should not function as self-appointed judges of law.

So, for example, while a service provider may choose voluntarily to take down particular material posted by a third party, including in response to a customer complaint, under no circumstances should a service provider be required to do so prior to a judicial finding that the material is illegal in the service provider's home nation. Nor should service providers be subject to punishment for failing to take down third-party material prior to a judicial determination that the material is illegal. Hotline operators should not be encouraged to become vigilantes enforcing their own notions of (il)legality and harmfulness.

Similarly, the Memorandum leaves unanswered the question of when hotlines and service providers should be required or allowed to turn over private data regarding speakers – e.g., their true identities or addresses – to law enforcement officials. I would urge a requirement that this information be provided only upon presentation of a judicially approved order.

Niam Chiang Meng

Chairman, Singapore Broadcasting Authority, Singapore

1. Singapore has decided to embrace IT and has invested heavily in developing a nation-wide broadband network for delivering of interactive multimedia services and fast access to the Internet. Singapore has the highest Internet usage in Asia with one in every four Singaporeans being Internet users. By the year 2002, there will be one computer for every two students in our schools to encourage them to access the Internet. Promoting healthy growth and development of the Internet is critical to Singapore's drive to become a knowledge-based economy.

2. We believe that the most effective way to promote the growth and development of the Internet while addressing society's concern regarding undesirable materials on the Internet is to create a government, industry and public nexus where self regulation and public education are supported by a light-touch policy framework.

3. Educating the public to be more aware, discerning and responsible in using the Internet is therefore a key component of our Internet policy framework. For the young, in particular, we see parental guidance as crucial. A key focus of SBA's initiatives is to empower the public with the tools to manage the Internet and convince them that they too have a part to play. One such tool we have in Singapore is the Family Access Networks which are offered by all Internet Access Service Providers in Singapore. The Family Access Networks are optional filtered services which offer parents, teachers and community groups a choice to have a safer environment for their children and students to surf the Internet.

4. We are also actively engaged in on-going efforts to put more tools into the hands of the public to manage the Internet more effectively. These include promoting a "whitelist" of useful and

121

educational sites, running online discussion forums for parents and promoting training packages to teach users to be more discerning and responsible when using the Internet. These public education programmes are also available in many countries in one form or another and we believe that there can be greater international co-operation and sharing of resources in this area of public education.

5. Another critical component in our efforts to address the problem of abuse of the Internet is getting industry to be more proactive in adopting good self-regulation practices such as website labelling and developing industry codes of practice. We believe that it is in the interest of industry for it to take on such responsibility since this will enhance consumer confidence and is ultimately good for business.

6. In Singapore, we encourage Internet Service Providers to take their own initiatives against offensive content. For example, all Internet Service Providers in Singapore have implemented Acceptable Use Policies for their customers pertaining to net abuses such as objectionable content, viruses and spamming. We are also working with the industry to develop industry codes of practice and promote the adoption of PICS compliant content rating schemes such as RSACi. We want to empower the public, especially parents, to make informed decisions about electronic media by means of an open and objective content advisory system which provides information, for example, about the level of sex, nudity, violence and offensive language in websites.

7. In line with these efforts, we are actively participating in discussions at international platforms such as ICRA, the Internet Content Rating Association, which aims to set an international standard for website labelling, building on the current RSACi system. I am therefore pleased to note that the Memorandum on Self-Regulation of the Internet includes a wide-ranging study of the key considerations in developing rating schemes. I would like

to urge industry and users alike to participate actively in the for-
mulation of a workable global ratings system.

8. To support our public-education and self-regulation efforts, Singapore adopts a light-touch approach where regulations are kept
narrow and minimal in order to allow industry maximum freedom to operate. For example, under our Class Licence Scheme,
Internet Service and Content Providers are given a set of simple
guidelines that provide a clear idea of what their responsibilities
are. This approach creates greater transparency and clarity on the
liability of Internet Service and Content Providers and makes it
easier for the industry to operate and grow. We do not regulate
individual websites, individual access to web pages, or personal
communications such as e-mail and chat groups. Organisations
who provide Internet access to employees for business use are
also not regulated in any way.

9. Given the borderless nature of the Internet, we fully support the
need for more international dialogue and co-operation in tackling
the challenges posed by the Internet. The Memorandum provides
a comprehensive overview of the key issues and offers much food
for thought on how the global community can act together to
develop a common global framework to manage this borderless
medium. I congratulate the Bertelsmann Foundation for doing a
remarkable job in creating greater international awareness of and
promoting self-regulation of the Internet. We in Singapore look
forward to working with the Bertelsmann Foundation to help
make the Internet a safer and richer place for everyone.

Jeffrey Cole

Director, UCLA Center for Communication Policy,
University of California, Los Angeles, USA

The Internet is well on its way to becoming the most important means of communication since the development of the printing press in the 15ᵗʰ century. There is almost no human activity that will not be affected by this technology and most activity will be transformed. At present, however, the vast majority of the world's people do not yet use the Internet. The next five years will be critical as the stage is set for the mainstream populations of many countries to participate on the Internet and create the beginnings of the first almost fully wired societies. In this critical period of the Internet's maturation as a medium for all people, it is essential that governments encourage Internet growth and provide support, and it is even more essential that governments stay out of the regulatory business.

The history of mass communications demonstrates clearly and repeatedly that self-regulation, rather than governmental control, is the most effective means of sustaining growth and nurturing content in the media. Self-regulation moves the burden of regulating content from the government to where it properly belongs: in the hands of users. During this important transformational stage of the Internet, particularly when non-users are overly aware of harmful content and less aware of the beneficial content (and non-users are the majority), there is great pressure for governments to regulate. Politicians can grab quick headlines by proposing to "do something" about this unappealing content, especially pornography and hate speech. Once a governmental effort to "clean up" begins, it becomes politically difficult for anyone to oppose the legislation, lest they appear to be supporting such awful content. In the United States, even though many legislators opposed the Communications Decency Act (CDA) both because of first amendment grounds and because it

124

was overly broad and difficult to enforce, many of these opponents were forced to "support" the CDA for political reasons. It fell to the courts, designed by the constitution to be immune to political pressure, to overturn the legislation. Ironically, the very same Congress that passed the CDA would have violated its own law (had it not been overturned) in September 1998 when it released the salacious details of the Starr Report on President Clinton onto the Internet.

Clearly an industry committed to regulating itself with the support of government and a people willing to take the time to learn the methods of self-regulation is, by far, the best method of dealing with content problems in the media. However, before self-regulation can become truly effective, there are several important issues that must be understood by all parties, i.e., the industry, the government and parents.

1. With very few exceptions, self-regulation does not eliminate "bad" content; it merely labels it and places it into proper categories.

The exceptions are content that is clearly illegal such as "child pornography" to which everyone must be committed to eliminate. If self-regulation is to work, all sides must understand that content that they find objectionable will survive and may flourish under this system. This means that people will have to accept the notion that occasionally they will be offended by the content they see on the Internet just as they are occasionally offended by what they see in the movies or on television. Filters and labeling will allow most people to keep unacceptable content (to them) away from their eyes and especially from the eyes of their children. Not all content will be labeled the way people want and from time to time they will see things they would rather not see. This is the price people must be willing to pay to participate in a free society. The alternative is for some governmental agency to screen everything before it is distributed (prior restraint) and eliminate anything that might offend anyone. This would ensure an Internet devoid of vitality and one so bland that it would quickly pass into oblivion.

In the United States the presence of an industry-applied rating system for film and television does not eliminate any content whatsoever (although some people are afraid that producers censor themselves or are censored by their companies to keep programming within acceptable ratings or limits). Tasteless films and television programs are still made, but are labeled with a rating that provides guidance to parents about the content. Many critics in government and advocacy groups are unhappy with ratings systems for the very reason that they do not eliminate "bad" content. Many would prefer to get this programming out of theaters, off the air or off the Internet. An authoritarian system where someone censors "inappropriate" content according to his or her standards is not a feature of self-regulation.

2. Parents must educate themselves about how labeling and filtering systems work.

None of these self-regulatory systems work if parents do not learn how to use them. If parents do not make the effort to learn this technology, the only systems that can result are ones that block everything or one that blocks nothing. It falls to the makers of filtering or labeling systems to make the technology as transparent as possible and the concepts of the system as easy to learn as possible.

In 1968, the Motion Picture Association of America (MPAA) devised a set of film ratings to provide guidance to parents about the appropriateness of films their children might want to see. The original system contained four ratings beginning with the tame G, and running through the harsher M, R and X. Today that system has evolved into five categories of G, PG, PG-13, R and NC-17.

Each film and all advertisements for the film contain these ratings. The only part of the system that is passive for parents is that children under 17 are blocked (in theory) from seeing a film rated R (unless with a parent or guardian) or NC-17. For the ratings to work, parents must learn the system and through experience learn the practical application of each rating symbol. This does seem to have happened rather well over the past 30 years.

It is less clear what is happening in the television world. After close to a year of turmoil over the design of the system, three of the four American broadcast television networks and almost all cable networks agreed to label programming with a TV-G, TV-PG, TV-14 and TV-MA (with additional ratings for programs created for children). In addition to these ratings, content descriptors of S (sex), V (violence), L (language) and D (dialogue) were added to the age-based ratings. The importance of this system is that it will ultimately trigger the use of the V-chip that will allow parents to block programming that exceeds the level they wish their child to see. In this way, the V-chip is analogous to the use of filtering systems on the Internet when applied by the user. Although the ratings have been on television programs for close to three years, it is not clear whether parents are learning what the labels mean and using the system. Furthermore, there is a serious question as to whether parents will learn how to program a V-chip and block the programming they select. Without parents taking the time to learn these systems, self-regulation simply does not work effectively.

When talking about the Internet, parents have an additional responsibility in a self-regulatory environment: they must, to the best of their ability, learn a little bit about how computers and the Internet work. This was never a problem in the television world because any parent knows how to turn a television on or off and how to change a channel. While computers and the Internet are almost as easy to use, a psychological barrier exists for some that are afraid of the technology. Of course, this will disappear as a problem in 20 years when today's 8-year-olds become parents. Until then, if parents are to apply filters and use labels, they must understand both the filtering systems and a little bit about the technology.

3. Parents must continue to talk with their children, watch their behavior and notice changes.

The best filtering system in the world does little ultimate good if parents are not actively involved in their children's lives. Parents must engage their children, talk about developments in their lives and ask them about how they use the Internet and what they find. While even the most devoted parent cannot always sit with their children while they are on-line, all parents must spend some time with their children exploring this world together even if the child has to lead the way.

The work our Center conducted on television violence over a three-year period concluded with a detailed list of recommendations to the television industry, government and teachers. The most important recommendation, however, was to parents to participate in their children's lives, listen to them and to occasionally get up early on a Saturday morning and watch their children watch television. This would allow them to see how the messages on television are internalized and whether their chidden are excited or repulsed by violent or other anti-social behavior. Watching with their children allows parents to explain the content and provide better understanding. Parents will be able to see the beginnings of problems with their child's behavior long before those behaviors become ingrained. None of this demand for parental involvement mitigates, in any way, the need for the industry to regulate itself. But parents must be active partners in the entire process.

These same recommendations are just as important in the Internet world. Self-regulation can and will work on the Internet. But to

128

work effectively, an added burden is placed on parents to be more than passive figures. The easiest system for parents is one in which the government or an ISP merely decides what is acceptable and blocks the rest. This would be tragic in stifling what is turning out to be the world's most open, international and interactive means of communication. For the system to thrive, parents must be willing to take on the added burdens of occasionally being offended, learning how the technology and filtering systems work and, most important of all, sharing the experience of going on-line with their children.

Chapter IV

Expert Reports

The Concept of Self-Regulation and the Internet

Monroe E. Price, Stefaan G. Verhulst[1]

1 The authors would like to thank Abraham Safdie, David W. J. Canter and Sanjeet Malik for their editorial assistance in the preparation of this article.

Introduction

This book addresses self-regulation of content on the Internet. Although Internet self-regulation involves many issues, such as e-commerce, technical protocols and domain names management, on-line content controls have initiated most public concern and debate. Throughout this book, emphasis is placed on the operational aspects and design of self-regulation. In this chapter we examine how self-regulatory entities relate to other quasi-legal and state institutions, how it is decided what powers the self-regulatory institutions wield, and how the use of self-regulation can contribute to the more effective and more efficient realisation of both economic and societal goals.

Self-regulation of the Internet has its special qualities, a product of the architecture of the industry, that extraordinary web of computers, servers, telecommunications devices responsible, in large part, for the flexibility, openness and convenience of communication. Self-regulation not only supports the open and decentralised network architecture of the Internet; self-regulation also forms a flexible response to the dynamic and on-going evolution of the sector and the emerging technologies. The development of these Internet technologies has led to outsourcing of operations to private entities and to encouraging third-party or "community" handling of a range of issues including content control.

The issue of content self-regulation on the Internet is a complex one, exacerbated by the inherently transnational nature of the Web, the economic and social importance of the newer services, the diversity of cultural norms in this area and the availability of technological tools to affect choices concerning content. The wide range of institutional, technological and social challenges presented by the growth of the Internet has led to government doubts about their capacity to do more than set the broad direction and pace of development. They have increasingly looked to the private sector as a resource for responsibility. The Internet community, seized with the idea of this new means of communication as calling for a very different relationship with government, has taken a similar approach to regulatory design.

In this first chapter, we examine elements of self-regulation that are usually taken for granted. A failure to have a deeper understanding of the mechanisms of self-regulation may hinder the development and implementation of policy. Such an examination also assists in determining the prerequisites and components of self-regulation as part of a comprehensive and systematic process that includes an appropriate role for government and for individual responsibility. In the Internet context, this exploration also illustrates how self-regulation is a means for ensuring economic growth based on emerging network technologies and an optimal combination of speech rights consistent with suitable protection of community interests.

1 Self-regulation: general concept and characteristics

1.1 Defining self-regulation

The initial problem of every approach to self-regulation lies with definition. There is no single definition of self-regulation that is entirely satisfactory, nor should there be. Self-regulation evolves as the nature of the Internet alters. Different profiles of self-regulation emerge that adjust to the varying aspects of the Internet that are regulated. Self-regulation has and will continue to have different meanings from sector to sector and from state to state, internationally. Furthermore, whatever its implication or suggestion, self-regulation is almost always a misnomer. It hardly ever exists without some relationship to the state; a relationship that itself varies greatly. The meaning of self-regulation shifts depending upon the extent of government coercion or involvement and upon accurate public perceptions of the relationship of private sector and state.

For these and similar reasons, there is a great hazard: governments, industries and users employ the term "self-regulation" frequently, almost indiscriminately. It is assumed to have a pre-determined meaning when it does not. A study on self-regulation in the Media Sector and European Community Law noted that "the term 'self-regulation' is often used as a matter of course, as if it were (1) a specific and defined term, and (2) an equally specific and defined regulatory practice. Yet in general, this is not the case" (Ukrow 1999: 11). From the outset, then, there needs to be an exploration of the variety of meanings of "self-regulation" and the implications of each grouping of them for the better management of social concerns with the new technology.

Different variables

Larry Irving, US Assistant Secretary of Commerce, observed: "At one end of the spectrum, the term is used quite narrowly, to refer only to those instances where the government has formally delegated the power to regulate, as in the delegation of securities industry oversight to the stock exchanges. At the other end of the spectrum, the term is used when the private sector perceives the need to regulate itself for whatever reason – to respond to consumer demand, to carry out its ethical beliefs, to enhance industry reputations, or to level the market playing field – and does so."[2] Even here, the range of variable meanings emerges. Because "self-regulation" is thought

---

2   When introducing a collection of papers analysing the prospects of self-regulation for protecting privacy (National Telecommunications Information Administration 1997).

to exist when private entities have been commanded to act or become the delegates of state power, the intertwining of state and private industry is implicitly recognized, although the "governmental nature of self-regulation" may differ across sectors (Baldwin/Cave 1999: 125). Questions arise: these include the propriety and clarity of delegation, the circumstances under which state functions can or ought to be carried out by private groups, the division of power and responsibility between the state and private groups. On the other hand, as Secretary Irving suggests, the private sector "perceives the need to regulate itself." The source of that need is often the threat of public regulation or a societal demand for increased responsibility by the private sector or economic factors. Other variables may include the extent of the role played by self-regulators, the degree of binding legal force that attaches to self-regulatory rules and their coverage of an industrial sector (Baldwin/Cave 1999: 126). These areas of indeterminacy are grounds for a statement in a recent Bibliography on Self-regulation on the Internet prepared for the OECD: "while there is broad consensus that self-regulation of the Internet is critical to its future growth, there is little consensus about how to achieve or implement a self-regulatory regime" (Internet Law and Policy Forum 1998).

Essentialist approach

To appreciate these various meanings and dimensions of self-regulation, the concept must be further dissected. An essentialist approach to self-regulation would require that all elements of regulation – formation of norms, adjudication, enforcement and others – be self-generated. Not only the rules that govern behaviour, but the mechanisms for their administration would arise from those whose behaviour is to be governed. Even "subcontracting" of rules might violate the purest ideal of self-regulation if the contractor is the government. Rules must be auto-generated in that ideal model. But it is rare that any form of self-regulation, save for cartelisation, really exists wholly independent of the force of the state and this may be especially true where the field of regulation involves content control on a medium of expression. Huyse and Parmentier distinguish between subcontracting (where the state limits itself to setting the formal conditions for rule-making while leaving it entirely up to the parties to shape the content), concerted action (where the state not only sets the formal, but also the substantive conditions for rule-making by one or more parties) and incorporation (where existing, but non-official norms become part of the legislative order by insertion into statutes or by declaring the product of private negotiations generally binding for a whole sector) (Huyse/Parmentier 1990: 260). Nor is the involvement of third parties in a self-regulatory body precluded. The important quality is the vector: maximising private or self-regulation as a supplement, substitute, or delegate of the state.

Self-regulation and other regulatory models

Another, though closely linked, way of defining self-regulation is determining its particular place and role among other regulatory models.[3] In reality the behaviour of industry players can in essence be governed and controlled through three forms of economic and social organisation: government organisation, industry self-organisation; and market organisation. Where any particular form of regulation falls on this spectrum depends largely on who gives impetus to

3   Joseph Rees somewhat idiosyncratically likens the general regulatory system in his landmark book Reforming the Workplace, to the proverbial iceberg: the tip being government regulation, while the massive body represents society's great array of private regulatory systems (Rees 1988: 6).

138

its development. Moreover regulation encompasses varying degrees of legal force and formal organisation. From what we have already said, it will be apparent that there is no clear demarcation between self-regulation and government regulation. The principal types constitute a continuum along which regulation is more or less formalised, with government or public regulation being the most formal (the so-called command and control type of regulation) and where non-compliance may lead to public or private law sanctions; and market organisation (laissez-faire approach) being the least formal and 'compliance' based upon voluntary action. In practice, however, the three forms overlap and create mutual inter-dependencies as a result of market or policy failures, or even wider public concerns – such as the protection of minors – which cannot be addressed purely by one form or another. Sinclair argued that "much of the current debate has been characterised by a choice between two mutually exclusive policy options: 'strict' command and control on one hand, and 'pure' self-regulation on the other. In fact, there is a much richer range of policy options, with most falling somewhere between theoretically polar extremes" (Sinclair 1997: 529). Many authors have concluded that self-regulation and formal legal systems work best when they are combined (Doyle 1997: 35–42). Furthermore, the mix between the two should shift depending on changes in the environment. Such changing conditions might include technological innovations. As an example, the evolving nature of the Internet has not only led to calls to regulate the Internet in a certain way but has also challenged the current regulatory regimes in place for other communications systems such as broadcasting and telecommunications. In this way, styles of regulation on the Internet might decrease government regulation and accelerate the shift for greater self-regulation in other media areas. Two-tiered regulation is especially relevant in industries and areas that are complex and transnational in character, with content regulation being an example. It is convenient and logical to consider these co-regulatory mechanisms as a form of self-regulation. Hoffmann-Riem calls this "regulated self-regula-tion" (Hoffmann-Riem 1996).

Self-regulation versus de-regulation and non-regulation

Self-regulation is different from de-regulation or non-regulation. De-regulation directly aims to remove any regulation perceived to be excessive and to hinder market forces. Self-regulation does not aim primarily to dismantle or dispense with a framework for private activity, but rather to change the actor who establishes this frame-work (Ukrow 1999: 15). Self-regulation is no alternative or substi-tute for elements of direct regulation, such as antitrust (Breyer 1982: 157). It is a technique, not a prescription for overall regulatory institutional design (Prosser 1998: 271). Considering self-regulation as the antithesis of legal regulation is thus far too simple a character-isation of the limits to law. We are concerned here, rather, with whether self-regulatory bodies can be an alternate significant source of "law" in the Internet. What we see, every day, is greater social demand for some form of control or supervision of what seems, inherently, to be beyond governance. This significant gulf between community aspiration and perceived limits on government capacity forces a thorough and almost painful search for each possibility of finding a remedy. Innovation of regulatory design is required in the Internet to resolve this dilemma.

Comparative approaches

Few existing discussions of self-regulation on the Internet pay attention to disparate meanings of self-regulation in various states. The very history of the relationship between business and govern-ment is so different in the major Internet states (we may look at the

US, Germany and the UK as a sample). It is inevitable that the patterns of "self-regulation" will differ accordingly. An international practice of self-regulation may emerge but it will have to be, in the first instance, an accumulation of national and regional experiences. Each state has different social demands, each state has a different constitutional structure, and each state has different traditions of industry-government co-operation in the fields of media and speech. No account of the emergence of self-regulation can be complete that fails to be not sensitive to these critical distinctions in practice. The expectation, function, structure and culture of self-regulation in the media is very different in Europe from the United States and in Germany from the United Kingdom, to give just two examples. One study of self-regulation and self-generation of standards (Canada and United States) demonstrated marked differences in the scope of co-operation with the government, shared standards, and the notion of self-regulation as a social and collaborative act (McDowell/ Maitland 1998). In the United States, partly because of the First Amendment tradition, self-regulation is distinctively a form of avoidance, confrontation, and studied separation from government. A comparative overview of self-regulation systems in all EU Member States within the media identified clear differences in meaning and structure of the self-regulatory systems within the individual EU Member States and in a comparative overview of these systems (Brohmer/Ukrow 1999). An understanding of these different traditions will assist a) in building common approaches where appropriate and b) in avoiding misunderstandings about the capacity of self-regulation across systems.

1.2 Regulation and regulatory tools

It is frequently said that the Internet is unregulable, or that regulation is beyond the control of the nation-state. The assumption of this book, and, of course, of this chapter, is that not only is some level of regulation possible, but that it can be undertaken by those involved in operating the Internet (Goldsmith 1998). It is important, however, to be clear about the differences between regulation by government and self-regulation by those largely operating apart from government. Regulation by government always implies the use of government power to ensure certain actions by third parties. Self-regulation, on the other hand, consists of a series of representations, negotiations, contractual arrangements and collaborative efforts with government. Self-regulation on the Internet is a subtle and changing combination of all of these forms of activity. Further, self-regulation can be seen as that range of activity by private actors undertaken to prevent more intrusive, and more costly action by government itself. In that sense, self-regulation can be explained as a collective economic decision, an intersection of maximisation of profit and expressions of public interest.

Justifications for and objectives of regulation

The starting point of every regulatory intervention, including self-regulation, must be the policy objective, not the means of achievement. In other words, the need and rationale for the rules and techniques to be imposed must first be identified. Justification for intervention arises out of an alleged inability of the marketplace to deal with particular structural problems. Other rationales are often brought up in political debate (and the details of a program often reflect only political force). Market failure forms the main rationale behind self-regulation, but a distinction must be made between

142

economic self-regulation and social self-regulation. While the former is concerned with the adjustment of markets or other facets of economic life, the latter "aims to protect people or the environment from the damaging consequences of industrialisation" (Hawkins/Hutter 1993: 199). Social self-regulation is thus usually taken to include mechanisms whereby firms or their associations, in their undertaking of business activities, seek to assure that unacceptable consequences to the environment, the workforce, or consumers and clients are avoided. Media regulation and especially content self-regulation, falls clearly under this category. Many scholars have listed the reasons why the media should be regulated.[4] European Commissioner Oreja summarised these reasons as follows:

"In order to give an answer to this question, the starting point is, of course, to recognize the crucial role that media play in our society. The role of the media goes much further than simply providing information about events and issues; media also play a formative role in society. That is, they are largely responsible for forming the concepts, belief systems and even the languages – visual and symbolic as well as verbal – which citizens use to make sense of, and to interpret the world in which they live. There are a certain number of public interest objectives which should be preserved in our societies, and which have a European dimension. In my opinion, these could be summarised as follows: ensuring plurality of ownership; ensuring fair and effective competition; ensuring diversity of content; protecting individual rights to privacy, free speech, etc; protecting intellectual property rights; maximising individual consumer choice and

---

4   Hoffmann-Riem lists among the fields of supervisory action *inter alia*: pluralism, diversity, fairness, and impartiality; social responsibility; maintenance of high quality programming and of cultural and linguistic identity; coverage of important events; protection against abuse of market power; strengthening national and regional industries; protection of consumers; and maintenance of standards in matters of violence, sex, taste and decency (Hoffmann-Riem 1996).

access to information, and, very importantly; ensuring a high level of protection of minors and human dignity" (Oreja 1999).

Much discussion about the development of the newer communications services and the growing globalisation suggests that new technology challenges these rationales. The European Green Paper on Convergence differed: "The fundamental objectives underpinning regulation in the Member States are not undermined by convergence" (European Commission 1997). "Nevertheless," it continues, "the nature and characteristics of convergence as well as the perceived need of industry actors for regulatory intervention to be limited and closely targeted, should lead public authorities at both a national and a European level to re-examine the role and weight of regulation in a converging marketplace." These differences led to the call for self-regulatory approaches. Public interest objectives do not become irrelevant or invalid as a result of technological change. The regulatory challenge within an Internet setting is thus to find appropriate legislative and other mechanisms to safeguard these policy objectives. A functional approach is needed, one which does not depend solely on technology or forms of delivery, but which recognizes the nature of the service and the character of the audience receiving it. However, in identifying the most appropriate legislative approach for controlling Internet content, two areas of complexity have to be taken into consideration. The first refers to defining the types of content that is unacceptable and/or illegal. The second is related to the different methods or platforms of exchanging information on the Internet.

Harmful and illegal content

A discussion of illegal, harmful or offensive content is always a complex matter (OECD 1997a) not unique to the Internet, even, or especially, in terms of definition. Several EU documents have out-

144

lined that it is necessary to differentiate between these categories of content (European Commission 1996) but a fully satisfactory definition is not given. The "Green paper on the protection of minors and human dignity in audio-visual and information services" (European Commission 1997b) produced broad agreement on objectives and the action to be taken within Europe.

Generally, the concept of "illegal" seems a relatively simple reference to content that is contrary to law. However this becomes a particularly difficult issue in the international context, where what is illegal in some countries is not necessarily illegal in others. It was only recently that Japan's lower house of Parliament banned the production and sale of child pornography. Furthermore this question can be exacerbated in a discussion of civil and criminal law, where "illegal" only refers to that which is a criminal offence and "harmful" might indicate that content which raises civil law issues because of "harm" to another party. What is considered to be harmful or appropriate depends on cultural differences and can be distinct according to different age groups. All this has to be taken into account in defining appropriate approaches to protect children against undesired material whilst ensuring freedom of expression.

Internet platforms

It is also important to keep in mind that (worldwide) web pages are only one of the platforms by which content is exchanged on the Internet. Other methods of information exchange include e-mail, ftp, newsgroups and real-time chats. As the KPMG review of the Internet Watch Foundation highlighted, each route has different characteristics and is used for different purposes and may require different regulatory and protective approaches. Chat and newsgroup platforms were, for instance, thought to be the most widely used communications platform on the Internet by paedophiles because of the difficulty in "traceability." Moreover filtering and blocking of such dynamic content has proven to be problematic and in some cases impossible. All this confirms that a multiple approach of regulatory tools will be necessary to control Internet content satisfactorily.

Self-regulatory tools

A wide array of self-regulatory tools have proven track records as substitutes for government regulation. They assume many forms, ranging from social control to formal contracts. Codes of conduct, voluntary standards, contractual provisions, accreditation, third-party certification, audits, best practices and performance goals and objectives have all withstood scrutiny in lieu of prescriptive regulation in a variety of industry settings, including the media. Dispute resolution is also an important element within a self-regulatory regime for the Internet (Katsh 1996).

Codes of practice or good conduct embodying mutual obligations by competing actors have an important role to play, but one of the most distinct means of enhancing protection and free speech on the Internet is the use of filtering and blocking mechanisms as described in the essay in this book by Balkin and Noveck. This is not to say that legal controls are unimportant but the shift from "hard law to software" (Wacks 1997) can clearly be considered as an empowerment of user's choice, (as opposed to an analogue broadcasting setting). Hence the major response to the call for self-regulation involves processes that promote filtering and rating systems. The institution of hotlines and complaint handling procedures by industry actors is also an important element of content self-regulation on the Internet. Hotlines – as Burkert describes in this book – can provide a mechanism for users to report illegal or harmful content that they see on the Internet. Based upon a public-private partnership they can have a crucial evaluation and monitoring function. In what

146

follows later in this discussion, codes of conduct will be addressed in greater detail. There are a number of industry initiatives underway directed at developing codes of conduct and a number of national governments specifically endorse codes as a front-line mechanism for addressing content issues. Moreover codes of conduct, as discussed above, may also offer a solution to content platforms that are difficult or impossible to filter and/or block, such as newsgroups or e-mail.

Regulatory process

Finally, in examining the design of self-regulation, one should also examine different components of the regulatory process which include: (i) policy-making, i.e., enunciating principles that should govern enterprises, (ii) legislation, i.e., defining appropriate rules; (iii) enforcement, i.e., initiating actions against violators; and (iv) adjudication, i.e., deciding whether violation has taken place and imposing an appropriate sanction. The point here is to determine, in each particular version of the exercise of regulation, how the roles are divided between the state and industry (Campbell 1999). For example, an industry may be responsible for the definition of standards for content (through developing a code of practice) but leave enforcement to the government. Industry may put its mark on official state legislation through effective lobbying, using state power to obtain results that could not be gained through private agreement. Self-regulation often means a division in which certain kinds of behaviour (incitements to violence, for example) are defined as prohibited by the state, while other kinds of speech behaviour (indecent conduct) are defined, labelled and policed by the industry. Similarly, enforcement may be divided with the state prosecuting for certain speech and the self-regulating entity self-policing and removing other kinds of speech.

147

1.3 Cost-benefit analysis

A fashionable way of looking at the characteristics and merits of self-regulation is to examine how it complements and addresses the limitations of government regulation. The increasing significance of self-regulatory mechanisms suggests that they offer a number of benefits that cannot be achieved through government regulation. Within the debate on self-regulation, however, a key question arises as to whether and in what ways self-regulatory systems can effectively monitor and control the behaviour of market players without generating the bureaucratic and legal costs of traditional regulatory regimes.

Costs

Implementing and complying with regulation entails significant costs, and efficiency losses associated with regulation can be high. Moreover, government regulation can be a blunt instrument and impose unintended costs (on the customers of other, competitive industries) without any tangible benefits (Ministry of Consumer Affairs, NZ, 1997). In contrast with command and control type of regulation, the "voluntary" nature of self-regulation implies, sometimes misleadingly, that the costs associated with compliance are lower and fall on those markets at which regulation is targeted.

It is, however, naive to suggest that self-regulation does not itself involve significant costs. For any system, regulatory or self-regulatory, costs are determined by a combination of the policy goals they envisage and the structures and dynamics of the economic and social activities they regulate. Monitoring and evaluative costs otherwise assumed by governments may be incurred directly by individual companies or indirectly by industry associations who will also generate significant amounts of third-party costs associated with governmental compliance procedures. To some limited extent, new

148

technology automates regulatory controls, procedures and compliance requirements, decreasing regulatory costs. But that would be true for direct regulation as well as self-regulation.

Enforcement and "free riders"

The very nature of a voluntary system, however, potentially creates a "free-rider problem" (OECD 1998) where some actors expend significant resources on the development, monitoring and implementation of codes and standards while others ignore their existence. This situation may not be entirely disadvantageous to more resourceful actors, as they can set benchmarks that can convey benefits in terms of consumer confidence and recognition in market formation and social responsibility. Commercial and social prominence is critical for the success of the major actors on the Internet as it is in any other medium (AOL is an example of the process[5]). And once a critical mass of participants has been reached, a "voluntary" system of codes and controls can become very hard to evade because of increased peer pressure and public expectations.

Self-regulation can quickly become moribund without strong and committed support for its development, implementation and enforcement. To be a living and working instrument, a code of practice or equivalent, must, in practice, be implemented with the agreement of the industry sector to which it applies. Whether governments may need to have reserve powers to ensure the effectiveness of self-regulation depends – as will be seen below – largely on this collaboration among industry players and on the type of societal goals and the

---

5   AOL's 1999 advertising campaign assured customers of their ability to determine access to content, using AOL's age-referenced system (http://www.aol.com). AOL has also enacted a "Safe-Surfing" campaign, outlining basic parental options in relation to children and Internet use (http://www.safesurfin.com/).

need to ensure that users are aware of their protection. But in any case "voluntary" and "preventive" self-regulation can be a sensible strategy to prevent considerable time and financial resources from being bound up in compliance activities.

Expertise and information

Another major limitation of traditional government regulation is that government agencies may lack the information and technical competence necessary to make the best policy decisions. On the Internet, a vast amount of data is collected by network operators, Internet Access (IAP) and Service Providers (ISP) on the use and abuse of networks. This information can consist of basic personal and commercial data such as users' names, addresses and also confidential information collected by technologies integrated into the network. Tracking of service site visits activity by users on a web-site is probably the most common data collected by IAPs and ISPs. The collection of these types of data has initiated competitive and consumer privacy concerns that need to be addressed (Birks 1997). The ability to gather this information in itself has opened a wide debate about the liability of these "mediating institutions."[6] Still,

---

6   The case against Felix Somm, managing director of CompuServe Germany, in Bavaria highlights these dilemmas facing governments, law enforcement agencies and the judiciary when defining liability for on-line content with regard to Internet service providers. On 28 May 1998, the Munich Judge imposed a two-year suspended sentence on Felix Somm. This was the first time in Germany that an online company manager had been held responsible for images available through the firm's gateway to the Internet. (*http://www.cyber-rights.org/isps/somm-dec.htm*). Goldsmith discusses the problems of legislative attempts at regulating content. (Goldsmith 1998: 1224–1226; Delacourt 1997). Meanwhile, the judgment has been reversed by the next instance and Felix Somm was freed from all charges.

150

the capacity enables the industry to identify and monitor key areas of content concern in a more effective way than government agencies would be able to do. The expertise that can only be effectively contributed and processed by the industry actors themselves can thus be mobilised within a self-regulatory structure to devise, subject to careful safeguards, "responsive regulation" (e.g., codes of conduct). Self-regulation should not, however, be a pretext for a new onslaught on privacy.

Free speech and globalisation

Self-regulation has the seeming benefit of avoiding state intervention in areas that are sensitive in terms of basic rights such as freedom of speech and information while offering social responsibility, accountability and user protection from offensive material. But private censorship can be more coercive and sweeping than its public form. And the dangers of constitutional violation are particularly striking where the self-regulatory entity is acting in response to government or as a means of preempting its intervention.

Self-regulation may better absorb the transnational conflicts inherent in the global architecture of the Internet. An emphasis on self-regulation may be a more effective alternative wherever one state is highly dependent on consensus with other states. Furthermore government regulation can be inflexible and not as adaptable to the rapid changes taking place in the Internet as other policy alternatives. Robert Pitofsky, Chairman of the Federal Trade Commission (US), explained recently that "[l]egitimate and fair self-regulation will become more important as the economy grows faster than government regulation" (Pitofsky 1998). He also referred to the fact that self-regulation sometimes is more "prompt, flexible, and effective than government regulation" and that "the judgement and experience of an industry also is of great benefit, especially in

151

cases where the government has difficulty defining 'bright-line rules.' Online content is clearly such a case."[7]

Thus, the professed advantages of self-regulation over governmental regulation include efficiency, increased flexibility, increased incentives for compliance, reduced cost, and minimised government intrusion in the speech field. However, a number of risks and limitations, besides the ones already listed, are also associated with self-regulatory approaches especially if they need to fulfil public interest goals as in the case of policing Internet content.

Democratic deficit and accountability

The "democratic deficit" or "corporatist character" (Schmitter 1985) of self-regulation in comparison with state regulatory activities can be seen as an important cost. The shift – within self-regulatory arrangements – of traditional public task fulfillment from specific and democratically legitimate regulatory institutions into a sector that consists primarily of private associations occurs at the expense of democracy and accountability.

The acquisition of power by groups that are not accountable to the body politic through the conventional constitutional channels may constitute an abuse. As John Braitwaithe has put it: "Self-regulation is frequently an attempt to deceive the public into believing in the responsibility of an irresponsible industry. Sometimes it is a strategy to give the government an excuse for not doing its job" (Braithwaite 1993: 91).

It is clear that legitimacy plays an important role within the

---

7   The U.S. courts recently invalidated the Communications Decency Act and granted a preliminary injunction against enforcement of the Child Online Protection Act. (Reno v. ACLU, 117 S.Ct. 2329 (1997); Reno v. ACLU, 31 F.Supp.2d 472 (1999)).

debate about government versus self-regulation. Part of the discussion is linked to the responsibility of mediating institutions to ensure transparency, accountability and consultation with interested parties. These are in general not perceived by the private sector as their primary objectives. Therefore, ensuring accountability when public interests are concerned should be a major concern in the design of a self-regulatory regime. Effective self-regulation requires active consumer and citizen participation at all stages of development and implementation. Without user involvement, a self-regulatory mechanism will not accurately reflect user needs and will not be effective in delivering the standards it promotes. It will fail to create confidence.

Self-regulatory institutions may not impose meaningful sanctions on industry players. Self-regulatory standards are, according to critics, usually weak, enforcement is ineffective and punishment is often secret and mild. If there is insufficient commitment to an enforceable code, the power of state regulation to effectively sanction contravention may be preferable. Finally, self-regulation can have an adverse impact on competition and market efficiency if the sector concerned attempts to use self-regulation as a way of restricting competition by, for example, limiting entry, driving up prices, or setting minimum standards of trading conduct that have little relevance to the needs of consumers. As a response to these concerns within the media field, European Commissioner Oreja recently stated that "self-regulation should not be used by major dominant operators to define 'rules of the game' that are best suited to their own interest to the detriment of small or more recent competitors[8]" (Oreja 1999; Page 1987).

---

8   However the opposite has also been claimed. One of the main reasons why self-regulation was introduced in the financial services in Britain was not only that it would lead to higher standards of business conduct, but that it was thought less likely than government regulation to inhibit innovation and international competitiveness (Rees/Cunningham 1997).

2 Analytical framework

It is difficult to deal with each and every area of indeterminacy involved in defining and then implementing notions of self-regulation. Also, it is impossible to consider each benefit and weakness self-regulation and its specific mechanism may have under each circumstance. Three areas, however, can be deployed to demonstrate the variety of meanings and implementations that can exist.

The first involves the scope of self-regulation: what, in a short-hand way, constitutes "the self." Self-regulation by business often means how businesses police themselves, what standards they use for their own conduct and what steps they deploy to see that those standards are followed. A second area focuses on what is meant by the "regulation" side of "self-regulation." While the inquiry into "self" deals with the issue of whose conduct, whose speech, whose uses are affected, and by whom, "regulation" deals with the tools that are used (such as denying access to those whose use is considered harmful) and the rationales or justifications behind the selected regulatory design. Mandating ratings or providing incentives for rating could be considered, in this sense, a form of regulation.

Finally, one needs to examine the background requirements for self-regulation, the varied institutional relationships that exist between industry and government, all within the self-regulatory banner. These relationships become even more complex in an Internet setting because of the need for international consultation and co-operation among states and private actors. States, industry and user associations are recognizing that the impact of any regulatory action will, in many instances, extend far beyond their frontiers. This is particularly relevant in the case of content on the Internet, given the significant role of culture and social values in these issues.

154

2.1 Self-regulating and mediating institutions

The self of self-regulation

The Internet is a consummate demonstration of the complexity of determining what ought to be included in the "self" of self-regulation. The Internet prides itself on being an autonomous interconnected, totally decentralised, set of communications networks. It includes a cornucopia of institutions that partake of self-regulatory characteristics. Standards and protocols are established by such entities. The process of establishing, registering and managing domain names is such a self-regulatory mechanism. Voluntary institutions, generated by the Internet and not by government, are the very backbone of efforts to deal with harmful content. W3, the entity seeking to develop protocols for websites that – among other things – can serve as the foundation for rating and filtering systems, is a paradigm of self-regulation. Self-regulation can refer to unmonitored, unaudited efforts by the single firm and it can extend to an elaborate process in which all users participate as well as all firms, with government playing roles that range from design, coercion, auditing, monitoring or acquiescence.

Individual versus collective self-regulation

Within this wide range of dimensions of the "self," it is important to distinguish between individual firm self-regulation (where an entity regulates itself, independent of others) and self-regulation by groups. Self-regulation may speak to the specific actions of each actor, but it often refers to a collective constraint by which individual actors are bound. In the Internet setting, one could consider as a matter of individual self-regulation the decisions by each entity that operates as a service provider or a bulletin board or program supplier as to

155

what they will post or what rules they will consider themselves governed by, including rules to rate or label content. Several major service and content providers (such as AOL, MSN, and others[9]) have developed explicit guidelines and user protection guarantees (especially for minors), often labelled "Netiquette" in order to establish and maintain confidence among their users.

This approach is by no means feasible only for large multinational enterprises though only such firms may have sufficient resources to reflect by a range of nationally defined tastes and requirements. In practice, in terms of social response to the Internet, self-regulation implies some degree of collective or community constraint, rules imposed upon each member or actor by an entity created by some or all the actors often under pressure from government. This collective action or, in some cases, the creation of a private regulatory entity, engenders outcomes that would not be reached by individual behaviour alone. As such, self-regulation is a process of "collective self-governance." It describes the situation of a group of persons, institutions or bodies, acting together, performing a regulatory function in respect of themselves and others who accept their authority.

Industry self-regulation

Industry self-regulation may also be described as a regulatory process whereby an industry-level (as opposed to a governmental or firm-level) organisation sets rules and standards (codes of practices)

---

9   Industry corporations are also working with public interest groups such as the Internet Education Foundation (*http://www.neted.org*) and America Links Up (*http://www.americalinksup.org*) to further consumer choice in content selection alternatives.

relating to the conduct of firms in the industry. This definition implies that industry self-regulation requires firms in the industry to decide to co-operate with each other, through industry associations. One of the important roles of these industry associations, within this context, is to make industrial and commercial life more responsible. Industry associations become, as such, "mediating institutions" between the state and the individual and are therefore well-placed to promote social responsibility and shared ethical practices among its members ("the industry"). This way of thinking about industry associations – as normative institutions – stands in contrast to how many economists or political scientists think about industry associations and their potential for self-regulation. Analytical models such as the public choice theory with its rent-seeking[10] language teaches us that associations of all kinds, including industry associations, rarely independently of coercion, establish behavioural norms for their members but to serve their private needs. One might prefer to think that industry associations not only serve private interests, but are also motivated by ideals, principles, and values (Rees/Cunningham 1997: 373).[11] In the end, however, the motivation is irrelevant. Associations embody contrary tendencies – primarily the push of self-serving economic (or political) interests, but modified to some extent by the pull of moral aspirations. Indeed, these moral aspirations may have an economic basis. This emergence of a social role for industry associations corresponds to a notable shift in power from the provident State to privatised and multinational enterprise, concomitant with a waning influence of governments and third-party organisations on market behaviour. This is especially relevant for the

---

10 Rent seeking can be defined as the actions and decisions of political actors that result in wealth transfers which reduce the economic well-being of society (Tollison 1982).

11 Important to mention, however, is that the authors agree that short-termism is one of the central challenges facing industry self-regulation.

157

Internet with its increasing globalisation of activity, decentralised architecture and growing networks of enterprises that operate across national boundaries in an array of contractual, equity and joint venture arrangements. In this environment many companies are facing pressure to be accountable even in the absence of explicit state command for non-financial benchmarks in what has been termed the "triple bottom line", a reference to economic, social and environmental performance.[12]

Self-regulation has proven to work best where there is a degree of coincidence between the self-interest of the industry, and the wider public interest (Cunningham/Grabosky/Sinclair 1998: 53). For instance, it is in the interests of both the Internet Service Providers and the general public to adopt new filtering mechanisms that protect users from offensive material and generate growing confidence. In the advertising industry, self-regulation has voluntarily emerged as the suppliers have perceived the benefit to be obtained from acquiring public credibility for their products and from creating an image of professional responsibility (Boddewyn 1991: 27). Such situations are referred to as "win-win." Where a substantial gap exists between the public interest and the private interest of the industry, it would be naïve to rely upon an industry association taking steps voluntarily in the public interest unless there is some external pressure to do so (the carrot and stick rationale). This may come from a variety of sources, the most important of which include the threat of direct government intervention (enforced self-regulation), broader concerns to maintain credibility and legitimacy (and as a result commercial gain), and the market itself.

12 The "triple bottom line" concept has received criticism for its potential to compromise three disparate forms of value on one balance sheet (Mayhew 1998).

Other industries

While structures of self-regulation vary across industries, its evolution on the Internet will share important common structural elements with other histories. The analysis we have made has its echoes in the work of J. J. Boddewyn, who, in his classic study of self-regulation in the advertising industry, found substantial support for a set of clearly relevant hypotheses concerning the effectiveness of such bodies (Boddewyn 1988). For example, he concluded that the existence of an industry-wide decision-making system (such as a capstone trade association) increases the probability of effective industry self-regulation. Industry self-regulation is more effective when it involves all interrelated levels. Just as a scheme that included only advertisers was strengthened if it included distribution systems (such as television networks), a self-regulatory system for the Internet would be strengthened if it included a range of content providers as well as service providers. He also found that the development and effectiveness of an industry self-regulatory system are enhanced by government threat and oversight. The corollary for an Internet context involves, as an example, monitoring and pressure of bodies such as the European Commission or national legislatures on the private sector to take productive action.

It was his view that the strength and effectiveness of an industry self-regulatory system is a function of its essentiality and non-substitutability. Put differently, self-regulation is most effective when, for reasons of practicality, technology and ideology, there is a coherent preference for self-regulation to government action. Further, the existence and effectiveness of industry self-regulation is not measured by formal rules alone, but also by cultural factors. The transnational character of self-regulation and the experience, in each state, of the relationship between government and business are examples of such potential influences.

Other "Boddewyn hypotheses" include the idea that industry

self-regulation is more likely in those situations where self policing can increase the overall demand for the industry's product and
many of the participants. States that encourage self-regulation must
convince industry that effective implementation, by enhancing
consumer credibility and reducing the threat of costly government
regulation, is self-benefiting. Industry self-regulation is more likely in
those situations where the externally imposed costs from not
undertaking such self-regulation would be greater than the cost of
undertaking such self-regulation. This conclusion recognizes the
careful calibration that enters the decision to model collective
self-regulation. It also suggests that, in a transnational sphere, the
calibration of costs in one national context may be different from
that in another.

Finally, the creation and improvement of an industry self-regulatory system are precipitated by the threat of governmental regulation. For all of the criticism of "jawboning" or other modes of
implying government intervention, the dialogue between government and industry is central to key structures of self-regulation.
Also, encouragement and support of industry self-regulation as an
instrument of public policy is more likely when the limits of
government intervention have become apparent. This may be true,
from the outset, in the area of content regulation where free
speech and similar concerns underscore the limited role for the
state.

The Internet

In the case of the Internet, the very decentralised nature of the
enterprise and the deregulatory ethic that pervades it makes defining
who is the self (object of self-regulation or who is included in its
ambit) especially difficult. In many discussions, governments have
failed to recognize that the Internet industry is not monolithic and

160

that there is no single "industry" that speaks for the whole of the Internet. Self-regulatory solutions are probably more appropriately developed on a sector-by-sector basis, on a timetable that fits the needs of that industry sector, and with due recognition and balancing of the extent of the perceived problem (risk of harm) against the risk of regulatory intervention (risk of diminished benefits) (Gidari 1998).

The fact that the Internet is relatively young and still booming also means that in many cases industries do not have a history of effective co-operative action (e.g. creation of industry associations in EU member states). An interesting example of such co-operation is the EuroISPA, the pan-European association of the Internet service providers' associations of some EU Member States (http://www.euroispa.org/members.html). The association was established when a number of such ISP associations signed the EuroISPA Memorandum of Understanding on 6 August 1997 in Brussels. On 10 September 1997 the signatories to the MOU met again and signed the agreement that formed EuroISPA EEIG, thereby creating the largest association of ISPs in the world. The purposes listed as rationales behind the creation of EuroISPA are:

"First, to protect and promote the interests of Europe as a whole within the global Internet, securing for Europe a premier position in the key industry of the new millennium. Secondly, to help deliver the benefits of this new technology of liberation and empowerment to individuals, while at the same time meeting the legitimate concerns of parents and others responsible for the weaker members of society. Thirdly, to encourage the development of a free and open telecommunications market, something of great benefit to society as a whole but essential to the healthy development of the Internet. And finally, to promote the interests of our members and provide common services to them where these cannot be had elsewhere."

These purposes also highlight the important role of industry

161

associations in the negotiations and bargaining with governments within a framework of co-regulation or enforced self-regulation.[13]

Competitive self-regulation

The multi-sectoral nature of many Internet services will also mean that a wide variety of self-regulating communities or mediating institutions can be expected to come into existence, and even within one given sector competing self-regulatory regimes may emerge. As Ogus has described: "competition of this kind is inherent in systems of private ordering: suppliers compete to attract consumers by the quality (as well as the price) of their products and services. Quality is, to some extent at least, a consequence of standards and other forms of control imposed internally by the management of a firm. The standards may reflect general regulatory requirements but more often they are voluntary, representing the firm's response to assumed consumer demand and, in some cases, incorporating industry-wide practices. To signal to consumers the relationship between standards

13 In an important contribution to the literature, Ayres and Braithwaite developed their model of "enforced self-regulation." Under this model, a public agency negotiates with individual firms regulations that are particularised to each firm, with the threat of an imposition of less tailored standards if it fails to cooperate. While the firm may thus formulate the rules, they are enforced by the public agency. The advantages are clear: as with other privately ordered systems, the rules are tailored to match the firm's circumstances and are less costly to adapt; there are incentives to identify least-cost solutions, which should encourage regulatory innovation; and firms would be more committed to the rules than if imposed externally. Moreover, the very fact of individualisation avoids the monopoly problem. On the other hand, the administrative costs would be high. This suggests that, for such a regime to be cost-effective, the firm must be large and the activity to be regulated must be one in which efficiency requires significantly differentiated standards (Braithwaite 1982).

and quality, some form of voluntary accreditation or certification can be used. Suppliers who aim at different quality standards, and have difficulty in communicating that fact to consumers, will have an incentive to establish a rival certification system" (Ogus 1997). When it comes to providing parental control mechanisms such as filtering and rating software – as described in the chapter by Balkin and Noveck – competition may occur (at the third layer) between white and blacklist filters, ancillary rating systems, and redemptive lists maintained by third-party raters. *It is important to note in this context that third party raters usually provide a commercial service which can be combined with the underlying self-regulatory mechanism.* The general policy implication of this analysis might be that where the public interest arguments for the state delegating its regulatory powers are strong, a variety of options for users should be stimulated.

There are, nevertheless, potential problems with these solutions. Users – more precisely adults and children – must be able to assess the quality of services provided by the competing options; otherwise there will be a "race to the bottom," with significant welfare costs. To remedy this problem, public and/or private institutional intervention may be desirable that lays down minimum quality standards that the self-regulatory regimes must presumptively satisfy. Such intervention would act as a proxy for insufficiently informed consumers (Ogus 1995). Also efforts to improve general media literacy need to be made. Hence the importance of developing awareness schemes to promote the best use of parental control systems.[14]

Secondly, there must be few significant externalities arising from

14 GetNetWise.org is such a scheme launched in Summer 1999 in the US by an industry coalition including AOL, Microsoft, Yahoo!, and groups like the National Center for Missing and Exploited Children and the Center for Democracy and Technology.

self-regulation. Regulation has its externalities, and so too does self-regulation. In the area of speech, the external impact of regulation is often carefully measured because state regulation may be "overinclusive," precluding speech practices that are not injurious and might otherwise take place. In the field of regulating indecency on television or the Internet, for example, some courts are concerned that regulation reduces the speech available to adults to that which is suitable for children. In Butler v. Michigan, 352 U.S. 380 (1957), the Supreme Court recognized the adverse impact on adults of state laws seeking to benefit children, and, since then, the external consequences of such otherwise beneficial regulation is awarded constitutional significance. Self-regulation inevitably requires the imposition of rules that affect third parties.

There is an ambiguity built in to the very term "self-regulation." Self-regulation implies, in the first instance, the exercise by firms within the relevant sector of a discipline over their own actions. On the other hand, it also sometimes suggests the exercise of power by firms over the actions of others, where it is they who are regulating rather than the government itself. As an example, one can say that it is self-regulation, in the first meaning of the term, if broadcasters agree that they shall not program material, before a watershed hour, that is potentially harmful to minors. But it may be self-regulation, in the second meaning of the term, if Internet Service Providers agree to block material that is pornographic or obscene.

Self and individual empowerment

There is an increasing social demand for breadth in the definition of "self" for self-regulation. If the function of self-regulation is to minimise harmful and illegal conduct on the Internet (particularly as it affects young people), then in this view, it must become more, rather than less extensive. Albert Gidari, Executive Director of ILPF has stated that, often, the "self" in self-regulation too narrowly focuses on the business sector alone. This narrow conception of self-regulation places too much of the burden on industry to solve the legal and policy issues and fails to recognize individual users of Internet services and other participants as "independent Internet stakeholders and possible administrators" in a larger self-regulatory regime.

One technique is to authorise or require industry to enforce norms against all Internet users. Another increasingly common approach is what is called "individual empowerment." Individual choice is celebrated in the very nature of the Internet where an individual self-determines what sites to visit, what content to view, and whether to do so anonymously or with the necessary identification to complete a transaction. In response to strong consumer demands, technological tools have been and are being developed to protect against inadvertent exposure to undesired content. In addition, technological complexity is giving way to pre-set preferences; information glut and disorganisation are being replaced by navigation tools, and third-party services that organize, rate or filter according to user instructions. Virtual communities of like-minded individuals form and re-form in an ever-expanding web of information-sharing connections. To be sure, not all individuals have or will achieve complete control over all aspects of electronic transactions. Therefore businesses, alert to consumer preferences, (will have to) respond to these demands by adopting social responsible practices. It is because of these external consequences that the question of the democratic source or legitimisation of self-regulatory activities arises. The power of Internet Service Providers to self-regulate becomes a matter of significant political activity specifically because that self-regulation changes the architecture of communication within society.

Industrial morality or social responsibility

The establishment of norms of behaviour is one of the most complex aspects, theoretically and practically, of collective-self-regulation. To "socialise" industrial life and business activities, an industry association often establishes a normative framework (e.g. enshrined in a code of conduct) for its members. Some may call this "industrial morality," but, to build on an aphorism, this morality may be to altruism what military music is to its civilian equivalent. Still, the articulation of norms, or processes that alter norms, is the basis of many self-regulatory activities with public interest objectives. How such social responsibility comes about is complex, given the wide variety of industries involved, but some common features may be listed (Rees/Cunningham 1997: 376–380).

An industrial morality is a form of moral discourse capable of challenging conventional industry practices ("this is the way we always do business"). Social responsibility provides a basis for shared understanding that can question, guide and set limits around economic considerations by giving a voice to other considerations of what is important for the industry, the consumers, and society such as protection of minors within the setting of the Internet. Self-regulation takes advantage of society's institutional pluralism to moderate the logic of one kind of institution (most notably, the market) by looking at it from the standpoint of another, in this case the parent or the guardian.

An industrial stance on behavioural issues is a product of conscious deliberation. It is the product of collective-industry reflection where industry officials question their customary ways of doing business, weigh the alternatives, and think through the consequences of their choices, including the economic impact of certain courses on their collective well-being. Social responsibility recognizes multiple values and commitments. An industry association, by developing its norms or establishing norms for third parties (like users of the

166

Internet), asks member companies to resist the single-minded pursuit of any objective, including profits. It asks them to become morally self-aware institutions capable of responsibly balancing economic self-interest with other values. An industrial morality is critical, as it presumes that any existing pattern of industrial conduct is subject to criticism and reconstruction in light of reflection and inquiry. An industrial morality creates a normative framework that defines and upholds a special organisational competence. For members of Internet service provider associations, it is the institutional capacity to promote information flow and access without offending large parts of its users. Social responsibility carries an expectation of obedience. This is not to say that an industrial morality is self-executing, but rather that great importance is attached to consent in the formation of an industry code of practice. An industrial morality provides a legitimate account of the industry's activities to the public. This is especially important for the Internet industry. Evolving and growing public concern with content freely available to everyone capable of accessing the Internet forces the Internet industry to develop an industry morality. When an industry's very existence is in question, there is a need for industry to make sense of its relationship to the norms and expectations that exist within its social environment. Hence the importance for the Internet industry of questioning its scope of responsibility.

Descriptions of the nature of norms on the Internet as self-generated are, however, too simple. The Internet, from the beginning, was a government-sponsored enterprise. In its early, happily chaotic period, the evolution of customs, free of government interference, proceeded apace. Custom, here as elsewhere, became the foundation for law, not necessarily a substitute for it. Industry sought the extension or freezing of this moment of the seemingly autonomous generation of norms. But it was governments from whom this extension of a customary or "unregulated" approach was sought. And it was easy to cloak a policy decision in the altruistic garment of law or regulation avoidance. The US position, and the position of others, on a moratorium on taxation of transactions on the Internet, or the policy against the imposition of other export-import duties, are examples of affirmative policy masquerading as a preference for self-generation of law. Essentially, these questions go to the nature of regulation or how norms are developed by a self-regulatory body. In the case of the Internet, norms are encouraged not through establishing an "industry morality" by the industry alone. The stubborn, dramatic and unfinished process of establishing a rating and labelling schemes is an excellent example of how norms develop through what might politely be called a "conversation" between industry and government. Among the key questions are whether, and in what circumstances, such rating and labelling efforts suffice to minimise the call for absolute content standards as difficult as they may be to enforce. A combination of techniques and processes – codes of conduct, rating and labelling and hotlines – may together serve as a way of melding industry conscience with industrial and social needs. The point is that while industry self-regulatory entities do a great deal of work in norm formation, that work must be perceived against a background of potential state coercion.

Institutionalising social responsibility and SRA

In its "collective form," self-regulation is sometimes a deliberate delegation of the state's law-making powers to an agency, the membership of which wholly or mainly comprises representatives of the industries or individuals whose activities are being regulated. Self-regulatory agencies can also be seen as a delegation of individual and user interests to a private body because of its specific expertise and knowledge. The "self" here can be institutionalised into (separate) self-regulatory agencies (SRA) (or in some cases cartels) that combine the governmental function of regulation – and in some cases enforcement – with the institutional and often legal structure and interests of a private body. They may impose conditions of membership (e.g. solely members of the collective or including outsiders) and expulsion and their own discipline. On the other hand, these self-regulation bodies may only articulate and foster norms, facilitating their adoption without enforcing them. Either way self-regulatory agencies play an important role, acting as intermediaries, linking different parts of society (Black 1996). So, despite the so-called disintermediation or the removal of intermediaries from the industry value chain (Negroponte 1996) as a result of the specific architecture of the Internet, the creation of SRA's may lead to a re-intermediation of the industry.

These self-regulatory agencies have the delicate task of helping to define norms, bringing them to public notice, and creating a sense of "industrial morality." One of the key tasks of an SRA might be to ensure accountability of its members through monitoring or enforcement of standards. One of the principal mechanisms to reach accountability is transparency. There are good grounds to believe that the effectiveness of self-regulation depends on the system's ability to produce and promulgate two kinds of information: (1) about the normative standards the industry has set for itself alone or by agreement; and (2) the performance of member companies in terms of those standards. The first step of public transparency is the public announcement of the principles and practices that the industry presumptively accepts as a guide to its role and also as a basis for evaluating and criticising performance. The next critical step is the development of an information system for collecting data on the progress of member companies in implementing the industry codes or practices. The process usually divides into two parts: (1) reporting by the members and (2) collecting and analysing of the data by the SRA. The third and final step in achieving transparency is the monitoring of performance. Building transparency into the social structure of the industry by those categories sets the stage for a "theatre of external judgement," and as transparency increases so does the likelihood of being called to account for one's industrial conduct (Rees/Cunningham 1997: 383–385).

Reaching accountability and social responsibility is thus an important task of every self-regulatory body. In carrying out its duties, the (self) regulatory body must, if it is to have any credibility, be seen as having reached its decisions and conducted its activities in an independent manner. This independence is especially important within the communications sector, given the role of media within citizen participation and democracy. Independence is virtually never absolute or complete, but the legal architecture of the body can be reassuring. Guarantees for independence include criteria such as institutional stability (as ensured in its constitution), the appointments system, the composition of the body, the disqualification conditions, the links established between government and industry and its financial and organisational autonomy (Robillard 1995).

"Audited self-regulation," is a US technique that illustrates the relational aspect of self-regulatory independence.[15] The conditions used are: "First, the private entity to which self-regulatory authority is granted must have both the expertise and motivation to perform the delegated task. Second, the government agency staff must possess the expertise to "audit" the self-regulatory activity, which includes independent plenary authority to enforce rules or to review decisions of the delegated authority. Third, the statute must consist of relatively narrow rules related to output-based standards. ... Finally, the agency's and delegated authority's decision must observe rules for notice, hearing, impartiality, and written records of proceedings and decisions" (Michael 1995: 192). These rules for monitoring would

---

15 This term refers to the delegation of power to implement laws or agency regulations to a nongovernmental entity where the federal agency is involved in verifying the soundness of rules, checking compliance, and spot-checking the accuracy of information supplied to it (Michael 1995).

apply to audits by self-regulatory bodies themselves, as well as to those of government auditors.

There are risks of regulatory capture when regulatory agencies become so closely associated with their subject of regulation that it becomes impossible to discern a divergence of interests; at such corporatist moments, the public interest, supposed to be protected by the regulator, may readily be compromised. Such risks may reasonably be heightened in a self-regulatory situation, where the regulators are drawn from and answerable to the industry concerned (Feintuck 1999: 141). Thus transparency, always a prerequisite for accountability as already highlighted, may be of particular significance in relation to self regulatory agencies, given their close relationship with those subject to their rules.

Other issues that arise: the duty or privilege of the SRA to co-operate with government, by, for example, disclosing abuses of a self-regulatory standard to government agencies; the extent to which there is any role for an official or quasi-official agency to have in reviewing or monitoring the performance of SRA and whether the SRA is clothed with any governmental or governmental-like powers of enforcement.

2.2 Government and third-party involvement

The particular rhetorical relationship between government and the self-regulatory body is most important when considering structure. There is a difference if self-regulation is a consequence of government threat (enforced self-regulation) or a consequence of a civic culture in which the government co-operates with industry (voluntary self-regulation). Self-regulation cannot totally replace government regulation entirely in the media and communications-related sectors (Federal Government Germany 1999). The state retains ultimate responsibility for protecting the public interest. This does not mean that the state must directly be involved in the activities of self-regulatory agencies but an interconnection will likely be needed to take sufficient account of compelling public interest considerations. If this interplay is to be a path to better regulatory policy in the Internet field then several points of broader relevance need to be made.

In general, one can identify four types of relationships with the state where the differences among them are delicate but significant: mandated self-regulation, in which the industry is virtually required by the government to formulate and enforce norms within a framework defined by the government. The development of a rating system for the V-Chip in the US falls within one of the first three depending on how one views the process (McDowell/Maitland 1998); sanctioned self-regulation, in which the collective group itself formulates the regulation, which is then subjected to government approval; coerced (or enforced) self-regulation, in which the industry itself formulates and imposes regulation but in response to threats by the government that if it does not the government will impose statutory regulation (the creation of the Press Complaints Commission in the UK); and voluntary self-regulation, where there is no active state involvement.

The possibilities can also be considered on two spectra, depicting degrees of autonomy from government and legal force respectively. Rules can be private to firms, groups or organisations at one extreme, to those approved by a government minister or some independent public authority at the other; in between, representatives of the public interest may participate in, but not conclusively determine, the decision-making. Rules may be formally binding, with non-compliance leading to public law or private law sanctions; codes of practice which presumptively apply unless an alleged offender can show that some alternative conduct was capable of meeting the regulatory goals satisfactorily; norms, the breach of which leads to non-legal sanctions, such as ostracism; or standards, with which compliance is purely voluntary.

In determining how to structure the symbiosis between the self-regulating entity and the state, a number of questions can be asked: Was the entity generated from within the industry or as a consequence of government action? Are the broad standards administered by the entity developed by the government or by the entity itself? Who appoints the members of any administering board? Does the board or entity or the industry require state intervention to protect them from liability? Does a consumer have a right of review within the self-regulatory process? Does a consumer have a right of review in the state's judicial system or other processes for review? Is there a public body that periodically reviews the work of the self-regulating entity? Does the industry act through a self-regulating board, or does self-regulation mean that each firm has some responsibility that they are privileged or required to exercise because of industrial consensus? If there is an entity, does it have enforcement powers (is it enforcement when an ISP removes content from a server?) Is there a duty or privilege of the entity (board or company) to co-operate with the state's law enforcement agencies (for example to monitor and then provide information of potential violation of a law)? Is the process of norm-refinement (what constitutes violence or improper material) wholly within the self-regulatory sector and if not how is it divided?

These questions are part of a taxonomy of self-regulation that is often overlooked. It is rare, as we have emphasised, that a self-regulatory body has (in terms of these questions) no relationship to the state. It is often the case – and this is certainly true in the Internet context – that the generation of self-regulation has its foundation in the possibility or fear of government regulation. In some states, the process of generating self-regulation is a co-operative effort, a suggestion by the state that self-regulation would be a more effective approach than the increase in the definition of illegal conduct by the state itself. In some states, self-regulation figures as a defensive response to a threat, either from political bodies or the public

173

sphere. Self-regulation becomes that body of action, by the industry itself, which can prevent the imposition of more extensive, more costly, more intrusive regulation by government. Self-regulatory entities that develop as a consequence of threat may have different cultures than those that develop as a consequence of negotiation and encouragement. Moreover, for some it seems unlikely that they would perform well in the absence of continuing government oversight and the threat of direct intervention. On the surface, autonomy, where self-regulation is a response to threat, could be defensive, less co-operative, less committed to a common goal. Self-regulation that results from a more positive relationship between state and industry might be more flexible, lead to greater working together, and have more of a spirit of shared experimentation.

Much clearer elements of autonomy are involved in who establishes the standards that are administered by the self-regulatory entity. In the arena of content control, one of the perceived virtues (though not unalloyed) of self-regulation, is the capacity of users to establish their own standards and not be governed by one standard developed by the government. However, the more engrafted with state power the self-regulatory body may be through setting certain standards in the architecture of speech, for instance; the more it is appropriate to scrutinise the nature of its approach to affecting content so as to insure that private does not take the place of public censorship.

Whatever standards are self-created by the private regulating entity, it still may have an administrative role with respect to standards that have been enacted as a positive prohibition by the state. In the Internet context, all states have laws that prohibit certain kinds of speech in whatever medium. These may include speech that incites violence, or speech that endangers national security in highly specified ways. While administration or enforcement of these prohibitions rests, usually, with the state, they can be administered by the self-regulating entity as well. More difficult is a description of speech regulating techniques that are different from those established by the

174

state. In almost every national setting concerning the Internet, self-regulation with respect to content will, increasingly, have one significant relationship to the state: a pact in which the service provider is willing to undertake affirmative actions to remove potentially illegal material from its servers, but requires immunity from the state for such actions. It is possible that contractual arrangements will entitle service providers (or others similarly situated) to remove what are deemed offensive materials, or cut off access to servers, or discontinue use by particular individuals or entities. But contract protection alone – and even that implicates the state – may not be sufficient if the self-regulating entity is to play the wider role that seems to be demanded of it. The state is being called upon to ensure that, within a particular ambit of action, the service provider will not be open to lawsuit, even if the removal of material proves to be erroneous or exceeding what constitutes illegality within the society. Such a provision was included as a so-called Good Samaritan law in the 1996 Telecommunications Act in the United States. It finds a curious mirror in a recent addition to the US Copyright Act (Section 512(c)) designed to deal with potential copyright infringement in the digital world. That law authorises the service provider expeditiously to remove or disable access to material that is claimed to be infringing a third party copyright. The statute provides very specific circumstances under which a service provider is notified as to potentially infringing activity. In Section 512(g), the statute provides that a service provider "shall not be liable to any person for any claim based on the service provider's good faith disabling of access to, or removal of, material or activity claimed to be infringing or based on facts or circumstances from which infringing activity is apparent, regardless of whether the material or activity is ultimately determined to be infringing."

Self-regulating entities will require this kind of immunity from liability if they are called upon to take down material thought to be harmful, especially if they do so expeditiously, without the kind of due process that would be required if the state were engaged in exercising content controls.

Even more so than in cases of disputed copyright infringement, there will undoubtedly be differences of opinion of what harmful content should be removed (either because of contract or because of codes of conduct or because of alleged violation of statute).

The state will be implicated in yet another way, this time to ensure greater freedom for the service providers. Increasingly, self-regulating entities require state assurance of a safe harbour. Again, the Communications Decency Act, even though struck down in part, is a model of what may come. In that statute, service providers could escape responsibility for delivering certain material to minors or displaying it to minors if they complied with specific techniques that were surrogates for actual determination of minimum age of addressee.[16] These included, for example, the use of credit cards (47 USCA 223(e)(5)(B)). Two elements are important here. Certain elements of self-regulation must be protected through state law. More significant, however, state law may itself rely on the self-regulatory mechanism to introduce comparable or acceptable mechanisms to determine what constitutes such things as a safe harbour. Three more elements of state involvement can be mentioned.

Self-regulatory mechanisms may be privileged in terms of their

---

16   47USCA 223(e)(5) It is a defence to a prosecution under subsection (a)(1)(B) or (d), or under subsection (a)(2) with respect to the use of a facility for an activity under subsection (a)(1)(B) that a person – (A) has taken, in good faith, reasonable, effective, and appropriate actions under the circumstances to restrict or prevent access by minors to a communication specified in such subsections, which may involve any appropriate measures to restrict minors from such communications, including any method which is feasible under available technology; or (B) has restricted access to such communication by requiring use of a verified credit card, debit account, adult access code, or adult personal identification number.

enforcement. We have already dealt with this in the analogy to the privileging of private entities to eliminate potential copyright infringers. More may be anticipated in terms of empowering the self-regulator. Second, the state may require, or at least excuse, actions, that otherwise might be violations of user privacy or contractual rights, by notifying law enforcement of possible harms that exist through particular uses of the Internet. Indeed, self-regulation might involve monitoring content, and a concomitant protected responsibility to evaluate and to report. Much of this is dealt with in Professor Sieber's chapter in this book. Finally, the state might require public review of the activities of the self-regulating entity and determine the composition of the reviewing mechanism. An interesting example of this was the announcement in September 1998 by the UK's Department of Trade and Industry (DTI) and the Home Office to carry out a review of the Internet Watch Foundation (Department of Trade and Industry 1999).

Third parties

The state is however not the only party that might develop co-regulatory arrangements with the industry. Sometimes, there may also be a possibility of harnessing third parties or "outsiders" to act as surrogate regulators; monitoring or policing the code as a complement or alternative to governmental involvement. It is possible to argue that self-regulation is rarely effective or legitimate without such involvement. The most obvious third parties with an interest in playing this role are sectoral interest groups such as consumer associations, trade unions or NGOs generally. Moreover with the individual empowerment made possible through the technologies of the Internet, the consumer him/herself may play an important role as co-regulator. A distinction between four major types of outside participants can be made: public members (also called "independents"), consumer representatives, experts and professionals. In practice, most self-regulatory systems use some mixture of all four types. Government agencies and officials can be considered as a fifth category of outsiders. They do not officially participate within a self-regulatory agency but informally guide, monitor and even threaten them (as discussed above) (Boddewyn 1988: 52).

This contribution of third parties or the so-called "co-opted" self regulation may be through their direct involvement in administration and auditing of the code itself (with often greater credibility of the self-regulatory scheme as a result), or in their capacity as potential victims of code malpractice, in taking direct action against firms that breach the self-regulatory program. One major consequence of harnessing the self-interest of consumers through self-regulatory programmes is that there is far less need for direct involvement of government. A major role of governments in these circumstances may be that of facilitator or broker (ensuring the effective involvement of appropriate third parties) rather than that of direct participant.

Non-member controls: summary

Self-regulators may thus be subject to government and non-member controls in a host of ways (Baldwin/Cave 1999):
- statutory prescriptions and objectives;
- rules that are drafted by or approved by other bodies or ministries;
- ministerial guidelines or criteria for consideration by the self-regulator;
- parliamentary oversight of the delegated legislation that guides the self-regulator;
- departmental purse strings and the influence that these provide;
- agency oversight;

- informal influences from government that are exerted in the shadow of threatened state regulation;
- judicial review;
- complaints and grievance-handling mechanism (e.g. ombudsmen);
- reporting and publication requirements laid down by government or parliament.

2.3 Codes of conduct

One form of industry self-regulation is the development of an industry-wide normative framework, a set of industrial principles and practices that defines right conduct as it spells out the industry's public commitment to moral restraint and aspiration. An evolving framework in many cases, it is usually drafted in very general terms at the outset because trust, co-operation, and technical consensus necessary for a more detailed agreement is lacking; but as co-operation and consensus grows, it is usual for more detailed norms to follow. Studies of the prevalence and contents of codes of conduct have shown that their use to define a socially responsible and ethical environment, and their effective implementation, must be a part of a learning process that requires inculcation, reinforcement and measurement (National Consumer Council 1986). One of the conclusions made by the Internet Law and Policy Forum was that "the history of self-regulatory initiatives proves that snapshot solutions are ineffective. Instead, the basic premise of self-regulation is continuous improvement to meet the needs of the particular business in the most efficient manner (with "needs" encompassing company growth and consumer demand as well as the prevention and detection of unlawful or liability-producing conduct). For example, third-party or internal audits are proven self-regulatory tools. Successful audits build on prior audit results and become management tools for future improved performance. The process is iterative and repetitive, resulting in best practices that often are adopted or emulated by others in the same industry to remain competitive" (Gidari 1998).

Codes of conduct are designed to protect an organisation's or industry's public image, and to a certain extent to enhance it, by declaring its moral standards to others. A hazard of industry codes is that while they may be useful and accurate descriptions of the organisational or industrial paradigm, they are likely to be only partially accurate, and even misleading descriptions of actual industry practices (Doig/Wilson 1998: 141). This is simply because the statements of aspiration or strategic intent emanate from a particular stakeholder (Johnson/Scholes 1997: 218). The question whether the association or body responsible for the code represents all the operators in a sector or only a small percentage of them is, therefore, a crucial one to answer.

There is a related danger of codes. While they appear to make the industry socially responsible and working for the benefit of those who use the services of the industry, the codes may become a means merely to sell the firm to customers and employees. One important criterion for judging the value of a code against this type of "window-dressing" is the degree to which its rules can be enforced. In this context, the strength of the association is crucial in terms of its ability to impose sanctions on its members for non-compliance with the code.

As to the Internet, several ISP associations have now developed or are in the process of developing different codes concerning, among other things, the protection of minors (BIAC/OECD, http:// www.oecd.org/dsti/sti/it/index.htm). Several secondary reasons suggest that industry-wide or profession-wide codes – with clearly comprehensive coverage – are more useful instruments of protection than those developed by small groupings of companies within sectors. From the user's point of view, an industry that is fragmented

180

and characterised by several rival associations, each with its own content protection code, is confusing. The co-existence of several different codes creates an overall picture that lacks transparency for the user. Particularly on the Internet offensive or illegal content is passed between different companies of the same sector. Situations can arise where the company evaluating the content is not subject to the same protection code as the company that receives it. This is a source of considerable ambiguity as to the nature of the rules applicable, and it might also render investigation and resolution of complaints from individual users extremely difficult.

The content of codes of conduct

Generally codes developed by the Internet service providers tend to focus on:
– co-operation with law enforcement authorities,
– clarification of liability and responsibility issues,
– approaches to privacy and handling personal data,
– investigation of complaints,
– procedures for addressing illegal or harmful content,
– promotion of technological tools to empower users.
As to illegal or harmful content the European Council Recommendation of 24 September 1998 provided an overview of what should be included in such a code (Council of Ministers 1998). Concerning the protection of minors, codes of conduct should address basic rules:
– on the nature of the information about Internet content to be made available to users, its timing and the form in which it is communicated. The most appropriate occasions should be chosen to communicate such information (sale of technical equipment, conclusion of contracts with user, websites, etc.).
– for the businesses providing online services and for users and suppliers of content. The rules should set out the conditions

181

under which the supply and distribution of content likely to harm minors is subject to protection measures such as: a warning page, visual signal or sound signal, descriptive labelling and/or classification of contents and age-verification systems.

– on the conditions under which, wherever possible, additional tools or services are supplied to users to facilitate parental control, including: filter software installed and/or activated by the user, and filter options activated, at the end-user's request, by service operators at a higher level (for example, limiting access to predefined sites or offering general access to services).

– on the management of complaints, i. e. on the provision by operators of appropriate management tools and structures to receive complaints without difficulty (through hotlines: telephone, e-mail, fax) and on the introduction of procedures for dealing with complaints (informing content providers, exchanging information between operators, responding to complaints, etc.).

Several additional observations are relevant. Whatever the content of such codes, transparency is a crucial element. When drafting codes, language should be plain and offer concrete examples to illustrate various provisions. A distinction may be made among principles, codes, and what might be called guidelines and recommendations, a distinction that relates to the strength of obligations imposed on industry. General principles are close to incontrovertible axioms that all members of the industry association should accept as self evident. Codes refer to explicit rules, whose violation is most likely to trigger some admonition or disciplining. Guidelines and recommendations are of a less binding nature because the problems are novel, fluid and/or hard to clearly circumscribe so that precise (or hard) rules are not possible. Honesty, decency, fair trading and the like are typically amenable to such looser treatment. In the field of advertising, self-regulatory systems are increasingly issuing recommendations rather than firm rules for fear that language that is too explicit increases the danger that voluntary codes will be transformed into laws and regulation. Appropriate rules for appeal and mediation procedures should also be included in a code of conduct.

Effectiveness of codes of conduct

The Working Group on the Protection of Individuals with Regard to the Processing of Personal Data of the European Commission (DG-XV) recently analysed the effectiveness of industry self-regulation, with results that can be adapted to content self-regulation (European Commission 1998). The four functional criteria they suggest for judging the effectiveness of a self-regulatory code are: level of compliance, support to users, impartiality of the arbiter and appropriate redress.

Level of compliance

The level of compliance is likely to depend on the degree of awareness of the code's content among members, on the steps taken to ensure transparency of the code to consumers, on the existence of a system of external verification (such as a requirement for an audit of compliance at regular intervals) and, perhaps most crucially, on the nature and enforcement of the sanction in cases of non-compliance.

When examining the types of sanction in place, it is important to distinguish between a "remedial" sanction which simply requires a service provider, in case of non-compliance, to change its practices so as to bring them into line with the code, and a sanction which goes further by actually punishing the provider for its failure to comply. According to the Working Group, it is this second category of "punitive" sanction which has the greatest effect on future behaviour by providing a strong incentive to comply. The absence of genuinely dissuasive and punitive sanctions is seen as a major weakness in a code. It can be argued, however, that a rigorous system of external verification (such as a public or private authority competent to intervene in case of non compliance with the code, or a compulsory requirement for external public audit at regular intervals) can provide strong incentives for a high level of overall compliance.

Important questions listed by the Working Group are: what efforts does the representative body make to ensure that its members are aware of the code? Does the representative body require evidence from its members that they have put the provisions of the code into practice? Is such evidence provided by the member company itself or does it come from an external source (such as an accredited auditor) and at what intervals is it provided? Does the representative body investigate alleged or suspected breaches of the code? Is compliance with the code a condition of membership of the representative body or is compliance purely "voluntary"? Where a member has been shown to breach the code, what forms of disciplinary sanction are available to the representative body (expulsion or other)? Is it possible for an individual or company to continue working in the particular profession or industry even after expulsion from the representative body? Is compliance with the code enforceable in other ways, for example by way of the courts or a specialist tribunal?

Support and help to users

A key requirement of an adequate protection system is that an individual faced with a problem is not left alone, but is given some institutional support. This institutional support should ideally be impartial, independent and equipped with the necessary powers to evaluate any complaint. Where the problem concerns illegal content on the Internet, there should be, at least, a preliminary evaluative inquiry, though such complaints must eventually be channelled to the proper law enforcement authorities. Details of this process are addressed in the chapters on hotlines and on law enforcement. Relevant questions for self-regulation in this regard are: is there a system in place allowing for evaluation of complaints from users? How are users made aware of this system and of actions taken in individual cases? Are there any costs involved for the user?

Impartiality of the arbiter

The impartiality of the arbiter or adjudicator in any alleged breach of a code is key. Clearly such a person or body must be independent in relation to the service provider. This in itself may not be sufficient to ensure impartiality Possibly, the arbiter should be independent from the profession or sector concerned, the reason being that fellow members of a profession or sector have a commonality of interests with the actor alleged to have breached the code or might otherwise be subject to a conflict of interest.

Appropriate redress

If the self-regulatory code is shown to have been breached, not only should a remedy be available to the user, but that remedy must be appropriate. Sanctions have a dual function: to deter the offender (and thus encourage compliance with rules) and to repair or cure a breach of the rules. The repair function seems to be more important to the Working Party. Additional questions would therefore include: how is it possible to verify that a member who has been shown to contravene the code has changed his practices and put the problem right? Will users deem that the sanctions have led to a situation in which the code is observed more fully?

It is difficult to assess the current status of self-regulatory practices in a comparative way. Often, self-regulatory efforts are non-public and not reported. They take different forms in different areas of the world. There are flaws in survey techniques as categories for description may vary between the surveying entity and the businesses or governments being surveyed. As the Internet changes, as social needs are defined, self-regulatory practices change and change rapidly. Some examples may, however, be given to demonstrate the institution of self-regulatory practices especially if it involved the creation of industry associations and the designing of codes of conduct.

Europe

The majority of efforts to self-regulate and consequently to draft codes of conduct for the Internet in Europe came in 1997 when there was an explosion of activity. To protect their interests vis-à-vis the intentions of government, working parties or industry associations were established then in Belgium (ISPA), France (AFPI), Ireland (ISPA), Italy (@IIP), and in Germany (ICTF/FSM). All have since drafted codes of conduct (see appendix) including references to mechanisms (rating and filtering) and rules to protect minors. Some of them also created a complaints mechanism or hotline (e.g. Newswatch (G), Meldpunt (Nl), IWF (UK), AFA (Fr)). These efforts were preceded by the earlier organisation of self-regulation of the Internet in both the Netherlands (NLIP est. 1995) and in the UK (ISPA est. 1995 and Internet Watch Foundation est. 1996). These forerunners have been followed more recently by efforts in Spain (Anprotel), Denmark (FIL), Austria (ISPA) and Finland (ISPA). Further, Internet service providers in Greece are in the process of setting up an official association and Sweden's leading Internet service providers are also in the process of holding discussions to create a framework for self-regulation in their country. Some of these efforts have also been combined across Europe through the creation of Euro-ISPA, the pan-European association of the Internet services providers' associations of the countries of the European Union. Other pan-European efforts include INCORE (Internet Content Rating for Europe), funded by the European Commission, to create a forum to examine questions of content rating and subsequent filtering and INHOPE (Internet Hotline Providers in Europe).

North America

There has been a great deal of activity in the US and Canada. In November 1995, the Task Force on Internet Use of the Information Technology Association of America issued a report on "Internet, Free Speech and Industry Self-Regulation." It concluded by stating that ITAA "believes a reasonable and rational middle ground exists that allows the Internet to continue to flourish, while at the same time giving parents and families the tools necessary to negotiate safely on the information superhighway. This approach recognizes the need for industry self-regulation rather than legislative intervention. ITAA intends to continue pursuing a balanced approach, what it views as the better alternative." This has been followed by several high level summits on Internet content and Child Protection and at the state level several ISP associations have been created. Examples are as follows: in Texas the non-profit Texas Internet Service Providers Association (TISPA) was founded in 1996. According to TISPA's bylaws, initiatives will be developed "to disseminate legislative, educational and other useful information and to inspire members to further inform themselves in the practical and ethical issues of the Internet industry" (http://www.tispa.org/bylaws.htm). State law requires all Texas Internet Service Providers to link to blocking and filtering software sites. In 1997, during the 75th Regular Session of the Texas Legislature, House Bill 1300 (HB 1300) was passed. HB 1300 requires Internet Service Providers to make a link available on their first World Wide Web page (home page) which leads to Internet "censorware" software, also known as 'automatic' blocking and screening software. The Florida Internet Service Providers Association was founded in May, 1996 "to facilitate discussion and educate the public about the importance of the Internet industry." A code of conduct was drafted that reflects general principles of good conduct (http://www.fispa.org/fispa_code.html).

In Canada the Canadian Association of Internet Providers (CAIP), created in 1996, has issued a voluntary code of conduct with an accompanying commentary (http://www.caip.ca/caipcode.htm).

International insert

A broad international effort to develop, implement and manage an internationally acceptable voluntary self-rating system was created in May 1999. Among the founding members of the Internet Content Rating Association (ICRA) are Bell Canada, British Telecommunications plc (BT), Cable & Wireless, Demon Internet, UU-Net, Geotrust, IBM, Internet Watch Foundation, the Electronic Network Consortium (Japan), EuroISPA, Microsoft, T-Online and the Bertelsmann Foundation.[17]

---

17 ICRA's mission is to develop, implement and manage an internationally acceptable voluntary self-rating system which provides Internet users world wide with the choice to limit access to content they consider harmful, especially to children. ICRA has received the RSAC assets including the RSACi system that provides consumers with information about the level of nudity, sex, language, and violence in websites.

188

Australia

On April 21, 1999, the Minister for Communications, Information Technology and the Arts introduced Internet legislation, known as the Broadcasting Services Amendment (Online Services) Bill 1999. Among the listed provisions, the Australian Broadcasting Authority (ABA) will be given powers to issue notices to service providers aimed at preventing access to prohibited material which is subject to a complaint if it is hosted in Australia. If the material is sourced overseas, the ABA is authorised to take reasonable steps to prevent access if technically feasible and commercially viable. Such "reasonable steps" are to be detailed in an industry code of practice to be developed in consultation with the ABA. There are several associations at the state level such as the South Australian Internet Association, the ACT Internet Association, the Tasmanian Internet Association and the Western Australian Internet Association. At a national level there is the Internet Industry Association (incorporating the Australian Internet Alliance, and the Internet Industry Association of Australia).

Asia

Some examples may be given from Asia. In Japan, the Electronic Network Consortium has developed its General Ethical Guideline for Running Online Services in 1996 (http://www.nmda.or.jp/enc/guideline.html). Similar guidelines, "Codes Of Practice For Internet Service Providers" were approved by the Telecom Services Association on January 30, 1998 (http://www.telesa.or.jp/e_guide/e_guid 01.html). To protect young people and public morals, a Practice Statement was developed that recommends guidelines for members of the Hong Kong Internet Service Providers Association (HKISPA) (http://www.hkispa.org.hk/) to follow in their provision of services insofar as the regulation of obscene and indecent material transmitted on the Internet is concerned. Finally, in Singapore, in exercise of the powers conferred by section 18 of the Singapore Broadcasting Authority Act, the Singapore Broadcasting Authority issued, with effect from November 1, 1997, the Internet Code of Practice (http://www.sba.gov.sg/netreg/code.htm).

3 Conclusions and recommendations: systematic self-regulation as a foundation

Given the competing societal interests in control of content on the Internet, meaningful and effective self-regulation is preferable to the exclusive exercise of government authority. Self-regulation has a greater capacity to adapt rapidly to quickening technical progress and to the transnational development of the new communications medium. In addition to flexibility, self-regulation presents the benefits of greater efficiency, increased incentives for compliance, and reduced cost. A carefully structured programme of self-regulation, often developed in co-operation with government, is harmonious with the new technology, mirroring the Internet itself as a global, essentially private and decentralised network of communication.

Effective self-regulation requires active consumer and citizen consultation based upon shared responsibility at all stages of development and implementation. Without user involvement, a self-regulatory mechanism will not accurately reflect user needs, will not be effective in delivering the standards it promotes, and will fail to create confidence. Moreover, the effectiveness of self-regulation and its enforcement will depend largely on the full collaboration and commitment among all industry players. Self-regulation can then yield a responsive, acceptable and systematic solution to current concerns.

The development of an effective self-regulatory regime for the Internet includes the formation of multiple, carefully considered, comprehensive and complementary mechanisms to achieve public interest objectives. The establishment of self-regulatory mechanisms that have a reservoir of social acceptance will, in general, be the product of public input and cooperation among Internet service and content providers, self-regulatory nationally and internationally active and state bodies.

Self-Regulatory Agencies (SRA), should be brought into being for the creation, promulgation and enforcement of self-generated codes. SRAs should stimulate public confidence by ensuring accountability, monitoring of members and enforcing standards.

Codes of conduct should be adopted to ensure that Internet content and service providers act in accord with principles of social responsibility. These codes should meet community concerns and industry needs and operate as an accountability system that guarantees a high level of credibility and quality. To be effective, these codes of conduct should be the product of and enforced by the self-regulatory industry entities themselves, though often in collaboration with government. Because of the transnational nature of Internet communications, coordinated activity among these agencies is an essential element of self-regulation.

There should be comprehensive use of rating and filtering technology and a mobilisation of content producers worldwide to empower users of the Internet to make more effective choices about programme content. Such technology is especially necessary for content directed to children or content that might, in the absence of mechanisms, enter homes without the capacity of guardians to exercise their judgment. Such a comprehensive system requires citizen content response and complaints systems, such as hotlines, that add to credibility.

In implementing codes, several additional principles are important. Effective self-regulation is not possible without support processes of law making and regulation. In addition, public education is essential to increase awareness of the means to filter and block content, to present complaints for effective redress and to obtain the level of compliance that is promised by the industry. Finally, techniques must be found to measure the effectiveness of self-regulatory measures and to determine what national and trans-national measures – if any – are necessary to compensate for their deficiencies. Codes of conduct should delineate both the standards for problematic content which they are attempting to enforce and the mechanisms through which this enforcement will occur, including provisions for co-operation with end-users as well as public authorities. Industry-wide codes are more useful instruments of protection than those developed by small groupings of companies within sectors. They are more comprehensive and transparent and reduce confusion among users.

For self-regulation to ensure public confidence, standards for protection of minors must be clear and effective. They should be transparent, and accepted by government as the mode for proceeding for the protection of youth. There are necessary, state-authorised conditions for self-regulation. ISPs must have the protected capacity to exclude potentially violative ICPs from their servers. And, in carefully specified instances, ISPs must have the protected capacity or "safe harbour" of handling and sharing information with law enforcement authorities, but the circumstances for such sharing should be circumscribed and the specific circumstances for sharing should be fully disclosed.

Bibliography

Ayres, Ian/John Braithwaite (1992): Responsive Regulation: Transcending the Deregulation Debate. Oxford: Oxford University Press.

192

Baldwin, Robert/Martin Cave (1999): Understanding Regulation. Oxford: Oxford University Press.

Birks, Peter (1997): Privacy and Loyalty. Oxford: Clarendon Press.

Black, J. (1996): Constitutionalising Self-Regulation. *The Modern Law Review, 59,* pp. 24–56.

Boddewyn, J.J. (1991): The Case of Self-Regulation. NY: IAA.

Boddewyn, J.J. (1998): Advertising Self-Regulation and Outside Participation: A Multinational Comparison. New York: Quorum.

Braithwaite, John (1982): Enforced Self-Regulation: A New Strategy for Corporate Crime. *Michigan Law Review, 80,* pp. 1466–1507.

Braithwaite, John (1993): Responsive Regulation in Australia. In: Peter Grabosky/John Braithwaite (eds.): Regulation and Australia's Future. Canberra: Australian Institute of Criminology, p. 91.

Breyer, Stephen (1982): Regulation and its Reform. Cambridge, Massachusetts: Harvard University Press.

Brohmer, Jürgen/J. Ukrow (1999): Die Selbstkontrolle im Medienbereich in Europa. Eine rechtsvergleichende Untersuchung. Saarbrücken: EMR.

Campbell, Angela J. (1999): Self-Regulation and the Media, 51 *Fed. Comm. L.J.* 551

Cunningham, Neil/Peter Grabosky/Peter Sinclair (1998): Smart Regulation – Designing Environmental Policy. Oxford: Clarendon Press.

Delacourt, J. (1997): The International Impact of Internet Regulation. *Harvard International Law Journal, 38,* pp. 207–235.

Doig, A./J. Wilson (1998): The Effectiveness of Codes of Conduct. *Business Ethics, 7,* pp. 141–149.

Doyle, C. (1997): Self-Regulation and Statutory Regulation. *Business Strategy Review, 8 (3),* pp. 35–42.

Feintuck, M. (1999): Media Regulation, Public Interest and the Law. Edinburgh: Edinburgh University Press.

193

Gidari, A. (1998): Observations on the State of Self-Regulation of the Internet. The Ministerial Conference of the OECD A Borderless World: Realising the Potential for Global Electronic Commerce. Ottawa, Canada: Internet Law and Policy Forum.

Goldsmith, Jack L. (1998): Against Cyberanarchy. *University of Chicago Law Review*, 65, pp. 1199–1250.

Hawkins, K./B.M. Hutter (1993): The Response of Business to Social Regulation in England and Wales: An Enforcement Perspective. *Law & Policy*, 15, p. 199.

Hoffmann-Riem, Wolfgang (1996): Regulating Media: The Licensing and Supervision of Broadcasting in Six Countries. New York: Guildford Press.

Huyse, L./S. Parmentier (1990): Decoding Codes: The Dialogue between Consumers and Suppliers through Codes of Conduct in the European Community. *Journal of Consumer Policy*, 13, pp. 260–287.

Johnson, Gerry/Kevin Scholes (1997): Exploring Corporate Strategy. New York: Prentice Hall.

Katsh, M. E. (1996): Dispute Resolution In Cyberspace. *Connecticut Law Review*, 28, pp. 953–979.

Mayhew, N. (1998): Trouble with the triple bottom line. *Financial Times*, 10 Aug. 1998.

McDowell, Stephen D./Carleen Maitland, (1998): Developing Television Ratings in Canada and the United States: the Perils and Promises of Self-Regulation. In: Monroe E. Price (ed.): The V-Chip Debate. New York: LEA.

Michael, Douglas C. (1995): Federal Agency Use of Audited Self-Regulation as a Regulatory Technique. *Administrative Law Review*, 47, pp. 171–205.

Negroponte, Nicholas (1996): Being Digital. New York: Vintage Books.

Ogus, A. (1995): Rethinking Self-Regulation. *Oxford Journal of Legal Studies*, 15, pp. 97–108.

Ogus, A. (1997): Self-Regulation. In: B. Bouckaert/G. De Geest (eds.): Encyclopedia of Law and Economics. Ghent: Edward Elgar/University of Ghent.

Oreja, Marcelino (1999): Seminar on Self-regulation in the Media (jointly organized by the German Presidency of the European Union and the European Commission). Saarbrücken (speech).

Pitofsky, Robert (1998): Self-Regulation and Anti-trust, http://www.ftc.gov/OPA/1998/9802/SE; FREG.HTM (visited July 14, 1999).

Prosser, T. (1998): Law and the Regulators. Oxford: Clarendon Press.

Rees, J. (1988): Reforming the Workplace, A Study of Self-Regulation in Occupational Safety. Philadelphia: University of Pennsylvania Press.

Rees, J./N. Cunningham (1997): Industry Self-Regulation: An Institutional Perspective. *Law & Policy, 19 (4)*, pp. 364–414.

Schmitter, P.C. (1985): Neo-Corporatism and the State. In: Wyn Grant (ed.): The Political Economy of Corporatism. London: Macmillan, pp. 32–62.

Sinclair, D. (1997): Self Regulation Versus Command and Control? Beyond False Dichotomies. *Law & Policy, 19 (4)*, pp. 529–559.

Tollison, Robert D. (1982): Rent Seeking: A Survey. *Kyklos, 35*, pp. 575–602.

Ukrow, J., (1999): Self-Regulation in the Media Sector and European Community Law. Saarbrucken: EMR.

Wacks, R. (1997): Privacy in Cyberspace: Personal Information, Free Speech and the Internet. In: P. Birks (ed.): Privacy and Loyalty. Oxford: Clarendon Press, pp. 93–112.

Internet sources

America Links Up *http://www.americalinksup.org* (visited July 14, 1999).

America Online, *http://www.aol.com* (visited July 14, 1999).

BIAC/OECD Internet Forum on Content Self-Regulation, *http://www.oecd.org/dsti/sti/it/index.htm* (July 14, 1999).

Canadian Association of Internet Providers, *http://www.caip.ca/caipcode.htm* (visited July 14, 1999).

Cyber Rights & Cyber Liberties, *http://www.cyber-rights.org/isps/somm-dec.htm* (visited July 14, 1999).

Electronic Network Consortium, *http://www.nmda.or.jp/enc/guideline/html* (visited July 14, 1999).

European ISP Association, *http://www.euroispa.org* (visited July 14, 1999).

Florida ISP Association, *http://www.fispa.org/fispa_code.html* (visited July 14, 1999).

Hong Kong ISP Association, *http://www.hkispa.org.hk/* (visited July 14, 1999).

Internet Education Foundation, *http://www.neted.org* (visited July 14, 1999).

Safe Surfin', *http://www.safesurfin.com/* (visited July 14, 1999).

Singapore Broadcasting Authority, *http://www.sba.gov.sg/netreg/code.html* (visited July 14, 1999).

Telecom Services Association, *http://www.telesa.or.jp/e_guide/e_guid01.html* (visited July 14, 1999).

Texas ISP Association, *http://www.tispa.org/bylaws.htm* (visited July 14, 1999).

Primary sources

Council of Ministers (1998): Recommendation 98/560/EC on the development of the competitiveness of the European audiovisual and information services industry by promoting national frameworks aimed at achieving a comparable and effective level of protection of minors and human dignity. Official Journal L 270 07/10/1998 p. 0048.

Department of Trade and Industry in the Home Office (1999): Review of the Internet Watch Foundation. London: KPMG and Denton Hall, *http://www.kpmgiwf.org/* (visited July 14, 1999).

European Commission (1996): Green Paper on the protection of minors and human dignity. COM (96) 483, final.

European Commission (1997a): Green Paper on the Convergence of the Telecommunications, Media and Information Technology Sectors, and the Implications for Regulation: Towards an Information Society Approach. COM(97)623. *http://www.ispo.cec.be/convergencegp/ 97623en.doc* (visited July 14, 1999).

European Commission (1997b): Follow-up to the Green Paper on the protection of minors and human dignity in audiovisual and information services. COM (97) 570, final. *http://europa.eu.int/ comm/dg10/ avpolicy/new_srv/comlv-en.htm* (visited July 14, 1999).

European Commission (1998): Working Document: Judging industry self-regulation: when does it make a meaningful contribution to the level of data protection in a third country? Adopted by the Working Party on 14 January 1998, DG XV D/5057/97.

Federal Government Commissioner for Cultural Affairs and the

Media (1999): Conclusions of the Experts' Seminar on Media Self-Regulation. Saarbrucken.

Internet Law and Policy Forum (1998): Bibliography on Self-regulation on the Internet, *http://www.ilpf.org/selfreg/selfreg2.htm* (visited July 14, 1999).

Ministry of Consumer Affairs (1997): Market Self-Regulation and Codes of Practice. A Policy Paper By The Ministry Of Consumer Affairs. New Zealand.

National Consumer Council (1986): Self-Regulation of Business and the Professions: An NCC Background Paper. London.

National Telecommunications Information Administration (1997): Privacy and Self Regulation in the Information Age, Introduction.

OECD (1997b): Co-operative Approaches to Regulation. Public Management Occasional Papers No 18.

OECD (1998): Working Party on the Information Economy: The Economics of Self-Regulation on the Internet. DSTI/ICCP/IE (98) 7, p. 6.

Cases

Butler v. Michigan, 352 U.S. 380 (1957).

Reno v. ACLU, 117 S.Ct. 2329 (1997).

Reno v. ACLU, 31 F.Supp 2d 473 (1999).

Filtering the Internet – A Best Practices Model

Jack M. Balkin, Beth S. Noveck, Kermit Roosevelt

1 Introduction

The rapid growth of the Internet during the 1990s has led inevitably to repeated calls for regulation of Internet content. The most widespread justification for regulation has been that the Internet contains material that is harmful to children because of its bad language, sexual explicitness or violent content.

Calls for protecting children nevertheless beg the question whether regulation is best achieved through government sanctions or through a combination of industry self-regulation and individual choice. We believe that industry self-regulation and facilitation of end-user choice through technology provide a better solution. Technological solutions like filters allow concerned parents and other Internet users to avoid harmful or objectionable material without violating the freedom of expression of Internet publishers. This chapter discusses the pros and cons of various filtering systems and proposes best practices for Internet self-regulation using filtering technology.

Many nations responded to fears about the Internet with legislation that tried to punish those who provided disfavored content. America's Communications Decency Act (CDA) is perhaps the most well-known example among many others.[1] The U.S. Supreme Court struck down the CDA as unconstitutional under the freedom of speech guarantees of the First Amendment to the U.S. Constitution, but Congress (and many states) promptly passed new legislation.

---

1   In a well-publicized case, a German court convicted the managing director of Compuserve Germany of assisting in the dissemination of pornographic material on the basis of the presence of such material in a Compuserve newsgroup. *See* Cyber-Rights & Cyber-Liberties 1999. The *Somm* decision imposes liability on a gatekeeper entity (Compuserve) rather than the actual content providers. Imposing gatekeeper liability may be more effective than trying to reach the actual content providers, but it is even less desirable from a free speech perspective. The judgment against Somm was later reversed on appeal.

Obviously, some governments may seek to control Internet content for reasons other than the protection of children. Some governments and some politicians may wish to control the viewing and reading choices of adults explicitly; others may attempt to control adults through the guise of regulation designed to protect children. In general, we think that regulations designed for these purposes are illegitimate interferences with freedom of thought and expression. Obviously we cannot prevent governments from engaging in antidemocratic practices or politicians from engaging in demagogic appeals. Rather, our arguments are designed to show why governments sincerely interested in protecting children should prefer self-regulatory solutions. Moreover, nothing in this chapter should be understood as opposing legal regulation of child pornography. Child pornography is unlikely to be dealt with effectively by filtering solutions. Filtering solutions generally require rating of sites. However, child pornographers are unlikely to draw attention to themselves by permitting rating or engaging in self-rating. The issue before us is the best way to guarantee adults access to content they have a right to view while allowing parents to shield children. We think that direct legal prohibitions on Internet content are a poor solution.

There are important and obvious problems with trying to impose such legal restrictions. National sovereigns usually legislate territorially, but the Internet crosses national boundaries effortlessly. A general international treaty on Internet content is highly unlikely, given the wide cultural diversity of the planet and the need for near universal participation in order to prevent technological end-runs. As a result, governments attempting to control Internet content through law have engaged in half-way measures: Each government has attempted to impose its own penalties on whatever content providers it can lay hands on. This practice combines unpredictable sanctions with near-total ineffectiveness because many content providers simply cannot be reached by many territorial governments.

201

Worse still, this haphazard arrangement can produce arbitrary and inconsistent patterns of prosecution that chill freedom of thought and expression without actually protecting children.

Some governments have considered requiring website operators to install age verification systems as a way of safeguarding children. Generally speaking, age verification systems require either the use of a credit card number or an adult verification code which can be purchased using a credit card. The credit card number or the age verification code is then typed in each time the user visits a site with content deemed inappropriate for children. The definition of what is inappropriate for children is determined by statute or administrative regulation. If a site contains such material, website operators are subject to fines or criminal sanctions if they fail to install effective age verification schemes.

Obviously, many of the same problems of territorial limitation apply to these proposals: much Internet content will come from beyond the territorial boundaries of governments requiring age verification, and each government will have different criteria about what is inappropriate for children. But age verification systems have other serious drawbacks. They are both problematic and ineffective as a general strategy for keeping children from inappropriate content. First, age verification strongly hinders Internet surfing by adults. Most adult users do not wish to have to insert an age verification identification every time they visit a new site, and they are even more loath to type in their credit card number. As a result, age verification will deter adults as well as children from visiting websites, particularly websites that adults have every right to visit.

Second, maintaining an age verification system is an expensive and complicated proposition for nonprofit organizations and for individuals who are not selling goods and services but simply wish to communicate with others. Age verification works best for commercial pornographers, because they already seek to sell adult customers goods and services, which are usually paid for by credit card. But

202

age verification is a genuine hardship for an organization like the National Abortion Rights League, or for the average individual who seeks to put content on the web that might contain material inappropriate for small children – for example, strong language or discussions of human sexuality. (We should add that adult verification requirements have virtually no effect on child pornographers, who are largely underground in any case.)

Third, most adult verification systems require only the use of a credit card to prove age. There is no guarantee that the person who holds the credit card actually is an adult. Moreover, there is a vibrant business on the Web for persons bartering false adult verification identifications and passwords.

At best we think adult verification schemes have a place in commercial pornography sites – and we note that many commercial pornography sites already include them – but we think that those sites can also adequately be dealt with through the use of filtering systems.

For these reasons, we believe that industry self-regulation and technological facilitation of end-user choice offer a better solution to the problem of harmful Internet content. Industry self-regulation does not mean mere forbearance by content providers; it also involves putting technological solutions in the hands of end-users to filter out content they do not wish to receive. Filtering through software specifications is the most widely supported technological method of blocking Internet content. Websites and other forms of Internet content receive ratings which can be read by a filter located in the end-user's browser or other software interface. In this chapter, we focus mainly on rating and filtering of content delivered on the World Wide Web; however the filtering solutions we recommend can be adapted to other forms of Internet content, including chat rooms and Usenet newsgroups.

A self-regulatory solution has two distinct but equally important components: the use of technology to facilitate choice by end-users, and location of that choice at a decentralized, or local level, rather than at a national or global level. Obviously whatever technological solutions individuals employ can also be employed by governments. Hence governments may be tempted to impose filtering centrally or hierarchically, upstream from their citizens. In this way governments may try to use filtering technology to block all content they deem inappropriate for their citizens to view.

The Information Society Project at Yale Law School strongly opposes such hierarchical filtering by governments. We emphasize that a self-regulatory solution must include both technological filtering and decentralization. Conceivably, governments may be more successful in blocking content through technology than through law, especially if their citizens do not know that their access to the Internet is being filtered without their approval. However, from the standpoint of freedom of thought and expression, state-imposed hierarchical filtering is no better than legal punishments and may in fact be much worse. The purpose of this study is to show how a decentralized technological solution that places choice in end-users about what and whether to filter can protect children and other citizens from being exposed to harmful or offensive content.

Because there is simply too much information on the Internet, filtering of some form will be inevitable. Market forces will demand and produce increasingly technologically proficient filters for different purposes. The most familiar of these are search engines, which grow in power and discrimination with each passing day. Thus, there is no need to ask whether filtering and filtering technologies should be implemented. They already are. The appropriate question is what kinds of filtering systems are desirable and for what purposes. Cyberspace is plastic and can be shaped into a wide variety of architectures. The choice of filters plays an important role in the architecture of cyberspace. Thus the choice we face in choosing filters is a choice about what kind of architecture cyberspace will have. This is an important and weighty decision, because architecture regulates human conduct and shapes human thought (Lessig 1998; Boyle 1997). Technology in practice is not neutral in its effects or in the values that it promotes or hinders. Moreover, filtering and rating systems will surely be used for purposes other than protecting children from harm. In this way they may have significant and unintended effects on the evolution of culture (Balkin 1996).

One argument against the development of filtering software is that it will be employed by governments or large private entities without the consent of end-users to censor private expression upstream. However, as noted above, we think that market forces will inevitably produce filtering systems of increasing proficiency. Moreover, opposing the development of filtering systems for end-users may have even worse consequences. Unless governments are assured that decentralized filtering will produce an acceptable degree of self-regulation, they will inevitably turn to legal sanctions that will stifle freedom of expression more directly. Thus, we should not avoid designing effective end-user filters because of a fear that they may someday be adapted by governments or other powerful entities for unscrupulous purposes. The fight against hierarchical filtering by governments is best carried on through political and legal pressure rather than by simply opposing technological development. Moreover, these criticisms overlook the fact that technology can also be used to fight hierarchical filtering, by developing effective methods to prevent or discourage governments from filtering Internet content upstream.

In order to avoid the dangers of upstream filtering by governments who fail to respond to political and legal pressure, we think it best to design the architecture of the filtering system to frustrate such attempts before they occur. Thus, we propose a system of *encrypted ratings*. Under this system, all ratings sent from web pages will automatically be encrypted with a weak (three to eight digit) encryption scheme. This encryption will take virtually no time to decode in the end-user's browser. However, a government's proxy server will have to decode each and every one of these ratings in order to decide whether the relevant web pages should be blocked. The cumulative effort required to do this will be prohibitive. If more than a small number of people try to use the Internet at once, decoding even weak encryption of all of these ratings will be sufficient to overload any proxy server. In short, the point of weak encryption of ratings is to use the bottleneck feature of upstream filtering against itself. If weak encryption of ratings is built into the filtering system, governments will be unable to filter upstream without their proxy servers grinding to a halt. As a result, all filtering will have to be performed at the end-user's browser. Thus, by designing the architecture correctly, we can actually promote free speech values. We can safeguard decentralization and end-user autonomy, and turn the tools of censorship against would-be censors.[2]

In the following discussions, we emphasize end-user autonomy as a central concern. Nevertheless, the expression "end-user" is necessarily a term of art. For example, if the goal of filtering is to protect

---

2   Even without encryption, end-users can take other steps to defeat upstream filtering. A second solution involves what we might call "trojan ratings." It involves sending targeted false ratings to the IP addresses of countries using hierarchical filtering. The point of trojan ratings is to create a credible threat against oppressive governments. If a government uses hierarchical filtering, private parties can threaten to sabotage it. It is not necessary for everyone to engage in this practice as long as a sufficient number of rated sites announce publicly that they will do so. While the first solution – encrypted ratings – is built into the architecture of the system, the second solution is a form of "civil disobedience" that individuals can employ based on the architecture of the system.

children, their parents or guardians are properly the relevant "end-users," even though the children use the computer.[3]

The aim of this report is to set out a best practices model for Internet filtering systems. The values that this model seeks to promote are the following:

---

3   We cannot hope to offer a general discussion of the problem of who is the "end-user" in this report, nor do we think it necessary, given that our basic concern is interactions between parents and children. We do suggest, however, that the decision by a third party that persons may not use a computer to access certain content from the Internet demands some sort of justification. The burden should be on the filterer to justify the denial of another person's access. The most plausible justifications for restricting access are that the third party owns the computer or that the third party has a relation of legitimate authority over the user. For privately-owned computers, the brute fact of ownership may often be a good enough reason, although a relation of legitimate authority will often also be present. Thus parents may restrict their children's use of their computers. (We also assume that private individuals should be able to restrict use of their computers by friends and social guests, even without a relation of legitimate authority.) Private employers may restrict employees' use based on ownership of the computer and legitimate relations of authority and workplace control. Nevertheless, restricting employee access may involve technological surveillance and invasions of privacy. These are separate questions that must not be overlooked.

Free speech values suggest that the government should be treated differently than private employers. We do not think, as a general matter, that governments should be able to impose mandatory filtering on government-owned computers if those computers are made generally accessible to the public. Nevertheless, certain important contexts, like computers used for educational purposes in public schools, may involve a relationship of legitimate educational authority that justifies filtering. By contrast, a general governmental mandate that citizens use filters or particular filtering settings on their own computers restricts the use to which private parties can put their own computers. This constitutes a genuine, and in our view, unacceptable threat to freedom of speech and conscience. Finally, we do not support the notion that governments may force parents to place filters on their computers in order to protect children; it should be up to parents, in the first instance, to decide what their children should be exposed to.

End-user autonomy

End-users, rather than intermediaries such as Internet Service Providers (ISPs) or nation-states, should decide whether and how to filter Internet access. As noted above, we oppose upstream or hierarchical filtering by governments. Equally important, meaningful choice by end-users requires a variety of filtering options that reflect different cultural values and ideologies. We hope to promote this variety by creating a market for filtering options and by carefully limiting the intellectual property rights in filtering systems that might allow third parties to restrain the market's operation. Finally, the system must feature a user-friendly interface that encourages actual use of its features and makes choice a real possibility for the vast majority of end-users. No system can truly promote autonomy unless most people can operate it fairly easily.

Protection of freedom of thought and expression for content providers

The point of using filtering systems instead of legal prohibitions of content is to allow individuals to publish what they want on the Internet while allowing end-users to filter out things they do not want. A good filtering system will respect the ideological diversity of content providers as well as end-users. It will not block pages whose content is unrelated to the criteria used for filtering, and it will not attempt to block pages because they are critical of the filtering system being employed. As a default rule, the system should not block unrated sites unless the end-user specifically requests this option. As we will discuss in more detail below, our preferred solution relies heavily on rating by content providers themselves, which is usually called "first-party" rating. First-party rating is not only more practical, it also places important decisions in the hands of content providers, for example, whether to rate the entire site, individual pages, or individual elements within a site, and, perhaps equally importantly, whether to rate at all.

Protecting freedom of expression is and must be a serious issue in filtering design. To understand why this is so, we must understand which speakers the burden of Internet filtering falls most heavily upon. When most people speak of protecting children from inappropriate content, they normally have in mind child pornography and commercial pornography. As we have pointed out previously, filtering systems are not particularly well-suited to dealing with child pornography. Because mere possession of child pornography is illegal in many countries, child pornographers do not wish to draw attention to themselves. They are unlikely to rate their sites as containing child pornography or to stay in one place long enough to be part of a list of rated sites by third parties. They are best dealt with through law enforcement and other devices of industry self-regulation like telephone hot lines. The same is true for people who use e-mail or chat rooms to entice children. They are unlikely to rate themselves as pedophiles.

Commercial pornographers, on the other hand, are in the business of making money. Hence they usually require a credit card or some other form of adult verification in order to enter a site. Obviously, these sites may have free "come-ons" designed to entice visitors. However, because their target audience is adults, it is not surprising that many commercial sites have signed up to be rated as adult sites by various forms of filtering software. Commercial pornography sites do not resist being identified as "adult." Being "adult" is part of their advertising. As a result, we think that commercial pornographers are the most likely to fit easily into our proposed filtering system.

It turns out then, that the burden of filtering is likely to fall most heavily on those persons who fit into neither of these categories – the vast majority of Internet speakers and publishers who are not in the commercial pornography business and who do not trade in child pornography. This includes political activists who discuss issues like human sexuality, abortion, rape, and drug use, take controversial and unpopular stands, as well as authors of artistic work with erotic themes. These speakers simply want to be able to reach audiences that are willing to listen to them. We should design a filtering system that ensures that they are able to do so.

Ideological diversity and flexibility

A good filtering system must be flexible enough to permit development of many different instantiations that reflect the wide cultural and ideological diversity on the planet. As values change over time, the system must be flexible enough to accommodate these changes.

Capacity for organic growth

Ideally, filtering devices should be both forward and backward compatible. New filtering software should be able to use specifications and read ratings currently in place. Older software should be easily adaptable to read ratings based on new specifications as they evolve.

Transparency

End-users must know when access has been blocked and why. For example, when access is blocked, filtering software should not simply display a generic error message such as "Error. Document not found." The software should instead explain that information has been blocked and give the reason for the denial of access, stating the basic criteria for the rating employed, for example: "Access to this site has been denied because the requested data contains content rated above 2 on the RSACi violence scale." The software should also reveal where the filtering has occurred – at the end-user's browser, or upstream, by a corporate intranet, an ISP, or a proxy server.

Transparency means different things for end-users, for people who assign ratings to websites, and for programmers who create implementations of a common filtering specification from which end-users may choose. For end-users, transparency means having enough information to make reasonable choices about which filtering system to use. Thus, the end-user must know the basic categories upon which filtering occurs. If the system involves scalar values that measure intensity, such as 0 to 4, the end-user must be able to ascertain what these different values mean in practice. For persons who rate websites – including people who self-rate – transparency means that the substantive meaning of different ratings is easily understandable and publicly available. For the programmers who create different ratings systems, transparency means that information about all aspects of the specification is fully public so that programmers can create different implementations. Moreover, it means that all aspects of the different implementations are public so that others can examine and criticize their work. Because end-users may lack programming expertise, what is transparent to programmers is not necessarily transparent to end-users or even to persons who rate websites; however, it is sufficient that anyone with programming skills can gain access to information about ratings specifications if they so desire.

Open source

As the discussion of transparency suggests, we advocate a basic filtering system with a set of specifications that can be implemented by anyone. The specifications will be public and free; no organization will hold intellectual property rights that allow it to constrain the use of the system. Network effects will probably lead to a certain degree of standardization, and we recommend that a nonprofit organization be created to oversee the development of an initial basic vocabulary of content descriptors. But the content of the system should be determined in large part by the preferences of end-users, website operators and public interest organizations; it should not be imposed from the top down.

Privacy

Some approaches to filtering – notably, certain implementations of the PICS-based system discussed below – raise troubling privacy issues, because the process of filtering generates and places in the hands of third parties a list of material requested by end-users. We must not allow filtering systems to erode end-user privacy.

Compatibility between
different rating systems

Filtering software must be able to accommodate different rating systems individually and in conjunction. Filtering software must allow different ratings systems to "talk to each other" and be applied seriatim or in combination. End-users who can turn to a large number of different rating systems have greater choice than those who must rely on a small number of systems. But end-users who can use different systems *together* have the greatest degree of freedom in constructing a filter to suit their particular needs.

These values are related, and each contributes to the central value of end-user autonomy. For example, transparency promotes autonomy because end-users who do not know that material has been blocked can neither readily evaluate the performance of a filter nor intelligently choose a different one. An open source approach also promotes autonomy, by giving end-users a voice in the development of the system. We can thus put our basic normative goal very simply: end-users should have a choice about whether and what to filter.

Filtering systems that attempt to offer a meaningful choice confront the same basic problem. For end-users to have real autonomy, they must be able to choose among a wide variety of ideologies and values embodied in different filtering systems. They must be able to choose a system that blocks what they want it to block and permits what they want it to permit.

The problem is who will do the rating. Generally speaking, rating is either done by content providers, called "first-party rating," or by separate organizations, called "third-party rating." Website owners who rate their own web pages are first-party raters; organizations like the Anti-Defamation League or companies like Cybersitter or NetNanny who rate sites are third-party raters.

The problem with third-party ratings is that there is too much material. Third-party rating is too expensive and time-consuming. Nor can end-users rely on first-party rating by website operators who rate their sites according to ideological criteria. Even if content providers were willing to self-rate according to these criteria, there is no guarantee that they would do so accurately. In short, first-party rating according to ideological standards is too unreliable. The task, then, is to construct a system that accommodates a diversity of ideologies while remaining inexpensive enough to be feasible and reliable enough to be useful.

213

Such a system must both describe Internet content and evaluate the description. It must, for example, both express the fact that a web page contains depictions of violence, and attach ideological significance to that fact by restricting or permitting access. The problem is how to achieve both tasks. Third parties can bring a consistent ideological perspective to bear in evaluation. But they cannot possibly describe all the content on the Internet. We might ask first parties to describe their content, but they cannot consistently evaluate it. Perhaps even more important, description and evaluation are not mutually exclusive categories. Descriptions of content are not entirely value-free, especially the content that most ratings systems would be interested in. Descriptions of nudity, language, violence and sexuality inevitably involve some normative or ideological evaluation.

Our solution relies on a division of labor between first and third parties. We ask first parties (website operators) to describe their content, but in terms that are likely to lead to convergent practices. In other words, we are less concerned with whether the descriptions are value-free (an impossible goal in any case) than with whether most first parties will apply them in roughly the same way. The goal is not ideological neutrality but predictable convergence in behavior. One might call these descriptions "objective" but a more accurate term would be "intersubjectively convergent."

We then ask third parties to produce "templates" that combine and rank combinations of these content descriptors in ways that match their ideological preferences. Simply put, a template takes the raw materials of content description and decides which combinations are better and which are worse with respect to a given value system. Thus, we do not ask third parties to be ideologically neutral – indeed, we specifically ask them to rank certain types of content based on their values about what is good and bad, and what is more or less harmful to children. The goal of third parties in the system is to set up basic standards of evaluation that will be applied to the

214

convergent descriptions of first parties. Because the basic task of third parties is to set up ratings templates, they do not have to rate every site, although they are free to rate particular sites individually and add those ratings to the mix.

Because ratings templates will be relatively simple and easy to set up, we expect many different organizations will be willing to create them. Our goal is to make it possible for an organization to set up a new template with only a day or two of work. Moreover, because the templates will be publicly available, organizations can model their efforts on previous templates, making the costs of template creation even smaller. Finally, because all templates will be based on a common language, end-users (or other organizations) can mix and match them to produce custom templates suitable to their ideological tastes.

This approach allocates to each group the tasks that they are most able and most willing to perform. Before explaining our recommendations in more detail, we will first discuss the history of different filtering systems and their pros and cons. Then we will discuss the technological devices out of which our system will be constructed.

2 Filtering systems

2.1 First generation filters

Filtering software is not new. Early approaches to filtering have tended to take two primary forms. One form screens documents before allowing access. If the screening detects forbidden words such as "breast," "sex" or "homosexual," access is denied. This technique deals with the twin problems of description and evaluation by performing a mechanical and very crude evaluation of all content requested. It judges content based on the presence or absence of forbidden terms. Unsurprisingly, text-based screening is very bad at recognizing changes in context: for example, text-based filters may block discussions of breast cancer and legal debates over homosexual marriage because they contain the words "breast" and "homosexual." The University of Kansas, having installed the text-screening Surfwatch program, found it had cut off access to its own Archie R. Dykes Medical Library. One way to mitigate the harshness of the automatic blocking rule is to delete the offending terms, but this leads to bizarre results, converting sentences such as "Traditionalists oppose homosexual marriage" to "Traditionalists oppose marriage" (Weinberg 1997: 460).

Text-based blocking software is still being refined, and more sophisticated approaches attempt to capture contextual subtleties by considering factors such as repetition and proximity of forbidden terms. But the refinement seems unlikely to produce a satisfactory system. Context is simply too complex for mechanical evaluation, and, more important, mechanical evaluation of pictures is still technologically quite distant.

The second major approach relies on third-party organizations to evaluate all content by individual inspection. Evaluators generate lists of acceptable and unacceptable sites; software then either restricts access to the unacceptable sites ("blacklisting") or allows access to only the acceptable ones ("whitelisting"). CyberPatrol, for example, offers both a "CyberNOT Block List" of sites deemed unsuitable for children and a "CyberYES List" of approved sites. Users can configure the software either to exclude the blacklist or to allow access only to the whitelist.

We have already noted that relying entirely on third-party rating is impractical given the volume of Internet content. Invariably both blacklists and whitelists are underinclusive. Blacklists miss some sites that should be blocked; whitelists omit some sites that do not contain harmful content. Indeed, the mere existence of both blacklists and whitelists acknowledges this failing, for a perfectly inclusive blacklist would be identical to a perfectly inclusive whitelist.

Even manufacturers of blocking software understand their inadequacies in covering the Internet; blacklisting software programs such as CyberPatrol are now usually compatible with PICS-based filtering, which will be described momentarily. But these programs are not only ineffective; they have other, equally serious failings. They also offend several of the values discussed above as a necessary consequence of their technological structure. First, blacklists are usually not transparent. Some blacklisting programs reveal to users that access has been blocked. But they need not do so. Moreover, once a site is blocked, the program does not have to offer any explanation, except that the program's raters found the site unsuitable based on their criteria. There is no requirement that these criteria be made public. Among existing blacklist programs, CyberPatrol offers some degree of transparency. It evaluates sites along fifteen different dimensions, from "violence/profanity" to "alcohol & tobacco." In effect, it contains fifteen different blacklists; end-users may activate as few or as many as they choose. CyberPatrol allows some information about why a site has been blocked, because it can disclose on which blacklist the site fell. Solid Oak Software's Cyber-Sitter, by contrast, maintains a single undifferentiated blacklist (Dobeus 1998: 633).

Lack of transparency is a serious problem for blacklisting software. Users of blacklist filters tend to be parents concerned about restricting their children's access to inappropriate material. But consensus at that level of generality about what should be blocked (material "unsuitable for children") does not translate into consensus about which sites belong on the blacklist. Even when more specific criteria are listed (e.g., "foul language") the basis for decision is not readily available. Decisions about individual sites are inevitably ideological, and blacklists force parents to accept the undisclosed ideologies of the third-party raters. Thus, blacklists tend to be not only underinclusive but also overinclusive; they block sites to which end-users do not object.

The list of sites blocked by common blacklisting programs is troubling: Jonathan Weinberg notes that CyberPatrol blocked the Electronic Frontier Foundation's censorship archive, the Animal Rights Resource Site, the League for Programming Freedom (a group opposing software patents), and Usenet newsgroups including alt.feminism, soc.feminism, and alt.support.fat-acceptance. Cyber-Sitter blocks the National Organization of Women website, the Penal Lexicon (a British site covering prisons and penal affairs), and web pages that criticize its blocking decisions (Weinberg 1997: 461–62).

Compounding the problems created by the lack of transparency is the second defect of blacklisting programs: they are not open source. Their blacklists are typically treated as proprietary information, withheld from end-users and protected by intellectual property rights. End-users have no voice in determining the content of the blacklist, and are in fact severely restricted in their ability even to learn which sites are blocked. (When the Netly News, a subsidiary of Time-Warner Pathfinder, created a search engine designed to allow end-users to find out which sites CyberSitter blocked, Cyber-sitter retaliated by blocking the more than 150,000 web pages on pathfinder.com.) (Wagner 1999: 762–763; Weinberg 1997: 462).

Withholding the list of blocked sites is not simply an arbitrary affront to transparency; it is a central feature of most blacklisting software. Blacklists employ lists of offending sites that are deliberately kept secret through technological devices and by legal protections like trade secret law. Third-party rating is labor-intensive and consequently expensive. The makers of blacklisting software sell their products to recoup these expenses and turn a profit. Because the value of blacklisting software consists primarily in its database of unacceptable sites, revealing a company's database of offending sites would undermine the market value of the product. Competitors could free-ride on the hard work done by the company's employees in locating and rating thousands of websites.[4]

Neither text screening nor blacklisting, then, is a viable way to construct a filtering system. Text screening is too crude. Blacklisting relies entirely on third parties; consequently it is expensive, underinclusive, and nontransparent. It gives end-users very little choice in the ideological content of the filtering system. The failings of text-screening and blacklisting filters show that first-party rating must be an essential component of any filtering system. In the next section, we look at various software solutions that take the first steps towards integrating the work of first- and third-party raters.

2.2 Filtering through software specifications: PICS, PICSRules, and RDF

2.2.1 PICS

The Platform for Internet Content Selection, (PICS) is a set of software specifications for filtering systems created by the World Wide Web Consortium (W3C). PICS allows the creation of labels that can be associated with individual Internet addresses (Universal Resource Locators, or URLs). Labels can also be associated with an IP address

---

4 Another argument is that transparency would give children a ready-made list of inappropriate sites. Indeed, most filtering systems can be inverted and used to seek out objectionable material. This concern seems relatively insubstantial however, given that the settings of filtering systems are supposed to be accessible to parents but not children; blacklists could similarly be protected by passwords known only to parents. More significantly, finding pornography on the Internet is anything but difficult. Simply searching for "PICS" (to say nothing of "sex") on Lycos will turn up a host of pornographic sites, and search engines devoted to pornography, like http://www.sexhound.com, also exist.

– the identifying address of a computer connected to the Web – in which case they apply to every document retrieved from that computer. The basic idea behind PICS is to create a standard for metadata: information about information. For example, if data consists of a picture on a page, metadata might include the statement that there is a certain type of picture on a page. A PICS label is essentially a statement about what data resides on the page at a certain URL. The statement generally takes the form of an assertion that the data has certain properties, for example, that it is a picture, that it contains guns, that it is violent, that it has been rated by a certain organization, and so on.

Different ratings systems will use different systems of labels; the PICS format simply outlines the basic format that all such systems must use so that they can be read by PICS compatible filters. Thus, strictly speaking, PICS itself is not a rating system; it merely provides common specifications for creating labels that are part of a rating system. The most well-known content rating system using the PICS software specification is RSACi, which was originally created and maintained by the Recreational Software Advisory Council on the Internet. (The RSACi organization has recently been merged into a larger organization, the Internet Content Rating Alliance (ICRA), which is now entrusted with maintenance and development of the RSACi rating system.) RSACi is only one possible implementation of the PICS software specification. It is not identical with PICS. We will discuss the advantages and disadvantages of the RSACi ratings system later in this report.

In the kinds of filtering systems we are concerned with, the properties used to describe data will be the categories and scales associated with particular rating systems. Thus a typical PICS label might say that the data at worldwarII.com/dday/omaha.jpeg (a fictitious URL, intended to designate a photograph of the Omaha beach landing) contains content rated 3 on the Violence category of RSACi, an Internet ratings system. A label may contain more than one assertion. The same label might also say that the document is a picture, that it is historical, or that it shows real-life combat. For labels to be useful, end-users must have filtering software that recognizes the properties "picture," "historical," and "real-life combat."

Programmers can associate PICS labels with entire websites, pages within those sites, or particular items on particular pages. A label associated with the hypothetical worldwarII.com website would apply to every document retrieved from worldwarII.com. If the documents differ significantly – say, a text description of the Lend-Lease program and a photo of Allied troops storming Omaha beach – there are advantages to creating different labels for each individual document. However, the more labels added, the longer it takes to rate a site and to filter the site when it is visited.

Using a PICS-based rating system to filter content involves several different tasks, and it is important to recognize that each of them can be performed by different parties (Resnick 1999). First, one must establish a rating system. A rating system requires the development of a standard vocabulary and categories for labels. By "vocabulary" we mean any description of content. By "category" we mean organization or grouping of vocabulary elements along a particular axis. For example, in the RSACi rating system "mild expletives," "moderate expletives or profanity," and "strong language, obscene gestures, or hate speech" are elements of the RSACi vocabulary. Note that the last two elements are *disjunctive*, that is, the rating applies if *any* part is satisfied. As we will describe below in more detail, disjunctive vocabulary elements create special problems for a ratings system.

RSACi organizes these vocabulary elements into a single "language" category, whose range of permissible values ("scale") runs from zero to four. Each scalar value from zero to four is associated with a different vocabulary element. Thus, "mild expletives" are assigned a scalar value of 1, "moderate expletives or profanity"

221

receive a value of 2, and "strong language, obscene gestures, or hate speech" have a value of 3. (Because this category is disjunctive, a site receives a 3 rating if it contains either a swear word, an obscene gesture, or a racial epithet.) A browser reading RSACi labels, with a "language" filtering setting of <3, will permit sites containing the first two groups of vocabulary elements but block those containing the third. A set of categories offered as a unit is a "rating system" or a "template" (W3C 1999d).

A ratings system can have many different categories, each containing many different vocabulary elements. For example, RSACi's rating system contains the categories "Nudity," "Sex," "Violence," and "Language." In RSACi each category has a five-point scale, running from zero to four, associated with different vocabulary elements.

As noted, PICS allows the creation of many kinds of ratings systems. For example, a different rating system, concerned with the medium of presentation, might have the categories "Picture," "Text," "Video," and "Audio." Each of these categories would probably have only two values on its scale: 1 (for yes) and 0 (for no). The vocabulary elements would thus be "Picture" and "No Picture," "Text" and "No Text," etc. Still another rating system, modeled on the Motion Picture Association of America (MPAA) ratings, might estimate the maturity required to view the rated material. It would have only one category, "Minimum Recommended Age." The scale within this category might run from 1 to 18, in which case the vocabulary elements would be "Suitable for Age 1," "Suitable for Age 2 and Under," "Suitable for Age 3 and Under," and so on. Or it might be a coarser five-point scale like the MPAA, with vocabulary elements "Suitable for All Ages," "Suitable for Pre-Teens," "Suitable for Young Teens," "Suitable for Older Teens," and "Adult."

As these examples should suggest, vocabulary elements may range from relatively "objective" descriptions that can be reliably coded by a wide variety of raters (e.g., "Picture" and "No Picture")

222

to relatively "subjective" descriptions that are likely to produce considerable disagreement in application (e.g., "Suitable for Young Teens"). Choosing between the reliability of vocabulary elements that will be coded similarly by most people and the ideological richness of more subjective vocabulary elements is one of the basic dilemmas for filtering systems. This dilemma is related to the choice between first- and third-party rating; if first-party rating is to be reliable, vocabulary elements must be "objective," not in the sense that they are value-free, but in the sense that they will produce convergence in rating because most people will apply them in the same way.

Because current filtering systems generally focus on protection of children, most rating systems use similar categories such as sexual or violent content, indecent language, and promotion of drug use. They vary considerably in the "objectivity" (expected convergence in rating) of their vocabulary elements. RSACi's elements are designed to promote behavioral convergence in rating, while SafeSurf's are more subjective and controversial. SafeSurf, unlike RSACi, tries to reflect common moral judgments (presumably those in the United States) about factors that make particular content more or less objectionable. Thus, for example, SafeSurf's "Nudity" category distinguishes between "Dictionary, encyclopedic, news, medical references" (value 3); "Classic works of art presented in public museums for family view" (value 4); "Artistically presented with full frontal nudity" (value 6); and "Erotic frontal nudity" (value 7). Hence the SafeSurf "Nudity" category may produce divergence in coding in many different ways. For example, people in different cultures or with different values may disagree about what is "artistic," and "erotic," as well as what is "classic."

The developers of PICS hope for a wide variety of rating systems in order to maximize end-user choice (W3C 1999f). Moreover, through a further development, PICSRules, they have made it possible to employ different rating systems in conjunction. We agree

223

that the homogeneity of existing rating systems is troubling. If third-party rating systems were cheaper to produce, greater diversity would be more likely. Hence one of the aims of our proposed system is to reduce the cost of creation.

Second, someone must rate sites by assigning labels to sites. To rate a site is to assign labels to content. A typical label for a website might look like this: "Nudity = 4; Language = 3; Violence = 5." Again, rating can be done by first-party content providers or third parties. W3C expects both first and third parties to be active in the rating of content, and we will also recommend a mixture of first- and third-party ratings. While we believe that a mixture of first- and third-party rating is preferable from a policy perspective, an equally important reason is that third parties will simply be unable to rate the entire Internet.

Third, labels must be distributed to those who request them for filtering. PICS-based filtering may be performed either by the end-user's browser, or by an entity further upstream – for example, a search engine, a proxy-server, or an Internet Service Provider (ISP). Upstream filtering – especially if not disclosed to or consented to by end-users – threatens free speech values. We thus recommend that filtering be performed at the end-user level. If filtering is performed upstream, the software should report this fact. It should also indicate that access has been denied and explain why.

Rating labels can be distributed either by website operators (first-party distribution) or by other organizations (third-party distribution). First-party distribution is probably the easiest and least costly method. Programmers can insert rating labels as a header in the language of a web page. Third-party distribution is more complicated, because the end-user has to fetch the rating labels associated with a particular web page from some other place on the Internet. W3C contemplates the existence of "label bureaus" which will store third-party labels and provide them to browsers (W3C 1999b). This creates a real danger of bottlenecks, as millions of web surfers request labels from a modest number of label bureaus. One can also store third-party labels in end-users' browsers. However, given the vast and growing number of websites, this approach is not feasible unless third parties rate only a very small fraction of websites. It is unlikely, in any event, that third parties will have the resources to keep up with the rapidly expanding Internet, and the system we discuss below contemplates a limited role for third-party raters.

Fourth, ratings will not work unless someone writes filtering software that can read the labels. The software required is actually quite minimal; it need be able only to read labels and follow instructions about restricting access based on what the rating labels say. We expect that in the future most browsers will incorporate filtering software, and indeed the most recent versions of Internet Explorer and Netscape Communicator are PICS-compatible.

Fifth, someone – either the end-user or another person – must choose among the available filtering settings permitted by the software. In short, someone must operate the filtering software to decide which ratings are acceptable and which are not. Once again, in general, we believe that this choice should be made at the end-user level. In other words, filtering settings should be specified in browsers, rather than upstream. This reduces the danger that filtering will be done without the end-user's knowledge or consent. This does not mean that third-parties should not develop and distribute their own rating systems, only that the end-users should be free to choose which rating systems to employ.

Sixth, and finally, filtering software must be installed and run. Generally, we also recommend that this take place at the end-user level, rather than upstream, in the interest of promoting end-user autonomy.

The PICS specification was designed to be flexible and to accommodate many different kinds of ratings systems. It has been enhanced by new specifications, including PICSRules, which we discuss next.

PICSRules, like PICS, is a development of W3C. It is a language for writing filtering rules that allow or block access to URLs based on PICS labels that describe those URLs (W3C 1999c). In general, PICSRules operate by specifying the organizations whose labels are to be consulted, and then articulating policies for applying those labels, specified according to their categories. For example, a PICSRule may instruct filtering software to look up the RSACi label for a particular URL. Then it may give instructions to use RSACi's violence and language categories in certain ways while ignoring its sex and nudity categories. In slightly greater detail: the "serviceinfo" clause of a PICSRule specifies the organizations whose labels are to be consulted and gives the URL of a label bureau from which to retrieve the labels. It also controls whether or not the rule will use labels embedded in the requested document. "Policy" clauses determine whether a URL will be accepted or rejected. They may direct the filtering software to accept or reject based on information coded in the URL itself or the scalar values of any categories of the labels specified in the serviceinfo clause. Once a policy clause instructs the software to accept or reject the URL, it does so regardless of later clauses. Thus earlier policy clauses have priority. A set of clauses defining preferences will be referred to as a "profile."

The importance of PICSRules lies in its ability to coordinate various rating systems through multiple policy clauses. A PICSRule could, for example, give the following instructions:

(a) Three particular URLs are to be accepted and four blocked. (These instructions use "AcceptByURL" and "RejectByURL" policy clauses.)

(b) Any URL rated by the ArtFriends service as having artistic content>2 is to be accepted. Any URL rated by People for the American Way as having political content>3 is to be accepted. (These instructions use "AcceptIf" policy clauses.)

(c) URLs not accepted under the first two clauses are to be rejected unless RSACi rates them as having violence<3. (This instruction uses a "RejectUnless" policy clause; it will reject all URLs rated higher than two on the RSACi violence category, and also all URLs not rated on that category.)

(d) URLs not disposed of by the first three rules are to be accepted. (This instruction uses the policy clause "AcceptIf 'otherwise'".)

This particular rule is broadly similar to filtering using the RSACi violence category alone and blocking unrated URLs, but it allows greater precision in articulating what is to be blocked and thus greater user choice in determining the ideology embodied in the filter settings. That is, it reflects the judgment that artistic or political content, as determined by ArtFriends and People for the American Way, is sufficient to redeem material rated as violent by RSACi standards. By employing rating systems developed by different organizations, PICSRules would allow a basic rating system to be refined and overridden by the avowedly value-laden judgments of organizations trusted by users.

2.2.3 RDF

The Resource Description Framework (RDF) is yet another framework for describing and exchanging metadata. As noted in the discussion of PICS, metadata involve statements or descriptions about properties of Web pages or individual documents on those pages. RDF provides a standardized and machine-readable syntax for making these statements and descriptions (Bray 1999; Cowan 1999; Flynn 1999; W3C 1999a; W3C 1999e).

A thorough technical analysis of RDF is beyond the scope of this report. In essence, RDF is quite similar to PICS; it can do anything PICS can. Both specifications allow the creation of statements about

Internet documents. As a sample statement, consider the proposition that worldwarII.com/dday/omaha.jpeg is a picture containing real-life historical violence. We have seen already that this proposition can be expressed in a PICS label, which can be attached to the document and read by a PICS-compatible browser. RDF permits parties to do precisely the same thing.

The syntax of RDF allows for the attribution of "properties" (specific characteristics with scalar values) to "resources" (anything corresponding to a URL). (We should note that the value of a property can also be a "literal" – i.e., any string of characters – but these do not play a significant role in filtering systems.) A specific resource together with a named property plus the value of that property for that resource is an RDF "statement." These three elements of a statement are called, respectively, the "subject," the "predicate," and the "object." A single RDF statement can attribute several properties, just as a single PICS label can express several different ratings. A description of worldwarII.com/dday/omaha.jpeg might consist of a single statement attributing four properties here, "picture," "real-life," "historical," and "violence." For the properties "picture," "real-life," and "historical" the scale would probably have only the values 1 and 0, corresponding to "Yes" and "No." The property "violence" might have a broader range of values – it might, for example, be the RSACi Violence category, in which case its scalar values would range from 0 to 4, and worldwarII.com/dday/omaha.jpeg would receive a 3. Website operators labeling their own documents need not use the RSACi properties; they would be free to use whatever properties they chose, and even those they invented. However, because the utility of metadata depends on the existence of a common vocabulary of properties, one can expect some degree of standardization in properties.

RDF differs from PICS in that it provides a more general treatment of metadata, and W3C plans to reformulate a future version of PICS as an application of RDF. W3C also aims to produce a conversion algorithm from PICS 1.1 to RDF. Presumably some form of RDF-based system will eventually supersede PICS-based filtering. The recommendations we offer here are consistent with either PICSRules or RDF treatments of metadata. For purposes of this discussion we will speak of PICS (including PICSRules) as the software basis of our proposed system, with the understanding that the system we propose can also be adapted to and supported by RDF.

3 Content analysis of Internet ratings systems

3.1 Ideological effects in the construction of rating systems

In this section, we examine the potential ideological biases of ratings systems that attempt to facilitate end-user choice. No ratings system can or should be value-free, but one of the goals of Internet self-regulation should be a filtering technology that is compatible with a wide variety of cultures, ideologies, and value systems. If there are many different rating systems in operation, the ideological slant of each is not a major concern, because end-users can simply pick the one that best matches their preferences. However, if network effects prevent a diversity of ratings systems, or cause ratings systems to converge toward a single model or a small group of models, then some end-users will either be forced to employ a system that does not adequately respect their values or face the choice of using no filtering system at all.

In fact, the market for rating systems does have very significant network effects. It is unlikely that website operators will be willing to rate their sites according to a large number of different or incompatible systems. As a larger number of websites rate according to a particular system, its value to end-users will increase. Similarly, as more end-users filter based on that system, the incentive for other website operators to self-rate according to that system will increase. This is especially so if end-users who filter block unrated sites. If network effects operate in a predictable way, one or two ratings systems will eventually emerge as a de facto standard.

We should distinguish between two different kinds of network effects. One of these is not troublesome; the other is. The first network effect is that ratings systems compatible with PICS and PICS/Rules may become a de facto standard. This means that there will be convergence toward an underlying software protocol but not toward a particular set of ratings categories, vocabulary elements or scalar values. Even if PICS becomes the basic software substrate for ratings systems, there can be many different PICS-compatible systems reflecting many different ideologies and value systems. Indeed, this was the original purpose behind the PICS specification. Moreover, because of the way that PICSRules are constructed, end-users can mix and match different ratings systems as long as they are all based on the PICS standard. This kind of network effect is not at all troublesome. In fact, it tends to promote diversity of rating and filtering systems.

The second kind of network effect occurs when a particular *substantive system* of rating becomes the de facto standard. For example, currently the RSACi system appears to have the largest base of rated sites. It has a fixed set of categories, vocabulary elements, and scalar orderings. Conceivably, network effects might also make RSACi the de facto standard for substantive ratings systems. We think this would be unfortunate, not because RSACi is a particularly bad ratings system, but because of inherent limitations in all ratings systems that code content as more or less appropriate for end-users. Simply put, all such ratings systems face a series of difficult tradeoffs, and all such systems reflect particular ideological biases. This is true even if the ratings system strives, as RSACi does, for value neutrality and objectivity. No single ratings system can adequately serve all end-users on a culturally diverse planet. If network effects produce convergence on one system, this will simply impose a particular ideological bias on all.

Value choices and ideological biases can enter into ratings systems directly or indirectly. They enter directly when the designers consciously attempt to promote a particular ideology or set of values. For example, a ratings system that coded Internet content for being "consistent with Christian scriptural values" or "inconsistent with Christian scriptural values" would be rather deliberately promoting a particular religious agenda. Nevertheless, value choices also enter into the process indirectly through tradeoffs that are inherent in any ratings system. To see why, we must consider the various constraints that will affect any such system.

1. Reliability and convergence in rating

If a ratings system relies on more than one person to rate content, it is important that most people rate according to the system in roughly the same way. For example, a system that relies on first-party rating must ensure that content providers around the world use the ratings criteria consistently. Sometimes this is expressed by saying that the categories and vocabulary in the ratings system must be "objective." However, there are at least two different senses of the word "objective." One means simply that the terms are likely to produce behavioral convergence: most people in most situations will apply them in roughly the same way. The other meaning of "objective" is "value-neutral" or "ideology-free." There is no guarantee that any ratings system can achieve this. The choices made by ratings systems always involve values, and those values are always contestable at some level. Hence, ratings systems at best can strive for objectivity-as-reliability.

Nevertheless, the more that a system strives for objectivity-as-reliability, the less likely it will be to adequately respond to and reflect people's differing ideologies and value systems. After all, such a system is designed to produce convergence despite ideological diversity. A reliable system will also be less likely to take contextual differences into account, for example, deciding whether expression is "artistic" or violence is "justified." As a result, a reliable system may be ideologically slanted toward an arbitrary or idiosyncratic set of values rather than toward "neutral" or "objective" ones.

2. Coarseness

All ratings systems feature differing degrees of coarseness. By coarseness is meant the number of categories into which the system divides the world (Balkin 1996). The more coarse a system, the more undifferentiated its judgments. A system that lumps homosexual and heterosexual intercourse, kissing and handholding into a single category of "sexual conduct" is more coarse than a system that distinguishes between kissing, handholding and intercourse, or between heterosexual and homosexual sexual conduct. A system that distinguishes racial epithets from sexual vulgarities is less coarse than one that treats both as instances of "bad language." The MPAA movie ratings system in the United States is quite coarse because language, nudity, sexual situations, and violence all contribute in the determination of whether a movie is rated G, PG, PG-13, R, or NC-17. Thus, a very violent movie, a movie with few well-chosen expletives, and a movie that features a nude love-making scene all may be rated "R" in the United States (meaning that no one under 17 is to be admitted without parent or guardian). The RSACi ratings system is much less coarse than the MPAA system because it has four separate categories each of which features five scalar values. Coarseness has ideological effects because different ratings systems impose a more differentiated or less differentiated vision of what is harmful or inappropriate for children. Deciding what categories count and how much will fall within them is often politically controversial.

3. Equivalency

Coarseness is the question of how many categories and degrees of ratings there are in the system. Equivalency is the question of what things the system treats as falling within the same category (e.g., "bad language") or category level (e.g., level 3 in the language category) (Balkin 1996). Thus, a system that places profanity, obscene gestures, and racial epithets in the same category level states that the three are just as bad or just as harmful for purposes of the ratings system. A system that treats homosexual kissing and heterosexual intercourse as "explicit sex" treats the two as equally inappropriate for children to view. Two systems can be equally coarse in that they have the same number of categories but they can make different things equivalent. For example, suppose system one has three categories, (1) profanity and hate speech; (2) nudity and (3) violence, while system two's categories are (1) profanity and nudity; (2) hate speech; and (3) violence. The two systems are equally coarse, but hate speech is treated as equivalent to different things. All ratings systems make certain things equivalent as soon as they create categories and establish category levels. But these decisions are some of the most ideologically controversial. For example, the decision to place hate speech in the same category with profanity is not ideologically neutral, nor is the decision to treat heterosexual and homosexual sexual activity as equivalent (or, for that matter, to distinguish between the two).

4. Scalar ordering

Many ratings systems have degrees of intensity or harmfulness within categories. As noted previously, the RSACi system has a language category in which level 1 is "mild expletives," level 2 is "moderate expletives or profanity," and level 3 is "strong language, obscene gestures, or hate speech." Level 3 has important equivalency effects: it makes hate speech equivalent to strong language and obscene gestures. Equally important, it treats hate speech as more troublesome than "moderate expletives" or "moderate profanity." Scalar ordering refers to situations when two or more elements placed in a category are not treated as equivalent but are ranked in order. Obviously there is more than one way to do this, and the choices are not value-free. For example, the decision to rank hate speech as worse than one kind of profanity or gesture but not as bad as another is not politically neutral. A particularly remarkable example of the political choices inherent in scalar ordering is RSACi's decision to rank sports violence at level 0, lower than any other form of violence (and equivalent to "no violence").

To see how these considerations interact in practice, we will discuss them in the context of what is perhaps the most widely used content rating system, RSACi. Because of the inevitable ideological effects of ratings systems, we believe that it is a fool's errand to settle upon or to accept a single content ratings system for first-party rating. Rather, the best solution is to create a flexible platform on which many different forms of first- and third-party rating can interact. This system will try to capture many of the real advantages of RSACi without the disadvantages that necessarily arise from a unitary content rating system.

3.2 The RSACi content rating system

The RSACi system is a set of categories, vocabulary, and scalar values built on top of the PICS specification. The original mission of the Recreational Software Advisory Counsel (RSAC) was to rate video games for violent content, bad language, sex, and nudity. In 1996 RSAC turned its sights on the Internet, and RSACi was born. The RSACi rating system is an adaptation of the video game rating system. The system has four categories, each comprising five sets of vocabulary elements. The categories are Sex, Nudity, Language, and Violence, and the vocabulary elements for each range from "None" through progressively stronger examples.[5]

RSACi ratings are generated by completing a questionnaire which asks about the presence of various vocabulary elements. The value for each category is determined by the highest valued vocabulary element present.[6] Like other PICS labeling systems, RSACi may be used to rate entire sites, particular pages, or particular documents on a page.

RSACi aspires to a substantial degree of "objectivity" in its vocabulary elements. What RSACi means by this is what we have called objectivity-as-reliability. The RSACi ratings are generated by

---

5   Of course, what constitutes a "stronger" example is a value-laden question, as is the determination of which vocabulary elements fall within a category. An ideal filtering system would allow end-users some freedom in defining their own categories, and we attempt to implement this ideal below.

6   The number of questions exceeds the number of vocabulary elements because RSACi's vocabulary elements are disjunctive. "Extreme hate speech" or "crude, vulgar language" both suffice to assign a "language" value of 4. Similarly, "wanton and gratuitous violence," "torture," and "rape" all suffice for "violence" value 4. We doubt the wisdom of disjunctive vocabulary elements. Deciding whether "extreme hate speech" and "crude, vulgar language" are equivalent is more appropriately left to end-users.

a series of yes or no questions about the presence of types of defined content. Because the definitions are explicit and turn on relatively uncontested concepts ("humans injured or killed with small amounts of blood" rather than "illegitimate violence against righteous people") RSACi expects that different people will tend to give the same answers about the same content. The RSACi system is objective in the sense that it does not require "subjective" judgments about, for example, legitimate violence or artistic nudity. This objectivity is obviously essential if self-rating is to be reliable.

In order to achieve reliability, therefore, the RSACi system thus tends deliberately to exclude contextual factors from the vocabulary elements. The SafeSurf rating system, in contrast, includes "Technical Reference," "Non-Graphic-Artistic," and "Graphic" (in ascending order of intensity) as vocabulary elements for categories such as "Profanity," "Violence," and "Nudity" (W3C 1999d). A depiction's technical or artistic nature is treated as a mitigating factor, reducing the depiction's assigned scalar value. RSACi's vocabulary elements make no distinction between technical and non-technical or artistic and non-artistic portrayals of nudity and violence. Nor do they distinguish between pictorial and textual portrayals.

The fact that RSACi strives for objectivity-as-reliability does not mean that it achieves another sort of objectivity: a rating system that has no ideological slant or bias. The RSACi system falls short of value-neutrality in several respects. RSACi's decision not to consider mitigating factors such as artistic or technical content might seem to avoid ideology: sexual or violent content will be coded for what it is, rather than how it is presented. But the rejection of the idea of mitigating factors is itself ideologically fraught; the perspective that equates Michelangelo's David, a Playboy centerfold, and a medical textbook because all feature frontal nudity is not neutral but embodies a particular (and idiosyncratic) ideological stance.

Second, and perhaps more serious, RSACi's vocabulary elements are constructed in disjunctive fashion. For example, "hate speech," "strong language," and "obscene gestures" all qualify for level 3 on the language category; thus, the level 3 vocabulary element of this category is effectively "hate speech, strong language, or obscene gestures." What this means, of course, is that the RSACi system treats "hate speech," "strong language," and "obscene gestures" as equivalent, indeed, identical. This is hardly an ideologically neutral decision. Whether we think that hate speech, strong language, and obscene gestures should be treated identically by the ratings system will depend on how we feel about the "harms" each may produce. The fear that children will acquire coarse habits of speech or conduct is surely distinct from the fear that they will acquire racial bias. And regardless of the qualitative difference, many Americans would probably find RSACi's categories of "obscene gestures" (e.g., extending the middle finger) and "strong language" (e.g., "dick") significantly less offensive than "hate speech," which includes the paradigmatically inflammatory "nigger."

The reason that the RSACi system seems to hold out the promise of objectivity as value-neutrality is its focus on the seemingly objective category of "harm." The RSACi rating system is explicitly oriented towards filtering out material that is harmful to children. The original rating system was developed by "a team of academics, psychologists, and educators" in response to the threat of congressional legislation on violence in computer games. RSACi describes its system as "based on the work of Donald F. Roberts of Stanford University, who has studied the effects of media on children for nearly 20 years" (Microsys.com 1999, W3C 1999d). The inclusion of different types of content as disjunctive components of vocabulary elements presumably reflects a judgment that these are equally harmful to children. This sort of judgment obviously depends upon the premise that "harm to children" is a concept that can be measured scientifically, so that the decision that "hate speech," "obscene gestures," and "strong language" are equivalent is not a value choice but an "objective" scientific truth verified by empirical evidence. Unfortunately, this is not the case.

In any event, RSACi's appeal to scientific data about "harm" does not explain the construction of its actual rating system. The appeal to science falls short in two ways. First, the RSACi vocabulary elements are too coarse to accommodate the social science data. The studies on which RSACi relies – and indeed the statements of Roberts himself – argue that the harm various content inflicts on children depends on context (Roberts 1999). For example, violence that is punished has different effects from violence that is rewarded; similarly, violence portrayed as a regrettable but necessary response to aggression has different effects from unprovoked violence. Seeking reliability, RSACi largely eliminates contextual factors from its vocabulary elements. But in so doing it eliminates the very factors that determine how harmful content is. The second failing is perhaps even more important. Social science data cannot provide an objective metric for the measurement of harm for the simple reason that "harmful to children" is a contested category. What counts as harm is an inherently ideological question. Presumably most people would agree that material that incites children to unjustified and unprovoked violence is harmful. If incitement to violence were the only danger, scientific objectivity might be possible. Nevertheless, we still face the difficulty that not all violence is necessarily harmful or socially undesirable. Police officers are required to exercise violence to preserve social order; soldiers are required to fight to defend their country, and physical force may be necessary (even if regrettable) in self-defense or to protect innocent third parties. But even if the terms "unjustified" and "unprovoked" could be given objective definitions, the Internet raises concerns far broader than incitement to violence. The danger of unfiltered access is that children will be exposed to the "wrong" values. Which values are wrong is obviously not a question to be settled by social science. Some parents may think their children benefited by

238

exposure to material suggesting that homo- and heterosexuality are orientations of equal dignity; others may think such material quite harmful.[7]

---

7   A final feature of the RSACi system is unrelated to content, but no less important. It is RSACi's response to the problem of first-party mislabeling and forgery. The problem is serious, for an RSACi tag – or any PICS label – is easy to forge. A website operator could simply write an RSACi tag without registering with RSAC or completing its questionnaire, or she could give false answers to the RSACi questions. The issue is significant because the legal rights and technological powers that third-party rating organizations may wield against first-party website operators will shape the legal and economic environment in which filtering takes place. Careful allocation of these rights and powers is essential to ensure that a filtering system does not collapse under the weight of high transaction costs or collective action problems.

RSACi is pursuing both legal and technological solutions to the problem of inaccurate self-rating. On the legal side, RSACi requires website operators to register their sites and enter into a contract before they are permitted to license RSACi labels (which RSACi refers to as "service marks"). The "Terms and Conditions" of use require website operators to acknowledge that RSACi "owns" its labels and "has established significant rights and valuable good will therein"(*See* RSACi 1999). They must also agree to RSACi audits and, if misrating is found, RSACi may terminate the license agreement or employ "corrective labeling, consumer and press advisories and postings on appropriate Web Sites." *Id.*

RSACi's technical solutions include the incorporation of digital signatures into its labels to make forgery more difficult and the development of a web crawler that will visit RSACi tags and compare them to the database of registered users to detect unauthorized use. A full discussion of the appropriate allocation of rights and powers is beyond the scope of this report. However, our general conclusion is that third-party rating organizations should have fairly broad technological powers but fairly narrow legal rights.

239

3.3 A critique of RSACi as a unitary system

Our discussion of blacklisting programs demonstrated why first-party rating must form an essential component of a successful filtering system. The RSACi rating system takes the opposite approach from blacklists: it relies almost exclusively on first-party rating according to a single substantive system. We now explain why its defects will make reliance on a unitary system for first parties inadequate as well.

RSACi was conceived as a complete and self-sufficient filtering system. It is superior both to first generation blacklisting systems and to the MPAA (Motion Picture Association of America) system that simply rates in terms of suitability for particular ages. It is more transparent, more flexible, and more "objective" in the sense of producing convergent and reliable coding. URLs are blocked not because their content has been deemed unsuitable but because they contain specific content that the end-user has decided not to receive.

Many of RSACi's flaws stem from its historical origins in video-game ratings. RSACi was not originally intended as a multipurpose filtering system, facilitating the choice of end-users with widely differing ideologies, desires, and purposes. Instead, its stated purpose is simply to protect children from "harmful content" as that term would be understood by a largely American audience. This narrow goal produces a system that is too coarse to be useful to end-users with divergent ideologies and values. In this sense, the RSACi system is ideologically too weak: it focuses on only a few ideological concerns and does nothing with respect to many others.

On the other hand, in many other respects the RSACi system is also ideologically too strong. It imposes an ideology that many end-users may not share. The fact that RSACi takes the goal of protecting children as a given creates the illusion that its "objectivity" extends beyond reliability to value-neutrality. The claim, made with varying degrees of explicitness by RSACi's proponents, is that the rating system encodes no contestable ideology but simply reflects and enforces the results of scientific studies about harm to children. However, this claim (or more accurately, this assumption) is simply not true. As we noted previously, RSACi is much too coarse to fully accommodate the scientific data on which it relies. The experimental literature has reached the unsurprising conclusion that the effect on viewers of depictions of violence depends heavily on context (Brown 1999). Donald Roberts, RSACi's in-house expert, identified nine contextual factors: 1) the nature of the perpetrator; 2) the nature of the victim; 3) the reason for the violence (whether it is justified or unjustified); 4) the presence of weapons; 5) the extent of the violence; 6) the realism of the depiction; 7) whether the violence is rewarded or punished; 8) the consequences of the violence as indicated by harm or pain cues; and 9) whether humor is involved (Roberts 1999).

RSACi's violence vocabulary elements do not accommodate all of these contextual factors. They do not take into account the presence of weapons or humor, the reason for the violence, whether it is rewarded or punished, or whether violence is presented as desirable or regrettable.[8] The result is a system that treats as identical depictions that are very different. Roberts comments, "It does not take a scientific background to sense that the consequences to viewers of a film like *Schindler's List* are quite different than the consequences of a film like *Natural Born Killers*." Yet oddly enough, the RSACi system would rate *Schindler's List* and *Natural Born Killers* identically: each contains wanton, gratuitous violence, and therefore each merits the highest rating (4). Similarly, Jonathan Wallace complains that the RSACi system would require him to rate "An Auschwitz

---

8   Surprisingly, even RSAC's video game rating system is more sensitive to context; it differentiates between violent depictions based on whether the target is threatening or non-threatening, and whether the violence is rewarded or not. *See* Roberts 1999.

Alphabet," a report on the Holocaust containing descriptions of violence done to inmates' sexual organs, as equivalent to "the Hot Nude Women site" (Weinberg 1997: 462–63).

The problem of context is important in another way. Avoiding the "harm to children" that comes from exposure to violent content is not a value-free goal. Even if exposure to certain kinds of violence produces aggressive behavior by children, it is by no means clear that all aggression is equally troublesome. Some forms of aggression – like standing up for one's rights, or being willing to protect other people who are being harmed, bullied, or attacked – may actually be socially valuable. It is by no means clear that children are harmed if they learn these lessons. Although some parents might be happy if their children were raised to be pacifist in virtually all circumstances, others might disagree. The real question is whether exposure to violent content creates socially undesirable aggression, and that is a question that the RSACi system does not purport to answer.

The problem of equivalencies pervades the RSACi system. By using disjunctive vocabulary elements, RSACi equates many types of content that many end-users may find quite different. Which types of content should be treated as equivalent is a political choice. RSACi's apparent belief that material harmful to children is both the universal target of filtering systems and a widely agreed-upon concept leads it to construct a system that is both too narrow and ideologically fraught. RSACi's set of categories is tailored to a narrow, secularized and Eurocentric notion of harm to children. Blasphemy, sexism, and homophobia, for example, are captured, if at all, by the vocabulary elements of "profanity" (treating something regarded as sacred with irreverence) and "hate speech" (devaluing a person or group on the basis of race, ethnicity, religion, nationality, gender, sexual orientation, or disability). But people disagree – often quite strongly – on what is sacred, and they also disagree with equal vehemence about whether content devalues a group or simply reflects basic truths and foundational values. For example, last year

U. S. Senate Majority Leader Trent Lott was quoted as describing homosexuals as sinners who are in need of treatment like kleptomaniacs. If Senator Lott's views were reprinted on a website, some parents would insist that it be filtered at a fairly high level because it demeans homosexuals, while others would find it entirely innocuous or at most a poorly expressed declaration of worthy religious sentiments.

Similarly, each RSACi category contains contestable value choices either in its construction of vocabulary elements or in its scalar hierarchy of better and worse vocabulary elements within each category. The Violence category, for example, treats "sports violence" the same as no violence; each gets a rating of zero. Yet the influence of sports violence on children is an area of increasing concern. Many parents might be concerned that a professional wrestling website will tempt their children to practice hammerlocks and piledrivers.

The Violence category also equates "rape" with "wanton, gratuitous violence." It does not distinguish between news stories, educational sites, and endorsements of rape or violence. As a result, news stories about the use of rape as a tool of war, date rape awareness sites, and pornography sites catering to "rape fantasies" are treated as identical.

The Sex and Nudity categories do not distinguish between homosexual and heterosexual content. Some parents may think that two men kissing is equivalent to a man and a woman kissing and therefore should receive the same rating. On the other hand, other parents may view the former as being as sexually explicit as a man and a woman having intercourse.

The Language category equates "crude language," which includes the standard obscenities, with "extreme hate speech," which includes advocacy of violence against racial, ethnic, and religious groups. Parents may well not want their children to encounter the word "fuck." Nevertheless, their reasons may be quite different than the reasons they do not want their children viewing a website urging genocide as a means of achieving racial purity. Some parents may find the "N" word much more troubling than the "F" word; some parents may think genocidal advocacy and the spread of prejudices and stereotypes to be much more harmful to the next generation than the spread of coarse language.

A good filtering system will be ideologically capacious even if it cannot be strictly neutral. Even if it inevitably makes value choices through its choices of category, it should allow users to select from among a variety of ideologies. By contrast, RSACi's attempts at neutrality by trying as far as possible to *eliminate* ideology. Nudity is nudity, regardless of whether it is artistic or educational. Violence is violence, regardless of whether it is endorsed or deplored. And criticism of groups is coded identically regardless of whether the defamed group is Catholics, atheists, or Satanists. But that is not the elimination of ideology; it is the imposition of an ideology – and a very peculiar one at that, a wooden and formalistic neutrality likely to undermine the ideological concerns of many different kinds of end-users.

These criticisms of RSACi should be understood in context, for RSACi is a significant advance on previous efforts at content filtering. Some of its defects are correctable. For example, RSACi could create separate "Sex" categories for homosexual and heterosexual content. But more important, many of these defects are inherent in any filtering system that relies exclusively on first-party ratings. To be useful, first-party ratings must be reliable. To be reliable, they must produce convergence in rating by different individuals. And if they are convergent in this way, they will be ideologically thin. They will not, by themselves, allow end-users to filter according to many different kinds of ideological preferences.

What the analysis of RSACi shows, then, is that a successful filtering system will require contributions from both first- and third-party raters. In the next section, we offer a new proposal that borrows the best features of RSACi while avoiding many of its disadvantages.

4 A proposal for a ratings system: the layer cake model

The central problem we face is to design a system that relies on both first and third parties, that is easy for raters to rate and end-users to use, that is flexible, that can accommodate many different value systems and ideologies, and can grow over time. The solution we propose aims to achieve all of these goals.

4.1 The basic model

Our proposal is to distribute the work of rating and filtering between first parties and third parties. One can think of the filtering system as a three-layer cake that sits on a plate. The "plate" is the software specification, which includes PICS, PICSRules, and (eventually) RDF. The first layer of the cake is a basic vocabulary that will be used by first parties in rating their sites. This vocabulary will consist of between thirty to sixty basic terms and expressions. The actual number will depend on a balance of considerations, including comprehensiveness and ease of use. Too many terms will be difficult for first parties to code. Too few will be insufficient to do the work of description.

For purposes of comparison, RSACi currently contains four categories of five levels each, or twenty basic vocabulary terms. This might suggest that RSACi contains only twenty vocabulary elements. In fact, several of the RSACi levels contain multiple terms, for example, level 3 of language contains "strong language, obscene gestures, or hate speech." This conjunction of terms is an important source of the ideological effects of RSACi's coarseness and equiva-

245

lency. When the vocabulary elements in RSACi are fully separated, the number is closer to forty, so that an upper limit of sixty elements is not unreasonable.

Unlike the RSACi system, first parties will not code their sites with scalar numbers. Instead, they will simply list all applicable vocabulary elements as a header in their web pages. They may choose to rate their entire website, individual pages within the website, or individual elements within web pages. We expect that most first-party labeling will rate the entire site to save time. But first parties will always have the option to offer separate ratings for pages and individual elements because they want specific parts of their site to be accessible to more people. The choice to differentiate parts of the site properly lies in the hands of the individual content provider, the party that wants to be heard and visited by others, and who therefore can best decide how much effort he or she wishes to invest.

The vocabulary elements should be chosen to be "objective" in the sense of objectivity-as-reliability described above. In other words, they should involve descriptors that most first parties will apply in roughly the same way. Objectivity-as-reliability will make the task of first-party rating easier and more predictable as well. The more controversial the descriptor, the more time first parties may spend agonizing over the right approach.

The second layer of the cake consists of ratings templates. They are created by third parties. Third parties will take the forty to sixty vocabulary elements and arrange them into categories and scalar orders. Different templates will have different degrees of coarseness. They will make different things equivalent, and they will rate elements in different scalar orders. Organizations that create templates do not have to include all of the vocabulary elements; they will include only those that are relevant to their particular ideological concerns. For example, assuming that the basic vocabulary elements are similar to those in RSACi, one template might make hate speech equivalent to strong profanity ("four letter words" in English) and

246

set both at level 3. A second template might differentiate between the two, and place hate speech at a higher level than strong language. A third might do exactly the opposite. A fourth template might treat hate speech as an entirely separate category from four letter words. A fifth might choose not to filter for hate speech at all, but focus only on profanity.

By separating the vocabulary elements from the construction of templates, we can better allow third parties to reflect their value systems while still preserving the reliability of ratings by first-party raters. We should not pretend that the choice of basic vocabulary elements has no ideological overtones. It clearly does. Any set of vocabulary elements at the first level will affect and restrict the kinds of templates that can be created at the second level. For example, if there is no vocabulary element for blasphemy, then third parties who wish to filter for blasphemy will have no codings from first parties to work with. In addition, every vocabulary element contains its own elements of coarseness and equivalency. A vocabulary element like "strong profanity" makes some expressions equivalent to others and does not permit further differentiation. Nevertheless, the goal is to allow a sufficiently diverse array of vocabulary elements at layer one to facilitate a wide variety of choices of template construction at level two. No system is perfect in all respects, but we think this approach is an improvement on a unitary system.

The basic point is that by combining a basic vocabulary at level one with flexibility at level two, we can achieve much greater diversity and provide more end-user choice than in a unitary system. At first it might appear that a common vocabulary at layer one will produce an unacceptable limitation of ideological diversity. In fact, precisely the opposite is true. If ratings systems existed with multiple and inconsistent vocabularies, network effects would soon reduce the number of ratings systems to a very small number. Because of the Internet's enormous size, any Internet ratings system must rely on the good graces of first-party raters. Most of these first parties are unlikely to code their sites for more than one ratings system. As a result, those first parties that seek to be rated will over time tend to converge on a smaller and smaller number of ratings systems, until at last there may be only one or two practical alternatives. This "winner take all" phenomenon is the predictable result of network effects. On the other hand, if first parties can be assured that all templates will be compatible with a fixed set of vocabulary elements, no template will necessarily dominate all of the others, because each template is, in principle, compatible with and combinable with all of the others. Ideological diversity thus is enhanced by having a common language at layer one, much in the same way that other common standards enhance creativity and diversity. It is the common set of standards at lower levels, in the "plate" (i.e, the software specification) and in the first layer of the cake (i.e., the vocabulary) that makes possible greater differentiation and diversity at higher levels.

Diversity can only be achieved if there are a wide variety of templates to choose from. However, because third parties do not have to rate individual sites in order to create templates, their costs are greatly reduced. Indeed, the point is to make templates sufficiently easy to create that many non-profit and ideologically driven organizations will want to create their own templates, which they will give away for general distribution. Thus, we do not expect that there will be a market for templates. Rather, we expect that many nonprofit organizations with ideological agendas will have an interest in making templates widely available to anyone who wants them. If template construction were expensive, the lack of a market would be a drawback. However, the system is designed to be inexpensive and easy to use. Indeed, we believe that an organization can probably create a new template in an afternoon, or at the most a few days. Moreover, because the content of these templates will be public and in the public domain rather than secret and proprietary, any organization can model their own template on the work of

248

previous organizations. In contrast to the first generation of filters, free riding on previous templates is positively encouraged. This should greatly speed up the process of template creation.

Note, moreover, that, at the second layer of the cake, the end-user is free to combine different ratings templates from different organizations. For example, imagine two templates, one from the Moral Majority that rates content based on suitability for age, and one from People for the American Way which rates according to language, nudity, sexual content and violence. An end-user (or yet another third party) might want to block out all content that either the Moral Majority or People for the American Way deem objectionable for children, only content that both templates deem objectionable, or content that the Moral Majority template filters except for content that People for the American Way rates as less than two on its language scale. Indeed, third parties might act as arbitrageurs between different ideological preferences of different organizations and attempt to offer end-users the best of both (or all) possible ideological worlds.

The combination of the first and second layers of the cake will achieve reliability in self-rating and accommodate a wide diversity of ideological concerns. Nevertheless, some might still object that a common vocabulary will not filter out everything that should be filtered and that a reliable first-party system will be insufficiently sensitive to context. The third layer of our cake is designed to address these problems by further refining the system.

The third layer of the cake is a set of third-party ratings of individual sites. Three types of third-party ratings are possible. First, existing third-party blacklist systems like those involved in CyberPatrol can be conjoined with the results of filtering from ratings templates. Although this solution is technologically feasible, we do not recommend it because of the transparency problems inherent in first-generation blacklist software.

Second, third parties can create their own PICS-compatible

ratings systems that can work together with or be superimposed on top of the layer two templates. For example, a group might create a ratings system that included contextual and ideological categories like "artistic" or "racist" or "insensitive to women." However, these ratings systems would be different from templates. The group would have to create the categories and vocabulary and also rate a large number of sites according to those categories and vocabulary. These ratings could then be combined with existing templates.

For example, parents concerned about their children's exposure to intolerance (as defined by certain trusted groups), pornography (but not artistic or educational material), and violence (but not in historical material) could opt for the following profile: Use the People for the American Way Layer Two template, and add the following modifications for Layer Three: Any URL rated above 2 on the NAACP's "Racist" category, The National Organization for Women's "Sexist" category, or the Anti-Defamation League's "Anti-Semitic" category will be rejected. Any URL rated above 2 on the National Endowment for the Art's "Artistic" category, the National Council of Teachers' "Educational" category, or the American Historical Association's "Historical" category will be accepted. (All of these categories refer to hypothetical additional ratings systems imposed at level three). Note that using these third party-ratings systems will require that end-users fetch rating labels from sites operated by these third parties or from a centralized label bureau. However, the most efficient storage method would be to put the ratings in the browser, periodically updated by downloads. This vision of integrated first- and third-party rating systems can provide great ideological richness and flexibility to layers one and two. However, it is costly for third parties, because they have to rate individual sites in addition to coming up with their own PICS-compatible ratings system.

A third possible solution is for organizations to create redemptive lists, i.e., lists of sites that, because of their context, should not be blocked even though their content falls within particular "objective" descriptor categories like nudity, profanity or racist epithets. Redemptive lists are a kind of whitelist. Because redemptive lists indicate sites that shouldn't be blocked, the collective action problems of constructing such lists tend to work in the opposite direction from blacklists: Individual website owners have strong incentives to identify themselves to sympathetic third-party organizations as sites that should not be blocked. This saves these organizations time in identifying and rating sites. Moreover, because organizations have ideological reasons to make sure that certain sites are not blocked, they have incentives to make their redemptive lists of sites available to other organizations with similar ideologies. This will result in a pooling of resources to create redemptive lists.

In short, layer three consists of traditional blacklist filters, ancillary ratings systems, and redemptive lists that can be combined with the results of filtering using layer two templates. Thus, an end-user could combine the Moral Majority's layer two template with a layer three redemptive list from an organization with very different agendas, for example those sites that People for the American Way has listed as acceptable for young adults on the basis of language and sexual situations. In this way the system can achieve considerable flexibility as well as ideological richness. End-users need not form these combinations by themselves. In the system we propose there is plenty of opportunity for interested organizations to act as ratings "arbitrageurs": They can produce combinations of ratings systems and offer them as a package to the general public.

4.2 Complicating the model: adding contextual judgments to the layer one vocabulary

Still further refinements of this system are possible. One of the biggest problems in designing a ratings system is accommodating judgments of context. For example, many people think that artistic nudity is preferable to nudity that is merely erotic and designed to titillate. The problem is that terms like "artistic" and "erotic" may not produce reliable convergence in first-party ratings. Different kinds of violence may be more harmful to children; variations in context may also be quite important. For example, violence by evil people that is suitably punished, or violence that appears as part of news reports may be less harmful than unpunished or so-called "gratuitous" violence.

One way of refining the system is to include contextual operators ("artistic," "news reporting", "cartoon" etc.) in the first layer vocabulary and then simply leave it up to template constructors whether to make use of these operators. Remember that a template does not have to include all vocabulary elements; it can be as coarse or as comprehensive as the template constructor wishes. Thus, some templates may use some of these contextual operators on the grounds that the tradeoff between reliability and contextual judgment is worthwhile, while other templates will strike a different balance and avoid them. Nevertheless, we note that the more contextual elements are added to the basic vocabulary in layer one, the larger the vocabulary becomes and the more time-consuming and burdensome for first-party raters. Therefore, we do not recommend adding a large number of these operators. Instead, we think the burden of deciding what is appropriate for children because it is "artistic" is best left to whitelists operating at Level Three. As we have noted previously, a whitelist system can sometimes be more finely attuned to ideologically sensitive judgments, and it can draw on the collaborative efforts of many different organizations.

Nevertheless, we do think that one can enhance the precision and ideological flexibility of the system at Layer One by adding a small number of contextual descriptors that can describe context in relatively reliable ways. For example, if contextual operators might include distinct descriptors for cartoon violence and sports violence.[9] Further, the vocabulary could distinguish between media: the system could offer distinct descriptors for text, audio, pictures, and real-time chat. These sorts of contextual descriptions would not sacrifice very much in terms of reliability.[10]

The demand for contextual operators is perhaps greatest in the case of news. News organizations regularly describe violence, and so it is understandable that they wish to be rated differently from non-news sites that contain violent depictions. We certainly do not

---

9   It might be desirable to incorporate other factors that the sociological literature finds relevant to the effect of violence on viewers, such as whether the violence is rewarded or punished, and what the reason for the violence is. These sorts of contextual distinctions require value judgments that are inconsistent with the reliability required of first-party labels – whether violence is "legitimate" is obviously a value-laden determination.

10   Still another way of increasing precision would be to offer different types of content descriptors that could be conjoined in a label when the label is generated. These types might include, for example, "media," "content," and "modifier." "Media" descriptors specify the medium of the content: text, audio, picture, chat, etc. "Content" descriptors specify categories of content, such as violence, sexual content, language, etc. "Modifier" descriptors specify content more precisely or more contextually; they might include such values as "political," "cartoon," "news," "medical," and "homosexual." First-party raters could rate for each type of descriptor; the types would then be conjoined to produce labels such as "text: violence (political)" or "picture: sex (homosexual) (medical)." Use of these conjoining types will work only if rating is done at the level of individual documents; otherwise, a web page that contains both political cartoons and pictures of violence might be labeled as "picture: violence (cartoon) (political)." RDF permits the labeling of individual documents, and that degree of precision seems desirable; it allows, for example, parents to decide that their children may read news accounts of violence but not see accompanying photographs. The problem with this solution is that many site operators will be unwilling to spend the time to rate pages, text, or photographs individually. Thus, although we offer this solution as a theoretical possibility, we are unsure whether it can be implemented practically.

rule out an experimental use of a content descriptor for news organizations. Nevertheless, there is some danger that non-news organizations will attempt to use this operator to prevent being filtered, and there will be inevitable controversy about what is or is not news. For these reasons, we think a better solution is to rely on whitelists for news organizations at Layer Three. Because the question of "what is news" is ideologically contested, we think it is better for it to be assigned to third-party raters, who can draw up lists of news organizations. Even if the advisory board ultimately decides to include a contextual operator for news organizations in Layer One, we think that a whitelist system provides an invaluable form of insurance in case first-party ratings about news do not prove to be reliable.

4.3 Open source and the creation of a ratings board

The task of constructing a preliminary set of content descriptors will require some degree of centralization and standardization at the beginning. There must be an initial standard set of vocabulary elements that first-party raters can use. We recommend the creation of a board of people for this purpose who have both interest and expertise in the problem of content filtering. We do not think that the board should be for-profit, nor should it be under the auspices or control of any business organization. Ideally, in addition to experts on civil liberties and Internet policy, the board should include social scientists who can advise about what kinds of content are more and less harmful to children. However, developers must recognize that "harmful to children" is a contested concept, and they must be aware that filtering will be used for purposes beyond protecting children. The members of the board must also be sensitive to cultural differences; in particular, content descriptors should not track only those concepts salient to Western cultures and Western preoccupations. Finally, the board should also strive to create easy-to-understand guides and questionnaires that reduce the number of questions and complications necessary for first parties in different places around the globe to produce acceptable ratings.

We recommend that elaboration and refinement of the rating system are conducted on an open-source model. The set of content descriptors will be part of the public domain, available for use by anyone at no charge.[11] New content descriptors can be proposed by anyone. The board in charge of constructing the preliminary set should periodically decide whether new descriptors will be approved as part of the standard vocabulary. Board approval, however, would be only an endorsement, neither necessary nor sufficient for practical success. Content descriptors that are not popular will simply remain unused; conversely, descriptors that are not approved by the board can nonetheless become widely used. What descriptors become used is simply a matter of choice for the first-party raters and the third parties constructing templates. As in other open-source situations, there will inevitably be feedback between the board and installed base of users and raters. Thus we think that the board will be responsive to features repeatedly demanded by persons who use the ratings system every day.

We thus envision that the board will not only oversee the development of the first generation of vocabulary elements, but also act as a clearinghouse for the open-source process that will result in successive updates. We do not think that "official" updates of the set of vocabulary elements should occur very often. One revision every

---

11 The reliance on first-party rating and the lack of intellectual property protection for content descriptors obviously raises the question of misrating. Misrating should be handled by technological means. Organizations whose templates are compromised by misrated URLs can maintain downloadable lists of corrected ratings for those URLs; browsers would give these ratings priority over imbedded descriptors.

two years is more than enough, primarily because it will require end-users to update their software and first-party raters to re-rate their websites. The board should assist in promulgating updates; it can also encourage users to download new software and first parties to update their websites based on changes to the first layer vocabulary.

4.4 End-user interfaces: how to ensure ease of use

Ease of use for end-users is an important consideration for any filtering system. Ease of use not only enhances the central value of end-user autonomy; it also helps ensure that people use the filtering system.

Ease of use is not inconsistent with a system that is both flexible and powerful. The proposal we describe features several different layers and many possible options for innovation. But it is important to distinguish between the complexity of the *filtering system* and the complexity of the *user interface*. A car is an extremely complex piece of machinery, but its user interface is designed to make it easy to drive. A cake can be baked from many ingredients, but this does not make it difficult to eat.

Software companies spend millions of dollars a year to make their user interfaces easy to use despite the complexity of the underlying software engines. We see no reason why this learning cannot be adapted to filtering, which, in many ways, involves a much less complicated piece of software.

We do not purport to design the actual user interface in this report: the interface will be integrated into the end-user's browser, and so the actual implementation is a job for professional software engineers. However, we do offer the following recommendations about how to enhance ease of use and thus promote end-user autonomy.

First, when the end-user purchases the computer, the dealer can offer to set up the filtering system at the point of purchase, just as dealers currently offer to install many other pieces of software.

Second, the filtering system should be accompanied by a step-by-step "wizard," akin to the devices Microsoft currently employs for its software suite. When the end-user boots up the computer for the first time, the wizard can ask "Do you want to protect your children from harmful content now?" and take the end-user step-by-step through the process. The end-user can choose to install a filter at that point or delay the process until later.

Third, access to filters should be easy to find and readily available to end-users whenever they are using their browsers. Buttons indicating access to the filter setting should be prominently displayed on the browser's main window, rather than hidden several layers down in the browser menu. The end-user should have the opportunity to turn filtering on or off with at most a few clicks of the mouse (and the typing of a password, in the case of turning off the filter).

Fourth, when adults are surfing the Net, they may not wish to be filtered. It is also important to remind them of the fact that they are being filtered. Therefore, when the browser blocks a site, it should not only tell the end-user that the site has been blocked, and why the site has been blocked, but also contain a small check box. Checking this box will allow the end-user to turn off filtering for the remainder of the session (i.e., while the browser is running) by typing in a password. The browser should also prominently display a button or toolbar that controls filtering settings so that the end-user can adjust filtering even if he or she does not wish to turn all filtering off. (Of course, changing filtering settings will also require the use of a password.).

Fifth, adjusting filtering ratings should be done with buttons and slides that allow settings to be changed with a few clicks of the mouse. If filtering templates are associated with particular languages or interest groups, they can be represented with icons (like national flags or other symbols) that make it easier for the end-user to identify their source and purpose.

Sixth, filtering wizards should make it easy for end-users to download new templates from the Internet and updated versions of older templates (including whitelists and other third-party ratings). End-users should also be able to quickly and easily create their own blacklists and whitelists by adding particular websites they encounter to lists of approved or disapproved sites.

An easy-to-use interface is perfectly compatible with a system that allows third parties considerable leeway in designing filtering templates and providing independent ratings and white lists. It is largely a question of good software design. The end-user does not need to know how many options are available to the template designer – the end-user only needs to know how to operate the software interface before him or her. End users do not need to know the details of the system and its complexities any more than they need to know how an engine works to drive a car or they need to know how to bake a cake in order to eat it.

End-users are not the only parties who need an easy-to-use interface. First party raters will also need help in rating their sites. Our proposed system contemplates that the Layer One vocabulary will contain between thirty to sixty basic terms. These terms should be organized and accompanied by questionnaires that help take the first-party rater through the system. Creating these questionnaires and testing them for ease of use can and should be an important task of the advisory board that designs the Layer One vocabulary. We also think that a software program or "wizard" could be designed to assist in this process. Finally, the system should be integrated into web authoring tools, so that authors and designers can easily integrate the system into their web content.

5 Conclusion

In sum, our proposed system consists of three layers placed on top of a software specification:

Layer One: A basic vocabulary for first-party raters.

Layer Two: A series of templates constructed by third-party raters that combine and rank these vocabulary elements in many different ways. In addition, multiple templates can be combined and added to refine the filter.

Layer Three: An assortment of blacklist filters, ancillary ratings systems, and redemptive lists maintained by third-party raters, that can be combined and added to the results of layers one and two.

The proof of the pudding, we recognize, will be in the construction of Layer One. Putting together the initial set of content descriptors will require important tradeoffs between precision, reliability, and increased workload for first-party raters. We do not think, however, that the tradeoffs are unacceptable. And we think that the result will better serve the interests of content providers and end-users alike than a unitary system of content rating and filtering.

Bibliography

Balkin, J.M. (1996): Media Filters, The V-Chip, and the Foundations of Broadcast Regulation, *Duke Law Journal* 45: 1133.

Boyle, James (1997): Foucault in Cyberspace: Surveillance, Sovereignty, and Hardwired Censors, *Univ. Cin. Law Review* 66: 177.

Bray, Tim (1999): RDF and Metadata, *http://xml.com/xml/pub/98/06/rdf.html* (visited April 24, 1999).

Brown, Jason (1999): Children and Television Violence, *http://www.compusmart.ab.ca/jbrown/Violence.html* (visited May 17, 1999).

Communications Decency Act, 47 U.S.C. Sections 223 et seq.

Cowan, John (1999): RDF Made Easy, *http://www.ccil.org/ ~cowan/ XML/RDF-made-easy.html* (visited April 24, 1999).

Cyber-Rights & Cyber-Liberties (1999): Felix Somm Decision in English, *http://www.cyber-rights.org/isps/somm-dec.htm* (visited April 24, 1999).

Dobeus, Jonathan (1998): Rating Internet Content and the Spectre of Government Regulation, *John Marshall Journal of Computer & Information Law*, 16: 625.

Flynn, John (1999): Frequently Asked Questions about the Extensible Markup Language, *http://www.ucc.ie/xml/* (visited May 17, 1999).

Lessig, Lawrence (1998): What Things Regulate Speech: CDA 2.0 vs. Filtering, *Jurimetrics* 38: 629.

Microsys.com (1999): Recreational Software Advisory Council Launches Objective, Content-Labeling Advisory System for Internet, *http://www.microsys.com/Profiles/RSAC_1.HTM* (visited April 24, 1999).

Roberts, Donald F. (1999): Media Content Rating Systems: Informational Advisories or Judgmental Restrictions?, *http://www.rsac. org.fra_content.asp?onIndex=36* (visited April 24, 1999).

RSACi, RSACi Terms and Conditions, *http://rsac.org/content/register* (visited May 17, 1999).

Reno v. ACLU, 117 S.Ct. 2329 (1997).

Resnick, Paul (1999): PICS Censorship, & Intellectual Freedom FAQ, *http://www.si.umich.edu/~presnick/pics/intfree/FAQ.htm* (visited April 22, 1999).

W3C (1999a): Extensible Markup Language (XML), *http://www. w3.org/XML/#faq* (visited May 17, 1999).

W3C (1999b): PICS Label Distribution Label Syntax and Communication Protocols, *http://www.w3.org/TR/REC-PICS-labels* (visited April 24, 1999).

W3C (1999c): PICSRules 1.1, *http://www.w3.org/TR/REC-PICSRules* (visited April 24, 1999).

260

W3C (1999d): Rating Services and Rating Systems (and Their Machine Readable Descriptions), *http://www.w3.org/TR/REC-PICS-services* (visited April 24, 1999).

W3C (1999e): Resource Description Framework (RDF) Model and Syntax Specification, *http://www.w3.org/TR/REC-rdf-syntax/* (visited April 24, 1999).

W3C (1999f): Statement on the Intent and Use of PICS: Using PICS Well, *http://www.w3.org/TR/NOTE-PICS-Statement* (visited April 24, 1999).

Wagner, R. Polk (1999) Filters and the First Amendment, *Minnesota Law Review* 83: 755.

Weinberg, Jonathan (1999): Rating the Net, *Hastings Comm/EntLaw Journal* 19: 453 (available at *http://www/msen/com/~weinberg/rating.htm*).

The Issue of Hotlines

Herbert Burkert[1]

1   The author wishes to thank the other lead experts and the members of the Bertelsmann network for their valuable input and the Bertelsmann Foundation for providing a challenging research environment. The responsibility for the outcome is, of course, exclusively the author's. The original is in English.

1 Introduction

Connotations

The term "hotline" evokes various connotations: It characterizes a connection, not necessarily limited to a telephone connection, between a sender and a receiver, where the connection is qualified by easy accessibility (the sender is aware of how to access the connection in advance), high availability and an ensured response system (the connection may e.g. be open on a 24-hour basis or assure response within a promised time).

We know of "hotlines" in the private sector where enterprises offer direct access to "help desks" or related services dealing with consumer and client requests over the telephone or via communication services offered via the Internet.

264

We find hotlines in the context of public services, as services providing information, offering communication or services which can be used to initiate a particular action.

In both areas the term is not only associated with easy availability and accessibility, but also stands for speedy contact with responsible personnel sparing the need to search through an organizational maze.

In the context of the European Commission action plan[2] the term has now entered the discussion on how to deal with problematic contents on the Internet.

However, even in such contexts we encounter a somewhat indiscriminate usage of the term "hotline." "Hotlines" may just be links to an information contact that provides less further information beyond what is already displayed on the web page pointing to the hotline; or, on the other end of the scale, a hotline may stand for an elaborate system of receiving, processing, verifying, evaluating, deciding and finally acting on complaints. Hotlines may be operated on a purely automated basis, or have individuals or elaborate organizations behind them.

In the context of the other chapters

Seen in context with the other chapters of this volume, the chapter on self-regulation by the different players in the Internet industry, on rating and filtering, and finally on law enforcement, hotlines may be defined as the *communication channel* for these contents concern response systems.

---

2   Decision No 276/1999/EC of the European Parliament and of the Council of 25 January 1999 adopting a multiannual Community action plan on promoting safer use of the Internet by combating illegal and harmful content on global networks.

Hotlines, under this aspect, are the – organizationally supported – link between users (the person or persons concerned with contents he or she has encountered), third parties (providing the information that raises concern), self-regulating bodies, organizations providing rating and filtering services and law enforcement.

Against this background it is obvious that the issue of hotlines only covers a relatively small area: Whereas self-regulation and law enforcement provide complementary approaches as responses by regulation and (public/private) enforcement action, whereas rating and filtering provide technical and organizational means by which eventually users themselves can respond to their concerns, hotlines are essentially means of communication, links from the outside (the Net, the user community) to the institutions involved in these processes of self-regulation, law enforcement (public authorities) and the providers of rating and filtering services.

It is on this communication role (and its organizational backup) that this chapter will focus.

Thus the issue of hotlines may be presented as dealing with questions on the expectations, typology, construction and evaluation of the communication infrastructure of contents concern systems.

Reservation: constructive and destructive response mechanisms

However, it has also to be observed already at this stage that seen from the more general perspective of contents concern response systems neither regulatory approaches (self regulation and law), nor enforcement initiated by these regulatory mechanisms, nor the technical and organizational approach of rating and filtering, nor finally hotlines are the only possible reactions to respond to contents concerns.

There are e.g. more aggressive forms to deal with contents concerns. However, since it is the purpose of these chapters to plead

266

for maintaining and enhancing the communication function of the Internet and to ensure that the Internet will remain a viable communication tool in future, we have deliberately excluded destructive responses. At the same time we cannot neglect in our chapter that by providing communication links to response institutions hotlines are vulnerable to any action taken against such institutions. So while not dwelling on more aggressive and eventually destructive response mechanisms we cannot and will not neglect that contents concern response systems may become the object of potentially disruptive and destructive actions. Since hotlines provide the "portal" to such institutions and their processes they will be particularly vulnerable to such destructive approaches. The issue therefore deserves attention under data security considerations.

In the context of the EC study on hotlines

This chapter should also be seen in context with a set of similar yet different approaches to hotlines taken in the European Commission-sponsored projects on these questions.[3] *This* chapter seeks to contribute to and supplement those approaches and their eventual findings by providing a more general framework for analysis in view of giving assistance to categorization, construction and evaluation efforts for hotlines.

---

3   See: the examination of hotlines in the context of the Daphne program (for further information see http://www.childnet-int.org/hotlines/daphne.html and http://europa.eu.int/comm/sg/daphne/en/index.htm (both sites as of June 15, 1999) and the coming activities under the Action Plan of the European Commission: European Commission: Action Plan on promoting safer use of the Internet. Technical Background Document Call for Proposals for setting up a European network of Hotlines – http://www2.echo.lu/legal/en/iap/proposals/99/hotlines_Tech.html (last verified June 15, 1999).

Approach of this chapter

The reader should keep in mind that dealing with hotlines when seen as communication channels (including their organizational backup) will result in a more functional, descriptive analysis. One should also keep in mind that contents concerns may range from a merely passing personal irritation to confronting illegal content. Because of this broadness and because of the need to deal with this whole range of concerns in the interest of the future of the Internet, we would like to address this issue in a manner that keeps it open to all kinds of contents concerns, not restricted to criminal law issues like child pornography (but also not excluding them). Illegal contents, and especially where not only the distribution but the possession of such contents is illegal, do, however, pose specific problems which will receive specific attention.

Against this background we would also not exclude from our consideration such hotlines which are entirely run by public authorities. These types of hotlines will become more common once more public resources become dedicated to such questions. These hotlines encounter particular questions if e.g. they are run in co-operation with private sector institutions.

Normative assumptions

Although primarily functional in its nature, the approach of this chapter is based on a number of normative assumptions which should not hide behind the functional language and need to be clarified from the beginning.

We assume that functioning communication channels are an essential element of democratic societies and that in order to function, communication channels need an environment and operational rules that honor these procedural *and* substantive values: namely

268

substantive and procedural due process, privacy and transparency. Only if these requirements are honored will hotline systems in the long run receive the legitimacy they will need for their general task: to contribute to a process of social learning in a new medium and for a new medium where we still have to learn when and whom to trust.

If one desires to operate a functional and trustworthy hotline system the following pages may at least be read as a sort of check list for once again going through the features of one's own concern response system.

Terminology

A concluding remark on terminology:

In the context of this report we shall use the term "user" for those persons or organizations which provide contents concern information to hotlines.

The term "third party" is used for such persons or organizations that are seen as originators of contents concerns, the user being the "first party" and the operators of hotlines being the "second party."

The term "hotline" generally – unless qualified otherwise – refers to the communication channel *and* the supporting organizational set up running this channel, be it
- based on an individual private initiative or run by a private self-regulating organization for its members, or
- run by a public authority organization, or
- constitute any combination thereof.

Contents

The chapter will start with looking more closely at the challenges and expectations which are facing hotlines (cf. 2).

In analyzing these expectations the function of hotlines in contents concern response systems will be developed, and based on this functional analysis a number of specification requirements for hotline systems will be introduced. These specification requirements cover substantive requirements as well as organizational and procedural requirements, the latter being largely a consequence of the organizational choice that has been made and of the legal environment in which the organization has to operate. (cf. 3).

While the requirements of Section 3 are largely to be seen as basic minimal requirements (at least in as far as substantive requirements are concerned, procedure depending largely on the legal conditions and choices of practicality) the specifications of Section 4 will deal with some possible variations and particularly examine the question of co-operation between hotlines.

Under Section 5 the elements thus developed will be brought into a categorization and evaluation framework – as a sort of an intermediate summary – that might be used for analytical purposes as well as a basis for developing construction and evaluation schemes for hotlines.

Section 6 comes to some basic conclusions as to the issue of hotlines and discusses some thoughts on possible future activities on contents concern communication.

2 Hotlines: challenges and expectations

Internet characteristics

One of the characteristics the Internet (although more precisely of specific services provided via the Internet) shares with some (other) media is that users do get exposed to content that they may not have expected. This may surprise those who primarily view (most) Internet services as individual communication. However, even if not targeted directly, when browsing, "surfing," or following suggestions from search servers any encountered page may contain unwanted, troublesome, outraging as well as surprising, amusing, and challenging material. It is the mixture of the deliberately sought for and the unexpected that perhaps constitutes one of the main attractions (and distractions) of the medium. To be able to profit from this opportunity, to make such encounters possible, while still allowing for highly selective approaches to information gathering and communication is one of the most important tasks in "Internet maintenance" and makes the medium so important for the freedom to seek and gather information, to develop and to exchange opinions.

Disturbances

Using any freedom is not risk-free, and there is always the possibility not only of encountering material with which one strongly disagrees, but which is also deemed to be harmful or judged as illegal.

Since such encounters occur in the world of traditional media as well, we and the social institutions have, by and large, often painfully, learnt how to deal with such encounters through procedures by which we hope to adequately balance the interests of those concerned, and which allows our institutions to act and/or to be seen to act effectively on these matters.

271

The Internet, however, is still in a transient phase as to its internal structure and also in the way it is perceived. Encountering illegal content or even only hearing repeatedly about illegal content being verifiably or even only allegedly available might well create a "broken window" effect[4]: The appearance of disorder is observed as a sign that public order cannot sufficiently be maintained, which in turn leads to more disorder. Transferred to the medium "Internet," such assumptions or observations increase already existing assumptions and observations on the insecurity of the medium which exist because of doubts about the identity of communication partners, the integrity of the data being exchanged and with regard to one's privacy rights.

Insecurity

Again such a feeling of insecurity (many of these insecurities are real enough, but the feeling of insecurity is already sufficient for the effects described) may as well occur in other communication processes, e.g. with regard to telephone communications. However, while we have not only learnt how *to deal with* contents concerns in the more traditional media, we also have culturally learnt *how to live with* varying degrees of insecurity, with communication risks; we have learnt how to decide which risk levels to accept and which to refuse, which "back-up" mechanisms to install.

In the transient cultural state of the Internet we are still in a learning process. As usual in such processes we seek to learn from the past, we use analogies, and try to transfer solutions from the more traditional media to new media. To some extent we shall also

---

4 This is a term borrowed and often reused from an article by Wilson and Kelling. Wilson, J.Q.; Kelling, G.L. (1982): Broken Windows: The Police and Neighbourhood Safety. *Atlantic Monthly* (March), pp. 29–38.

try to consciously make use of what we see as the specific new qualities of the new environment, the new advantages. And to some extent these new qualities, whether technical, economic, organizational or psychological, will find their way into our traditional solutions, whether we intend it or not – and often this may happen in a manner which we do not expect. Responsible politics of technological change cannot and should not ignore feelings of insecurity that accompany such processes.

Perceiving traditional mechanisms of maintaining order as impotent in such a period of change has a re-enforcing effect on the perception of danger and insecurity – the "broken window" effect mentioned above. Such effects tend to be highly undesirable in any community, and even more so in a medium that still carries positive connotations of cultural exchange, community building, political re-vitalization, and lately, economic prosperity.

On the other hand equal attention must be paid to concerns that response systems may develop a chilling effect if they do not follow substantive and procedural due process, transparency and data protection rules, and rules on the freedom of expression. Rather it should be made clear that the operation of such response systems is to contribute to maintaining communicative freedoms.

Contents concern response systems are necessary to manage these disturbances. Among the elements of such systems, hotlines (again, the notion always including its organizational infrastructure) carry the burden maintaining the communicative performance of such systems.

Trust and empowerment

If one intends to profit from the advantages the medium offers in spite of its risks, it becomes essential to create an environment of trust and to encounter any feeling of helpless exposure to the medium with user empowerment. Consequently processes and institutions have to be developed, tested and implemented, and learning processes have to be initiated that help to create such trust and empowerment. What makes this task so difficult in this case is not only that social learning processes are difficult to predict (and thus to plan), but that the learning process itself has to basically take place in the very same medium one needs to learn about. Processes and institutions of trust building and empowerment have to be perceivable and easily usable on the selfsame medium which they try to enhance while they are still being developed. This brings to mind the "software trap": the user for whom software is to be developed remains its constant test object.

A note of caution

Being available on the medium, these mechanisms of trust and empowerment are bound in to share the fallacies of the medium. While considering hotlines as a developing but nevertheless hopefully efficient and effective way to deal with contents concern one should remain aware that this tool remains exposed to the same information security risks as any other means of communication on the Net. So trust (and security) considerations should always be present when elaborating specifications, considering construction, and evaluating concrete examples.

This observation also makes it obvious that the process and institution being implemented reflect processes and institutions of trust building one is already familiar with in the "real" world. It may well be that in the years to come this necessity will lose its urgency; for the time being it is an essential requirement.

This process occasionally creates ambiguities. Traditional institutions, public authorities, operate by "old" rules, slowly adapt "new" rules, testing their interpretation against the old rules. Re-

274

sources have to be shifted, new infrastructures established. Ways have to be found so that public authorities may make use of these additional input channels to reach out to communities that otherwise bypass them.

To bridge the transition new private/public forms of co-operation are tentatively developing. These testing processes occasionally create new uncertainties and uneasiness among participants. Adaptability has to be weighed against predictability and clarity.

It is against this background that specifications for hotlines as communication elements of contents concern response systems have to be developed.

As the starting point for such systems we have already identified: concern for contents, the need to respond, the search for empowerment, the uncertainties of the medium, tentative self-regulation, difficulties to identify public authority and to judge its effectiveness as well as its efficiency.

The need to respond in such an environment leads to the need for the communication links of contents concern response systems
- to be available for talking back, to be heard, to help to initiate action in diverse cultural and geographical environments;
- to be visible, but also to be transparent as to their functioning and consequences;
- to help to reduce ambiguity;
- to connect reliably and efficiently to bodies that seek to establish trustworthiness and to connect with organizations that wish to make use of these channels as information gathering as well as information distribution mechanisms.

In short the expectations specification requirements for hotlines will have to meet are
- availability,
- transparency,
- reliability.

3 Specification requirements for hotlines

The performance expectations do not immediately lead to an ideal type of hotline or even to minimal requirements for hotlines, simply because of the large variety of possibilities in communication design. What may be done, however, is to establish a list of basic substantive requirements and lay out the general confinements for organizational and procedural variety.

Substantive requirements

As a set of minimal substantive requirements for any organizational choice for hotlines we have already identified – however in a very general way – availability, reliability and transparency. Although these requirements are very general and have a mainly functional character, they carry with them a number of normative implications that must guide the design process.

Organizational and procedural considerations

Hotlines as elements of contents concern mechanisms must ensure communicative action and reaction, as well as interaction. The term "action" refers here to the "message" that is supposed to initiate the contents concern response process, whereas "reaction" comprises the whole of the response mechanism. Such a response mechanism might eventually imply a dialogue with the initiator as well as the originator or transporter of the contents.

How this dialogue is organized is a question of basically three organizational choices. These choices and their consequences must be seen as being set in concrete normative environments, which may be changeable, but which currently at least may still have their gray

276

areas of interpretation, diverging practices, discretion and opportunity, but which nevertheless make their impact felt on users, self-regulating bodies and third parties alike.

3.1 Substantive requirements

As we have seen the mere term "hotline" evokes associations with availability, transparency and reliability. Any hotline, regardless of the organizational set up in which it operates, has to meet these functional requirements to deserve its name. In the specific environment of the Internet, however, these requirements are not as trivial as they may seem at first glance.

3.1.1 Availability

Hotlines have to stay available. This concept of availability comprises – in our understanding – visibility and readability, and it also means establishing robust and timely communication links.

Visibility

Hotlines have to be visible. This requirement is not as easy as it seems: on the Internet, to express it in a simplified manner and to reword a famous phrase, nobody is visible until "hit" by a browser. Commercial players have been aware of this problem and have developed a number of mechanisms to address it.

To name a few of these mechanisms: designing sites so that they are more easily found by search engines, buying into search engines to achieve preferential treatment, ensuring presence in portals, negotiating and establishing links with other well-visited sites, reaching out to traditional mass media and attracting attention from there.

A particular problem of visibility may occur when hotlines are run in an organizational environment where providing a communication link for handling contents concerns is not the main purpose, but embedded in a broader approach. A site might e.g. be dedicated to improving the situation of children in general (social, medical, educational situation). As part of its operation it might run a hotline regarding concerns about child pornography. In such contexts it must be ensured that contents concern hotlines are not mistaken for feed-back mechanisms for these general concerns.

Readability

Visibility, however, is not only ensured by mere presence, by developing a sort of "brand" recognition. What is also needed is simple readability. The main barrier to readability is language. To the extent that the medium is becoming multilingual, response systems have to decide consciously how to meet language demands.

Again this a problem that is not always easily solved. While it seems that borderlines of nationality and geography may loose some of their importance, language – although English seems to be developing to the universal language (for the time being) – is now more clearly seen as the new separation factor. Technical progress (automated translation) may help to reduce this problem, but it will hardly be able to address differences in underlying language cultures.

On the other hand hotlines may take a completely different strategy by *expressly* limiting their reach to a language region, a state or even a smaller geographical area in addition to limiting their availability to specific subject areas.

Particularly where hotlines are run by law enforcement agencies

278

or are closely connected to them, such an approach might receive some preference because it could help to overcome criminal procedure law problems.

Communication links

As hotlines serve as communication channels in contents concerns response systems a careful choice of media links is necessary. Accessibility via the Internet has to be the fundamental technical requirement, since any enforced media change reduces usability. A user e.g. should not be forced to logout so that the telephone line can be used for a phone call or a fax. For merely practical reasons alternatives to direct response via the Internet should, however, be provided.

Privacy protection

Entering via the Internet poses privacy protection problems. At their point of entry hotlines should therefore clearly advertise their privacy policies since *informed* consent will remain the main[5] basis for the legitimate handling of user data (if we take the privacy regulations in the European Union's Directive as a guidance).[6] In

---

5   There may be – depending on the circumstances – also other legitimate reasons like an overriding public interest in the processing.

6   DIRECTIVE 95/46/EC OF THE EUROPEAN PARLIAMENT AND OF THE COUNCIL of 24 October 1995 on the protection of individuals with regard to the processing of personal data and on the free movement of such data: "Art. 2. (h) 'the data subject's consent' shall mean any freely given specific and informed indication of his wishes by which the data subject signifies his agreement to personal data relating to him being processed." "Article 7: Member States shall provide that personal data may be processed only if: 7.(a) the data subject has unambiguously given his consent; [...]."

further processing the information the same attention has to be paid to privacy considerations eventually applying to the data of the third party against whom a complaint is made.[7] In these cases consent cannot necessarily be expected and one would have to resort to regulations on processing in the public interest, to be found either in general data protection laws, or if the processing is done by public sector authorities, very often also in criminal procedure laws.

Anonymity

Connected to the issue of privacy is the question whether hotlines should allow anonymous input, and once such input is accepted whether such anonymity should be honored under all circumstances. The general rule to be followed here is that *if* anonymity is accepted and thus advertised at the point of entry it should be honored unless there are clearly compelling obligations not to do so and such a possibility should be stated at the entrance. Otherwise hotlines run the danger of losing trust, and with trust their purpose.

Whether to accept anonymous input, however, seems rather a question of practicality and experience with handling such messages than a fundamental question. Hotline operators have to decide for themselves if they prefer getting the broadest input possible and then to sort out what might be relevant and acceptable for further processing or whether already signaling a barrier at the point of entrance is more efficient for them.

It should be remembered, however, by all parties concerned in the communication process that anonymous communication – in the context of the Internet – is not always also unidentifiable communication (since communications may be traced unless special additional

---

7   In such cases public interest overrides, a legal obligation or specific data protection rules in criminal procedure laws may apply.

precautions are being taken) and non-anonymous information is not always identifiable information (since identities might be forged).

Data security considerations

This leads us to a more general and by no means negligible issue: data security. The entry points of hotlines as well as further processing must provide sufficient security for their users, the third parties whose data might eventually be processed over these lines, and for those operating hotlines.

Operators of hotlines should also be aware that contents concern response systems might themselves become subject to responses by those who resent such systems and might want to block or harm their operation.

From the users' perspective there is another problem to be considered, a problem which is not restricted to data security as such but affects the security of the whole of the response system: users might want to receive assurance that they are dealing with a contents concern response system that is genuine, that exists as advertised.

While the problem of secured identity of contents concern response systems does not yet seem to be an issue it might easily become one if such hotlines are established in politically controversial environments.[8] It may be advisable, as soon as the tools for verifying identity become more widespread, to ensure their use by the operators of hotlines. For the time being, at the point of entry, hotlines should at least provide some assurance by referring to a verifiable physical address and by naming the people and organization(s) responsible for operating the hotline and – as the case may

---

8   See such discussions in Australia on the occasion of the introduction of a controversial bill against Internet pornography: Sydney Morning Herald of Wednesday, June 9, 1999 at http://www.smh.com.au/ (as of June 10, 1999).

281

be – naming the person(s) and organization(s) for which the hotlines are being operated.

The particular issue of newsgroups

Newsgroups do not pose particular problems for hotlines. Reports on contents concerns may be entered as any other reports from other services. Hotlines accepting such complaints should advertise accordingly.

Newsgroups do pose occasional problems when news are to be taken down. This, however, is an enforcement problem that is being dealt with in the chapter by Sieber.

Newsgroups, of course, provide other means for direct response beyond just sending a the response message to the newsgroup in question. For reasons explained in the introduction, however, we leave such considerations aside.

Time

Another element that decides on how availability is perceived is time.

Time with regard to contents concerns is of crucial importance. The term "hotline" suggests timely if not speedy response. Maximum response time should therefore clearly be mentioned at the point of entry.

Such time specifications can, of course, only refer to time spans within which a user will receive a "receipt" indicating that the input has been received and will be processed. Such response could be provided automatically, although one might want to combine such a response with personal communication with the user should further information become necessary. If automated response mechanisms are being used (for indicating that the complaint has been received and is being processed) the automatic system should be identified as such so as not to become a credibility risk. A backup mechanism should be in place for human intervention.

In most cases the time span within which the input will be fully processed up to the moment of the final decision or action cannot and therefore – again for reasons of trust maintenance – should not be advertised to the users. However estimates could be given (and again be marked as such). If only for reasons of internal efficiency, rules of internal procedure for handling information inputs should provide for standard time limits and warning mechanisms should be established if such self-set time limits cannot be met. By publishing the internal rules of procedure (see directly below the section on transparency) hotlines and their support systems would give assurance to users that time has indeed been recognized as a crucial factor and is taken seriously.

Finally, operators of hotlines should be aware that both initial response time, (after placing the complaint) and total processing time will affect the way in which hotlines are perceived as being efficient.

3.1.2 Transparency

Transparency, in our view, is perhaps the most essential requirement for hotlines to function adequately as communication channels for contents concerns because transparency is a basic normative requirement put on organizations and their procedure in democratic societies. Furthermore in a period of transition in communication cultures trust building and trust maintenance systems are of crucial importance, and in order to achieve trust transparency has to ensured.

Point of entry

Throughout the previous analysis of substantial requirements we have already referred to a number of transparency obligations for hotlines:

- the need to describe the conditions under which input will be processed including whether anonymous input is accepted and under which conditions;
- the limitations on input with regard to subject, language and geographical area;
- the need to present a privacy protection policy and to point to data security risks;
- the need to inform on when a first response can be expected, whether this response is operated automatically, and what the average processing time may be.

Description of organization and procedure

Furthermore users should find all necessary information on the type of hotline organization they are faced with. While the organization types and options will be described in more detail below, in terms of transparency the most crucial information that needs to be given is the relationship the hotline has to law enforcement. This information is necessary because law enforcement operations are strictly bound by procedural law. While procedural law may provide areas of discretion the exercise of discretion is often again bound by practice, court interpretation of discretion and/or precedent. Such strict rules may strongly affect the status of a potential informer particularly when the possession of material is already a criminal offence.

Hotlines as a mechanism for obtaining evidence?

It should therefore be obvious, in our view, that law enforcement agencies when operating hotlines themselves should clearly identify themselves as law enforcement. And indeed, as more resources are dedicated to the web presence of public authorities, more and more hotlines run by public authorities become visible and should be visible on the net.

We feel, however, that hotlines should not be used to obtain evidence clandestinely that would otherwise not be obtainable through them.[9] In the current transition period we are still in a learning process as to which of the "old" rules we wish to apply in a new environment. Public authorities in such an environment have their own learning processes. But they do learn in an environment with stricter rules and less flexibility. Law enforcement has to wait for the legislator before adaptation can take place. Under such circumstances, if one wants to maintain the valuable input function that is provided by hotlines, one has to look for a more flexible mode of operation. To provide such flexibility is one of the many possible roles for private hotlines. They, however, can only be trusted if their relationship to public authority hotlines and public authorities is clearly defined and that advance definition is being honored by subsequent practice.

Private hotlines may then help to overcome entrance barriers to provide possible evidence and may – after clearly advertising this policy – eventually channel it to public authorities. Where law enforcement agencies suspect that such non-law enforcement hotlines do not process complaints or evidence properly they should address these organizations directly.

---

9   The issue to what extent law enforcement should and could use stealth techniques – other than faked hotlines – to obtain evidence is outside the scope of this chapter.

Setting up hotlines under a pretext – and this applies to private organizations as well as to law enforcement agencies – is likely to destroy trust in communication generally and would fundamentally jeopardize the whole of the hotline exercise.

The organization and the full procedure should be described to the user at the point of entry in a manner that can easily be understood (e.g. using graphics). If self-regulation and public authorities co-operate in running the hotline, particular attention should be put to explaining the organizational co-operation and possible consequences.

The description at the point of entry should make clear to what extent, if at all, evidence should be provided by the user and how it can best be secured.

Transparency during the process

Ideally, users should be able to track their complaint or information input at any time through the processing system.

But this is rather a matter of additional design options than an issue of fundamental requirements. We, however, regard it as essential in terms of transparency of procedure that the user is informed about the final outcome of the procedure that she or he has initiated, although as we shall see this may not always be possible. Such information is owed to the initiator and it is necessary for building and maintaining trust in the whole of contents concern response systems. Also users should be made aware that adverse decisions might be taken against them or that adverse developments may threaten them.

Reports

Hotlines and contents concern response systems in general are not only interactive devices linking concerned users, self-regulating or independent private organizations, rating and filtering systems, third parties, and law enforcement. Hotlines also operate in the eye of the general public, and what is reflected by the general public will become important for the process by which the Internet becomes a fully accepted part of our culture of communication. Hotlines therefore should be aware that not only do they operate under the scrutiny of law enforcement agencies, users and third parties, but under the scrutiny of the general public that is watching and commenting on this medium.

It is therefore, in our opinion, not only useful, but necessary, certainly during the phase when hotlines still seek acceptance, that hotline supporting institutions not only keep track of their processed complaints (this may prove necessary for law enforcement and exculpation purposes anyway)[10] but that they produce reports on their activities for the general public at regular intervals.

3.1.3 Reliability

Users of the Internet are constantly made aware, sometimes painfully, that things do change fast on the Internet. By and by, users lose their certainty that communication channels and organizations supporting them will still be around when they look for them the next time. Hotlines should therefore give some assurance that at least they are planned for medium term, if not long term existence. Contents concern response systems and in particular their communi-

---

10 This recording procedure should, of course, properly be announced in the data protection policy at the point of entry.

cation channels to the Net have to be viable, or at least steps are needed that would help to ensure this viability.

Financial resources

Viability of hotlines is (also, but not exclusively so) a matter of financial resources dedicated to their purpose. In order to obtain visibility hotlines need financial subsistence. Although in part such financial resources may be substituted by providing direct aid (Internet service operators e.g. providing contents concern hotlines for free or contributing in kind to their operation) other if not all financing has to be shared among those who eventually will profit from their operation because of trusted and increased use of the Internet. Such cost sharing schemes may eventually also include users, but they should not be made to bear the main burden since other groups can generate more direct (financial) gain from a more broadly accepted operation of the Net. In any case, costs for running and maintaining such systems should not be underestimated and appropriate precautions should be taken to make them financially sustainable.

Organizational backup

Hotlines need to be attended to by professional personnel. Unprofessional handling and neglect will be recognized quickly, and this perception will affect other contents concern response systems as well. Organizers should therefore ensure appropriate organizational backing, appropriate procedures and, most of all, personnel to run these communication channels that is able to do this in a professional way and to keep them running. It should be remembered that in the eyes of the general public the effect of the hotline exercise will at least also co-decide the fate of self-regulatory concepts (although, as we pointed out, hotlines are not merely restricted to self-organizing bodies).

Monitoring, evaluation and co-operation

Quality assurance for processes and institutions require oversight and monitoring. Hotline operators should be encouraged (as is already the case for the European Union) to co-operate, not only by properly organizing links between their hotline systems but by co-operating on quality assurance for their hotlines. They might agree e.g. on evaluation criteria and administer procedures that would measure existing hotlines against such criteria.

Eventually a rating system or at least "a seal of approval" scheme could be developed co-operatively which would help to increase the quality and the viability of such systems, as well as transparency for the users.

3.2 Organization and procedure

There are a number of organizational and procedural choices to meet the general expectations with regard to hotlines and specifically the demands of availability, transparency and reliability.

We have already referred to the basic option of having
- independent private individual initiatives, or self-regulating operations by private organizations
- operations by public authorities
- organizational combination of the above.

There are two basic questions such an organizational choice has to face: how to comply with the legal environment in which the hotline system is expected to operate and what the basic requirements are as to the internal procedure of the chosen option.

3.2.1 The question of the legal environment

How do compelling legal obligations influence the choice of organization and procedure for privately operated hotlines?

There is, however, another problem which might also be affected by the legal environment but which is, in the absence of compelling legal obligations, rather a question of specification variation: how should private hotlines design their co-operation with law enforcement authorities? While the first question is a normative question directly affecting the internal structure and procedure of hotlines, the second question is more a question of how they organize (and are left to organize) their *external* relations.

Public sector restraints – private sector opportunities?

When dealing with transparency issues we had briefly alluded to the relationship between public authority hotlines and privately operated hotlines. Sieber has described the normative environment (and possible changes) in detail in the following chapter of this volume. This part of this report concentrates on design consequences resulting from these normative considerations. Sieber's observations may – for this purpose – be summarized as follows. Choices for hotline design are limited

(1) *if* there is a legal obligation to inform law enforcement authorities at a very early stage (having information on certain contents immediately leads to a duty to inform public authorities), and/or

(2) *if* there is a legal rule against possession of certain contents material and/or

(3) *if* there are not – either explicitly or by observing (predictable) rules of discretion or opportunity that accord certain privileges to institutions like hotlines (with or without perhaps demand-

290

ing the observance of some additional rules for such institutions to obtain such privileges).

Hotlines have to be designed (in terms of organization and procedure) to minimize the legal risks for their users and operators. Mechanisms have to be developed so that, if necessary, possession can be taken by public authorities of relevant evidence, without legal risks for the users. A broader spectrum of choice may exist in the area of harmful material (unless in this area there are – depending on the relevant legal system – similar risks).

If on the other hand there are no such restrictions or if there are privileges granted (perhaps in connection with certain safeguards) then there is a broad range of organizational and procedural choices. Currently, in the transitory period, however, private bodies including self-regulation organizations are left with little choice. They have to respond to contents concerns and they have to be seen to respond. They cannot afford to wait until more public authorities are fully established on the net. They have to find suitable solutions to respond to a broad range of complaints. Therefore there might be cases when such organizations are faced with the need to take evidence even if the possession could be illegal, simply to relieve the users of hotlines from such risks. They have to find solutions fast, solutions that are acceptable to users who are their customers, and to law enforcement.

If dealing with illegal material is itself regarded to be a criminal offence, public authorities are under an obligation to react against the user. This in turn may reduce the chance to obtain relevant information at all.

To get around this problem the legislator could intervene. The legislator might change the rules on illegal possession. However, for criminal policy reasons such changes might be difficult to achieve. The legislator might privilege certain hotlines under certain conditions. Such changes might be obtained more easily. But it is difficult to predict in which direction changes may occur and how long such changes will occur. Still, contents concern response systems have to operate in this transition period and their presence is particularly needed.

This situation has a number of consequences:

- As already pointed out under the aspect of transparency, public authority hotlines should clearly be recognizable as such and should at their point of entry provide adequate warning of possible legal consequences when information is being provided by users or where users are uncertain about the legal consequences of providing such evidence.

- At the same time, in order to keep the contents concern response system intact, users might be referred to private sector hotlines, operating in an adequate self-regulatory environment and meeting the substantive requirements pointed out above as well as the procedural requirements described in more detail below and provide for – again a transparent procedure – where information might be referred back to public authorities.

This approach might currently be useful in a situation where public sector hotlines still have to establish visibility and obtain necessary resources and in order to reach out for audiences which for social, cultural or technical reasons, are still difficult to reach.

In the long run, however, under the aspect of efficiency, more important even for reasons of transparency, if not legality, it would be preferable to have a broad range of entrance points and hotlines available among which users could then choose according to qualitative criteria and select the hotline they are most comfortable with and which provide for contents concern response without ambiguity.

And indeed, looking at some existing hotline operations, even if their policies are transparent, it is not always clear whether they are operating in an environment that does not have such legal limitations as described under conditions (1) and (2) above, or whether they operate under a scheme which is either explicitly or implicitly protected under a scheme as described under (3). Particularly if operating under condition (3) it is not always clear whether such considerations will also be extended to a particular case in question. In such situations private operators have to clearly state the risk and avoid giving the impression that a user is moving in a "safe harbor" environment.

The problem of ambiguity

Communication analysis ambiguity, while occasionally socially useful by allowing action under strong if not contradicting constraints, is perhaps the most important impediment of current hotline systems. This is so regardless of their internal organizational and procedural structure, because ambiguity is an "environmental" factor of their operation. Their operations become highly risky, if they operate under a "private face" and give procedural assurances which, should the rather informal rules of discretion and/or opportunity change, they may no longer be able to guarantee.

Legal policy and functional considerations

This is not the place to argue the advantages and disadvantages of specific legal policies. However, it is the purpose of this chapter to point out some mainly functional implications of possible choices made.

Not to provide for exemptions or privileges will in the long run make private endeavors in that field difficult to continue. While there might still be incentives for the private sector to at least symbolize co-operation with law enforcement there is little attraction in merely channeling incoming information to public sector authorities. Even more so, also in areas where there would be space for private sector action because there are no compelling legal obligations, there would remain few incentives (beyond image considerations) to keep running private hotlines. Although one useful function might still be to run them as feedback mechanisms to contents rating and filtering organizations, they would have to be designed differently to serve this purpose. Rather, we would be left with basically two types of private hotlines: hotlines which operate for contents concerns that do not lead to compelling legal action and hotlines which, in case of compelling legal action merely channel concerns to public authorities. These options would have to be clearly shown at the point of entry. Still, private sector operators would have to take decisions to channel concerns correctly. This is not an easy task, and it is a task with high responsibilities because of the risks involved for users (and third parties) that might still confound their purpose. This would transfer an image not only of complexity but also of risk and might discourage the use of hotlines generally, even in areas where there would be no compelling legal constraints.

On the other hand, to provide for exemptions if not privileges is to open up a variety (if not competition) of contents concern mechanisms. Not all of these competing systems might prove themselves to be more beneficial than public authority hotlines. But in all a variety of hotline systems could develop, carving out their own specific areas of competence and mechanisms – where necessary – in co-operation with public authorities. New resources to address content concerns could be employed. Self-regulation bodies and those co-operating with them would continue to see incentives for trying to become particularly effective at addressing specific areas of concern. As in any such situation a greater effort will have to be made to allow for independent evaluation and to provide for market transparency.

Again these are legal policy questions that need to be weighed by the legislator, who might have different answers depending on the circumstances of the day and long term assessments being taken, elements that cannot sufficiently be analyzed in the context of a text that is limited to functional aspects of hotlines. We do feel, however, that societies may generally fare better if they provide for a broad range of alternative channels of communication. Some of these channels already receive legal protection as privileged information (as it is the case in most countries for communication with an attorney), or they may at least receive social recognition (as communication with journalists in some countries). These are risks which in our societies we have consciously taken because we feel that such channels must stay open not only for functional reasons but also because we feel that this is how a society should work. If the Internet because of its communicative potential is an environment where similar risks should be taken so that trust may develop and we may eventually harness the potential of the medium, then the burden of risk should be adequately distributed. Hotlines as communication links offer users the opportunity to obtain speedy and effective response. Operators of hotlines focussing first of all on providing such response by addressing the content side should not be left with the risks that might develop from not being able to address the author problem at the same time with equal efficiency. While we might regard some of the "private" hotlines operating right now as taking such risks as forerunners to achieve at least social and perhaps legal recognition, it would clearly be preferential if such channels would indeed receive express legal recognition.

None of these arguments should be read, however, as to imply that currently there cannot already be self-regulation, or forms of co-operation between the state and self-regulating bodies using hotlines. We only argue that it would be desirable if the "rules of engagement" for those using hotlines were defined more clearly and, if, in the long run, the legislator would allow for cases of privileged information, as it is the case for traditional media already.

3.2.2 Procedural choices and minimum requirements

The procedural analysis will start with the standard "internal" procedure where there is no need to involve public authorities. Legal obligations may require either an "external procedure" (where input is exclusively handled by public authorities or at least immediately channeled to them) and more complex "mixed procedures" (see also the chart at 5.1). Again – the variety of choices would depend on the mandatory rules set by the legal system.

Typical procedure

Against this background the typical procedure would run as follows[11]:
(1) The input by the user would be confirmed (information of the user).
(2) The hotline organization would check the input as to whether the formal point of entry criteria it has set in its policy are met. It would also verify the input to the extent to which the claimed contents concern can be found as described by the user.
(3) If the entry criteria are met and verification has been successful there will be an internal evaluation procedure as to the qualitative criteria with the purpose of determining whether further action is needed (evaluation). This decision-making process will have to follow the criteria prescribed in a policy placed at the entry point of the hotline.
(4) If this evaluation leads to a decision that no further action is needed – for reasons of transparency – the user should be informed accordingly.

---

11 The best example in practice we have come across so far – and which indeed has served as a starting point for our more general procedural reflections (although we did not follow this example in all points) – may be found at: http://www.internetwatch.org.uk (as of June 15, 1999).

If there is a decision on further action the third party has to be addressed. Such a third party may or may not have been subjected itself to such an action (within a self-regulatory organization). In the latter case the action has merely the character of a notification. In cases of illegal content notification of the authorities may also be required, with or without notification of that third party depending on the circumstances but also the policy concerns of the hotline.

If a third party has subjected itself to the self-regulatory procedure it is necessary – for reasons of due process – to give that party a hearing, or the third party may simply decide to take the action required. Again, a handover to public authorities may be required for compelling legal reasons. Being subjected to a self-regulatory procedure, however, might carry with it privileges as to liability.

However, providers suject to a self-regulatory regime that takes action according to the requirements should be privileged in a legal proceding.

(5) Finally a record of this procedure should be kept and, depending on the transparency policy that has been decided, the user should be informed on the outcome.

Particularly the last step, informing the user on the outcome, is not always easy to realize. This is mainly the case when the procedure had been "externalized" at some stage, since public authorities do – it seems – rarely inform the private sector hotline of the final results of its operations.[12]

---

12 At some time it might be useful to undertake some quantitative research – across hotlines – on how many "externalized" procedures have actually lead to formal enquiries and how many of these enquiries have led to final convictions. Such empirical verification would, however, require an appropriate tracking system both for private hotlines and public authorities.

Externalizing procedures

Depending again on the regulatory environment a decision to externalize the procedure might have to be made earlier than described above: already at the evaluation or at the verification stage. If there are compelling rules the user may need to be told how to handle the evidence problem and/or to turn to a public sector hotline directly, or to hand in the information and the hotline would forward it for the user, if privileged accordingly, providing the user perhaps with a sort of receipt statement.

Minimum procedural requirements?

As shown above, the scope of organizational and procedural variety depends on the strictness and margin of appreciation that is left to private actors. So it is difficult – unlike with regard to substantive requirements – to talk about minimum procedural requirements. But provided that there is room for internal procedure then the minimum procedural rule would be the right to a hearing for the third party.

4 Specification variations

We have analyzed so far a number of basic requirements (or minimum substantive requirements) for the quality and (as far as there is room for such an approach left by the legal environment) for the organizational and procedural design of hotlines, resulting from basic performance expectations in the Internet environment.

The following considerations address a number of design variations that are left to the discretion of hotlines which may be taken and which, in our view, would have a beneficial effect on the whole of contents concern response mechanisms.

It is also under that heading that we shall address the problem of co-operation with other private hotlines, but also with public sector hotlines and public authorities in general.

4.1 Internal variations

Anonymity

Some of the possible variations in internal substantive rules and procedures have already been alluded to when dealing with these requirements as basic requirements. Providing for anonymous communication at the point of entry may e.g. be regarded as such a variation.

Design considerations

Remembering that availability and transparency are among the qualitative requirements for the design of hotlines one can still imagine a broad variety of how entry points should be designed in practice. Again those intending to set up hotlines should not under-estimate both the effort that has to go into this design process and the implementation process itself. While this kind of design is nor-matively of secondary importance, it may be crucial as to whether people will actually be attracted to these hotlines.

Indeed looking at currently available hotlines in the area of contents concern one encounters broad variations, from the highly professional to the more – it seems – improvised.

Symbolic value

Beyond the basic substantive and procedural requirements, beyond mere design considerations hotlines have a symbolic value indicating that those operating these hotlines share at least ethical concerns with users.

Added value: hotlines as feed back mechanisms

Beyond generating good will, adding to elements of corporate or organizational identity, added value may be created for the functioning of the other contents concern response systems: hotlines may help to provide statistical data on Internet contents concerns for self-regulating bodies (and law enforcement agencies). Furthermore the kind of input provided through hotlines may give feedback on issues important for self-rating and filtering mechanisms pointing to areas where users feel such new mechanisms may be needed, or where they are felt to have become obsolete.

If such extended use is to be made of hotlines, not only do input formats have to be adjusted to this purpose, but also such additional use has to be made transparent to the users, and – for privacy protection reasons – to be made dependent on their informed consent.

4.2 External variations: co-operation with other hotlines

4.2.1 *Among private hotlines*

There is no essential requirement that private hotlines co-operate with other private hotlines. There is, however, a growing number of hotlines, with regard to industry sectors, subject areas, and countries and regions.

Such hotlines might compete with each other once the advantages of operating hotlines become more visible. Public authorities will have to develop standards for hotlines if the legal situation provides special privileges to those using such services.

In the current situation, however, there is simply growing complexity rather than competition. This complexity does not necessarily facilitate the choice of these hotlines. This uncertainty may affect all hotlines. For the future we have already argued for "market quality" and "market transparency" for such systems. While some "natural" separation between these services is created by language, language does not always provide a valid dividing line.

There are also "aggregation" processes under way; industry sectors join across national boundaries and form organizations on the regional if not on a global level. But also these new aggregates may be confusing as to what information inputs they would take and how they would process them. Evaluative processes (see below) will bring some structure. Special information services may develop in the market to provide "consumer guides" for hotlines, if not for contents concern response systems in general.

Some of these "consumer offers" will also have to be addressed by the co-operation between hotlines. Hotlines may operate in the same area but in different countries or language areas. Joining their efforts would increase their efficiency.

The first problem, however, that has to be overcome is to know about each other, particularly when such hotlines have started from individual initiatives. Again initiatives should be supported that seek to create at least descriptive inventories that might be used by hotlines seeking co-operation.

Outsourcing of hotline activities?

Small providers realizing the advantages of hotlines might want to outsource hotline activities individually or together with others rather than joining an association. Such a model is particularly interesting in cases where legal advice has to be sought. Outsourcing, however, might create problems in addition to those already inherent in a successful hotline operation.

Indeed, the underlying assumption of our observations is an association model rather than an outsourcing model. The association model is, of course, functionally a (controlled) transfer of obligations as well. Following an association model rather than a model with varied and varying outsourcing partners, however, has the advantage that the members of the association decide together on the hotline operation and are also willing to take consequences should a concern affect any of them. There is also more likely be a broader circle of providers helping to sustain such an operation. In the more individual outsourcing relationship dependencies between an outsourcer and the outsource operator might develop more easily which could affect the proper operation of a hotline which, in turn, might affect the whole of the contents concern approach.

International co-operation

Hotline mechanisms as well as their supporting organizations are currently and will continue to develop most likely on a national basis since this still seems to be an important pattern for users to view the complexity of the Internet. However, concern creating contents does not necessarily follow this pattern. Hotlines, in order to fulfil their functions, will therefore have to co-operate internationally.

Such international co-operation could also help to overcome, in principle, in cases of illegal content, problems international law enforcement co-operation is still facing.

However, such co-operation, in the interest of the legitimation of hotlines and thereby in the interest of their long-term effectiveness, would have to observe at least the same requirements as the operation of hotlines outlined above, namely material and procedural due process, data protection and data security, reliability and transparency. As to transparency in this context, hotlines should make their accords of co-operation transparent to users and third parties.

Such accords could then become recognized internationally and – once the international legal environment is developing accordingly – lead to mutual recognition of privileges under similar conditions as they could become recognized on the national level.

The difficulties of such co-operation should not be underestimated. Such co-operation may have to cross cultural lines, language lines, lines between different legal cultures. Still such co-operations could make use of their flexibility, not being bound by sovereignty issues, being based on mutual agreements of providers sharing similar concerns. Such co-operations could also help to provide a forum for a continuing international dialogue on shared and differing values in different societies being brought so close together now through the advantages of this technology.

4.2.2 Between private sector hotlines and public sector hotlines or public sector authorities

As long as this co-operation occurs between private sector hotline operators solutions might be negotiated, discussed internally, agreements reached and published, although technical and practical problems may continue to occur. Public authorities or public sector operated hotlines from one country seeking co-operation with the private operator of their country or of another country pose yet a different problem.

As already pointed out, the legal system in which a private hotline operates may set up certain mandatory requirements as to what information it would be allowed to carry and in which circumstances internal procedures have to be "externalized" and thus "co-operation" has to be initialized. Such rules follow directly form substantive and procedural law and leave little room for specification variations.

The question remains how to handle informal requests of co-operation by public sector hotlines or public sector authorities.

First of all it is our opinion that requests for informal co-operation between public sector hotlines and private sector hotlines and their operators should be kept to a minimum. We have stated above under basic requirements that hotlines should operate under clearly formulated and publicly accessible policies of operation. It goes without saying that public sector hotlines have to operate under their respective procedure laws; they are part of exercising public authority and these procedure laws are meant to check the exercise of public authority. If these procedure laws contain regulations on how to engage with private sector operators these rules should be followed; if the procedure laws do not contain such rules such rules should be established in the proper rulemaking process under public scrutiny.

Such strictness is particularly necessary in cases of transborder co-operation with public authorities. This strictness is necessary if one recalls that contents concern response systems, and thus hotlines, do not only operate in areas where international consensus is widespread, but also in areas that are close to the rights of freedom of expression and political activity, areas in which there is a high variance in interpretation. In such cases it is likely that the private sector operator is in no position to judge what consequences informal co-operation would have for third parties. In many cases there are also (national) legal obligations *not* to engage in such informal co-operation (secrecy laws, rules on discovery concerning foreign private and public sector parties, privacy protection laws) and there may consequently be risks of civil and criminal liability. Since these consequences cannot sufficiently be judged by the private sector party whose co-operation is sought by the foreign public authority it is advisable that the private sector party invites the requester to seek official co-operation through the appropriate channels. It might also be advisable to protocol the request and the response to that request.

It would be unrealistic to assume that there are not, at least on the national level, situations in which efficient law enforcement would require speedy action, but which – if all the formal rules would have to be followed, or even if one would have to wait till these formal rules are well established on the regulatory level – would simply come too late. These situations may still occur rather frequently while public authorities have to develop appropriate resources to meet their tasks and where such co-operation could bridge the gap at least until these resources are fully developed. In such situations private sector operators will be caught in the occasional yet classical practical dilemma of law enforcement agencies: be formal and inefficient or be efficient yet informal? Court cases on the admissibility of evidence give evidence of this dilemma and how to arrive at a proper balance.

But such casuistic approaches are of no help to the private sector operator faced with a co-operation request. Public authorities would view the legal basis of their co-operation request (outside cases of mandatory co-operation, of course) as consent. For private sector operators such consent is not necessarily viewed as consent in terms of having a choice, nor would they always regard their consent as informed consent. The private sector operator might worry as to the consequences with regard to third parties which in turn might claim liability compensation. While this problem might be solved by the recommendation put forward on this point by Sieber, co-operating hotline operators might still face liability outside contractual obligations (legal liability), even from outside their own country, if they have "consented" to rather than followed formal obligations.[13]

As shown by the court cases on the admissibility of evidence a clear cut solution is not easy to find. However, as a minimum rule of designing for such cases a general protocol of co-operation between public authorities and private sector operators should be established which is made transparent to users and third parties, the elements of these protocols should become part of the contractual arrangements and the by-laws of the organizations running hotlines, and there should be an individual protocol on each individual case in a manner that would make it admissible as evidence should the need arise. It is then indeed up to the user whether to entrust information to hotlines which follow such a policy for his or her concern, or whether, for reasons of clarity, using a public sector hotline directly would not be preferable.

5 Categorization and evaluation

Organizational choices, and substantial specification requirements as well as procedural variations may now be put together in a categorization scheme. Such an exercise may serve various purposes:
- to help to categorize the world of existing hotlines and thus have a tool for further analytical purposes,
- to develop a tool kit for the construction of future hotlines, or at least to serve as a sort check list for such purposes,
- to create a tool with which existing hotlines could be evaluated.

---

13 Although they might (successfully) claim circumstances that may lead to their exculpation. However, the risks to have to prove this in court will still remain.

Not all the elements which we have discussed so far are suitable for all these purposes. Organizational choices and procedural constructions (as we have seen above depending largely on what the legal system tolerates) are of a more descriptive nature, and can be used in the context of analysis as well as tools for construction. The substantive requirements are more of a qualitative (if not normative) nature and therefore are more suitable for the purpose of evaluation, although their elements may also be used for analytical as well as constructive purposes.

In this chapter we therefore merely try to provide a summary systematization of what has been presented above where – as we think – the summary on organizational and procedural variations could provide a basis for a typology of hotlines (for analytical and construction purposes), whereas beyond that purpose the summary of substantive basic requirements would also open itself for evaluative uses.

5.1 Categorization

Organizational choices

Under organizational aspects we can categorize (or analyze or construct) hotlines as follows:
- hotlines as part of private non-collective initiatives,
- hotlines as part of self-regulatory agencies or associations that represent a particular group interest,
- hotlines run by public authorities, and
- co-operative variations of these three basic types.

Types of procedure

Under procedural aspects we can identify basically three types of procedures:
- internal procedures
- internal procedures with transfer points to external procedures (mixed procedures)
- external procedures with some initial functions for internal procedures (letter boxes) but with the main emphasis on the operation of a public body (external procedures).

If we describe these procedures in a more detailed manner set in parallel we arrive at the following picture.

Substantive requirements

The third kind of typology may be generated by looking back to the basic substantive requirements which we have discussed. This descriptive typology can also be used for analytical as well as for constructive purposes.

At the same time, these are basic requirements. Therefore they can be used to analyze concrete hotlines not only as to whether they fulfil these basic requirements, but also to what extent they might go beyond these requirements, and may thus provide for a basis for comparative evaluation.

Such evaluation may become important in contexts where running a hotline may serve as possibility to escape from liability, and where consequently certain threshold requirements would have to be met.

Such an evaluation sheet might look as follows:

Basic substantial requirements	Tools used	Rating (In which degree have the requirements been fulfilled?)
Availability - visibility - readability - privacy protection - communication security - time		
Transparency - at the point of entry - of organization and procedure - of process - reporting in general		
Reliability - financial resources - organizational backup - monitoring, evaluation		

5.2 Implementing evaluation systems for hotlines

In the market

If indeed the operation of hotlines will play an essential role in determining liability, methods will have to develop to determine under which conditions a contents concerns response communication channel may be called a "hotline" for this particular purpose, and when – in more detail – these criteria are fulfilled and what may be missing.

Whether in this process hotlines will have to become objectively verifiable (How long per day has a hotline to stay open? How often has input to be checked? How fast has a verification and an evaluation process to take place?), will they may become subjected to a rating system, and who would be authorized to run such a system, are still open questions.

Some of these elements, at least, would have to be described in an accompanying regulation or, less preferable, in successive court decisions, should there be legal consequences drawn from running a hotline. Other criteria and supplementary rating systems might well develop in the market because of consumers' and operators' needs.

In the context of self-regulation?

In any case, if the legal system becomes more open to self-regulatory mechanisms and thus lets hotlines function beyond mere letter boxes, in cases connected to illegal content it is also likely that, while the procedures might become (or remain) in our wording "internal," more "external" obligations will be placed on them, and mechanisms will develop which check more formally on the fulfillment of these "external" obligations.

Seen from the more general aspect of self-regulation it may well be the case that whatever procedural flexibility may be "gained" by privileging self-regulation mechanisms will have to be "paid back" by more rigid external standards and mechanisms to ensure that these standards are being kept.

Whether this is going to be the course that contents concerns systems in general and hotlines specifically will go, is currently difficult to predict.

However, there are already indications that while self-regulatory procedures may be accompanied by more rigid external control mechanisms, but leave them at least operational, there is also another trend according to which self-regulatory mechanisms will be incorporated into "external" rules in a manner that they will hardly have any self-regulatory quality.

310

This is at least one way to read the "notice and take down" requirements of the US Digital Millennium Copyright Act.

In the context of law enforcement

These regulations might serve as an indicator that hotlines may well become the integrated part of a regulatory approach rather than to operate as a self-organized mechanism. Certainly, under such conditions not only the evaluation but already the establishment and operation of hotlines, at least those operated for exculpation purposes, will become more, if not highly formal. This might in the long run affect visibility, response time, transparency, privacy protection and data security, as well as transparency, co-operation procedures and cost regulations.

For all these conditions criteria will have to be developed, both for the implementation and the evaluation, and at the same time mechanisms would have to be maintained to allow competition for better solutions. In such an environment of increased and more formal information, operators might well reflect whether it is worthwhile to maintain hotlines with complex evaluation systems rather than simply deal with notices "to take down," in this case issued not by "owners" but by public authorities.

However, to adopt such a solution from the realm of property rights (already dangerously close to rights of freedom of expression) would have predictable chilling effects on the new medium and with regard to its ability to transport adversary content.

Another future for evaluating hotlines?

However, if these consequences are taken into account, and taking into consideration that the presence and visibility of public authorities will increase on the Net anyway, other alternatives may be more practical that nevertheless observe the special conditions under which the providers of services on the Internet are operating. "Alternative channels" of communication just like privately run hotlines with their internal decision-making procedures might at least be given a chance. These alternative channels have sufficient incentives to address specific content response issues also beyond the need of exculpation. Such incentives will come from the overall (and commercially) beneficial effects in terms of visibility, status and trust.

To generate such positive consequences hotlines will still need to be comparable among themselves and against objective criteria. In any case, whether under public guidance, or motivated by private interests in the continuing function of the Internet, communicative channels of contents concerns will not only further develop but they will also generate procedures of evaluating such contents concern response systems.

We also feel that this development will not be restricted to hotlines as such but will and already does affect contents concern response systems in general, whether these evaluative systems will develop through better insight, user demand or political pressure.

We therefore assume that in the future we shall see more institutions developing whose task will be to provide some sort of independent quality assurance for such systems on the net. These quality assurance systems will not only have to take into account to which extent the task of handling contents concerns are met, but also how, and to what extent they will allow contents to be exchanged. If this balance is kept, and when contents issues finally receive the same reasonable amount of attention as in the more traditional media, then indeed contents concern response systems, hotlines as their communication channels, and systems evaluating these response systems will have served their task to contribute to a general cultural acceptance of the Internet as a medium of our time.

6 Summary, final observations and future perspectives

6.1 Summary

Contents concerns play an important role in the acceptance of the Internet as a culturally incorporated medium. To address these concerns in the interest of harnessing the potentials of the medium, contents concern response systems are being established and improved more consciously. Self-regulating mechanisms, self-rating and filtering as well as co-operation with law enforcement are important elements of such systems. To connect these systems with their users hotlines are established and managed as communication channels.

The quality, rules, procedures and organizational contexts of these hotlines play an important role in the acceptance, functioning, and effectiveness of these other parts of contents concern response systems.

As the communication element of contents concern response systems, hotlines have to fulfil the quality requirements of efficient communication as such. This makes availability, reliability, and transparency the main qualitative requirements of such hotline systems.

Since hotlines process crucial information that may have wide-ranging effects on all users, third parties and organizers, in order to obtain and maintain legitimacy and by legitimacy eventually trust, operators will not only have to follow functional requirements but also normative requirements. Therefore – apart from concrete legal obligations that may be placed on operators anyway – substantive and procedural rules of due process, data protection and data security, as well as freedom of expression principles have to be observed when operating these communication channels.

As to the organizational set up there is a broad choice of implementation possibilities depending basically on self-regulatory, or public authority, or "mixed" mechanisms. This flexibility provides the opportunity to adjust the organizational structure to the particularities of the contents concerns the response system is eventually dealing with.

In this capacity hotlines as communication channels for such systems can operate as valuable input systems for the other parts of the contents concern response systems. To exploit hotlines for these purposes again presupposes transparency as well as honoring data protection and data security obligations.

However this process is not an easy one. Hotlines (as well as the other parts of contents concern response systems) operate in regulatory environments. With regard to certain information these environments set up compelling rules which information may be handled in which way. These regulations tend to reduce the flexibility of organizational and procedural choices. In such an environment, if self-regulatory mechanisms continue to operate they will do so in a more formal and more closely scrutinized manner. While the choice will be left with the legislator on how to strike the balance, there are clearly a number of consequences which should be avoided: whatever solutions are developed, and particularly if they contain a regulatory mix between private and public approaches, they must show a "clear face" to the user. This is particularly important for the fragile initial phase of information input into such systems as provided by hotlines.

To the extent in which providing hotlines will become (one of several) criteria for exculpation and avoiding liability it is even more likely that the requirements and rules of operation for hotlines will become more formal.

What will develop with certainty with this process are evaluation schemes for hotlines, assessing their availability, transparency and reliability as well as assessing their organizational structure and procedural means for efficiency, effectiveness and due process.

6.2 Final observations

In short, moving to more self-regulation may move more erstwhile "public" obligations into the private sector or move "self-regulating forms" into the public sector. Whatever the direction competitive advantages perceived for self-regulation and user empowering processes might well turn out differently. Hotlines, relying on broad communicative input, may be particularly affected by such rigidity.

As to hotlines and their functionality, what has to be avoided in the meanwhile, is that uncertainty and ambiguity apparent in this transition process has detrimental effects on the efficiency, if not the legitimacy of hotlines as communication channels in the service of contents concern systems.

These lines rely on input, even more they should encourage input to provide a sense of empowerment to users. To be able to continue to do that, however, it is necessary to make clear what will happen to the input, how concerns are being taken care of, what kind of procedures they will set in motion, and most important of all, what will be the risks for the users.

For this purpose it is necessary that hotlines operate in an environment that is clearly defined, as to rules, procedures and consequences. If for reasons of opportunity a larger area of discretion is left to the private sector, or to forms of co-operation between the public and the private sector, again the rules for such operations should be transparent. If for reasons of legal policy, symbols of self-regulation are adopted by public regulation, or public sector strictness becomes the underlying feature of self-regulation in the private sector, this requirement of transparency becomes even more important, so that users will not be misled by such symbolic forms.

Hotlines, when they operate with an open face and a clear profile, can continue to serve as assurance that one is not a lone surfer on a vast net, but that there are institutions out there, not only public authorities but also private organizations and maybe other individuals who share the same concerns. This knowledge alone can contribute to user empowerment and increasing trust in the new medium.

If, in addition, hotlines prove themselves as trustworthy and efficient, and follow the rules of fairness and due process, and if they use the net efficiently to make this known, then in the long run hotlines and their supporting organizations may contribute to finally incorporating the Internet into our culture, as a challenging and therefore not risk free medium, a medium, however, that is equally responsive to our concerns for trust and security as it is challenging, a medium on which we can exchange contents as well as our concerns for content.

But this knowledge would have become a banality by then and that would be the final proof of cultural incorporation.

6.3 Future perspectives

Till this stage is reached one can probably not avoid that contents concern response systems and in particular their communication channels, hotlines, will become indeed more formal and more scrutinized. In this process they might well lose some of their innovative and dynamic impetus which has helped to create them in the first place.

So finalizing this chapter might very well be the starting point to reflect on future developments and supplementary steps to be taken.

All reflections so far have relied on rating and filtering, on self-regulation and law (state intervention) and eventually on hotlines as the communicative part of these contents concern systems. Reflections on the role of hotlines in this system do, however, also invite questions on whether the contents concern system should not in itself be expanded beyond the model discussed in the context of this project and the activities of the European Commission.

If we look back at our initial reflections we identified two basic needs for the process of culturally incorporating the Internet: Empowerment (present in rating and filtering, self-regulation and hotlines) and establishing (and maintaining) trust.

We should therefore not forget that there are other if only supplementary methods for trust generation and maintenance and user empowerment. In particular we should not forget that not all contents concerns deal with illegal or harmful content, and that not all concerns are contents concerns.

To extend our approach along the lines of empowerment and trust would then mean

– establishing and increasing user education not only as regards the technical side of handling the net, but providing means to handle the psychological, social and political impact of the medium by empowering identity and autonomy of the individual user and groups of users;

– providing alternative response structures that would ensure that counter positions would be as effectively presented as the contents to which there is response; i.e. mechanisms to help to establish diverse opinions, to encourage exchange and dialogue.

Within these systems of encouraging contents exchange (rather than contents concern response systems) new approaches could be developed to make the concern element manageable:

– One of these approaches is zoning i.e. designing contents differently for different kind of spaces, marking in advance areas that provide by their designation certain expectations as to the communication contents and style to be encountered and thus reducing the risk of unwanted exposure. Although the inherent danger of "out-zoning" discontent should not be neglected, such zoning approaches, for certain areas, would serve both empowerment and trust building.

- All response mechanisms discussed so far seem to lack a substantive phase for deliberation and some mechanism to seek for legitimacy outside the internal verification and evaluation processes described above. It may well be that such mechanisms could serve as an add-on to hotline procedures, but this would certainly affect the time scale in which response is generated and thus may affect the "valve" performance that is needed for the medium.
- Another element that could be added to contents concern systems as we see them in operation so far, is a more widespread use of moderation mechanisms (instead of directly involving enforcement processes), beyond simply inviting information input from the user and response from the third party. Such moderation systems could serve as buffers to the intervention by public authorities and may thus allow more and different types of interactions than those used by hotline systems up to now.

Such supplementary approaches might help us to remember that the Internet is an interactive medium not only in the sense of a "concern – response" model but as tool encouraging communication.

Legal Regulation, Law Enforcement and Self-Regulation: A New Alliance for Preventing Illegal Content on the Internet

Ulrich Sieber

319

1 Introduction: the emergence of a new alliance

1.1 The current unpleasant situation

On the eve of the new millennium in today's information society, the relationship between the Internet industry and the law enforcement sector is not in an ideal state. According to a survey carried out in 1998 by the German Federal Crime Office (BKA) in 25 countries, most of the police authorities questioned described the relationship between the police and Internet service providers as "bad" or "bad to non-existent."[1] This poor relationship applies to various areas, but represents a particular problem with respect to the responsibility on the Internet for illegal and harmful contents. Here, an unnecessary confrontation between the Internet industry and law enforcement agencies has arisen. This confrontation originated in the field of child pornography, but spread to all other forms of illegal and harmful contents in the Internet.

In 1998 in Munich, a local first instance court sentenced the former managing director of CompuServe Germany to two years imprisonment on probation for illegal distribution of child managing director of CompuServe Germany to two years imprisonment on probation for illegal distribution of child pornography and contents glorifying violence. The sentence was based on a misinterpretation of the German Teleservices Act and the facts of the case; the accused – an honorable business executive – was not in any way personally involved with child pornography, as is the case for the majority of other representatives of the Internet industry. It was only in the second instance case in November 1999 that he was acquitted (Sieber 1999a; 1999g). Unfortunately, this experience is not just a German peculiarity. In France, the chief executive of France Net was arrested on similar counts, and he described his personal feelings in

---

1   See http://www2.echo.lu/legal/en/comcrime/sieber.html (As of: 22 March 2000).

320

an article entitled "Comment devenir pédophile en 24 heures?" (How can one become a paedophile in 24 hours?).

This threat of legal responsibility for the Internet industry goes far beyond the issue of pornography, content glorifying violence or hate speech. It also includes defamatory statements, unfair competition and copyright infringements which are not only prosecuted by the police with respect to criminal responsibility but also by citizens and private organizations seeking civil law remedies. In Italy in 1998, for example, the police seized and closed down a well-known server of a nonprofit organization due to defamatory statements contained therein which had been forwarded to this server by third parties. Similarly in the US, online service providers whose servers had been abused by third parties disseminating defamatory statements faced a considerable number of civil claims by those affected. Moreover, it will only be a question of time before European copyright owners will sue network, access, and service providers for assisting third parties in copyright infringements due to their provision of the necessary IT infrastructure: Once these organizations become more involved and if no cooperative solutions can be developed, the whole issue of Internet industry responsibility for illegal and harmful contents will be aggravated.

The threat of joint liability on the part of the Internet industry for all these contents has severe consequences: For industry, these do not only include possible criminal sanctions and civil damage claims. If some recent criminal and civil judgments were to be regarded as binding precedents, they would force the Internet industry to implement costly but inefficient control measures and could also lead to censorship and severe barriers to the free flow of information. A confrontation between the two parties would also be extremely detrimental to law enforcement, which in many ways depends on productive cooperation with the private sector. In such a confrontation, all parties and interests concerned – especially the fight against illegal contents and the protection of children on the Internet – would lose out.

In order to avoid such undesirable consequences, it is essential to analyze the legal and sociological origins of these present problems.

1.2 The underlying problems and their solutions

The legal origins of the above-mentioned problems arise from the fact that courts apply the traditional rules of aiding and abetting, and complicity found in criminal and tort law to the Internet industry in a very broad manner: Running an IT infrastructure – itself highly valuable to society – is considered assisting the perpetrators who are abusing the networks. In criminal matters, these traditional rules of assistance can be based on the intent of the accessory, in civil matters (e.g., copyright infringements), the negligent omission to fulfill controlling obligations can be sufficient. This general and traditional approach of co-responsibility often stems from a lack of knowledge of the technical aspects involved. Many politicians and large parts of the public are still not capable of differentiating between the responsibility of the authors of illegal statements and the role of providers, let alone between the different positions of access, network and host service providers. In order to avoid such an over-zealous and general approach, a reasonable framework of liability and a predictable legal environment are essential.

However, it is not merely the external problem of the Internet industry's co-liability that needs correcting. One must also look at the sociological origins of the problem and determine why many European countries follow the present detrimental approach. The public wants to see results in the fight against illegal and harmful content on the Net. Since in many cases the actual authors of these contents cannot be tracked back and prosecuted, the representatives of the Internet industry are held responsible. Therefore, removing child pornography and other illegal content on the Net in an effective way appears to be the best way to avoid such "scapegoat liability."

Thus, the requirements needed to stop the present confrontation between the Internet industry and law enforcement are as follows: i) to limit the responsibility of the Internet industry for third-party content to a reasonable and technically feasible degree, and at the same time, ii) intensify the actions against the *real* perpetrators. Bluntly speaking, this leads to a carrot and stick approach: The more successful Internet industry and law enforcement are in prosecuting the real perpetrators, the easier it will be – in parliaments and courtrooms – to fight an excessive "scapegoat liability regime" which is to some extent taking the Internet industry as hostage.

For that reason, the analysis of the present legal situation raises strong arguments in favor of an effective industry self-regulation, and of efficient law enforcement with respect to illegal and harmful content on the Internet. These arguments supplement and support the economic arguments in the chapter of Stefaan Verhulst and Monroe E. Price, which illustrate that effective measures against illegal and harmful content are in the industry's own interest, since the Internet must be a safe place to be accepted by society and by parents in particular. As a consequence, Internet industry and law enforcement agencies are not adversaries with conflicting interests, but rather ideal partners: They both share the common interest of making the Internet a safe, crime-free platform for the worlds of business, science and leisure. This is especially in the interests of children and other potential victims to which illegal and harmful contents on the Internet can create grave harm.

The consequences of this result are clear. On the one hand, the Internet industry should endeavor to better understand the work of law enforcement agencies so that these law enforcement bodies can help the Internet industry and the user enjoy a crime-free Net. On the other hand, law enforcement agencies should endeavor to better understand the underlying technology so that Internet providers are not viewed as the primary problem but as a potential ally in the fight against crime on the Internet. With respect to this aim, industry self-regulation and law enforcement could form an ideal partnership combining the strong points of both regulatory systems in pursuing their common interests.

1.3 The main differences between legal regulation and self-regulation

The establishment of a scheme of self-regulation in addition to legal regulation first requires an analysis of the differences between these two forms of regulation, especially the strong and weak points of both systems.

Self-regulation has various advantages over legal regulation:

- Self-regulation is implemented by the parties which are directly concerned with the respective problems. They have at their disposal the necessary remedies to solve the problems immediately (such as the technical know-how and capacity to promptly block illegal and harmful content or the log files necessary to trace back the perpetrators). Law enforcement agencies on the other hand, first have to familiarize themselves with the relevant problems and then resort to industry to get factual problems on the Net solved.
- Self-regulation is more flexible and often offers a quicker response than legal regulation. Industry can change its practices and select new and better ways immediately, whereas legal regulation is bound to the rule of law which often requires difficult and time-consuming parliamentary processes to change the relevant legislation.
- Self-regulation is also more "international" than legal regulation. The Internet industry, and especially multinational companies, can easily work together on an international level. The decisions of law enforcement agencies, on the other hand, (such as a search and seizure order) are only valid on the territory of the issuing state and require time-consuming processes of mutual and judicial

cooperation (often having to go through official channels within the respective ministries of justice) in order to be enforceable in other states.

However, there are also considerable strong points to legal regulations:

- Legal regulation is binding for all citizens addressed by that legislation. Contrary to that, self-regulation is non-binding and often does not affect all parties concerned (such as all content providers or all host service providers on the Internet).

- Legal regulation is by nature enforceable by defined and generally available state force, whereas self-regulation per se depends on this state force to be compulsorily enforceable (this also applies to minorities within the "self" of regulation which do not act responsibly).

- Legal regulation is based on a democratic parliamentary decision. Self-regulation – depending on the "self" of regulation – is often only represented by a specific interest group (such as the Internet providers) without participation of other concerned parties (such as parents or educators). For that reason, legal regulation has often a stronger moral authority than industry self-regulation. This might be especially important when dealing with private "censorship" of illegal contents.

As a consequence, illegal content cannot be fought effectively by only one of the two regulatory systems. A mere system of industry self-regulation would not be enforceable and could not be generally applied, since not all market participants would take part in a self-regulatory system without pressure and sanctions. Similarly, a mere system of law enforcement would be doomed to failure due to the technical, fast-changing and global nature of the Internet, which can only be managed best in cooperation with the parties directly concerned.

1.4 The optimal dual system of Internet regulation

The various advantages of self-regulation and legal regulation lead us to the conclusion that an ideal regulatory system for fighting illegal content on the Internet has to *combine both forms*. Such a combination, however, should not just involve the isolated existence of both regulatory forms parallel to one another. The optimal system for achieving specific results can only be reached through a mutual and interactive existence of both where each complements the other in relevant areas.

Some examples help to illustrate this. Self-regulation can, for example, be made enforceable by legal means, e.g., if non-binding agreements of self-regulation are incorporated into binding contracts which are armed with sanctions agreed by the contracting parties. Similarly, legal enforcement can be supported by industry self-regulation (e.g., by concrete tip-offs by Internet providers with respect to the location of illegal contents, to perpetrators or to relevant evidence). Moreover, the dearth of democratic representation of concerned parties in the development of many forms of self-regulation can be counterbalanced by involving various interest groups or by enacting self-regulatory agreements in legal provisions.

These examples illustrate that the coordination of the two regulation systems can be developed in a creative process, preferably involving dialogue between all the parties concerned. With respect to this process the question arises whether it is limited merely within the realms of creativity and effectiveness or whether any further rules or limitations arise when combining the two regulatory schemes.

1.5 The basic role of law

The coordination of the two regulation systems must respect one fundamental rule and limitation, based on the hierarchy of the two regulatory systems, namely: In cases of conflict between these two forms of regulation, existing legal regulation (hard law) has primacy over self-regulation (soft law). When developing the coordination between the two regulation systems, it must therefore be kept in mind that existing binding legal regulations will supersede self-regulation. An example for this could involve the conflict between the transfer of evidence provided for under self-regulation and civil liberties regulated by law. Such a delivery of evidence to the police would not be possible if this infringes on the secrecy of telecommunications or the protection of privacy of Internet users. In many cases, failure to respect legal regulations could even have severe consequences for self-regulatory schemes, exposing all parties concerned to criminal liability. An example for such consequences would be where a hotline requests that all incidents of child pornography found on the Net be e-mailed to them, but the transfer (by users) or even the possession (of the hotline) of such content constitutes a crime within the relevant jurisdiction.

However, the need to respect the rule of law applies not only to industry but also to law enforcement agencies. This means that existing legal regulations have primacy over enforcement practices. It would therefore not be possible for law enforcement agencies to come to an agreement with industry not to prosecute Internet providers in specific cases if this violated a legal duty to prosecute all crimes (as is the ground rule for prosecution in many European states). As a consequence, it is not easily possible for law enforcement agencies to freely determine "best practice" approaches, since all parties involved are bound by the rule of law. In particular, the acts of law enforcement agencies are regulated by law in great detail in order to protect citizens against state arbitrariness and abuse of power.

When trying to implement best practices within the present context both for private sector self-regulation and police law enforcement, one must therefore first take into account and analyze the binding legal framework. Only within this framework can best-practice approaches be evaluated *de lege lata*. And only on the basis of this existing framework can proposals for law reform be developed *de lege ferenda*.

Yet, when developing best-practice approaches for industry and law enforcement agencies, the primacy of law can be superseded by law reform. This is especially important since any regulation is a dynamic process and must be steadily adapted, especially in the fast changing area of information technology. This ever-changing process and dynamism of the law also covers the relationship between legislation and self-regulation, which can be adapted if better solutions for the coordination of the two mechanisms are found. As a consequence, the present analysis must not only deal with the development of regulation and self-regulation according to the present law, but also with respect to law reform.

However, the possibility of law reform does not permit a neglect of existing legal regulation and a reversion to the free development of best-practice approaches. Especially with respect to the practical implementation of best-practice approaches, it is important to know whether they can be applied in accordance with existing legislation. If this is the case, the implementation in most cases is relatively easy and can be done by the concerned parties themselves (e.g., industry or law enforcement agencies). On the other hand, if law reform is required, the legislator must be addressed, which requires a time-consuming process. For that reason, it is important to first analyze the existing basic legal framework with respect to Internet content concerns before turning to the development of law enforcement and self-regulatory practices and best-practice approaches. This sequence of analysis is also important with respect to an efficient description of the present empirical situation, which is to a great extent defined by existing legislation.

This leads to the following consequences: we first need an analysis of the basic legal framework for Internet content regulation, before turning to best-practice approaches for law enforcement and

328

then to the coordination of self-regulation with legal regulation. This consideration determines the sequence of this report. Each section will aim to find best-practice approaches for an optimal dual regulation and a new alliance of state and industry regulation for preventing illegal and harmful contents on the Internet. The following chapter on legal regulation aims at setting the ideal basic framework both for industry and state regulation (infra 2). The chapter on law enforcement seeks to provide best-practice solutions for effective state prosecution supported by industry efforts (infra 3). The final part on self-regulation will develop principles for optimizing legal compliance and legal enforcement of industry self-regulation (infra 4).

2 Legal regulation: providing the basic framework

A complete legal framework for the development of self-regulation with respect to illegal and harmful content on the Internet would touch a broad variety of legal issues. It would not only include the above-mentioned question in how far the Internet industry is responsible for third-party content. It would additionally have to cover various questions of substantive criminal law, such as: What are the various criminal law provisions on illegal and harmful contents on the Internet (e.g., pornography, hate speech, defamation, copyright infringements, illegal gambling, etc.)? What are the main differences between the various national statutes, and is there any possibility of finding a common denominator for various national legal regimes providing minimum rules? In addition, many issues of procedural law would have to be solved, such as: Do law enforcement agencies have a duty to prosecute or do they have a margin of discretion? What are the (formal and substantive) requirements for providers to hand over the data of their users to law enforcement agencies? In some cases, the questions of procedural law would also require an analysis of telecommunications law and data protection law. Examples of such questions are: Can voluntary cooperation between Internet providers and law enforcement agencies (e.g., by offering access to customer data) constitute an infringement of privacy or violate the secrecy of telecommunications? To what extent can providers support foreign prosecuting agencies? All these questions are important for benchmarking an ideal practice of law enforcement by the police and an ideal coordination of self-regulation and legal regulation.

A comprehensive comparative study of these questions is not possible within the scope of this project. Such a study is also not desirable within the present context, since it could overlap with the work of other international organizations dealing with the international harmonization of substantive criminal law, criminal procedural law, copyright law or data protection law. Moreover, an analysis of these questions is not possible here since many of their solutions are to be found within a context much wider than the scope of the present study (see Sieber 1998a).

Therefore, the following analysis of the legal framework is limited to the question of the responsibility of Internet providers for third-party content. This question is the central starting point for any deliberation of Internet self-regulation by the Internet industry. It is important not only to analyze the underlying technical questions and various legal responsibility regimes, but also to develop proposals and best practices for the legal regulation in this decisive area of law which provides the basic legal framework both for law enforcement and Internet self-regulation.

The following technical findings on these questions (infra 2.1) originate from a detailed technical analysis on the technical control possibilities of Internet providers (Sieber 1999a). The subsequent legal comparative analysis (infra 2.2) is based on a comparative study of illegal and harmful contents and the responsibility of Internet providers on behalf of the German Ministry of Justice (Sieber 1999c;

1999e). The recommendations for legal policy (infra 2.3) are based on a study for the European Commission with respect to computer crime (Sieber 1998a) and on legal opinions, prepared for the German Ministry of Research with respect to the new German Teleservices Act (Sieber unpublished).

2.1 The underlying technical aspects

The legal responsibility of Internet providers cannot be developed theoretically at the legislative table using parallels to existing traditional media. Instead, when assessing the responsibility of Internet providers, any legal discussion must first be preceded by an analysis of the technical possibilities of action by the provider. With respect to this question and the resulting legal responsibility regime, the persons responsible for the network infrastructure must be differentiated according to functions. Among the persons active in computer networks, the following function-carrying operatives – with differing possibilities of control – should be differentiated:

- network providers (providing the network),
- access providers (providing access to the network),
- host service providers (providing the computer systems – known as servers – through which the data is not only transmitted but also stored).

In principle the network and access providers have very limited possibilities of controlling and barring contents transferred on the Internet. From a technical perspective, this lies above all in the large amount of data conveyed on the Internet, in the encryption of data (which already occurs through the mere use of differing algorithms), and in the impossibility of carrying out a real time control of the content transferred. However, a comprehensive monitoring of the flow of data by network and access providers would not only be technically impossible but also undesirable for policy reasons. It is not just public contents which are conveyed over the Internet but also – in many formats, often unknown and encrypted – private correspondence and other confidential information. An effective "filtering" solution would therefore require an extensive control mechanism and ultimately an encryption ban. This would mean not only a blatant violation of the right to secrecy of telecommunications, but also a complete monitoring of citizens. This was indeed attempted – unsuccessfully – in the People's Republic of China, but is unimaginable in a constitutional democracy. "Isolation strategies" within computer networks spanning the globe – which formed the basis of the above-mentioned Munich state law suit against the former managing director of the German company CompuServe GmbH (Sieber 1998b) – are therefore no longer feasible. Possibilities of control for access and network providers would only then come into consideration in specific cases where particular data are evaluated before their transfer (e.g., by so-called labels or watermarks), identified as being safe from manipulation, and could – without violating the secrecy of telecommunications – be analyzed in real time. Furthermore, several generalized blocking methods with respect to specific data collections (such as specific server addresses or Internet services) are possible; however, these control mechanisms can easily be circumvented and can also have a detrimental influence on the free flow of information and on free speech. For that reason, a responsibility of service providers merely providing transmission or Internet access, without additional storage or content functions is only possible in certain exceptional situations.

Effective solutions for preventing illegal content from entering global data networks therefore cannot function mainly as a form of dataflow control, but rather should concentrate – through closer European and international coordination – on the host service providers, who store illegal content for a prolonged period. The technical analysis shows that host service providers who are responsible for the server systems frequently cannot reliably control their data store because of the large amount of data. However, where these host service providers have knowledge of illegal content, then a control and possible barring of known data is possible and often also reasonably expected. In legal terms, the possibility of an effective "notice and take down" procedure arises in particular. This means: The host service provider with awareness of and, in particular, with concrete knowledge about illegal content, can be obliged to control and to delete or block the named data. On implementation of such a "notice and take down" procedure (e.g., by criminal law sanction of an omission to block illegal content where knowledge thereof exists), Internet users, performing rights societies and other associations can contribute to a "clean Internet" by means of appropriate notifications to the provider, supplemented by internationally networked reporting offices and hotlines. They, in addition to victims and users (without having a monopoly gateway for notices), can inform the relevant providers.

There is therefore agreement among experts within the area of network technology that an appropriate "notice and take down" approach is the most effective solution in the fight against illegal content in data networks. For this reason the European Commission has also been promoting similar projects since 1998.[2] On the other hand, national "isolation strategies" (in particular, the blocking of particular Internet material abroad) have generally proven to be ineffective (Sieber 1999a). This technical insight has already – especially in recent years, albeit in differing ways – influenced the respective responsibility regimes in many countries. However, not all countries' legislating bodies possess this insight!

2   See http://www2.echo.lu/iap/position/de.html (As of: 22 March 2000).

2.2 The various responsibility regimes

2.2.1 Regulation models and legislative techniques

Upon legal comparison, the provisions on the responsibility of those in charge of the Internet infrastructure appear as differing regulation models, which, however, overlap to some extent and can be found as a combination of several approaches in individual legal systems.

– In numerous legal systems, the responsibility of Internet providers for communication offenses of third parties is still regulated solely according to the provisions of the special part of criminal law in conjunction with the general criminal law principles on the differentiation between positive action and omission, the guarantor's duty in criminal law as well as the general rules on secondary participation. Very broadly speaking, it can be asserted that these rules frequently lead to an extensive exclusion of responsibility for network and access providers as well as a limited responsibility for host service providers where they have knowledge of illegal content. However, it also occurs that stricter responsibility regulations are derived from the general criminal law norms.

– Some legal systems additionally use special press law regulations particularly relating to the "cascade liability" of publishers and editors, as well as other solution methods based on press law, which either can apply to the Internet by analogy, or were expressly made applicable by the legislator. However, there can be considerable differences between these provisions in the various legal systems: In some cases they lead to liability privileges for the Internet provider and in others to a tightening of liability. The solution methods based on press law are aimed primarily at particular censuring obligations of the provider for contents under his control, at an identification of offenders by the provider as well as an obligation of the service providers to appoint a responsible agent. However, the current legislative reform is

334

tending not to an application of solution methods based on press law but rather to the development of independent norms for electronic communication services.

–   More recent approaches in different legal systems take account of the peculiarities of communication in computer networks and provide, either in cross-section regulations applying generally (e.g., in Germany and in the corresponding directive proposal by the European Commission) or in provisions affecting specific areas of the law (as in the USA for example), independent responsibility regulations for mass communication in computer systems, in particular on the Internet. Above all, a differentiation is made here between the responsibility of the network and access providers (who are widely granted a full exemption from criminal responsibility and a far-reaching exemption from civil liability) and the responsibility of host service providers (who, with knowledge or awareness of illegal contents, must take reasonably expected barring measures). Here the approach involving a "notice and take down" procedure is increasingly being imposed on the host service providers. This means that host service providers, upon notification of illegal content, must bar or delete the appropriate data. A system can therefore be created, which – in connection with internationally networked hotlines and reporting offices and incorporating the network user – can lead to a worldwide removal of illegal content on the Internet. Proactive control obligations of the host service provider on the other hand, are usually not adopted, but do appear in some legal systems (in particular, Sweden).

–   Certain legal systems regulate the responsibility for Internet contents not, or not entirely, by statute, but rather grant public or half-public bodies certain competencies. Such a "procedural model" for the responsibility of individual providers on the Internet exists in the form of an "administrative model" in Japan. A corresponding procedural approach for the determination of what material is harmful to minors has existed for some time in Germany in the traditional media area; following a supplementation of the Act on the Dissemination of Publications and Media Content Harmful to Youth (GjSM) this is now also applicable to the Internet. Similarly in Australia, illegal content on the Internet are now classified by the Australian Classification Board or the Classification Review Board. In France, there are proposals to integrate such interdiction orders into criminal procedural law.

- A special objective going beyond these approaches of regulating responsibility is found in more recent proposals – especially in the U.S. – which are not only geared to the regulation of control measures by the Internet providers, but provide for further specific obligations of the Internet providers. These include above all the free provision of filtering software by the Internet providers. With the help of this filtering software, a minor's confrontation with harmful material can be avoided; however, the relevant proposals are not suited for the fight against child pornography and other "absolutely" (i.e., prohibited also with respect to its being passed on among adults). Moreover, proposals exist – in particular in the Netherlands – aimed at the identification of offenders by the Internet providers. More recent US reform proposals aim to require Internet providers, upon gaining knowledge of child pornography material, to give notice thereof, as well as to no longer allow convicted offenders Internet access.

- In the Anglo-American legal systems above all, much emphasis is given to the self-regulation of those affected, besides legal measures. Firstly, the development of codes of conduct is promoted, under which Internet providers agree to observe certain rules and in some cases to co-operate with the criminal law enforcement authorities. In various countries, especially in Australia, these codes of conduct are closely interwoven with the legal system. The codes of conduct of international online providers could, in the form of a "soft law," thereby prove to be a forerunner of a

336

"worldwide uniform law." In addition to this, there are industry-controlled areas of content and filtering techniques. Finally, reporting offices or hotlines are encouraged, sometimes involving state bodies. The hotlines are intended to draw the attention of host service providers to illegal contents, so that the relevant data can be deleted and must be deleted – in accordance with the above mentioned "notice and take down" procedure.

2.2.2 Content criteria for responsibility regulations

While the choice of one of the aforementioned regulation models is not mandatory in determining the contents for responsibility regulations, it is often connected with the content criteria. This connection between the formal regulation model and the material content of the provisions is based above all on the current standpoint and level of technical knowledge of the persons responsible for legislative reform.

– Where legal doctrine and literature adopt general liability norms and regard provider responsibility solely as a question of overcoming technical consequences, the result is at times strict responsibility regulations. With respect to general civil liability provisions, this is stressed in some parts of German legal literature by referring to strict liability, which is used elsewhere with respect to new industrial-technical dangers. However, the new information-based aspect of the issue is not considered (in particular the effects of the responsibility regulation on freedom of expression and protection of telecommunications secrecy and privacy).

– Countries that do not place emphasis on the peculiarities of electronic communication in computer networks, but rather on the parallels to the traditional media, tend towards a "publisher's" liability for the providers of online services, servers and network services. Even where such a conformity with solution methods based on press law exists, the know-how on technical control possibilities by the provider and the protection of tele-communications secrecy and privacy are not given much consideration. On the basis of this approach, the access and network providers are therefore usually burdened with control duties, which, in turn, is usually incumbent on the "reasonableness" requirement; this then leads to complicated technical and legal issues in the assessment of individual cases.

- Countries or supranational organizations who, on the basis of experience with the Internet, develop special solution methods for electronic information and communication services, are quickly faced with the technical realization outlined above, that access barring is of limited technical and legal value at least at the present time, and that, in addition, a complete content control of large volumes of data is technically impossible. Especially in countries with a strong tradition of free speech and/or privacy protection, it is realized that this Internet-specific differentiation between access providing and host service providing is necessary in order to protect constitutional values on the Internet (such as freedom of information, secrecy of telecommunication or privacy protection). As a consequence, a simple qualification such as "what is illegal off-line must be illegal online" is considered to be correct with respect to content providers, but cannot easily be applied with respect to the responsibility of technical Internet providers, given the cross-border nature of the problem and the mixed roles that service providers perform. In the majority of countries with Internet-specific responsibility legislation, these criteria lead to the exclusion of (criminal) responsibility for access and network providers as well as to a limitation of liability for the host service provider with knowledge or awareness of illegal content. The recognition of this technical reality thereby is combined with the development of specific regulative approaches,

338

particularly the "notice and take down" procedures, which can be expanded through the use of internationally networked hotlines and reporting offices to become an effective means of fighting illegal content in computer networks.

2.3 Recommendation of best practices

2.3.1 Legislative technique

When evaluating the different international methods with the aim of recommending best practices, it is first necessary to decide if a specific legal regulation on responsibility for computer networks and electronic communication services is necessary. The answer to this question must be in the affirmative because of the special technical control problems in computer networks and the legal peculiarities of a responsibility regulation for information systems (under which the principles of freedom of information and the safeguarding of the secrecy of telecommunications are to be taken into account). Therefore, the solution to the difficult question of responsibility cannot be left to the criminal courts on the basis of general criminal provisions on secondary participation. The same applies for the civil law dogma on allocation of responsibility. Otherwise, legal certainty, which is necessary for the quick development of the Internet and an effective protection against illegal content, and common competition conditions within the information industry, would not be guaranteed for many years to come. But likewise, the general press law regulations (in particular on cascade liability) are also not suited to the peculiarities of computer networks and electronic communication systems. The criteria of legal certainty, the free cross-border flow of data and an effective fight against illegal content therefore clearly bolster the need for a specific legal regulation.

A further question arising with respect to the legislative technique is whether responsibility in computer networks – as in Germany and in the recent directive proposal from the EC Commission – should be legislated in a general cross-section regulation for all legal areas or whether – as in the USA – a more comprehensive differentiation according to individual causes of liability and legal areas is necessary. The general cross-sectional regulation has the advantages of providing the service providers with legal certainty and uniformity. However, the concept of regulations for specific legal areas also depends largely on the precision of the legal regulation. Provisions like those in the USA naturally require a more careful consideration of specific facets arising in the particular legal areas, for example with respect to the amount of information necessary to equal "knowledge" of illegal content in the field of criminal responsibility (e.g., child pornography) or in the domain of copyright law with respect to awareness of facts or circumstances from which illegal activity is apparent. If workable technical measures are developed for copyright protection (for example the labelling of protected works by "watermarks" or copyright management systems) then a special responsibility regulation for copyright infringements could also take account of peculiarities of this kind. It would therefore appear a general cross-sectional regulation is preferable; indeed, this does not rule out supplements and amendments relating to specific legal areas, particularly in the case of detailed provisions.

With respect to the legislative technique, it is also necessary to examine to what extent statutory provisions should be complimented by procedural models, by which means, for example, yardsticks for technical access control systems could be flexibly laid down. This procedural route should only be followed – bearing in mind the administrative costs involved – when legal administrators are not in a position to quickly implement the legal proposals. However, a necessary basis for such a solution based on the judiciary involves not only specialized judges, but also an adequate legal technique which avoids technical definitions, yet provides guidelines for future

340

interpretation of the content. In the event that the procedural model continues to be followed because of unsatisfactory judicial results, it is then necessary to examine to what extent a process of self-regulation of those affected should be incorporated into this model.

2.3.2 *Content of responsibility regulations*

The remarks above, relating to the issue of which regulation model should be adopted, show that the contents of a responsibility regulation should not be orientated along the lines of traditional solutions based on press law, but rather the technical peculiarities of information and communication services. Due to the existing technical control difficulties described above, as well as the protection of information freedom and telecommunications secrecy, this leads almost invariably to a differentiating solution in criminal law, as is the case in German and US law and in the recent EC Commission directive proposal. In practice this means an exemption from criminal and tort liability for the access and network providers, while for the host service provider the "notice and take down" procedure described above should be applied, which limits criminal and tort liability to cases where the provider has knowledge (or – in specific areas such as copyright infringements – awareness of facts and circumstances from which illegal activity is apparent) and which excludes proactive monitoring obligations. More comprehensive proposals – in particular concerning access bars for specific IP addresses on the part of access providers or monitoring duties on the part of the host service provider – should be left to be covered by claims for injunctions in civil law and actions under administrative law, instead of introducing legal uncertainty into a criminal procedure unsuitable to clarify future technical control possibilities.

Within this differentiating solution, specific legal clarifications could be necessary, not only – as was the case up to now – with respect to proxy-cache servers, but also for links, search engines and other forms of information location tools (Sieber 1999b). In individual areas (e.g., copyright infringements), it may prove necessary, following the US model, to create particular regulations – e.g., with respect to knowledge or awareness of illegal content – or to legally incorporate more recent technical developments, e.g., in the domain of "watermarks" used to identify material protected by copyright.

This differentiating model would create the ideal legal framework for industry self-regulation. It would provide the Internet industry with the necessary scope to develop "notice and take down" procedures to be administered by self-regulatory agencies such as hotlines. Adopting such "notice and take down" procedures and hotlines would limit criminal sanctions to acts clearly constituting criminal offenses and form an effective industry mechanism for enforcing self-regulation (supra 2.2 and 2.3.3). At the same time, the state would still retain its arsenal of administrative orders should industry self-regulation not function properly.

Additionally, legal regulations aimed at preventing illegal contents in computer networks could help bring industry self-regulation and new technical solutions into even more use. Future efforts should therefore incorporate further legal and non-legal models going beyond the responsibility regulation. An example for supplementary legal provisions are the proposed obligations in the USA and France to install filtering software, or to provide available information on infringers. A further example is the US proposal of a duty on the part of the provider to notify the authorities in cases of serious crime. Since these additional measures concern the coordination of legal regulation and self-regulation, they are dealt with in the following chapter. The present chapter and the recommendation therein are limited to the basic legal model of responsibility.

Recommendation: Creating a basic responsibility framework

The fight against illegal content in computer networks is a complex task, which can no longer be appropriately overcome with classical responsibility regulations or methods based on general press law. Rather, specific statutory solutions and other additional legal measures are required. The basis for the development of these solutions necessarily involves consideration being given to the technical characteristics of computer networks. It must also consider the legal peculiarities of a responsibility regulation for information systems, which have to take into account the protection of information freedom, telecommunications secrecy and the right to privacy. Furthermore, the responsibility regime should enable and enforce industry self-regulation as far as possible.

An analysis of the legal solutions available relating to the issue of Internet provider responsibility worldwide shows that national and supranational instruments which are ideally fulfilling these aims should limit and clarify civil and criminal liability of the Internet industry for third party contents in a differentiated way.

As in the US legislation and the EU draft directive on electronic commerce, access and network providers should not be responsible for third parties' illegal content transmissions taking place in real-time through their networks, since international information flows cannot be controlled and must remain free. Exceptionally, if obligations for access and network providers to restrict access (e.g., to specific Internet addresses) should exist at all, then they should only be based on binding administrative orders or civil law injunctions (subject to means of legal redress before their enforcement).

Service providers merely storing third party contents should be held liable only if they have concrete knowledge of illegal information (or – in specific areas such as copyright infringements – awareness of facts and circumstances from which illegal activity is apparent), and if a removal of illegal content is technically possible and can reasonably be expected. The regulation of such "notice and take down" procedures or the establishment of such policies should specify the requirements for a proper notification of that host service provider. The legislation could also define rules allowing service providers to remove or disclose illegal activity in cases of uncertainty, including an exemption with respect to the contractual liability of Internet providers in cases where the provider, acting in good faith, blocks what he believes to be illegal content. The Digital Millennium Copyright Act in the USA, for example, provides a liability limitation for the service provider if it simply takes down material of which it receives notice is illegal, and protects the service provider from liability if that notice turns out to be wrong.

Within this differentiated liability regime for host service providers (storing third party content) and access and network providers (only transmitting third party content), the role of caching as well as specific information tools (such as search engines or links) should be clarified. One might also develop specific rules or procedures in cases where illegal content can only be removed or blocked together as a package of data, the vast majority of which is legal (as is the case, e.g., with the closing of a newsgroup containing only a small percentage of illegal news or the blocking of a server with only a small percentage of illegal websites).

Such a legal regulation could be an ideal prerequisite for developing and fostering industry self-regulation. "Notice and take down procedures" for the legal responsibility of host service providers can become a decisive link between legal regulation and Internet self-regulation. Self-regulatory bodies such as hotlines could evaluate user complaints and other information on illegal content and inform the responsible host service provider about justified complaints thus providing for their knowledge of, and the resulting duty to remove, the said content.

The relationship between the legal system and self-regulation must be analyzed in more detail and in a broader context in chapter 4. However, in order to fully understand and develop the relationship between legal regulation and self-regulation, it is first necessary to complement theoretical law with law in practice, in particular by examining the area of law enforcement in more detail.

3 Law enforcement: securing effective prosecution

State law enforcement is the basic arsenal to prevent, detect, investigate and prosecute illegal content on the Internet. This state reaction is essential for various reasons: It guarantees the state monopoly on power and public order, it is democratically legitimized and directly enforceable and it secures justice, equality and legal certainty.

In all democratic states subject to the rule of law, the activities of law enforcement agencies are, to a great extent, determined by substantive and procedural law. With respect to illegal content on the Internet, these include in particular the above-described responsibility laws, the specific prohibitions of criminal laws on illegal content as well as procedural law provisions on coercive powers, the use of evidence and obligations/discretion for prosecution. A detailed comparative analysis of these legal questions has been undertaken in the COMCRIME Study for the European Commission (Sieber 1998a) and further comparative legal work in this area is presently being carried out by the Council of Europe, the European Commission and the G-8 Working Group on High-Tech Crime. However, the work of law enforcement also depends on political and administrative structures, allocation of funds, technical know-how and international cooperation.

These provisions and factors vary to a great extent in different countries. Since it is neither possible nor desirable within the present context to repeat the above-mentioned comparative study or to duplicate the work of other international bodies on the harmonization of criminal procedural law by undertaking a further comprehensive legal analysis of all these issues, the following chapter focuses on a description of the law in action. This must be kept in mind when implementing the resulting recommendations at the end of the analysis. Since these recommendations take the form of best practice methods, their implementation into each legal system must give consideration to existing legal rules. Thus, the incorporation of these recommendations will require legal amendments in some countries while in other legal regimes this may be possible on the basis of existing law.

The results and recommendations of this chapter are not only founded on the above-mentioned previous studies. In addition, they are based on a written questionnaire distributed via the Network of the Bertelsmann Foundation to representatives within law enforcement, Internet industry and other administrative and private organizations, and – with the help of the German Federal Crime Office (BKA) – among participants of the G-8 Working Group on High-Tech Crime (Lyon Group). Based on the results of the questionnaire, 25 face-to-face interviews were conducted with law enforcement representatives from Germany (including representatives from the Federal and State Crime Offices), the United Kingdom (from New Scotland Yard, the National Criminal Intelligence Service and other regional police forces), the USA (including representatives from the F.B.I. and the US Department of Justice), Australia, Singapore, France and the Netherlands. Interviews were also carried out with representatives from the Internet industry (including Internet watchbodies), hotlines and child protection organizations.[3] Due to the limited amount of time available for the present study, it cannot claim to provide a complete picture of the law in action but rather a

---

3   I am most indebted to Mr. Ivan Waide for conducting the interviews, and for his help with the present study.

cross-section of "online law enforcement," in order to provide best practice approaches supporting a new alliance of law enforcement and industry.

The following section concentrates on those questions which are essential for an effective control and prosecution of illegal content by law enforcement agencies. Therefore, it deals especially with the need to create effective organizations (infra 3.1), determine the main focus of practical law enforcement (infra 3.2), ensure an effective gathering of evidence (infra 3.3), improve international law enforcement (infra 3.4) and – most important in the present context – develop a better cooperation between law enforcement and Internet industry (infra 3.5).

3.1 Creating effective organizations

3.1.1 Developing adequate structures and types of organizations

The organizational structure of "law enforcement" involved in combating illegal content on the Internet is a complex one. Even by separating the task of law enforcement into the functions of prevention, detection, investigation and prosecution, it already becomes clear that in most countries a complex combination of various different bodies are involved in the process. The responsible bodies in the various countries can be of a state, administrative, private or hybrid nature. This structure is further complicated by the fact that they can be structured either in a centralized or decentralized way. Moreover, the task of law enforcement with respect to illegal contents is tackled within most countries using a combination of both specialized and non-specialized units.

The existence of a multilateral and diverse combination of organizational bodies involved in the prosecution of illegal Internet content is a natural and historical consequence of having to quickly adapt to a relatively new phenomenon, namely the spread of illegal content on the Internet. Such a multilateral approach, however, has several disadvantages: The complex variety of bodies renders a coordinated approach difficult, particularly with respect to law enforcement agencies. Most cases relating to illegal content on the Internet are still reported at the local level, yet there is perceived to be a general lack of resources and the necessary know-how to effectively deal with these notifications and subsequent investigations at this level. It is sometimes difficult to clearly define and allocate competencies, and some local law enforcement agencies are uncertain where expert help can be sought with respect to particular investigations. The lack of clearly defined competencies and points of contact also presents a problem to foreign law enforcement agencies seeking assistance in particular transnational cases.

Recommendation: Creating effective organizations

In each country it is a top priority to create adequate law enforcement bodies to combat computer crime and the problem of illegal content on the Internet. This is necessary for all levels of law enforcement, including prevention, detection, investigation and prosecution, and can be achieved by developing centralized units and/or a better coordination of existing competent bodies.

Especially in federalist countries, the law enforcement organization must reflect the federal political structure. Nevertheless, an effective fight against computer and Internet crime will require some centralized units. These can act as centers of excellence for computer crime issues, lending informed support and training to local forces when required. They can also help coordinate national and international law enforcement, determine trends and emerging threats and thus prioritize scarce resources and law enforcement activities in this area.

If more centralized organizations are created in federalist systems, fears of an overly centralized and bureaucratic organization can be overcome by staffing the relevant bodies representatively and at least partly with rotating personnel from decentralized agencies, thus also improving training, personal contacts and co-operation within and between the various bodies. Similarly, any centralized approach should ensure that competence is reserved for local law enforcement agencies, who can provide a more timely response to individual cases at a local level and play an indispensable role in the mechanics of the investigation (e.g., by using their local knowledge for search and seizure of evidence). They could then resort to a national unit or focal points where a particular level of expertise is required.

Furthermore, it is vital to coordinate the activities of the competent organizations on a higher level. This applies both on the national and supranational level (e.g., with respect to coordination by Interpol, Europol and G-8). This could be achieved by introducing national/international operational and investigative best practices to ensure the quality of investigations, avoid redundant work and facilitate interagency case referrals. Theses "standards" should be developed in a collaborative process and could cover topics such as case management, information sharing, preventive measures, training and the selection of law enforcement personnel.

A better coordination of law enforcement activities can also be achieved by improving communication channels between the various organizations. It is necessary to create "focal points" within the respective bodies, which can serve as points of reference for operational enquiries at a national and supranational level. These points of reference should possess technical expertise where the necessary know-how is readily accessible and where valuable training and scarce resources can be best exploited.

In addition, the work of law enforcement should be supported by, and coordinated with, appropriate administrative bodies and private organizations. In particular, private bodies can play an important role in the prevention and detection of illegal Internet content, e.g., by providing preventive and educational campaigns or operating "hotlines" processing notifications of illegal Internet content.

3.1.2 *Providing sufficient resources*

Computer crime is threatening the backbone of our information society. Illegal and harmful Internet contents especially pose a grave risk for children since they can seriously affect their lives, physical and social development. It is therefore necessary to funnel adequate resources into combating these dangers. However, the empirical study shows that the availability of sufficient funding for computer crime in general and the prevention, detection, investigation and prosecution of illegal and harmful contents in particular, varies considerably from one country to another.[4]

The general consensus of law enforcement, however, is that there is a major lack of resources among law enforcement for effectively combating illegal Internet content as well as other forms of computer crime. While the level of funding allocated by government to law enforcement in general is often perceived to be adequate, there is widespread agreement that individual law enforcement agencies are not directing enough of these resources towards combating computer crime and illegal contents but are instead prioritizing other, more traditional crime-types.

---

4   In the 1998 Budget, the US Congress provided the FBI with $10 million for one national initiative alone, known as "Innocent Images," directed at online child pornography and child sexual exploitation investigations. This allowance by Congress is reviewed and given to the Innocent Images program on an annual basis. In contrast, estimates have put the UK budget in this area at less than £2 million.

350

Recommendation: Providing sufficient resources

There should be sufficient funding for adequate personnel and material (especially technical) resources within law enforcement agencies dealing with computer crime, which is jeopardizing the fundamental foundations of today's information society. More priority should be given to this area both at the levels of allocation to, and reallocation of resources within the competent authorities.

It is therefore essential that prosecuting agencies should allocate more of their budget to the computer crime area, both at the central and local level. These funds must be distributed with respect to both general computer crime (e.g., fraud, hacking, espionage and terrorism) and specifically to combat illegal Internet contents (e.g., child pornography and enticement, bestiality, hate speech and copyright infringements). In both areas, sufficient funds must be available for all stages of law enforcement. In order to achieve adequate funding, greater awareness should be created of these dangers and the serious effects they are having.

3.1.3 Ensuring adequate training

The speed of evolution of Internet technology is presenting law enforcement with new technical challenges. Traditional methods of detecting crime, gathering evidence, identifying and tracking down the perpetrators and obtaining efficient prosecution will experience more and more changes as technology itself advances. Challenges already exist with respect to detecting Internet crime in an environment where no border controls exist and where the "goods" are intangible masses of information, sometimes encrypted, passing in real time or both. Likewise, encryption, anonymous accounts and the transnational nature of the Internet also make the process of gathering evidence and identifying the perpetrator more difficult.

351

These are just a few of the challenges which law enforcement is facing, and as technology evolves so too shall these challenges.

The provision of training and level of technical expertise varies substantially from jurisdiction to jurisdiction and within different levels of national law enforcement. It would appear to be better at the national/federal level, but generally there is perceived to be a lack of such IT expertise or adequate training within all levels of law enforcement, ranging from police forces through to prosecutors and judges, particularly at the local level. This deficiency usually derives from a lack of resources. Indeed, many law enforcers complain that no IT training whatsoever is being offered to prosecutors and judges at the local level. A further factor for this lack of IT know-how among law enforcers is the fact that in many countries such as Germany and the United Kingdom, neither IT training nor online law enforcement forms a core element of the basic law enforcement training given to new police recruits.

However, in the USA it appears that law enforcement at the Federal level is relatively well-equipped to cope with the new challenges which online law enforcement is facing. Federal organizations such as the FBI possess special units that are often well-trained and funded. Indeed, the FBI actively engages in providing training programs both for its own personnel and representatives from other law enforcement agencies at the local level. The level of IT training and expertise is also perceived to be higher at the national level in other countries such as the UK. Besides the provision of training, technical expertise is also drawn from the civilian sector in many countries.

It is most essential to realize that not only the criminal, but also the law enforcer can take advantage of this new technology. For example, while the nature of the Internet and its relative anonymity allow the paedophile to reach a wide audience without having to disclose his identity, these very same attribute allows law enforcement to covertly monitor his activity. It is therefore also vital that law enforcers are taught how to make best use of the new medium within all legal means to obtain an efficient prosecution of illegal content.

Recommendation: Ensuring adequate training

Law enforcement agencies dealing with computer crime must possess adequate technical know-how to ensure efficient prosecution in a highly technical and fast changing environment. This includes both the ability to proactively use the new technology to detect crime and the expertise to efficiently investigate and prosecute high-tech crime. To this end, the training must not only be comprehensive but also ongoing.

It is essential to create at least a basic awareness of the underlying technical issues among local police forces, prosecutors and the judiciary. This could include general computer literacy courses and the study of IT and data networks. Beyond this, law enforcement should be skilled in "tracking" the perpetrator. Here, the training should cover specific aspects of online law enforcement, including tracing procedures, the identification of the offender, automated tools, network protocols and server structures. Law enforcement must also be able to carry out flawless investigations without jeopardizing their case. In this area, the training should concentrate on search and seizure procedures, forensic analysis skills, best practice operational methods relating to the investigation and the underlying legal issues.

An international training symposium for law enforcers would not only raise awareness and know-how of the relevant issues but also encourage supranational law enforcement and international cooperation through the promotion of personal contacts among law enforcement agencies and common law enforcement practices.

3.2 Determining the main focus of practical law enforcement

3.2.1 Prioritizing crime types

The dawn of the information society has witnessed the widespread introduction of ever-advancing computer technology and with it the development and emergence of crime types within the field of computer crime. These include, in particular, illegal content and activities within electronic communications. Law enforcement therefore needs to allocate appropriate priority to computer crime within the context of traditional crime and in turn to specific (emerging) forms of computer crime, where particular dangers are perceived. Since the process of law enforcement with respect to criminal activities perpetrated through electronic communications involves prevention, detection, investigation and prosecution, it is vital that within this process, law enforcement affords each of these areas the priority it deserves.

Recommendation: Prioritizing crime types

Law enforcement's responsibility for fighting crime applies as much to the computer environment as to the traditional environment. Within the context of general crime, law enforcement is being increasingly confronted with computer crime and since all forms of computer crime pose a major threat to individuals, industry and society in general, law enforcement must allocate this area sufficient priority.

However, within the area of computer crime, law enforcement is faced with the problem of illegal activities generally (such as fraud, hacking, terrorism and espionage) and specifically, the problem of illegal Internet content (e.g., child pornography, hate speech and copyright infringements). With respect to their danger potential, law enforcement should afford both these crime types the attention they require.

Within illegal activities, increasing attention should be afforded to the emerging problem of Internet fraud and hacking, while within the area of illegal content, priority should be given to child pornography and exploitation and furthermore to bestiality and other pornography, hate speech, copyright infringements and defamation.

3.2.2 *Concentrating on the real perpetrators*

In the case of illegal content on the Internet, law enforcement can try to prosecute the content providers and/or make Internet service providers responsible for the content stored on or accessed via their computers. According to the empirical research of this study, law enforcement agencies claim that the overwhelming majority (on average 90 percent) of law enforcement activities is allocated to tracking down and prosecuting the authors/content providers, as opposed to the service provider. There is broad consensus that the content providers are the "main" perpetrators.

With respect to the prosecution of Internet providers there is widespread agreement among law enforcement that they should only be prosecuted where they clearly contravene the above described responsibility regimes (supra 2.3). However, it also emerges that varying and sometimes contradictory approaches from law enforcement representatives arise within the same jurisdiction – with respect to particular case scenarios. This would suggest a lack of appropriate legal provisions or proper legal clarification in some countries and/or a possible lack of understanding of these laws by law enforcement agencies with respect to the responsibility of Internet providers.

In general, it has been found in the course of the empirical study that increasing technical know-how on the part of the interviewees leads to a greater reluctance to apportion liability on mere access providers. In combination with the above technical analysis of control possibilities in the Internet, this finding supports the fact that an adequate training of law enforcement with respect to these data processing and technical aspects is not only in the interests of law enforcement agencies and the prevention of crime, but also in the interests of the Internet industry.

Recommendation: Concentrating on the real perpetrators

When prosecuting illegal content, law enforcement agencies should concentrate their efforts on tracking down and prosecuting the real perpetrator (e.g., the content provider producing or publishing the illegal content). Internet providers and self-regulatory bodies (such as hotlines) should be seen as natural allies in the pursuit of this goal. They should not be regarded as the primary problem and should therefore only be prosecuted where they contravene the above-described responsibility regimes (e.g., intentionally failing to remove illegal content from their servers after receiving adequate notification).

3.2.3 Introducing preventive measures

As has been discussed above, the fight against illegal Internet content, as with any crime, involves prevention, detection and investigation, and prosecution. Since law enforcement is charged with the task of combating such crime, the focus of their work should allow for adequate measures being taken at all these stages. However, in most countries, a lack of resources usually means that priority is given to the investigation and prosecution stages. Furthermore, in many other countries, there is simply a lack of priority given to preventive measures and activities are concentrated on detection, investigation and prosecution.

Nevertheless, in some countries, law enforcement agencies are

356

active in taking such preventive measures. In the United Kingdom, regional police forces have been proactive in providing parents and children so-called "safe-surfing" tips and information concerning the potential hazards of using the Internet. In several countries law enforcement is supported by private bodies with respect to preventive measures, particularly in the form of awareness campaigns. In the USA for example, one such initiative, dealing with the problem of online enticement of children, has been undertaken by the National Center for Missing and Exploited Children (NCMEC). In the UK, the Internet Watch Foundation has published a brochure in conjunction with industry and law enforcement relating to safe surfing.

Recommendation: Emphasizing preventive measures

Law enforcement agencies should not only concentrate on detection, investigation and prosecution of crime, but also ensure that adequate preventive measures are taken with respect to the fight against illegal Internet content. This will not only help curb the existing problem but by rendering the activity and medium less seductive, it will help prevent problems on a much greater scale in the future.

Appropriate measures include education of parents and children of the risks of "surfing," including tips on filtering software, and best practices for Internet use (e.g., placing the family computer in an open, communal room). In order to prevent online child enticement, children must be warned of the dangers of "online" conversations with strangers, in particular that they should never give their personal details or agree to meet strangers in person. Awareness campaigns should also be used to encourage users to act as responsible citizens reporting any illegal activity accidentally uncovered while surfing, thus helping in the overall detection process and ultimately contributing to a cleaner Net. Especially in the field of prevention, there are many opportunities for developing a productive cooperation between law enforcement and the private sector.

Law enforcement can take further preventive measures by investing in more skilled personnel and equipment, and in the development of new technologies (e.g., automated "tools") in conjunction with industry to combat the problem and help them stay apace with the determined criminal. Prevention should also involve making the public (and the criminal) more aware of law enforcement capabilities with respect to prosecuting offenders. If there is public knowledge about police capabilities to patrol the Net, act undercover or trace back, this can serve as an effective deterrent.

3.3 Ensuring an effective gathering of evidence

An efficient prosecution of illegal content on the Internet depends on the identification of illegal content followed by the identification of its author and an effective procurement and preservation of evidence on the part of law enforcement during the criminal investigation. In order to identify illegal content and its author, law enforcement agencies in the various countries employ a number of methods. These include the use of notifications from third parties and searching the Net manually, either overtly or covertly. Where further investigation is required, coercive powers such as search and seizure in automated information systems, wiretapping and eavesdropping or duties of action or cooperation of witnesses become relevant.

3.3.1 Using third-party input

Law enforcement can gain knowledge of the existence of illegal content on the Internet either through their own investigative activity or by relying on third-party notifications. In the case where law enforcement receives input from third parties, such notifications usually stem directly from individual users, Internet service providers or hotlines.

Generally, law enforcement still relies heavily on their own investigative activity with respect to the identification of illegal content on the Internet. In those cases where law enforcement receives third-party notifications, the vast majority of these stem from individual users (on average approximately 75 percent). Some law enforcement agencies provide special telephone numbers for users to call, or E-mail addresses on their homepage where URL addresses containing illegal content can be left. Only a small percentage of third-party notifications come from Internet providers. An increasing number of such leads come from hotlines. The proportion of third-party notifications received by law enforcement from hotlines is comparatively large in the UK, while in the USA, hotlines provide a valuable source of leads at the federal level, but would appear to play a small role at the local level. This shows that there is a great and unused support potential in the form of users, providers and hotlines, which could be mobilized by law enforcement to support in the fight against illegal content.

3.3.2 Patrolling the Net

Various law enforcement agencies, especially at the national/federal level, are actively involved in patrolling the Internet for illegal content. Generally it is found that they use all means within the rule of law to identify such content. This includes manual, overt and covert searching, and the use of specific software, including advanced search programs.

For example, in Germany, proactive patrolling of Internet chatrooms led Bavarian police to undercover paedophile activity, which ultimately resulted in the successful, internationally coordinated Operation "Bavaria" (infra 3.4). Such effective "sting" operations again show that Internet technology, in this case anonymity, can also be used to the advantage of the police.

In some countries, such as the USA, law enforcement takes a more proactive role in the gathering of evidence, particularly with respect to the problem of child online enticement within the Internet. Under the "Innocent Images" program (supra 3.1.2), FBI agents initially went online posing as children under fictitious screen names only in chatrooms. Investigations have now been extended to newsgroups, Internet relay chat and fileservers. Well-defined administrative and operational protocols have been developed by the FBI into best practice approaches, which help avoid problems likely to jeopardize a prosecution, such as entrapment. All online undercover contact is archived and stored in a database allowing prioritizing of more serious offenders. Each undercover session takes place only in predicated areas of the Internet where criminal activity is known to occur, the conversation is fully documented and the agents always play a passive role in online conversations, allowing the target to take the lead at all times. Once an individual has been targeted as a potential or priority offender, subpoenas and coercive powers may be issued to the relevant online service provider to obtain all available identifying information. All relevant data is then gathered together, including conversations and images downloaded while in contact with undercover agents, and the case can then be presented to the US Attorney's Office for prosecutive action. Since the inception of the Innocent Images initiative in 1995, the FBI has been very successful in prosecuting cases involving computer-sex offenders travelling between American states to meet minors they enticed on the Internet.

3.3.3 Developing and applying coercive powers

Legal aspects

The prosecution of illegal content on the Internet pose various general problems of criminal procedural law, e.g., with respect to the competencies for patrolling the Net and the issue of possible entrapment. As in other areas of computer crime and computer-based investigations in the data processing and data communication area, the prosecution of illegal content faces the further challenge of adapting traditional coercive powers to suit the data-processing environment. This is especially the case with respect to search and seizure in automated information systems, wiretapping and eavesdropping as well as duties of active cooperation of witnesses. Difficulties also arise with respect to mutual cooperation in international cases. As far as illegal content is concerned, further problems exist with respect to the collection, storage and transfer by service providers to law enforcement of (usually unverified) user identity and other relevant data and log-files. Administrative duties to store (especially traffic) data also play a decisive role. Most of these – more general – questions of criminal procedural law have been dealt with in the COMCRIME report for the European Commission (Sieber 1998a) and are currently being discussed in international organizations (e.g., Council of Europe and also the G8 Group on High-Tech Crime).

One concept is, however, especially worth mentioning, which is currently being developed within the respective working groups of the G8 Group on High-Tech Crime and the Council of Europe. This is the process of "fast-freeze quick-thaw" whereby a preservation order would oblige providers to freeze evidence in a fast procedure, and law enforcement should then try to obtain the necessary judicial order for delivery. Under this process, the provider does not have to store as much data as general duties for keeping log-files would require, no important data is lost, law enforcement receives the information it needs and the problem of data protection is avoided since the delivery of data has been authorized by the relevant national court and the stored data does not relate to innocent third parties but merely suspected offenders.

Recommendation: Creating adequate legal powers for investigation

Based on the respective recommendations of international and supranational bodies (especially the Council of Europe and G8), it is essential to have adequate legislative powers with respect to computer-based investigations, in particular, adequate coercive powers for search and seizure, wiretapping, eavesdropping as well as duties of active cooperation of witnesses. It should be especially helpful to make available a preservation order, which could "freeze" evidence in a fast procedure and thus leave the decision about its delivery to a court judgment. In addition, legislation could create more defined obligations on the part of the Internet provider with respect to the collection, storage and transfer to law enforcement of data relevant to investigations. Specific powers or legal clarifications should also be created by the legislator with respect to powers to patrol the Net and to act undercover as well as powers to actively participate in dialogues with potential perpetrators (also clarifying the borderline between legal undercover activities and illegal entrapment).

However, the development of these coercive powers must be based on a careful balancing of the need for effective prosecution on the one hand, with the protection of citizens against a too far-reaching intrusion into their private life, on the other.

Practical aspects

Prosecuting illegal content is faced by considerable practical difficulties. In particular, methods of encryption represent major challenges for law enforcement. It may occur that law enforcement gains power to search and seize a computer only to find the data encrypted and non-intelligible. Indeed, in their recent report entitled "Project Trawler" the UK National Criminal Intelligence Service states that "widespread effective use of robust non-recovery encryption by criminals will seriously damage law enforcement's ability to fight serious and organized crime."[5]

Law enforcement is facing other common difficulties in this area. These include the problem whereby the relevant data sought by law enforcement has already been deleted by the service provider, has never been recorded, has never existed or is false. Anonymous and fake accounts pose a serious problem for law enforcement and even though the provision of false subscriber details may constitute fraud, it remains difficult to trace the offender. Problems also occur where "whois" databases contain missing or false information and there can sometimes be difficulties obtaining information on foreign sites within the established registries. The lack of adequate mutual legal assistance can also be a major problem in tracing and identifying the perpetrator in transnational cases. There is widespread agreement among law enforcers that such problems are seriously detrimental to an efficient prosecution.

5   See NCIS Report "Project Trawler" (June 1999) at http://www.ncis.co.uk (As of: 22 March 2000).

Recommendation: Ensuring effective evidence-gathering

The process of detecting crime and gathering evidence should rely on all legal means available. Important sources for obtaining notification and evidence include complaints from users, input from industry and notifications from hotlines.

It should also include law enforcement agencies actively patrolling the Net themselves. Undercover searches within the Internet are highly effective means of obtaining evidence, but should be exercised within the rule of law. While conducting such searches it is especially important to respect the borderlines of national law prohibiting entrapment of citizens. In such cases strict administrative and operational protocols should be followed to ensure an efficient prosecution and avoid problems of entrapment.

One of the most efficient means to track down perpetrators is the development of efficient trace-back procedures on the Internet (e.g., by using log-files). The creation of a global database incorporating all existing registries would assist in the process of retrieving particular data, including domain names, IP addresses and the location of servers. Generally, there should be better cooperation between law enforcement and the Internet industry, involving an exchange of information.

3.4 Improving international law enforcement

The Internet does not have respect for national or international borders. Illegal content which can be accessed domestically are often hosted on servers abroad. This creates various problems and questions for law enforcement. These problems arise both on the legal and practical level.

3.4.1 *Creating the legal requirements*

The legal problems in cases of international law enforcement are manifold and concern both substantive and procedural law. Problems of substantive law are created by the fact that criminal provisions relating to specific computer crimes differ from country to country. What is illegal in one country may be legal in another. An example of this would be where right-wing extremist material is stored on a server in Denmark (where it could be legal) and is easily accessible on the Internet in Germany (where it is illegal).

Similar differences exist with respect to criminal procedural law. Indeed, in some cases there is no proper legal basis in the foreign country, which would allow the gathering of the necessary evidence. In some countries, therefore, it is possible to use coercive measures with respect to gathering evidence from the Internet providers if necessary, in others, the only option available is asking for their cooperation.

Further difficulties arise with respect to other differing national legislation, for example with respect to data protection laws or telecommunications secrecy. In particular, difficulties can arise with respect to the storage of user data by providers for longer periods.

With respect to mutual assistance, these differences of substantive law can create problems since mutual cooperation often requires "double criminality" (i.e., the particular behavior must be illegal both in the state requesting legal assistance and in the executing state). The differences of procedural law cause problems in mutual assistance procedures since a state can only provide legal assistance which is legal under its criminal procedural law. Moreover, mutual assistance is a lengthy process often involving tedious diplomatic channels.

Finally, problems arise with respect to the competent jurisdiction. It is sometimes unclear for example, if a state has jurisdictional power to prosecute if a server is stored in a foreign country but can be easily accessed domestically. These issues are currently being discussed in work being carried out by several international organizations (esp. Council of Europe and G8 Group on High-Tech Crime) and their efforts in this area should be supported.

Recommendation: Fostering international harmonization of law and international cooperation

Law enforcement within the Internet must be internationally efficient since it deals with perpetrators and data which are not limited to national boundaries. As a consequence, it is vital to have harmonized or fairly uniform rules for substantive criminal law, especially common minimum standards for the fight against illegal activities or content on the Internet in accordance with international and supranational recommendations (e.g., by Council of Europe, EU, OECD, G8). Since country-specific blocking of content is hardly possible, it is difficult to fight content which is illegal in one country and legal in another.

A similar harmonization of law is required in the field of criminal procedural law with respect to coercive powers, evidential rules and data protection law and telecommunications secrecy. In a matter involving mutual assistance, a state can only provide those legal measures that are permitted under its law. There should be an effective and fast means of prosecution which can quickly transcend national borders, especially by electronic searches across borders, effective freezing of evidence and witness conferencing. The process of mutual legal assistance should be streamlined, allowing cross-border prosecutions to evolve more quickly. It should be based more on direct contacts, facilitated by the creation of "focal points." The introduction of an international "Preservation Order" could further help foster supranational law enforcement.

International law enforcement does not only create difficult legal problems. A similar problematic situation arises on the practical level. Although there have been some successful international law enforcement operations, many practical problems still exist.

The success of Operations "Starbust,"[6] "Bavaria"[7] and "Cathedral"[8] have shown that an effective international coordinated law enforcement is possible. These investigations targeted paedophiles using the Internet as a means of communicating with fellow paedophiles and who were exchanging and distributing child pornographic images online. However, in practice many problems arise which make the process of international law enforcement difficult. The main problem is the lack of any efficient exchange of information, ongoing cooperation or coordination of law enforcement activities in general. A common complaint among law enforcement agencies is the lack of any proper infrastructure and focal points

---

6   A tip-off by US Customs led British police to identify an individual involved in the dissemination of paedophilic images on the Internet. Further investigation uncovered other perpetrators throughout the world and cooperation within law enforcement in numerous jurisdictions ensured coordinated arrests to prevent tip-offs.

7   Operation "Bavaria" concerned a similar effort led by Bavarian investigating authorities who uncovered paedophiles disseminating and exchanging child pornographic images within Internet Relay Chat (IRC). The operation involved cooperation between numerous police authorities and led to simultaneous house searches in Germany, United Kingdom, Canada, Norway, Sweden and Switzerland. Thousands of child pornographic images were seized and several persons arrested.

8   Operation "Cathedral" involved law enforcement agencies from 15 countries successfully breaking the "Wonderland" paedophile ring, and as a result, over a quarter of a million paedophilic images were seized from computers in Europe alone, as well as thousands of videos, CDs, and floppy discs.

within many foreign agencies, which hinders coordination of activities and causes costly delays in the investigation and prosecution.

The G8 working group on High-Tech Crime has been studying some of these problems and developing solutions since January 1997. Some of the measures taken include the formation of a 24-hour point of contact to help coordinate law enforcement. Each of the countries involved have similar contact points, where, for example, expert advice and assistance with respect to securing evidence in a particular case can be obtained. The G8 Group wish to spread these contact points to other countries and to this end are working together with international organizations such as Interpol and the EU. Moreover, they are currently drafting a uniform hi-tech training software program covering the search and seizure of evidence. This is to ensure that all law enforcers practise the same procedures, since only in this way can evidence be mutually recognized. Such endeavors by the G8 Group will help contribute to better international law enforcement and should be supported.

In general, it is necessary to develop a more efficient cooperation between individual national law enforcement agencies on an international level. This could be achieved by developing better communication channels, in particular an international police network of "focal points" for issues relating to online law enforcement and a more unified, secure communication system. Such a communication system has already been developed and successfully introduced in the USA to foster law enforcement cooperation between the federal and state levels (known as "LEO" or "Law enforcement online"). The introduction of an international "online law enforcement database" has also been advocated. In particular, with respect to mutual legal assistance, the emphasis should be moved away from formal and often lengthy diplomatic procedures to direct, practical cooperation between the competent law enforcement authorities. Further proposals include an international training symposium specifically to help standardize law enforcement training on the supranational level (see the G8 example above). This would not only create international minimum training standards with respect to online law enforcement but also encourage cooperation in general on the unofficial level. It is widely believed that such forms of harmonization on the practical level would contribute enormously to a more effective prosecution of illegal content at the supranational level.

Recommendation: Implementing practical solutions for international law enforcement

From a practical law enforcement viewpoint, there must be a more efficient cooperation between individual law enforcement agencies on an international level.

Official diplomatic procedures for formal legal assistance should be replaced by more direct cooperation of the competent police agencies. This could be achieved by developing better communication channels, in particular the creation of "focal points," secure communication systems and common databases within law enforcement agencies.

An international training symposium specifically to help standardize law enforcement training would not only create international minimum training standards and lead to common practices with respect to online law enforcement but also encourage cooperation in general on the unofficial level.

Such forms of harmonization on the practical level cannot only contribute to a more effective prosecution of illegal content at the supranational level, particularly in the absence of appropriate legal harmonization, but can eventually help facilitate and compliment such legal harmonization. However, practical solutions can only function properly when accompanied by the aforementioned legal harmonization and while respecting the rule of law, which is a basic requirement for the protection of citizens' freedoms, especially in criminal proceedings.

3.5 Developing better cooperation between law enforcement and Internet providers

An effective prevention, detection, investigation and prosecution of illegal Internet contents requires fruitful cooperation between law enforcement and Internet providers. This could be especially improved by fostering mutual understanding between law enforcement and industry, enabling an exchange of views, introducing mutual training courses, providing technical support where possible and creating clearly defined conditions for providers to transfer evidence.

3.5.1 Improving mutual understanding

The relationship between the Internet industry and the law enforcement sector is not in an ideal state. In some cases, an unnecessary confrontation has arisen between the two, originating in the field of child pornography and relating to a threat of legal responsibility for the Internet industry. However, there is some indication that the situation may be gradually improving.

The situation is particularly positive in the United Kingdom and USA. In the UK, the Internet Watch Foundation reports that service providers working in tandem with them have always cooperated with law enforcement when potentially illegal material has been identified on their servers. In addition, there are quarterly meetings currently taking place between law enforcement and the service providers in the United Kingdom. These discussions, which have been facilitated by government, are designed to tackle some of the issues raising problems in this cooperation, including data protection and the provision of information relevant to an investigation. A similar result can be found in the USA, where some of the service providers have established 24-hour points of contact for law enforcement.

370

However, considerable problems are still perceived by law enforcers to exist in the relationship between law enforcement and Internet industry. In particular, some providers are considered to be "not law enforcement-friendly" and reluctant to cooperate for differing reasons. In the USA, some complaints are heard from law enforcers that this reluctance is a result of uncertainty about their obligations to provide details of subscribers holding anonymous accounts when requested to do so by law enforcement. This has necessitated court orders resulting in costly delays in the prosecuting process. In other cases law enforcers report how some providers vary their willingness to cooperate according to the gravity of the case in question, and become less cooperative in less serious cases.

In other countries, particularly in Germany and France, questionable criminal prosecutions and convictions of corporate Internet industry representatives with respect to the dissemination of third party illegal content within their technical infrastructures have seriously set back the relationship between law enforcement and Internet industry. Indeed, in Germany, many law enforcers have admitted frankly that such a deterioration occurred following the proceedings against the Chief Executive Officer of CompuServe GmbH.

In all countries, there is a broad consensus among law enforcers that they experience particular difficulties with respect to some of the smaller service providers, or those not belonging to service provider associations. Such associations often have their own "codes of conduct", which is to be respected by all the providers who join. Many law enforcers therefore express the desire that all service providers should at least be subject to such codes of conduct to ensure compliance with certain minimum standards or alternatively be subject to some form of mandatory licensing system, where misconduct by a provider would lead to a withdrawal of the licence. Law enforcement experience special difficulties where service providers do not store particular data, including IP addresses. When

371

this data is requested, the data is sometimes not available. However, such problems do not necessarily stem from a lack of willingness to cooperate, but rather individual service provider procedures, which happen to hamper law enforcement activities. Indeed, in other cases, difficulties arise from service providers because some measures they are being asked to take, or which could help law enforcement generally, are not technically possible, or would conflict with other existing laws, such as data protection.

Nevertheless, it appears that a more positive situation is developing in many countries, where there is a broad consensus among law enforcers that a large majority of providers are interested in good cooperation with law enforcement. For example, in Germany, a federal state police authority has recently been consulted during the development process of certain software solutions by a provider. However, law enforcers also see some problems within their own organization. In particular, many law enforcers believe there is a lack of transparency within the police/law enforcement organization, thus making cooperation with providers difficult. Another common complaint is the lack of understanding for the underlying technical issues, which sometimes leads to police placing false or impossible demands on the providers.

Recommendation: Encouraging general cooperative measures

Both law enforcement and Internet industry can and should contribute to a better cooperation. Law enforcement should treat Internet providers as potential allies in the fight against illegal content on the Internet, not as the primary problem, concentrating their activity instead on the real perpetrator. There should be greater appreciation by law enforcement of the technical difficulties providers may face in combating illegal content. The responsible law enforcement agencies should ensure their organizational structure is transparent to facilitate cooperation with service providers.

372

On the other hand, service providers should understand that law enforcement also work in their interest by aiming for a safe, crime-free Net, which can be enjoyed by everyone. Internet providers should also have a clear understanding of their obligations under existing law.

3.5.2 Providing training and exchange of views

Due to the fast-changing technology of the Internet, prosecution agencies and judges are usually not familiar with the latest technologies applied by the Internet industry. Training courses of law enforcement officials provided by the Internet industry as well as the regular exchange of views could be of considerable help. Such exchange programs are also in the Internet industry's own interest, since they can avoid misunderstandings which could create unnecessary law suits against them or unrealistic demands with regard to the gathering or safeguarding of evidence.

Recommendation: Providing training and mutual understanding
There should be a regular exchange of views between Internet providers and law enforcement agencies in order to discuss common points of interest and to exchange law enforcement know-how with technical know-how. Training courses for law enforcement agencies provided by the Internet industry could support the development of personal contacts, mutual understanding, further discussion and the effectiveness of law enforcement generally. Law enforcement should provide training and advice as and when needed.

Both sides should exchange information and know-how through discussion forums, building mutual understanding based on trust and ensuring transparency in the relationship through ongoing dialogue.

3.5.3 Promoting general logistical support

There are various other measures with which the Internet industry could support law enforcement without any legal implications. This is especially the case with respect to general logistical support. It is recommended that such support measures be undertaken.

> **Recommendation: Promoting general logistical support**
> If there are no legal obstacles, the Internet industry should support law enforcement agencies in the fight against crime thus helping them make the Internet a safer place. This could include:
> – the creation of focal contact points within the Internet industry
> – the availability of these focal contact points within the Internet industry for emergency situations, accessible 24 hours
> – the provision of technical support in appropriate cases as needed by law enforcement
> – the undertaking of all commercially reasonable steps to try to verify the identity of their subscribers, while protecting their subscribers' privacy
> – the definition of voluntary data formats for frequently used requests for information
> – the freezing of evidence in urgent cases in accordance with data protection law
> – the informal handing over of general information about the availability of data and evidence (not involving illegal disclosures of personal data)
> – the advising of users that any posting, transmitting, accessing or storing of illegal content might result in serious legal consequences for them, including removal or blockage of illegal material, or termination of service
> – the requesting of users to notify hotlines or a specific hotline about any illegal content on the Internet so that the hotlines can consider further action with respect to this content.

3.5.4 Reacting to requests for evidence with respect to personal data

With respect to other means of support, legal problems and limits have to be considered. This is especially the case if law enforcement agencies ask for evidence in the form of personal data of third parties, especially of customers of the Internet providers. This data can be protected by telecommunications secrecy, privacy legislation and in contractual law. In some countries, problems with privacy legislation not only arise if Internet providers transfer data, but in some cases even if they store personal data for a longer period than prescribed by data protection law.

In order to overcome these obstacles, and to enable an effective prosecution, the criminal procedural codes of all countries lay down detailed procedures for handing over and searching for evidence. One of the main safeguards of these procedures for protecting civil liberties is the requirement of a decision from an independent judge. The providers, as well as the prosecuting agency must respect these procedures and safeguards as well as privacy laws. They must understand that the fulfillment of these requirements and laws is essential in order to avoid criminal and contractual liability of Internet providers especially with respect to infringements of the telecommunications secrecy, infringements of privacy laws and of breaches of contracts. Similar problems arise in the private sector if private victims (e.g., of copyright infringements) try to prosecute perpetrators. In these cases, the Internet providers may have to respect obligations towards their customers laid down by telecommunications secrecy law, privacy law and their contracts.

**Recommendation: Transferring personal data
in a legal manner**

The transfer of personal data from IT providers to the law enforcement agencies must be in accordance with the formal requirements laid down in the criminal procedural codes (especially
requiring the decision of a judge) and in the data protection legislation in order to protect the secrecy of telecommunications and
privacy rights. Similarly the transfer of personal data from providers to private victims must be in accordance with privacy legislation and data protection law. However, if these requirements
are fulfilled, Internet providers should cooperate with the police
and private victims in a constructive manner.

In order to further support law enforcement agencies and private victims and move the focus off providers and onto the individual criminals, the Internet providers could consider incorporating into the user agreements adequate data protection notices,
which, in serious cases, would allow the disclosure of personal
data of the user to public or private enforcement bodies investigating alleged illegal activity by the user.

*3.5.5 Considering self-initiated transfer
of evidence by providers*

Positive action by Internet providers, especially self-initiated transfer
of evidence, would be the most effective support which Internet
providers could give to law enforcement. Generally each citizen has
the possibility and right to make such a notification. However, in the
case of Internet providers, telecommunications secrecy and privacy
protection with regard to their clients could pose a hindrance.
Except for very serious cases of crime, the conflict between the right
to make notifications and the secrecy obligation of Internet providers could create legal problems. In order to solve these questions

one could consider specifically regulating the rights and obligations of Internet providers, especially with respect to the delivery of personal data of clients in serious cases of crime. For that reason, one should carefully examine a US proposal of the duty on the part of the provider to notify the police in certain cases of serious crime (Sieber 1999a). Such a proposal should be considered especially in cases of child abuse and child pornography.

An additional practical possibility to enable active support to the police by Internet providers is shown by the US practice: In the USA, some Internet providers only transfer anonymous data to law enforcement agencies, e.g., the picture of an abused child, without delivering the personal data (such as the sender/recipient of the picture). If the police considers the picture illegal, it will seek to obtain a judicial order requesting the personal data be provided in, or prior to commencing, criminal proceedings. However, it is not quite clear whether such a practice would be in accordance with the legal regulations in Europe: a specific and express regulation of the rights and obligations of Internet providers concerning duties to make notification could therefore be preferable.

Recommendation: Ensuring legal clarification relating to self-initiated notification

The self-initiated notification to the police and/or private organizations by Internet providers relating to illegal content could be one of the most effective means of industry support for law enforcement. In some cases such support infringes the secrecy of telecommunications and privacy protection. However, in serious cases, especially in cases of child exploitation and child pornography, such active duties of Internet providers, by way of self-initiatives to deliver data to the police, could be considered.

The legislator should therefore examine the legal duties and rights of Internet providers relating to notification duties, in particular the transfer of personal data of alleged criminals and violators of legal rights to law enforcement agencies and to private victims. This requires a balancing of the privacy interests of the user, of the prosecution interests of law enforcement agencies and private victims, as well as the role of Internet providers in the prosecution system. The development of these rules should be based on an international comparative analysis in order to create a globally effective and protective system.

As long as there are no clear legal regulations for self-initiated notifications with respect to serious crimes such as child pornography, the Internet providers should consider following the US practice of transferring illegal data to the police – without transferring personal data – thus giving the law enforcement agencies the option to obtain a judicial delivery order.

4 Self-regulation: ensuring legal compliance and enforcement of industry measures

An ideal regulation system coordinating legal regulation and self-regulation on the Internet has to specifically combine and interweave both regulatory systems. Since law enforcement as well as the support of law enforcement by Internet providers was already dealt with above the legal aspects of self-regulation remain to be discussed.

An ideal combination of the two regulatory systems should involve two main links between self-regulation and legal regulation: the basic requirements for the legality of self-regulation (infra 4.1) and the legal enforcement of self-regulation (infra 4.2).

4.1 Legal compliance

Since existing legal regulation has primacy over self-regulation, there is a basic requirement for any form of self-regulation, namely, that it is in accordance with existing legal regulation. Considering the above-mentioned legal framework, this leads to the following requirements for internal procedures, contract clauses and codes of conduct, for age verification systems and filtering techniques, and for hotlines.

4.1.1 Defining illegal content

The basic requirement of any Internet self-regulation is the definition and/or description of illegal content which should not be tolerated. Within a particular company, this not only raises difficulties with regard to internal procedures for the relevant employees dealing with illegal content, but also presents problems with contractual clauses between providers and their subscribers prohibiting certain acts of the users. Within a cooperative self-regulation regime, it is furthermore especially relevant for codes of conduct. For all these purposes, therefore, defining illegal content can generally give rise to certain problems.

Conformity with legal content regulations

The description of illegal content in internal procedures, contractual clauses and codes of conduct first poses the risk that these descriptions are too restrictive and do not fulfill all legal requirements, in particular, that they do not cover all those contents classed as "illegal" either in criminal law, media law or in the laws protecting the press. A complete description of illegal acts in such a code of conduct is especially difficult since in many cases in the Internet it is not clear which national legal system should apply to a computer system accessible from many countries. Even if a complete description of illegal activities was possible, it could soon be outdated since the law is a dynamic process, which is always changing due to new legislation and new jurisprudence. For that reason, the content description problem within internal procedures, contracts and codes of conduct cannot be solved by detailed lists on illegal content but only by providing a dynamic and general reference to existing legal obligations. In addition, providers and users should be aware that the legally binding norm is the law and not descriptions within codes of conduct of what could constitute illegal content.

> **Recommendation: Describing illegal content**
> Internal procedures, contracts and industry codes of conduct describing illegal content can play an important role in informing providers and users about the illegality of certain types of content. However, the relevant descriptions should be based on a general and dynamic reference to existing law. It should be made clear that in general, private regulation does not supersede existing law. Concrete descriptions of illegal content are certainly helpful for reasons of clarity. Nevertheless, if they are used, it should be made clear that these descriptions are only examples or minimum requirements for illustrating the most important legal obligations.

The conflict between civil liberties and users' rights

In order to comply with legal content regulation (especially under criminal law), the Internet industry might be tempted to avoid legal risks by censoring content in a far-reaching way. However, such a

380

strategy would lead to an unwanted private censorship infringing the civil liberties of users (especially free speech) and giving rise to civil claims by users e.g., against their host service providers, especially within contractual relationships. Aside from contractual relationships, difficult legal questions arise whether and to what extent civil liberties are only protected against the state, or also against private organizations. These legal problems become even more acute if a specific content regulation originates from an extra-territorial application of foreign law. As a consequence, industry self-regulation does not only face the problem of insufficient regulation but also of over-regulation and censorship.

> ## Recommendation: Respecting civil liberties
> When erasing or blocking illegal content, Internet providers should not be over-reactive. Besides criminal law, they must also respect the civil liberties and information rights of their users, to avoid accusations of private censorship and breach of contract.

The "international trap"

In searching for a balance between legal requirements for blocking illegal content and respecting civil liberties, Internet providers face some specific problems which could be called the "international trap," the "evaluation trap," and the "contractual trap."

The "international trap" for global Internet providers is created by two factors. First, there are some different evaluations of fundamental values within the various states. The value of free speech for example plays a great importance in the public discussion of some states (e.g., the US) whereas in other countries it is more limited by social interests or in some cases by historical developments. This can lead to the result that some content might be illegal in one country but at the same time protected by civil rights in another. An example for this is Nazi propaganda, which can constitute a crime in Germany or Austria, but is legal or even constitutionally protected under freedom of speech in other countries such as the US, Canada and Denmark. Different attitudes can also exist with respect to sexually explicit content where there are countries more "liberal" (e.g., Denmark, the Netherlands, France) only protecting restricted and defined legal interests with respect to children, and countries with extensive and strict criminal legislation protecting public morals (such as Canada, US, UK and many Asian countries).

Secondly, there are many arbitrary technical differences between the national legislations, which could easily be harmonized by adopting a rational approach. This can be illustrated in the area of child pornography, which has been in the public focus of the discussion on liability of Internet providers. Among many other examples, various legislations differentiate e.g., with respect to the age limit under which minors should be protected from exposure to pornographic material (which at present ranges from 14 to 18 years), criminal sanctions in cases of fictitious pornographic illustrations (in particular the image editing of pictures of minors), and the extension of an absolute prohibition to the mere transfer of pornographic material containing animals, violence and other obscene material. Further differences arise with respect to the liability of "consumers" for procurement and possession, the requirement of intention, and with respect to penal sanctions (which, in the case of providing access to child pornographic illustrations for example, vary from six months to 15 years).

Internet providers might try to escape this "international trap" by country-specific blocking techniques. However, such country-specific blocking of content is technically difficult and could easily destroy the advantage of global networks by creating barriers to the free flow of information. For that reason, the "international trap" could be better avoided by harmonizing international laws, establish-

382

ing international minimum rules, and restricting the "extra-territorial" application of national law for the Internet.

Recommendation: Avoiding conflicts of law

Under any responsibility regulation, it is impossible for international online services and Internet providers to take into consideration content regulations existing in all the countries from which their data can be accessed. The problem of respecting all these laws and avoiding conflicts of law can only to a limited degree be solved by country-specific blocking of content, which destroys the advantage of open global networks.

For that reason, solutions should be found mainly by national lawmakers and the international community with respect to the international harmonization of law and the limitation of the extra-territorial application of laws in the Internet (especially by establishing a link between the physical location of the relevant server and the respective jurisdiction). Content offered through the World Wide Web should not fall under the jurisdiction of any state from which the server can be accessed.

Since finding such solutions requires considerable time, industry should take a lead and develop international minimum rules for content regulation (to be applied alongside and in accordance with the applicable national law). Such minimum rules might then be a forerunner for similar hard-law regulations created by an international cooperation of regulatory bodies.

The "evaluation trap"

Even if clear (and internationally valid) standards for content regulation existed, Internet providers in many cases are still faced with the "evaluation trap." Due to the vague legal clauses of the respective laws (e.g., dealing with "pornographic" or "obscene" content) it is extremely difficult, especially for small providers, to judge whether certain types of content are illegal or harmful. For example, with respect to child pornography or generally known and widely used software packages, it may be relatively easy to ascertain that specific sites are violating the law; on the other hand, it may be much more difficult to determine if defamatory or obscene material or individual software is illegal. In these latter instances, it is appropriate for industry to create self-regulatory bodies or develop procedures to help Internet providers evaluate the legality or illegality of specific contents. Examples for such self-regulatory bodies are the German "FSM" (Freiwillige Selbstkontrolle Multimedia Diensteanbieter e.V.) and the British IWF (Internet Watch Foundation). An example for procedures relying on trusted third parties is the cooperation of various providers with specific companies.

> ### Recommendation: Assisting in the evaluation process of illegal or harmful contents
>
> It is extremely difficult for Internet providers to evaluate the legality or illegality of specific data. Industry self-regulation should therefore create organizations, which can help Internet providers in this evaluation process. This task could be integrated into the work of hotlines or self-regulatory bodies. It could also be achieved by cooperation procedures with appropriate third parties or government authorities.

The "contractual trap"

Since illegal content is difficult to evaluate and a final judicial decision by the courts might take years, Internet providers could be faced with conflicting demands from the police on the one hand (demanding that certain "illegal" content be blocked) and by users on the other hand (claiming the same content as "legal" and threatening the provider with a law suit in the case of illegal blocking). As illustrated above, this dilemma can also be solved by the law. The Digital Millennium Copyright Act in the USA, for example, provides a liability limitation for the service provider if it simply takes down material, of which it receives notice is illegal, and protects the service provider from liability if that take-down turns out to be wrong. If there are no such legal solutions, these conflicts can be avoided by special contractual clauses in the agreements between the providers and users and by the creation and contractual recognition of an arbitration board, for example, within the above-mentioned hotline.

Recommendation: Creating contractual clauses allowing the blocking of contents

In order to avoid conflicting demands being placed on Internet providers by the police (demanding the blocking of illegal content) and by clients (requesting their civil liberties for the same content), the contracts between providers and users should not only give the providers a right to block illegal content but also content which they believe is likely to be illegal. These rights should include the possibilities of removing such content from the servers or limiting access to specific content.

In cases of serious and repeat offenders, the contracts should also include a right to terminate subscriber accounts. In order to provide expeditious and effective decisions in this process, the contracts could make reference to, and recognize the binding nature of, decisions of self-regulatory bodies (such as hotlines). For cases involving serious offenders, the contracts might also provide clauses allowing the disclosure of user details to government or private sector associations investigating allegedly illegal activity on the user's site.

4.1.2 Determining the appropriate procedures for dealing with specific types of contents

In addition to defining illegal content, Internet providers also have to determine the appropriate procedure with respect to dealing with these contents. This procedure could range from removing or blocking to merely tolerating the presence of illegal contents. The appropriate procedures for dealing with the various contents is defined in the above-described legal responsibility provisions as well as in the specific laws on illegal content. The internal procedures of companies as well as codes of conduct must make sure that their procedures are in accordance with these laws. In doing this they must, in particular, differentiate between illegal and harmful content.

Illegal content

Illegal content is defined as content whose transfer is illegal per se. An exchange of this content between adults, and in some cases, even their possession by adults, is illegal. The best known example for such contents is child pornography, which is generally forbidden in most countries. The same applies to copyright infringements. Therefore, the provision of filtering techniques does not give any privilege for the dissemination of such contents. Instead, removal and blocking techniques must be applied. These techniques must be in accordance with responsibility legislation, which – as illustrated above – is different in the various countries. Based on the above-proposed notice-and-take-down-procedure for host service providers, an appropriate recommendation for the Internet industry would be.

Recommendation: Removing and blocking illegal content

Illegal content must be removed or blocked in accordance with general responsibility rules and specific prohibitions. According to the above-proposed legislation, access and network providers would only be under an obligation to block access in case of binding administrative orders or civil law injunctions. Host service providers would have to promptly remove or block illegal content where knowledge or awareness thereof has been attained. The deletion of illegal content is required if the respective provisions criminalize the possession or knowing assistance in the possession of the said content (which in many countries is the case with respect to child pornography); blocking of content (also for adult users!) is required if only the transfer or offering of the content is prohibited.

Age verification systems developed for the host service providers and filtering/rating techniques developed for the end-user (especially adults with respect to children) must not be applied in conjunction with illegal content (e.g., child pornography). Similarly, with respect to this content, filtering does not provide any privilege since the transfer of such contents is not only illegal with respect to children, but also among adults.

Harmful or unwanted contents

With respect to content harmful to minors but legal among adults, the various laws describe illegal acts in different ways. In many cases, they forbid, for example, the accessibility of such material to minors and/or the public distribution of this material. However, in most legal systems, it is quite *unclear* which technical barriers are necessary to prevent "accessibility to minors" or "public accessibility." It is, for example, controversial which technical safeguards are required for age verification systems (e.g., permitting the offer of pornographic or obscene material exclusively to adults). Furthermore, it is also unclear whether filtering techniques employed at the level of the individual household should be recognized by law, e.g., with respect to indecent or inappropriate material, if they can be circumvented by minors. Similar problems arise in those legal systems which, in addition to the material harmful to minors, prohibit a category of "unwanted (especially sexual) material" which must not be sent to adults without their consent. Here the problem arises with regard to which protection systems (such as descriptive labelling, notices or other visual or audio signals) are required to ensure appropriate consent to the receipt of such material. Only in a few legislative systems, such as in German and US legislation, it is specified that the application of filtering techniques excludes "accessibility" of specific material to minors. Clarification and the international coordination of relevant provisions are particularly necessary in this area.

Recommendation: Defining the legal privileges of age verification, filtering and rating techniques

Lawmakers should give more consideration to the feasibility of age verification systems, filtering and rating techniques as well as signalling procedures. In particular, they should draft codes according to which certain age verification systems and filtering techniques exclude responsibility for harmful content. If criminal laws require age verification systems for Internet providers, there must be a corresponding and consistent privacy legislation providing the possibility of differentiating between adult and minor users.

4.1.3 *Excluding criminal liability for the work of hotlines*

As already mentioned, the criminal law of all countries differentiates between illegal content (which are illegal even for adults) and harmful content (which are legal with respect to adults but illegal with respect to children). Especially in the case of some illegal content (such as child pornography), many legal systems do not only criminalize the transfer of such content but also its possession. These criminal laws could *conflict* with the work of hotlines. Users could incur criminal liability by transferring illegal content to the hotlines; likewise, the members of the hotlines could be accused of promoting such illegal acts of transferring illegal content and of illegal possession of said content.

Only in a few legal systems are there clear exceptions providing for the legal transaction and possession of illegal contents. These usually apply to the police or with respect to other activities arising as a necessary consequence of professional duties. For that reason, one might consider the creation of similar special *legal privileges* for hotlines. However, such privileges would have to face the concerns of prosecuting agencies that hotlines for illegal content could also be set up by potential perpetrators, e.g., paedophiles looking for illegal content. To prevent this, licensing systems could be established for hotlines set up to handle illegal material. Nevertheless, as long as no such clear privileges are available under the applicable laws, hotlines must avoid infringing existing criminal law provisions by a proper regulation of their business, in particular by specific notifications to the users.

Recommendation: Ensuring the legality of hotlines

The handling of illegal content by a hotline and users collaborating with hotlines create the risk of criminal liability, both for the user and for the staff of the hotline especially with respect to the transfer and/or the possession of child pornography and certain other illegal content. Potential legal privileges stemming from the legitimate aim of hotlines are difficult to evaluate in most legal systems. In order to avoid any legal risks, hotlines should therefore not only operate in accordance with privacy legislation, but also avoid violating these criminal provisions by a proper regulation of their business. They should request their users not to send them illegal material but only to give notice of their existence or to transfer an exact description of where the illegal content can be found on the Internet. Similarly, hotlines should avoid storing illegal content if the possession of such content is a crime.

Since such procedures could lead to the loss of important evidence, legal clarifications (or in some countries with prosecuting discretion, agreements between prosecuting agencies and hotlines) might be necessary to enable storage of illegal content for reasons of safeguarding evidence and other legal purposes. Such privileges might be restricted to reliable hotlines (especially where coregulation with the police exists) or require a licensing system.

4.2 Legal enforcement of self-regulation

As illustrated above, the weak point of self-regulation (soft law) in comparison with legal regulation (hard law) is the missing binding nature and enforceability of self-regulating codes. However, several techniques exist which empower self-regulation by legal means, thus making it enforceable.

4.2.1 *Enforcing codes of conduct*

Industry codes of conduct of Internet providers lack any binding nature both for the Internet providers and for the user. However, various techniques exist which could *empower* these codes of conduct. Since the possibility of making these codes binding by law (either expressly or by general clauses) on a worldwide basis is not a realistic option in the field of Internet self-regulation, the main option for making them binding is their incorporation by means of contract. Such contractual enforcement of non-binding codes of conduct is a well-known technique in the field of privacy protection where it is used to allow the transfer of personal data in countries with an unsatisfactory level of privacy protection. With respect to illegal content on the Internet, the same technique is used to impose certain obligations upon Internet users. In this context, it is interesting to note that in some countries, the codes of conduct of Internet providers historically originated from contracts between the users and the providers. This illustrates that codes of conducts of Internet providers (e.g., containing international minimum rules with respect to illegal content) could be incorporated into the contract between the provider and their clients.

In addition, an agreement between various providers or between providers and the hotline could create legal obligations on the part of providers. In these contracts, the providers submit themselves to legally enforceable (contractual) sanctions and orders from a court of arbitration.

Recommendation: Enforcing codes of conduct

In order to make codes of conduct enforceable and to create internationally consistent minimum rules with respect to illegal content, the respective codes of conduct should be incorporated into the contracts between the Internet providers and their clients, in agreements between providers themselves as well as in agreements between providers and self-regulatory bodies such as hotlines.

4.2.2 *Applying age verification, filtering and rating techniques*

The use of filtering and rating technology is an important component in protecting children from harmful content. However, as illustrated above, these filtering techniques are only relevant in the legal sense if they are seen as fulfilling relevant legal requirements (e.g., excluding the "accessibility" of the classified content to minors). Therefore, the use of filtering techniques should be encouraged not only by economic but also by legal means limiting liability of providers in order to develop the appropriate legal framework for user empowerment.

Additional and special enforcement measures might be necessary especially for self-rating systems. Self-rating systems depend to a large degree on the capabilities and honesty of self-raters. To avoid false rating, a system of positive and negative incentives could be created. Positive incentives could be economic (e.g., tax) advantages. Negative incentives could range from a mere warning to a blocking of contents, fines and even criminal sanctions in the case of persistent and internal misrating.

> **Recommendation: Supporting the use of self-rating systems**
>
> The creation of a rating system depends to a great extent on the reliability of self-rating. For that reason, the self-rating system could be stabilized by positive incentives as well as deterrent sanctions. Such positive incentives could not only be provided by provisions against harmful contents which specify that the responsibility of providers is excluded if certain minimum requirements regarding the application of filtering and rating techniques are fulfilled.-Tax law and economic administrative law could also give financial incentives for filtering and rating techniques. Sanctions could range from a mere warning to a blocking of contents and fines, and criminal sanctions for deliberate false rating.

4.2.3 Supporting decisions of self-regulatory agencies (especially hotlines)

The evaluation of illegal content by self-control bodies can be a great help for providers, especially in grey areas like pornography. Centralized self-regulatory agencies can collect relevant information for the above-described difficult legal evaluation process, which would otherwise not be available, especially for small Internet providers lacking in-house specialized legal advice. This can be especially important in the above-mentioned cases of the "evaluation trap" in which the Internet providers are facing liability against users in cases of unjustified blocking. However, due to their very nature, the decisions of these self-regulatory bodies do not generally exclude the responsibility of Internet providers with any certainty, since the final evaluation as to illegal content is assigned to the courts. This means that a self-regulatory body could evaluate specific Internet contents positively, but a later court decision could find the opposite. In order to avoid such controversies and uncertainties, it should be considered whether a certain "evaluation power" could be transferred to self-regulatory bodies. Such delegation does not seem possible for clearly illegal content or obvious copyright infringements. However, it could be introduced with respect to certain contents detrimental to minors and in certain grey zones. This could be done by various legal and non-legal techniques.

Full legal recognition

A model of "full legal recognition" of decisions of self-regulatory bodies can be found in Germany within the "Bundesprüfstelle für Jugendgefährdende Schriften". According to section 9 of the "Gesetz über jugendgefährdende Schriften und Medieninhalte" (GjSM), this "examination agency" consists of representatives from a broad spectrum including the arts, literature, the book trade, publishers, voluntary and public youth organizations, teachers' and religious organizations (however, up until now containing no representatives from the online industry). These representatives are proposed by their respective organization and appointed by the Federal Ministry for Family and Youth Affairs. The decisions of this body are published in the official journal of the Federal Republic of Germany. Section 21 of the Act on the Dissemination of Publications and Media Contents Harmful to Youth (GjSM) makes it a crime to contravene against these decisions. A similar system exists in Australia.

> **Recommendation: Recognizing the decisions
> of self-regulatory bodies**
> Individual national legislation could consider whether decisions of certain broadly representative self-regulatory bodies (especially in cases of harmful content) should be legally recognized and enforced, e.g., by creating but also limiting criminal liability in certain cases to violations against the decisions of these bodies. This requires that the decisions of these bodies can be challenged in appropriate legal proceedings.

Limited legal recognition on a subjective or procedural level

For many legal systems, a full legal recognition of the decisions of such self-regulatory bodies on an objective level could be too far-reaching. These systems should therefore consider giving credit to the decisions of such self-regulatory bodies either on the *subjective or on the procedural level*. On the subjective level, for example, a limited legal recognition with respect to criminal liability could be given to a positive evaluation of a specific content by a reliable self-regulatory body, even if this decision is not recognized by the courts at a later stage, by excluding the responsibility of the provider. In judicial systems where discretionary powers are conferred upon prosecuting agencies, consideration could also be given to the decisions of such regulatory bodies before deciding whether to prosecute.

> **Recommendation: Considering self-regulatory body decisions on a subjective or procedural level**
> If decisions of reliable self-regulating bodies regarding the legality or illegality of contents are not fully recognized legally, the prosecution agencies should at least consider their decisions, either on a subjective or procedural level. On the subjective level, this would involve evaluating the particular facts of the case in question, especially if the provider relies on a false decision, or on the procedural level, giving consideration to such findings in determining whether to prosecute.

Factual legal recognition

A third and most interesting approach to empower the decisions of self-regulatory bodies, especially of hotlines, can be based on the fact analyzed above, that responsibility of Internet providers in most countries requires actual knowledge of illegal content. On this basis, hotlines could be used in a filtering capacity within the criminal prosecution process against Internet providers. If the hotline could be promoted in a way that users would direct their notifications on illegal content not to the provider but to the hotline, the hotline could serve as a *filter* which would not only concentrate police work on essential cases but also factually exclude liability of providers. If the hotline would judge a content as legal, it would not pass the complaint to the respective provider. In this way, the provider would not have knowledge of the data and would therefore not be liable due to the lack of knowledge. This would apply even if the decision of the hotline turns out to be false. If the person making notification is not content with the decision of the self-regulating body, he could still address himself directly to the Internet provider.

If, on the other hand, the hotline evaluates certain content as illegal, it could transfer it to the provider who should block the information. Only in cases where the provider does not follow the advice of the hotline, would the hotline transfer the data to the police. Such a system would not only empower the decisions of the hotline with effective sanctions but also concentrate police work on serious cases, and at the same time, avoid any problems of proof with respect to the *mens rea* of the provider.

Recommendation: Collaborating by means of an international hotline scheme

Hotlines should try to collect user complaints to evaluate them and only transfer justified complaints to the respective provider. The host service provider would then have a chance to block the content. Only in cases of refusal to follow justified blocking advice would the hotline transfer the case to the police. Based on a "notice and take down" procedure on the part of Internet providers, such a proceeding would not only concentrate the work of the law enforcement agencies to the more serious cases but also restrict liability of the Internet provider if the self-regulatory body would evaluate the content as legal and not give the respective notice to the provider. Such a system could be especially effective if industry could develop a hotline portal, which would attract and pass on all user complaints to locally competent hotlines.

Abbreviations

ABA	Australian Broadcasting Authority
CDA	US Communications Decency Act
COPA	US Child Online Protection Act
CR	Computer und Recht (German Journal)
FSM	Freiwillige Selbstkontrolle Multimedia Diensteanbieter e. V. (German voluntary self-control association of multimedia online service providers).
GJSM	Gesetz über jugendgefährdende Schriften und Medieninhalte (German Act on the Dissemination of Publications and Media Contents Harmful to Youth).
ISPA	Internet Service Provider Association
IuKDG	Informations- und Kommunikationsdienstegesetz (German Act on Information and Communication Services).
IWF	Internet Watch Foundation (UK)
MDStV	Mediendienste-Staatsvertrag (German Länder Media Services Convention)
MMR	Multimedia und Recht (German Journal)
NCMEC	National Center for Missing and Exploited Children (USA)
NCIS	National Criminal Intelligence Service (UK)
NJW	Neue Juristische Wochenschrift (German Journal)
OJJDP	Office of Juvenile Justice and Delinquency Prevention (USA)
OSA	Australian Broadcasting Services Amendment (Online Services) Act 1999
StGB	Strafgesetzbuch (German Penal Code)
TDG	Teledienstegesetz (German Teleservices Act)
U.S.C.	United States Code
ZUM	Zeitschrift für Urheber- und Medienrecht (German Journal)

Bibliography

Recent literature of the author providing more detailed references:

Sieber (1999a): Verantwortlichkeit im Internet. Munich, C.H. Beck.

Sieber (1999b): "Multimedia-Strafrecht", in: Hoeren/Sieber (eds.), Handbuch Multimedia-Recht, Munich, C.H. Beck, part 19.

Sieber (1999c): Kinderpornographie, Jugendschutz und Providerverantwortlichkeit im Internet. Eine strafrechtsvergleichende Untersuchung. In: Bundesministerium der Justiz (ed.): "reihe recht," Mönchengladbach, Forum Verlag Godesberg.

Sieber (1999d): *Multimedia und Recht (MMR) Supplement 2/1999*, "Die rechtliche Verantwortlichkeit im Internet. Grundlagen, Ziele und Auslegung von §5 TDG und §5 MDStV," pp. 1 et seq.

Sieber (1999e): *Zeitschrift für Urheber- und Medienrecht (ZUM)*, "Die Verantwortlichkeit von Internet-Providern im Rechtsvergleich," pp. 196 et seq. English translation: *The Computer Law and Security Report (CLSR)*, "Responsibility of Internet Providers – A Comparative Legal Study with Recommendations for Future Legal Policy," pp. 291 et seq.

Sieber (1999f): *Neue Juristische Wochenschrift (NJW)*, "Internationales Strafrecht im Internet," pp. 2065 et seq.

Sieber (1999g): *MultiMedia und Recht (MMR)*, "Aufbruch in das neue Jahrtausend: Für eine neue Kultur der Verantwortlichkeit im Internet," pp. 689 et seq.

Sieber (1998a): COMCRIME Study for the European Commission, "Legal Aspects of Computer-Related Crime in the Information Society." See http://www.jura.uni-wuerzburg.de/sieber/comcrime/comcrime_www.pdf

Sieber (1998b): *Multimedia und Recht (MMR)*, Comments on AG München "CompuServe" Judgment, pp. 429 et seq.

Sieber (1997): *Computer und Recht (CR)*, "Kontrollmöglichkeiten

zur Verhinderung rechtswidriger Inhalte in Computernetzen,"
pp. 581 et seq., p. 653 et seq.

Sieber (1996): *JuristenZeitung (JZ)*, "Strafrechtliche Verantwortlichkeit für den Datenverkehr in internationalen Computernetzen," pp. 429 et seq., pp. 494 et seq.

Some of these articles are available under "http://www.jura.uni-
wuerzburg.de/sieber/art_engl.htm."

Chapter V

Representative Survey on Internet Content Concerns in Australia, Germany and the United States of America

Renate Köcher

1 Introduction[1]

Concerns about harmful content have been a part of electronic media long before the development of the Internet. In the Federal Republic, 72 percent of the overall population called for bans and restrictions on violent content on television during the first half of the nineties, and 43 percent called for restrictions on sexual content. At the same time, 62 percent were convinced that measures and controls need to be coordinated on an international level and that solo efforts on a national level are practically hopeless.[2]

---

1   Results of representative surveys conducted in the United States, Australia and the Federal Republic of Germany. A project of the Bertelsmann Foundation, Germany, in cooperation with the Australian Broadcasting Authority (ABA). The questionnaire can be found at http://www.bertelsmann-stiftung.de/internetcontent
2   Source: Allensbach Archives, IfD-survey 5076.

The revolutionary changes that have taken place in communication technologies render traditional ideas about controlling media content obsolete. Because of the freedom of access for both providers and users worldwide, the wide variety of offerings and the individualization of use, the offerings and use are judged to be beyond any centrally coordinated state control. In view of the importance of the media for the dissemination of information, for the shaping of opinions and for the discussions of moral values in society, the concept of abandoning efforts to control and restrict media content can not be viewed as satisfactory. Surveys show that the majority of the population generally does not want to view the media as an unrestricted space that is totally disconnected from society's values but is looking for possibilities to ban certain content such as child pornography or crude violence. However, ideas about the practicability of such bans are diffuse; the discussion about control and selection in the new media has just started and is at different stages of development in different countries, depending on the degree of distribution of the new information technologies and the activities of opinion-shaping groups. For example, the discussion is on a different level in the United States due to the much larger saturation of Internet technology compared with Germany, where a large majority can not as yet refer to personal experience when it comes to assessing the risks associated with the Internet.

Despite different experiences, there is an international consensus with respect to the essential assessments of the risks and the possibilities for controlling misuse on the Internet. Representative surveys conducted simultaneously in the United States, Australia and Germany support this statement. A comparison of these three countries is especially interesting since they clearly differ not only with respect to the extent of Internet use but also in their discussions about unwanted media content and past efforts at control.

The survey was made by phone in June 1999 in all three countries. The data from each country is representative for the population above the age of 18. In Australia, a shortened questionnaire was used due to budgetary constraints; as a result, a comparison of some of the results can be made only between the United States and Germany. To assure that the sample survey would include a sufficient percentage of Internet users, the sample size differed in the three countries as follows:

- 1 003 subjects in the United States
- 1 200 subjects in Australia
- 1 423 subjects in Germany.

Since Internet usage in Germany is clearly lagging behind the other two countries, above all the United States, the sample was disproportionally structured in Germany through an over-sampling of online users. However, the online users enter the overall results according to their participation among the sampled population so that the representative nature of the results is preserved. The study can thus base its results on the judgement of subjects with Internet access, in the United States 698 subjects, in Australia 718 subjects and in Germany 605 subjects. Questions about how the population assesses the risks associated with the Internet, what Internet content is considered undesirable, who the population believes is responsible and can be trusted to make a difference and how it perceives concepts of self-regulation were at the center of the survey.

2 Extreme national differences in the extent of Internet use

The revolutionary development of communication technologies is reflected in the equipment found in individual households. Within just a few years, PCs and, increasingly, Internet use have spread in the households. In Germany, which is still lagging behind the development in the United States and Australia, the development is currently very dynamic. The number of households having one or several PCs has increased since 1995 from 23 to 40 percent.[3] In the population aged 14 to 54, who are essentially leading this dynamic development, the majority has one PC available in the home; the percentage of Internet users in this age group has almost doubled since mid-1997, from 9.7 to 17.6 percent.[4]

Despite this dynamic development, the number of German households with access to modern communication technologies and Internet lags far behind that of other industrial nations. So far, only 14 percent of the German population over the age of 18 have direct access to the Internet in their home, workplace or through other means; in contrast, 70 percent of the American and 60 percent of the Australian population are connected to the Internet:

Graph 1: Percentage of the population with access to the Internet

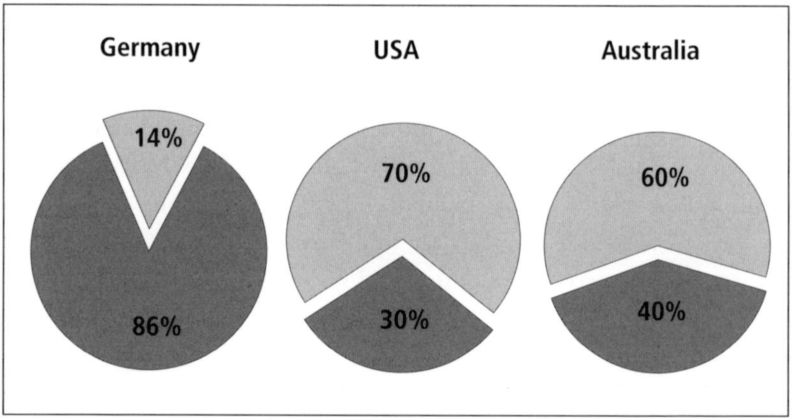

Question: "Do you yourself have access to the Internet at home, at work, or at some other location?"

Basis: Germany, USA, Australia; population 18 years and older

---

3   Source: Allensbach advertising carrier analysis 1995 and 1999.
4   Source: Allensbach computer and telecommunication analysis 1997 and 1999.

In all three countries, private Internet access plays the largest role: 46 percent of the American population over 18 have Internet access in their homes, 31 percent (additionally) at their workplace, and 14 percent elsewhere:

Graph 2: Possibilities for Internet access:

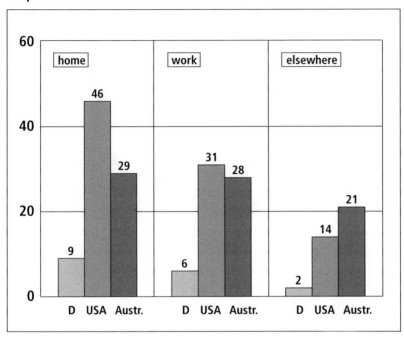

Question: "Do you yourself have access to the Internet at home, at work, or at some other location?"

Basis: Germany, USA, Australia; population 18 years and older

The possibilities for children to access the Internet also differ considerably in the three countries included in the survey. 61 percent of American parents and 55 percent of Australian parents say that their children have Internet access at home or elsewhere, but barely one fifth of the German parents can make this claim.

Graph 3: Internet access of children

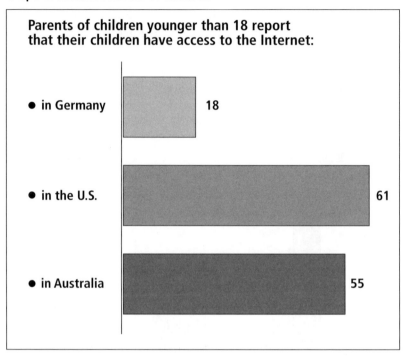

Parents of children younger than 18 report that their children have access to the Internet:

- in Germany — 18
- in the U.S. — 61
- in Australia — 55

Question: "Do your children/does your child have access to the Internet? Not just at home but, e.g., at school or at someone else's home?"

Basis: Germany, USA, Australia; population 18 years and older

The extent of personal experience with the Internet is an important factor in comparing opinions about the Internet and about dealing with problematic content in the United States, Australia and Germany. The American and the Australian population can make an informed judgement based on personal experience, whereas the opinions of the German population are, for the most part, thus far shaped by presumption, hearsay and by following the on-going public discussion. The overwhelming majority of the German population presumes that the computer and Internet technology will drastically change every-day life; 87 percent of the German and 86 percent of the American population are convinced of this. In the professional field, 43 percent of the people working in Germany have already had an experience whereby the new technologies drastically changed their working life, a development that is judged to be positive by the overwhelming majority as a relief and enrichment.[5]

Since the percentage of individuals having professional or private experience is, however, essentially smaller in Germany than in other countries, the assessment of the new technologies in general, and of the Internet in particular, is thus far influenced by insecurity and skepticism to a noticeably greater degree in Germany than in the United States or Australia. In Germany, the belief that the Internet brings with it more advantages than disadvantages also clearly prevails. Individuals in America and Australia, who have more personal experience with the Internet by far, are, however, far more convinced of the opportunities of this technology than the German population: 73 percent of the American and 70 percent of the Australian population, in contrast to 57 percent of the German population, attribute mainly positive effects to the Internet.

In all three countries, the attitude towards the Internet is age-dependent; by far, the younger generation is more convinced of the advantages of the new communication technologies than the generation of their parents or grandparents. The decisive age threshold beyond which Internet technology is judged with clearly more reservation occurs strikingly early in Germany, between mid-30 and mid-40. Whereas three quarters of the Australian and American population in this age group mainly attribute advantages to the Internet, only 53 percent of the Germans in this age group share this opinion:

5   Source: Allensbach archives, IfD-survey 3296.

Graph 4: Generation-specific attitudes towards the Internet

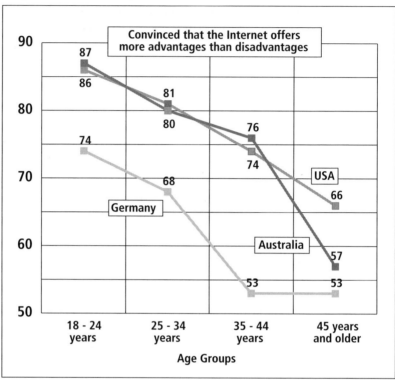

Question: "Judging by your own experience thus far or what you have heard or read about the Internet up to now, would you say the Internet has more advantages or more disadvantages on the whole?"

Basis: Germany, USA, Australia; population 18 years and older

Generally, the younger generation is more open-minded towards technical innovations. However, this is by no means a law of nature. Long-term analyses in Germany[6] show that this pattern was for the most part suspended during the seventies and eighties. Whereas the generation of the below-30 year-olds stood out with an above-average enthusiasm for technology and interest in technological innovations during the fifties and sixties, this attitude changed during the seventies and eighties, an era that was marked by controversial discussions and skepticism towards progress. The above-average openness of the younger generation towards technology reemerged only during the nineties; this process was essentially promoted by the development of modern communication technologies that were understood as a revolutionary transformation of everyday life.[7] At the same time, the younger generation has considerably more experience with the possibilities afforded by the Internet. The more personal experience there is, the more positive the assessment of the Internet will be. Internet users in Germany assess the Internet in a way that is similar to American or Australian Internet users. This supports the theory that the above-average skepticism among the German population relates, above all, to the relative inexperience of Germans with this new technology and not to another assessment of their personal experience. 77 percent of Germans with Internet access are convinced that there are advantages associated with this technology, 81 percent of the American and 86 percent of the Australian users share this belief.

6   Federal Republic of Germany.
7   Renate Köcher: Einstellungen zu Technik und Kernenergie in Deutschland. In: *Energiewirtschaftliche Tagesfragen. Zeitschrift für Energiewirtschaft, Recht, Technik und Umwelt* 1998, No. 1, pp. 50–53.

Table 1: The advantages of the Internet prevail
(Germany, USA, Australia – Population 18 years and older)*

> *Question:* "Simply judging by your own experiences thus far, or what you have heard or read about the Internet up to now, would you say the Internet has more advantages or more disadvantages on the whole?"
>
> | | Germany | USA | Australia |
> | ---------------------- | ------- | --- | --------- |
> | More advantages | 57 | 73 | 70 |
> | More disadvantages | 10 | 14 | 9 |
> | Evens out | 18 | 6 | 5 |
> | Undecided, no opinion | 15 | 7 | 16 |
> | | 100 | 100 | 100 |
>
> Persons with Internet access in:
>
> | | Germany | USA | Australia |
> | ---------------------- | ------- | --- | --------- |
> | More advantages | 77 | 81 | 86 |
> | More disadvantages | 4 | 11 | 5 |
> | Evens out | 15 | 5 | 5 |
> | Undecided, no opinion | 4 | 3 | 4 |
> | | 100 | 100 | 100 |
>
> Source: Allensbach Archives, If D-survey 4210 (tel.), June 1999

* All values in percent

At the same time, individuals with Internet access know more than the average population about the risks associated with the Internet. 90 percent of German Internet users, 86 percent of American users and 78 percent of Australian users attribute the Internet with great risks in part.

Graph 5: Risk assessment

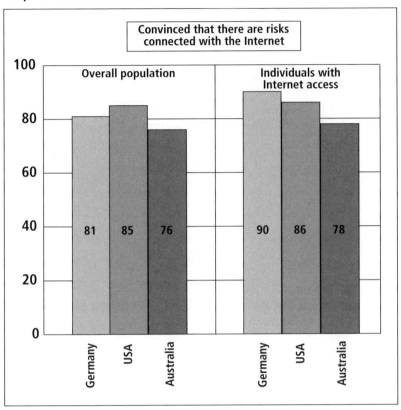

Question: "Would you say that the Internet also entails some risks or wouldn't you say so?"

Basis: Germany, USA, Australia; population 18 years and older

Most, however, do presume limited risks; a quarter of the American and German population believe the risks are considerable; for Australia, there is no comparable data available. But the question asked in Australia about the kind of risks involved with the Internet allows for the conclusion that the extent of the risks is considered to be as high as in the other two countries. When thinking about risks

411

on the Internet, the German and American populations first think of data protection and threats to privacy, the Australian population first thinks of the dangers of inappropriate Internet content to young people. Generally, spontaneous associations show that the discussions about risks on the Internet have taken a different course in the various countries and have, in part, made different progress. 31 percent of the Australians and a good fifth of the Americans spontaneously think of child protection when thinking about risks connected with the Internet, as opposed to only 6 percent of the Germans. In Australia, not only is the theme of child protection enhanced at an above-average level, but also pornographic content, organized crime and misuse of credit cards.

Table 2: Internet risks
(Germany, USA, Australia – Population 18 years and older)*

Question to individuals who believe that the Internet also entails some risks: "What risks do you associate with the Internet? Can you tell me which risks you're thinking of?"			
	Germany	USA	Australia
Data protection, privacy issues	24	22	17
Pornography	17	13	25
Risks in banking businesses	11	11	23
credit card misuse	3	7	20
fraud regarding payments	2	1	1
General: data misuse	6	3	3
Child protection, content unfit for minors	6	21	31
Hackers, uncontrolled access to all data	5	6	3
Threat of isolation	5	2	1
Criminality, illegal content	5	8	12
Danger of addiction	4	3	3
Cost, financial losses due to 'false' purchases	4	4	7
Forgery, manipulations	3	8	4

	Germany	USA	Australia
Glorification of violence, violent content	3	2	5
Viruses	2	3	4
Copyright not protected	2	1	1
Economic criminality	2	1	1
Misuse for the purpose of spreading propaganda	1	1	2
Espionage	1	1	1
Chat rooms, contact with sexually perverted, criminally sick or addicted persons	–	4	5
Other	5	4	4
No opinion	10	12	3
Do not believe that risks are connected with the Internet	19	15	24

* All values in percent

Parents who have children below the age of 18 show above-average concern about child protection in connection with the Internet. This applies, above all, to Australia, less so to the United States and, interestingly, hardly at all to Germany.

Individuals who have children below the age of 18 and access to the Internet connect the issue of risks on the Internet spontaneously with problems regarding child protection:
- Germany: 7 percent
- USA: 28 percent
- Australia: 40 percent.

The results reflect the differences in the status of the discussion about the risks in the various countries. The theme of child protection plays a major role in the public discussions taking place in the United States and Australia; in Germany, it thus far exists only in a nascent state. Appropriately, parents in Germany dedicate less attention to this issue in connection with the development of the Internet. German parents are not at all convinced that the Internet contains no content that might pose a danger to young people; this becomes clear when asked directly about youth protection. However, for the most part, they have not yet formed an opinion, which is also due to a lack of personal experience. 35 percent of the German parents of children under the age of 18 do not feel competent to make a judgement about whether content unsuitable for their children can be found on the Internet. In Australia, only 12 percent, and in the United States, only 6 percent of the parents have no opinion with respect to this question. 91 percent of the American parents, 79 percent of the Australian and only 63 percent of the German parents recognize dangers for their children in some areas of the Internet. From the German parents who themselves have access to the Internet, 82 percent perceive risks to their children; only about 14 percent do not feel competent to make a judgement about this question.

Table 3: Content inappropriate for children
(Germany, USA, Australia – Population over 18 years)*

Question: "Are there certain contents and sites on the Internet that you would say are inappropriate for your child or children?"			
	Persons with children younger than 18 in:		
	Germany	USA	Australia
Yes	63	91	79
No	2	3	9
Undecided/don't know	35	6	12
	100	100	100
	Persons with Internet access in:		
	Germany	USA	Australia
Yes	82	95	82
No	4	2	10
Undecided/don't know	14	3	8
	100	100	100

* All values in percent

414

Only the risk of chat rooms is considered to be lower by German parents than by American parents, even if they have personal Internet experience. Chat rooms have thus far played a less significant role in German Internet use than in America. Indeed, only two thirds of German Internet users know about chat rooms; in the United States, it is 90 percent. Whereas American parents with Internet access are already aware of chat rooms at a level that is above average, German parents with access to the Internet know less about this form of online communication than the average: 42 percent do not know about chat rooms, another 18 percent have not formed an opinion about whether chat rooms represent a problem with respect to the protection of young people. Among those who are prepared to make a judgement, there is a balance between concern and reassurance, contrary to American parents, whose judgement is extremely critical: 73 percent of the American parents with Internet experience perceive a problem with regard to the protection of youth in chat rooms.

Table 4: Chat rooms as a problem for child protection
(Germany, USA – Parents with Internet access)*

Question: "In general: do you think that the (so-called) chat rooms pose a problem when it comes to the protection of children and young people or don't you think so?"		
	Parents with Internet access in:	
	Germany	USA
Think they are a problem	20	73
No, not a problem	20	15
Undecided/don't know	18	3
Don't know chat rooms	42	9
	100	100

* All values in percent

415

2.1 Personal experience with inappropriate content

Thus far, only a minority of users has had personal experience with inappropriate content. One fourth of the users in Australia, one fourth in Germany and 35 percent in America have already encountered inappropriate content at some point during their Internet sessions. According to those who have personal experience with the Internet, the greatest perceived problem is the dissemination of pornographic content, followed, with some distance, by depictions of violence and political propaganda; with respect to political propaganda, reports thus far are exclusively about radical right-wing content. Six percent of the German users have already noticed propaganda on the Internet, 5 percent clearly attribute this kind of content to the radical right-wing scene. In the United States, 4 percent of the users complain about right-wing content. Pornographic content, however, is noticed much more frequently by Internet users than extreme political messages and depictions of violence. One in 5 Americans, almost the same number of Germans and also 15 percent of the Australian users have already encountered inappropriate pornographic depictions on the Internet.

Users who themselves have encountered offensive content are convinced at a level above average about the risks of the Internet. The assessment of the risks involved with the Internet is dependent upon personal experience, but only in a limited way. Those who are convinced of the risks of the Internet thus far can not, for the most part, refer to personal experiences with inappropriate content. In Germany 71 percent of the users who attribute risks to the Internet have thus far had no experience with inappropriate content.

Table 5: Personal experience with inappropriate content
(Germany, USA, Australia – Persons with Internet access)*

Question: "Have you, yourself, discovered anything on the Internet that you felt was disturbing in some way to you?"			
If: 'Yes, I have': "What was it that you discovered?"			
	Persons with Internet access in:		
	Germany	USA	Australia
Yes, I've discovered something	27	35	24
It was about –			
Pornography, sexual depictions	18	20	15
Depictions of violence, directions for violent acts, (building bombs), call for violence	7	5	7
Political propaganda	6	4	2
with right-wing radical content	5	4	2
with left-wing radical content	–	–	–
Sects	–	–	–
Other	2	5	3
No response	1	6	3
No, haven't discovered anything	72	64	76
No response	1	1	–
	100	100	100

* All values in percent

In their risk assessment, many refer to the contents and examples offered by traditional media. The extent of pornographic content and the glorification of violence on television is being criticized by large circles of the population. Altogether, the American and German populations agree that much of the content that is shown on television and on the Internet today is problematic; the desire to interfere with control mechanisms is appropriately widely spread. Women along with the general population group 45 years and older have an especially critical view. Two thirds of the German and American women consider the development of media content to be an extremely serious matter; contrary to this, German and especially American men consider this problem to be much less of a problem. 64 percent of the American women but only 47 percent of the American men consider the developments to be extremely problematic.

Table 6: A lot of media content is disturbing
(Germany, USA – Population 18 years and older)*

Question: "Thinking of all the things being shown on television and on the Internet nowadays, do you think the trend is going in a very disturbing direction or do you think a lot of this is exaggerated, that the trend is not so bad at all?"			
Germany	Overall	Men	Women
Very disturbing direction	61	55	66
It's not so bad at all	24	30	20
Undecided	15	15	14
	100	100	100
USA	Overall	Men	Women
Very disturbing direction	56	47	64
It's not so bad at all	35	45	26
Undecided	9	8	10
	100	100	100

* All values in percent

At the same time, the majority is convinced that they are not helpless in the face of these new developments in the traditional and the new media but that they can protect themselves from unwanted content. This also applies to the protection of children and minors: the majority of the population in all three countries and an over-

418

whelming majority among Internet users is convinced that parents can prevent their children from coming into contact with inappropriate content. People with Internet access are more optimistic with regard to this question than individuals who have no Internet experience.

Table 7: The majority perceives options for control
(Germany, USA, Australia – Population 18 years and older)*

Question: "Do you think there are ways for parents to prevent their children from viewing inappropriate content or sites on the Internet?"			
	Population in:		
	Germany	USA	Australia
Yes, there are possibilities	58	83	61
No	23	11	21
Undecided	19	6	18
	100	100	100
	Persons with Internet access in:		
	Germany	USA	Australia
Yes, there are possibilities	68	86	68
No	23	11	21
Undecided	9	3	11
	100	100	100

* All values in percent

3 National differences in the definition of inappropriate content

The definition of offensive content that may pose a danger to children can hardly be given in universally valid terms. The definitions are characterized by national culture, religious beliefs, political ideas, and the individual's history of socialization and sensitivity.

419

With respect to essential questions there is, however, a consensus carried by the majority of the population and beyond national borders. A large majority of the population in all three countries pleads for the blocking of racist messages: 79 percent of the German, 63 percent of the American and 60 percent of the Australian population are in favor of the blocking of such messages in all circumstances. This international consensus is also present when it comes to pornographic content. It is, however, just as clear that the threshold for shame varies, depending on the culture. Whereas the majority in all three countries wishes to avoid pornographic content, nudity is hardly viewed as offensive in Germany but is seen as considerably offensive in the United States. Only 13 percent of the German population, in contrast to 43 percent of the Americans, generally want to ban nudity from traditional media and the Internet. On the other hand, the German population is more offended by obscene language, which is considered to be less disturbing particularly by the American population.

Given the experiences from and the confrontation with their history, the German population is especially sensitive when it comes to politically radical content. 58 percent of the Germans but only 26 percent of the Americans want to avoid contact with radical right- or left-wing content on the Internet. The depiction of violence is also considered much more problematic in Germany than in the other two countries. 61 percent of the German, 39 percent of the American and 41 percent of the Australian population consider violence to be such a problem that they would block it from the Internet.

Graph 6: Internet content that should be blocked

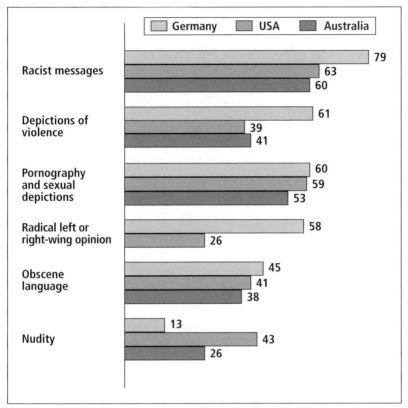

Question: "There are also things on the Internet which are not actually illegal, but which some people consider unsuitable for themselves or their children and would like to black out or block access to. Other people do not think these things are unsuitable and would like to view them. If it were up to you, which content would you personally block by all means, if it were technically possible, which would you only block under certain cirumstances and which wouldn't you block at all?"

Basis: Germany, USA, Australia; population 18 years and older

3.1 Gender-specific attitudes towards disturbing content

The critical attitude towards depictions of violence, pornography and nudity does not represent an appeal for a rigorous censorship of all media content. Most are aware of the fact that a general ban on depictions of violence, for example, is hardly in line with the principles of a free society and would massively curtail the free flow of information. Thus, the recipients are inevitably confronted with depictions of violence in news programs. The majority wants to differentiate between violence that is shown in an informative program, such as political news or sports reports, or in the context of entertainment. Most also differentiate between nudity in informative programs such as news or medical reports and that in films. Women make a stronger distinction than men, especially with respect to the depiction of nudity. The judgement of men and women differs noticeably in the United States when it comes to this question. Whereas a small majority of the men hold the opinion that the context is irrelevant when it comes to the depiction of nudity, two thirds of the American women base their assessment on the editorial context.

Table 8: The context of the depictions is decisive
(Germany, USA – Population 18 years and older)*

	Germany		USA	
	overall	women	overall	women
Question: "On television, nudity is shown in movies, on the news, in medical documentaries or on other programs. Would you say the type of program or context in which nudity is shown makes any difference to you or makes no difference to you?"				
Makes a difference	56	60	57	66
Makes no difference	39	35	40	31
Undecided	5	5	3	3
	100	100	100	100

Question: "And does it make any difference to you whether violence comes up in movies, on the news, on sports programs, or on other programs or doesn't it make any difference to you?"

| | Germany | | USA | |
	overall	women	overall	women
Makes a difference	64	65	55	63
Makes no difference	31	30	41	31
Undecided	5	5	4	6
	100	100	100	100

* All values in percent

This stronger tendency of women to draw a distinction depending on the context is, given the above-average tendency of women in all three countries, of importance when considering restrictions of Internet content and the blocking of as much inappropriate content as possible. In particular, depictions of violence, nudity and pornography are generally considered to be a bigger problem by women than by men. The differences between men and women are especially large in the United States and the smallest in Germany. If the share of men who appeal for a restrictive approach to content is set to 100, the share of women is always above this level. When it comes to the depiction of violence, in Germany the share of women who want to ban this kind of content from the Internet is almost 20 percent above that of the men, in the United States and Australia it is over 70 percent above the index value.

Graph 7: Tendency towards blocking specific content

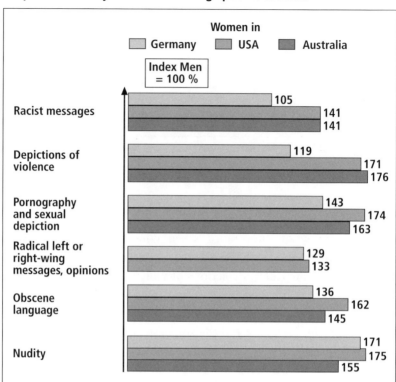

Women in
Germany USA Australia

Index Men = 100 %

Racist messages
105
141
141

Depictions of violence
119
171
176

Pornography and sexual depiction
143
174
163

Radical left or right-wing messages, opinions
129
133

Obscene language
136
162
145

Nudity
171
175
155

Question: "There are also things on the Internet which are not actually illegal, but which some people consider unsuitable for themselves or their children and would like to black out or block access to. Other people do not think these things are unsuitable and would like to view them. If it were up to you, which contents would you personally block by all means, if it were technically possible, which would you only block under certain cirumstances and which wouldn't you block at all?"

Basis: Germany, USA, Australia; population 18 years and older

In all three countries, between two thirds and three fourths of all women appeal for the blocking of pornographic content on the Internet, among men this share varies between 40 percent (Australia) and 49 percent (Germany).

424

Graph 8: Tendency towards blocking pornographic content

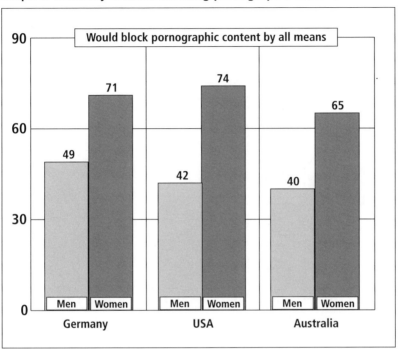

Question: "There are also things on the Internet which are not actually illegal, but which some people consider unsuitable for themselves or their children and would like to black out or block access to. Other people do not think these things are unsuitable and would like to view them. If it were up to you, which contents would you personally block by all means, if it were technically possible, which would you only block under certain cirumstances and which wouldn't you block at all?"

Basis: Germany, USA, Australia; population 18 years and older

Beside the strong objection to pornographic content, the American sensitivity towards depictions of nudity primarily goes back to the female population, as well. 54 percent of the American women, but only 31 percent of the American men want to generally ban depictions of nudity from the Internet.

Graph 9: Tendency towards blocking violent depictions

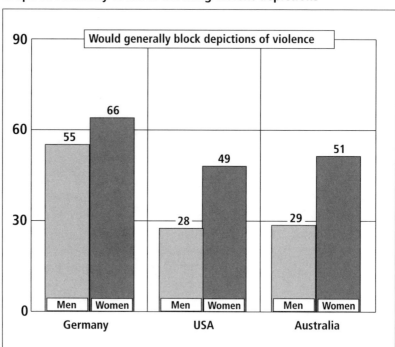

Question: "There are also things on the Internet which are not actually illegal, but which some people consider unsuitable for themselves or their children and would like to black out or block access to. Other people do not think these things are unsuitable and would like to view them. If it were up to you, which contents would you personally block by all means, if it were technically possible, which would you only block under certain cirumstances and which wouldn't you block at all?"

Basis: Germany, USA, Australia; population 18 years and older

The lower discrepancy in the comparison between the attitudes of women and men in the US and Australia towards depictions of violence does not go back to a more harmless assessment by women in Germany but to an unusually rigorous attitude of German men compared to other countries. The majority of them appeal for a general ban of violent depictions on the Internet, an attitude that is shared by only 28 percent of the American and 29 percent of the Australian men. German women also appeal for restrictions at an above-average level compared with the other two nations.

3.2 Generation-specific attitudes towards inappropriate content

Not only is the consensus between men and women wider in Germany than in the United States and Australia, but also between the generations. The assessment in all three countries depends upon age; people over the age of 45 are in favor of prevention of such content on an above-average level, but the 18 to 24 age group views such controls on a level that is below average. Whereas 18 to 24 year-old Germans, in a limited way, have a different attitude compared with people who are middle-aged and older, the strict dividing line between this age group and the rest of the population is striking in both the United States and Australia. Especially depictions of violence, but pornographic content as well, are considered significantly less problematic by the 18 to 24 year-old Americans and Australians than the middle-aged and older people. In the case of racist content, the young German generation has an above-average tendency towards favoring a general ban – an attitude that is slightly below the average level in the same age group in the U.S. and Australia. With respect to other radical political content as well, a consensus embracing all generations can be observed in Germany, whereas the young American generation perceives fewer problems in this area than the average of the American population.

Graph 10: Different attitudes of different generations towards blocking specific content

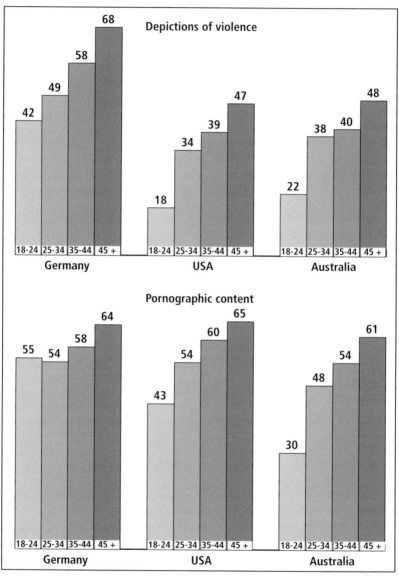

Question: "There are also things on the Internet which are not actually illegal, but which some people consider unsuitable for themselves or their children and would like to black out or block access to. Other people do not think these things are unsuitable and would like to view them. If it were up to you, which contents would you personally block by all means, if it were technically possible, which would you only block under certain cirumstances and which wouldn't you block at all?"

Basis: Germany, USA, Australia; population 18 years and older

Interestingly, parents of children with Internet access tend less towards a restrictive attitude than the average of the parents. This applies to pornographic and obscene content as well as for depictions of violence or radical political messages. Whereas, for example, almost two thirds of the German parents want to block out pornographic content by any and all means, this is the case among only 49 percent of the parents whose children have Internet access. 60 percent of all parents do not accept depictions of violence, but only 48 percent of the parents whose children use the Internet. The same tendency can be observed in Australia and, in a more restricted way, in the United States. Among other factors, this is based on the fact that only a minority has had direct negative experiences in the course of their personal use of the new medium and has encountered content that they would like to block by any and all means.

Table 9: Parents of children with Internet access worry less
(Germany – Persons with children younger than 18)*

Question: "There are also things on the Internet which are not actually illegal, but which some people consider unsuitable for themselves or their children and would like to black out or block access to. Other people don't think these things are unsuitable and would like to view them. If it were up to you, which contents would you personally block by all means, if it were technically possible, which would you only block under certain circumstances and which wouldn't you block at all? I shall now read a few items to you."

	Persons with children younger than 18:		
	overall	Internet access:	
		yes	no
I would block by all means:			
Racist messages	82	74	85
Pornography and sexual depictions	63	49	66
Depictions of violence	60	48	62
Right- or left-wing radical opinions, messages	58	46	60
Obscene language	45	30	46
Nudity	11	9	10

* All values in percent

Table 10: Parents of children with Internet access worry less
(USA, Australia – Persons with children younger than 18)*

> *Question:* "There are also things on the Internet which are not actually illegal, but which some people consider unsuitable for themselves or their children and would like to black out or block access to. Other people don't think these things are unsuitable and would like to view them. If it were up to you, which contents would you personally block by all means, if it were technically possible, which would you only block under certain circumstances and which wouldn't you block at all? I shall now read a few items to you."

I would block by all means:

USA	overall	Internet access:	
		yes	no
Racist messages	68	65	73
Pornography and sexual depictions	67	66	70
Nudity	48	45	52
Depictions of violence	45	41	50
Obscene language	42	41	44
Right- or left-wing radical opinions, messages	26	23	32

Australia	overall	Internet access:	
		yes	no
Racist messages	62	62	64
Pornography and sexual depictions	58	52	65
Obscene language	41	35	49
Depictions of violence	38	31	48
Nudity	30	24	35
Right- or left-wing radical opinions, messages	–	–	–

* All values in percent

The majority of all parents, like the majority of the parents whose children have access to the Internet, want to be able to block out the possibility to shop via the Internet using any and all means. German parents, like the overall German population, are more disquieted about the possibility of uncontrolled purchases by children than their American counterparts. 72 percent of German parents and 55 percent of the American parents of children younger than 18 want to block this possibility by any and all means. Here, too, personal experience reduces the amount of concern rather than raising it. Whereas 72 percent of all German parents of children below the age of 18 absolutely want to block out the possibility of their children shopping on the Internet, only 65 percent of the parents whose children have Internet access share this opinion. This result and the fact that uncontrolled purchasing by children hardly played any role in the risks spontaneously associated with Internet use allow for the conclusion that this is not a serious concern of parents but rather a widespread belief that prophylactic measures should be assessed positively in this area.

Table 11: Majority of parents would block possibility for shopping
(Germany, USA – Population 18 years and older)*

> *Question:* "You can also shop on the Internet, that is, you can order merchandise. Would you prevent children from purchasing merchandise online by all means or only under certain circumstances, or wouldn't you prevent them from doing so?"

Germany	Population overall	Parents of children younger than 18	
		overall	with Internet access
Prevent by all means	73	72	65
Prevent under certain circumstances	18	19	20
Would not prevent	6	7	11
Undecided/don't know	3	2	4
	100	100	100

USA	Population overall	Parents of children younger than 18	
		overall	with Internet access
Prevent by all means	56	55	53
Prevent under certain circumstances	35	38	41
Would not prevent	5	5	4
Undecided/don't know	4	2	2
	100	100	100

* All values in percent

4 An appeal for personal responsibility

Given the widespread desire to shield oneself and, above all, young people from certain content on the Internet, the question arises about who should be entrusted with the responsibility of fulfilling this need. Research with respect to the control of inappropriate content in traditional media reveals that the population is well

aware that technological progress has changed the initial conditions upon which any kind of control measure would be based
and that, hence, the original and at least somewhat efficient control mechanisms can no longer be relied upon to function effectively. The overwhelming majority does not question that the
legal authorities should increasingly interfere in cases where clearly illegal content, such as child pornography, are concerned. 79
percent of the American and 86 percent of the German population appeal for a clear expansion of police controls of illegal content on the Internet and prosecution of those responsible.

Table 12: The overwhelming majority asks
for increased police monitoring
(Germany, USA – Population 18 years and older)*

Question: "You are able to access some things on the Internet which are illegal, such as child pornography or instructions for making bombs. Do you think police authorities should monitor the Internet more heavily?"		
	Population overall in:	
	Germany	USA
Yes, we need more police monitoring	86	79
No, I don't think so	7	16
Undecided	7	5
	100	100
	Persons with Internet access in:	
	Germany	USA
Yes, we need more police monitoring	78	77
No, I don't think so	15	18
Undecided	7	5
	100	100

* All values in percent

At the same time, the overwhelming majority has doubts as to whether police monitoring can efficiently counteract inappropriate and illegal content on the Internet. Internet users are more skeptical than the general population when considering the possibilities of the legal authorities to control illegal content:

Have doubts that the misuse of the Internet can be efficiently monitored through police measures:		
	Population overall	Internet users
Germany	72 percent	77 percent
USA	63 percent	66 percent
Australia	71 percent	77 percent

The assessment of who can best control misuse on the Internet displays strikingly different national perspectives. The Australians trust the Internet users themselves to best accomplish this task, followed by online service providers, other agencies such as government or independent agencies, and the producers of websites. The Americans clearly place the highest level of trust on the users themselves, followed by the online service providers and organizations specialized in child protection or with a special moral authority of some other kind.

Contrary to this, the German population places trust on politics and law enforcement authorities to a noticeably greater extent, while it only gives a small amount of credit to the Internet users themselves. Whereas 48 percent of the Australian and 36 percent of the American population consider the individual Internet user as the best guarantor of an effective control of inappropriate content, barely one fifth of the German population shares this opinion. In contrast, 28 percent of the German population places trust on politicians, but only 2 percent of the American and 12 percent of the Australian population.

However, Germans have far more confidence in online providers such as AOL and T-Online than in police and justice. 39 percent of Germans think that their competence is particularly high.

Graph 11: Supervision of Internet content

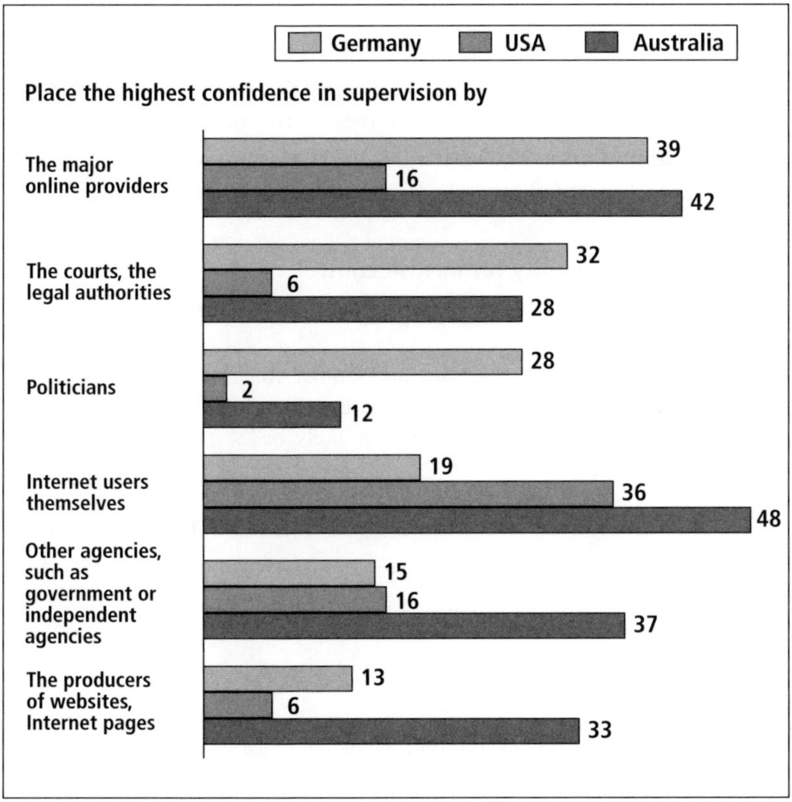

Question: "Who do you think would be most able to ensure the supervision and selection of Internet content, in whom would you have the most confidence?"

Basis: Germany, USA, Australia; population 18 years and older

The theory that the minimal amount of trust placed by the German population on the users themselves to control the content that enters their computers from the Internet goes back to a lack of experience with the medium is not confirmed. If this was the case, German Internet users' trust in their own capability to control Internet content would be corresponding to that of the Americans and Australians. German Internet users believe themselves to be significantly less capable to fulfill the task of content control than do Australian or American users, and they trust in politics, the justice system and the legal authorities to an above-average degree. American Internet users primarily perceive the users themselves as the best guarantors of an efficient content control, Australian users also mainly trust the users themselves in connection with the large online providers.

Table 13: Responsibility for misuse control
(Germany, USA, Australia – Population 18 years and older)*

	Persons with Internet access in:		
	Germany	USA	Australia
Question: "Who do you think would be most able to ensure the supervision and selection of Internet content, in whom would you have most confidence? Would you say that would likely be ..." (multiple responses possible)			

	Germany	USA	Australia
The major online providers	53	17	47
The courts, legal authorities	35	6	26
Politicians	20	1	9
Internet users themselves	29	41	52
Other agencies	10	14	39
The producers of websites, Internet pages	18	6	34
Other	4	11	8
Undecided/don't know	5	10	5
	174	106	220

* All values in percent

The German population generally has an above-average tendency towards state-sponsored interventions and controls. This also becomes clear with respect to the question of whether child protection on the Internet is better safeguarded by parents or by government authorities. The majority of the German and the American population favors control by the parents; in the United States, however, there is a much wider consensus with regard to this question than in Germany. 83 percent of the American population favor leaving the control of what children can see on the Internet with the parents. In Germany, only 57 percent of those polled share this opinion, whereas 31 percent want to defer to governmental institutions and control authorities. German and American parents of children with Internet access differ even more with regard to this question than the average population. 37 percent of German parents whose children have Internet access would prefer placing the protection of their children from inappropriate Internet content on governmental authorities rather than fulfilling this task themselves, in the United States, only 11 percent feel this way.

Table 14: Preference for personal responsibility
(Germany, USA – Population 18 years and older)*

Question: "Do you think it would be better if parents could decide for themselves what their children are able to view on the Internet or do you think it would be better for the government agencies to decide what children can and cannot view?"		
Germany	Population overall	Persons with children younger than 18 and Internet access
Better if parents decide themselves	57	49
Better if government agencies make the decisions	31	37
Undecided	12	14
	100	100

USA	Population overall	Persons with children younger than 18 and Internet access
Better if parents decide themselves	83	84
Better if government agencies make the decisions	12	11
Undecided	5	5
	100	100

* All values in percent

In general, Americans very clearly support the principle of personal responsibility and freedom from governmental regulations. This not only applies to attitudes about the control of inappropriate content on the Internet but also about media content in general. The idea that violence and pornography in movies should be subject to state censorship is foreign to the American population. 69 percent would assign responsibility to the viewers, and only 26 percent of the American population would want to assure from the onset, through bans and state censorship, that such scenes do not appear on the screen at all. The attitudes in Germany are completely different: 59 percent of the German population would like to prevent from the onset such scenes from appearing at all, and only 36 percent would assign responsibility to the viewers themselves. The attitude of the American population is characterized by a clearly greater amount of trust placed on personal standards and possibilities; the attitude of the German population, however, is marked by the model of a strong state control.

438

Table 15: American plea for personal responsibility
(Germany, USA – Population 18 years and older)*

> *Question:* "Now thinking about television for a moment, people often say that there are television programs that have violent scenes or sexually explicit scenes and that these programs should be banned. Do you feel we should try to prevent these programs from appearing on television or should it be up to the individual to decide which programs to watch?"
>
> | | Germany | USA |
> | ------------------------------ | :-----: | :-: |
> | Should prevent from appearing | 59 | 26 |
> | Up to the individual | 36 | 69 |
> | Undecided/don't know | 5 | 5 |
> | | 100 | 100 |

* All values in percent

Such divergent ideas concerning the division between the roles of the state and of its citizens have evolved over the centuries and can not be resolved in the short term. There may be indications that the younger generation in Germany is coming closer to sharing the American perspective. With a clear majority, 18 to 24 year-old Germans hold the opinion that in the end the individual should be able to decide upon the media contents he or she wants to see and wants to avoid. However, when it comes to other questions, individuals in this age group display typically German patterns of attitude. The discrepancy between 18 to 24 year-old Germans and Americans with regard to the question about whether parents or governmental authorities should decide about the contents accessible to children on the Internet is even greater than among the general population. 88 percent of young Americans and only 58 percent of young Germans would leave this decision up to the parents. The question about the predetermined control institutions also does not show a clear tendency towards liberalization: young Germans may consider the Internet users themselves more capable than do Germans who are 35 years and older; but at the same time young Germans would also rely more on the justice system and legal authorities than on the individual.

In the United States, 18 to 24 year-olds also call for a control of media content on the basis of personal responsibility at an above-average rate, while those over the age of 45 show an above-average tendency to defer to general bans and governmental controls. And yet, the preference for liberal solutions and personal responsibility is also very clear among the American population over the age of 45, as opposed to Germans in the same age group. All generations are characterized by a different understanding about the distribution of power between the citizens and the state and thus a different level of trust in their own capabilities.

Table 16: Differences based on gender and generation
(Germany, USA – Population 18 years and older)*

Question: "Now thinking about television for a moment, people often say that there are television programs that have violent scenes or sexually explicit scenes and that these programs should be banned. Do you feel we should try to prevent these programs from appearing on television or should it be up to the individual to decide which programs to watch?"

Germany	Gender		Age Groups			
	Men	Women	18–24 years	25–34 years	35–44 years	45 years and older
Should prevent from appearing	47	69	39	51	52	66
Up to the individual	47	27	57	43	44	29
Undecided/don't know	6	4	4	6	4	5
	100	100	100	100	100	100

440

USA	Gender		Age Groups			
	Men	Women	18–24 years	25–34 years	35–44 years	45 years and older
Should prevent from appearing	18	34	11	20	25	34
Up to the individual	77	61	87	76	70	60
Undecided/don't know	5	5	2	4	5	6
	100	100	100	100	100	100

* All values in percent

5 Broad acceptance of a system of voluntary self-regulation

The very diverse ideas about who can best be entrusted with the control of content on the Internet are based, on one hand, on different state traditions and, on the other, on the status of the discussion about misuse control on the Internet in each country. The lower tendency of the German population to assign this task to the Internet service providers and, above all, to the users does not represent a rejection of self-regulatory concepts. Rather, it goes back to fundamental beliefs that ascribe greater latitude for the state to evolve without reflecting upon the impact it will have on individual freedom. In part, the differences also reflect the fact that the discussion about the dangers of Internet content and the possibilities for controlling misuse and abuse is still in a nascent state in Germany.

That the above-average tendency of the Germans to defer to the state when it comes to the control of potential misuse does not represent a rejection of self-regulatory concepts is shown in the extraordinarily positive reaction to concepts of voluntary self-regulation. If the possibility for every Internet user to block out certain content is mentioned, the reaction in Germany is just as positive as in the United States and Australia. Approximately eight out of ten citizens in all three countries welcome such a possibility; the share of the population that considers such mechanisms unnecessary is even the smallest in Germany with 13 percent.

Table 17: In favor of personal selection
(Germany, USA, Australia – Population 18 years and older)*

> *Question:* "Anyone can publish information, pictures or even video re-cordings on the Internet. Regardless of whether or not it's technically possible, do you think it would be a good idea if everyone could set their computers so that certain Internet contents would be blacked out auto-matically, so that they would never appear on users' screens, or do you think that's not necessary?"
>
> | | Germany | USA | Australia |
> |------------------------|---------|-----|-----------|
> | Yes, good idea | 79 | 78 | 77 |
> | No, not necessary | 13 | 17 | 18 |
> | Undecided/don't know | 8 | 5 | 5 |
> | | 100 | 100 | 100 |

* All values in percent

There is also a broad consensus that the filtering should be effected autonomously by the users so that the individual user can decide which content is blocked. The Internet users appeal even more unanimously for a self-regulatory control than the average of the population. The broad consensus between the German and the American population shows that concepts of self-regulation are as popular in Germany as they are in the United States, provided that the population perceives them as a realistic alternative.

Graph 12: Pro filter setting by the individual

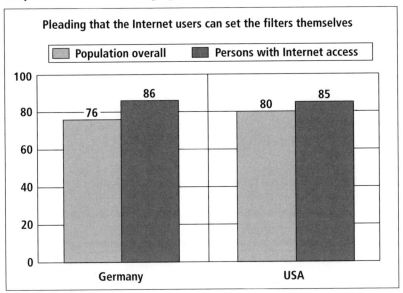

Pleading that the Internet users can set the filters themselves

Population overall   Persons with Internet access

Germany: 76 (Population overall), 86 (Persons with Internet access)
USA: 80 (Population overall), 85 (Persons with Internet access)

Question: "Would you prefer that computers have a preset filter that automatically filters out certain content or would it be better for users to be able to set the filters themselves?"

Basis: Germany, USA, Australia; population 18 years and older

Given this wide acceptance of self-regulated selection of content, it comes as no surprise that a concept whereby the online service providers offer aids to facilitate selection for the users in connection with the appropriate selection technique meets with the interest and approval of the overwhelming majority of the population in all three countries. This system was concretely presented to the polled individuals as follows:

"A system has now been developed that enables users to filter the Internet sites and pages they have access to in their homes. It works like this: all Internet providers mark their pages with symbols indicating whether the page contains depictions of violence, sex or

443

other such things. All Internet users can then set their computers at home so that certain topics and depictions are automatically blacked out."

This concept meets with overwhelming approval in all three countries included in the survey. 90 percent of the Australian population, 84 percent of the German and 83 percent of the American population consider this system sensible and useful. Those who already have access to the Internet are even more unanimously positive towards the system than the average of the population.

Graph 13: Very positive resonance of a system of self-regulation

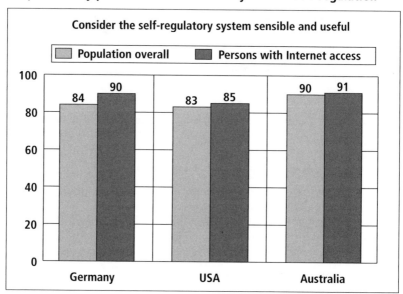

"A system has now been developed that enables users to filter the Internet sites and pages they have access to in their homes. It works like this: all Internet providers mark their pages with symbols indicating whether the page contains depictions of violence, sex or other such things. All Internet users can then set their computers at home so that certain topics and depictions are automatically blacked out. Do you think this is a useful system on the whole or do not you think so?"

Basis: Germany, USA, Australia; population 18 years and older

444

The system that was presented presumes a cooperation between Internet providers and users. The providers have to develop criteria for the classification of content that are accepted by the users as sensible and in line with their personal moral and social values. Only through such a systematic rating of content does it become possible for individual users to control the selection of content without having to check specific cases.

The widespread approval of a system for rating the suitability of Internet content for young people, comparable to the rating system used by the movie industry, shows just how great the interest in the classification of Internet content is, especially in connection with child protection. 86 percent of the German, 79 percent of the Australian and 75 percent of the American parents of children younger than 18 would consider such a system of classification that would indicate the suitability of content for specific age groups useful.

Necessarily, the acceptance of a system of control based on classification standards stands and falls with the consensus or dissent with regard to the criteria that the classification of media content will be based upon and with the reputation of the insitutions that are given the resposibility of creating the classification. In Germany, such an institution does not yet exist, whereas in the United States, the Recreational-Software-Advisory-Council on the Internet (RSACi) was founded in 1996; providers can classify their websites according to RSACi standards. The categories that exist thus far are noticeably influenced by American values and tastes; however, the Bertelsmann Foundation is striving to develop an internationally valid rating system in collaboration with business entities from the Internet industry. This survey is not able to make specific recommendations – within the given framework – in as far as a consensus could not be achieved. This question requires a more complex survey in which test subjects are confronted with certain media content and asked for an assessment within the framework of a given rating system. The general interest in a system that provides parents with a prophylactic selection without having to check individual cases is, however, extraordinarily great.

Table 18: Wide approval of a classification of Internet content according to its suitability for certain age groups
(Germany, USA, Australia – Population 18 years and older)*

Question: "Movies are rated according to whether they are appropriate for children and young people of certain ages. If there were some kinds of ratings like this for the Internet, do you think that would be useful or not so useful?"			
	Germany	USA	Australia
Would be useful	82	69	78
Not so useful	13	25	18
Undecided/don't know	5	6	4
	100	100	100
	Persons with children younger than 18 in:		
	Germany	USA	Australia
Would be useful	86	75	79
Not so useful	11	22	18
Undecided/don't know	3	3	3
	100	100	100

* All values in percent

5.1 Problematic chat rooms

Chat rooms' contents evade a predetermined classification and therefore represent a specific problem. However, other forms of classifications are possible such as the classification as "highly monitored chat room," "monitored chat room" and "not monitored chat room." Such a possibility to allow access by children e.g. only to monitored chat rooms is perceived as very positive. 79 percent of the American

446

Internet users with children younger than 18 and 44 percent of the German parents with Internet access welcome this concept. The lower approval in Germany does not, however, represent a rejection of this concept. Only 7 percent of the German parents of children with Internet access consider such a monitoring system unnecessary. This share is even lower than in the United States. Moreover, the lower approval in Germany is mainly associated with the reduced familiarity with chat rooms and the differing status of the national discussion. In the thus far barely developed discussion in Germany about inappropriate content on the Internet, chat rooms have hardly played any role at all. 35 percent of the German Internet users do not really know anything about chat rooms, and even 42 percent of the parents who have Internet access are not familiar with them. In the United States, however, only a small minority has no knowledge about how chat rooms function and the risks associated with them. Hence, a comparison can only be made based on those individuals who can make an assessment that is at least based on the level of a basic common denominator. On this basis, the German results, for the most part, adjust to the American results. In Germany, 76 percent of the parents who know about chat rooms have a positive attitude towards the monitoring of chat rooms, in the United States, 87 percent.

Table 19: Wide approval for monitoring chat rooms
(Germany, USA – Persons with Internet access)*

> *Question:* "A system has now been developed that can monitor chat rooms, giving users the choice of visiting chat rooms that are closely monitored, not so closely monitored or not monitored at all. Do you think a system like this, where users can set their computers so children only have access to monitored chat rooms is good or do you think it's unnecessary?"

Germany	Population overall	Parents of children younger than 18	
		overall	discerning persons
Think it' s good	49	44	76
Think it's unnecessary	10	7	12
Undecided/don't know	6	7	12
Don't know chat rooms	35	42	–
	100	100	100

USA	Population overall	Parents of children younger than 18	
		overall	discerning persons
Think it's good	76	79	87
Think it's unnecessary	12	11	12
Undecided/don't know	2	1	1
Don't know chat rooms	10	9	–
	100	100	100

* All values in percent

5.2 Competitive advantages through classification

The success of classification systems depends not only upon the acceptance of the classification criteria but also upon the participation of content providers. Since the rating is voluntary, a high level of participation can not be presumed. The attitudes of the population in all three countries show, however, that the efforts of Internet providers to facilitate the selection and blocking of sites for their users via the classification of Internet content could become a competive advantage for providers. Approximately half the population in Germany and the United States and 57 percent of the Australian population leans towards making such a commitment by the providers a selection criterion for choosing a provider. Approximately one out of two current Internet users in all three countries expresses that such a voluntary self-regulation could play an essential role in their decision with regard to registering with a provider.

448

Table 20: Voluntary self-regulation – a competitive advantage
(Germany, USA, Australia – Population 18 years and older)*

> *Question:* "In order to access the Internet, you have to sign up with a service provider. Now assume a provider tries to attract new customers by offering to filter out Internet content that is harmful or disturbing to young people before it ever appears on users' screens. When choosing an Internet service provider, would you say this would be an important aspect in making your decision, or are there other options that are more important to you?"

	Germany	USA	Australia
Yes, an important aspect	48	50	57
No, other options are more important	35	40	32
Undecided/don't know	17	10	11
	100	100	100

Persons with Internet access in:	Germany	USA	Australia
Yes, an important aspect	47	50	52
No, other options are more important	48	44	43
Undecided/don't know	5	6	5
	100	100	100

* All values in percent

Both women and parents of children younger than 18 tend towards considering this criterion in their choice of Internet providers on an above-average level. Given that a provider has a sensible classification system and advertises it aggressively, 59 percent of the German, 60 percent of the American and even two thirds of the Australian parents can imagine that this would be a decisive factor in the selection of an Internet provider. The above-average interest of women in all three countries in blocking out inappropriate content is also reflected in a strong preference for Internet providers with the appropriate classification contents. In all three countries, the majority of the female population leans toward making their decision concerning an Internet provider dependent upon the provider having an appropriate classification system in place:

Graph 14: Above-average interest of women in filtering systems

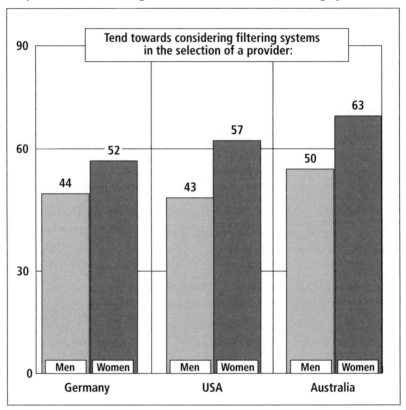

Question: "In order to access the Internet, you have to sign up with a service provider. Now assume a provider tries to attract new customers by offering to filter out Internet content that is harmful or disturbing to young people before it ever appears on users' screens. When choosing an Internet service provider, would you say this would be an important aspect in making your decision, or are there other options that are more important to you?"

Basis: Germany, USA, Australia; population 18 years and older

6 Positive attitude towards hotlines

Aside from filtering software that enables the users to block certain content from their computers, hotlines represent another possibility to have inappropriate content examined and, if necessary, to have it eliminated from websites. In Germany, such a hotline thus far exists only in the form of the "voluntary self-regulation of the multimedia service providers" (Freiwillige Selbstkontrolle der Multimedia-Diensteanbieter, FSM), and in Great Britain, in the form of the Internet Watch Foundation. The disadvantage of such hotlines is that, by their very nature, they can only become active after the fact, i.e., only after a user has submitted a complaint about inappropriate content. Despite this handicap, hotlines that enable users to complain about content are assessed as being extremely positive. 80 percent of the German population, 70 percent of the Australian and 66 percent of the American population have a positive attitude towards hotlines. In all three countries, the concept of hotlines is welcomed by parents of children younger than 18 to an above-average extent.

Table 21: Unanimous approval of hotlines

(Germany, USA, Australia – Population 18 years and older)*

Question: "In some countries there are hotlines you can call when you find dangerous content on the Internet. These kinds of hotlines are often run by independent organizations that are trying to rid the Internet of such content. Do you think it's a good thing that there are hotlines of this kind in some countries or don't you think they help much?"			
	Germany	USA	Australia
Yes, a good thing	80	66	70
No, doesn't help much	11	21	17
It depends	3	4	6
Undecided/don't know	6	9	7
	100	100	100
	Persons with children younger than 18 in:		
	Germany	USA	Australia
Yes, a good thing	86	71	76
No, doesn't help much	8	18	14
It depends	2	3	4
Undecided/don't know	4	8	6
	100	100	100

* All values in percent

A complaint via a hotline is considered more effective than a report to the local police. Especially the American population, but also a relative majority of the German population, is convinced that a complaint via a hotline would be more successful than informing the police. In both countries, a clear majority of individuals with Internet access believe that a hotline system would be superior to the possibilities of intervention by the police.

Table 22: Preference for hotlines
(Germany, USA – Population 18 years and older)*

Question: "Which do you think is more effective: calling a hotline when you discover something highly offensive or dangerous on the Internet or informing the police?"		
Germany	population overall	Persons with Internet access
Hotline	41	54
Police	34	24
Undecided/don't know	25	22
	100	100
USA	population overall	Persons with Internet access
Hotline	50	53
Police	29	26
Undecided/don't know	21	21
	100	100

* All values in percent

The question concerning who should provide and finance such a hotline again revealed distinct national differences. The American population believes that this is most likely a job for the large companies running the Internet, followed by private initiatives and the individual service providers. The Australian population mainly thinks of the state and the large companies running the Internet, as does the German population, although in reversed order. Here, the experience with the Internet partially changes the assessment, which is especially noticeable in Germany. German Internet users are convinced that the large companies running the Internet should be responsible for hotlines.

Table 23: Who should finance the hotlines?

(Germany, USA, Australia – Population 18 years and older)*

Question: "In your view, who should set up and finance these kinds of hotlines? Would you say this would most likely be a job for ...?"			
	Germany	USA	Australia
The government, the state	37	18	30
The major companies which run the Internet	38	30	27
The individual Internet service providers	12	19	15
Private initiatives	13	24	11
Other	1	1	3
Undecided/don't know	9	8	14
	110	100	100
	Persons with Internet access in:		
	Germany	USA	Australia
The government, the state	37	17	28
The major companies which run the Internet	47	29	24
The individual Internet service providers	15	20	18
Private initiatives	16	27	12
Other	2	1	4
Undecided/don't know	3	6	14
	120	100	100

* All values in percent

Of course, such a question concerning hotlines extends beyond the scope of the current discussion, and most questions have to necessarily go unanswered. At the same time, this question is of lesser importance for Internet users; the fundamental question about the possibilities of control of content on the Internet is of far greater interest to the users.

The results of the survey show that the population on an international level considers the control of content on the Internet to be an important task. The majority wants to counter inappropriate content and welcomes control mechanisms that leave the responsibility for the selection with the users but also offer them efficient criteria and procedures to make the selection without having to check on individual cases. With the continuing expansion of Internet use and increasing experience with inappropriate content, the interest in such selection mechanisms will continue to rise. The data already shows that the participation in systems that provide the recipient with the ability to consciously select or reject content can become an essential competitive factor for the providers of Internet content.

Chapter VI

Self-Regulation on the Internet
A Bibliography

Markus Behmer, Bettina Trapp[1]

The following bibliography, compiled in the summer of 1999, aims at providing an overview of English and German sources in the areas of Internet policy and regulation. It is by no means complete but should be a useful starting point for further research in this area.

Books and Articles

Albaran, Alan B. (ed.) (1998): Global Media Economics: Commercialization, Concentration and Integration of World Media Markets. Ames: Iowa State University Press

Allard, Nicholas E./David A. Kass (1997): Law and Order in Cyberspace: Washington Report. Comm/Ent, 19, pp. 563 passim

---

[1] Research assistents, Commiunication Science Institute, University of Munich, Germany.

Ayers, I./J. Braithwaite (1992): Responsive Regulation. Transcending the Deregulation Debate. New York/Oxford: Oxford Univ. Press

Bär, Wolfgang: Strafrechtliche Kontrolle in Datennetzen. Multimedia und Recht, 1 (9), pp. 463–468

Baldwin, Thomas F. (1996): Convergence: Integrating Media, Information and Communication. London [et al.]: Sage

Balkam, Stephen (1998): Sex, Lügen und Selbstregulierung. Bertelsmann Briefe 140, pp. 22–23

Bangemann High Level Group on the Information Society (1994): Europe and the Global Information Society: Recommendations to the European Council. Brussels: European Commission

Barrelet, Denis (1998): La publication du nom d'auteurs d'infractions par les médias. Media Lex, 4, pp. 204–212

Barrett, Daniel J. (1996): Was Sie schon immer wissen wollten: Gauner und Ganoven im Internet. Bonn: O'Reilly/International Thomson

Bartosch, Andreas (1998): Das Grünbuch über Konvergenz: ein Beitrag zur Diskussion auf dem Weg in die Informationsgesellschaft. Zeitschrift für Urheber- und Medienrecht, 42 (3), pp. 209–220

Bartsch, Michael/Bernd Lutterbeck (eds.) (1998): Neues Recht für neue Medien. Köln: O. Schmidt

Beck, Klaus/Gerhard Vowe (1998): Zwischen Anarchie und Zensur – Zur Regulierung internationaler computervermittelter Kommunikation. In: Siegfried Quandt/Wolfgang Gast (eds.): Deutschland im Dialog der Kulturen. Medien – Images – Verständigung. Konstanz: UVK Medien, pp. 349–366

Beck, Klaus/Gerhard Vowe (eds.) (1997): Computernetze – ein Medium öffentlicher Kommunikation. Berlin: Spieß

Becker, Jörg (1998): Massenkommunikation und individuelle Selbstbestimmung: Zur Entregelung staatlich-technischer Informationsprozesse. Aus Politik und Zeitgeschichte, B 40, pp. 3–12

Bender, Gunnar (1998): Fahrgemeinschaften auf der Datenautobahn: Rechtskontrolle multimedialer Unternehmensverflechtungen in Deutschland. Kommunikation und Recht, 1 (10), pp. 428–432

Beniger, James R. (1986): The Control Revolution: Technological and Economic Origins of the Information Society. Cambridge, Mass. [et al.]: Harvard University Press

Bensoussan, Alain (1998): Internet: aspects juridiques. Paris: Hermes (2 ed.)

Biernatzki, William E. (1997): Globalization of Communication. Communication Research Trends, 17 (1), pp. 1–30

Birks, Peter (ed.) (1998): Privacy and Loyalty. Oxford: Clarendon Press

Black, J. (1996): Constitutionalising Self-Regulation. The Modern Law Review 59 (1), pp. 24–56

Blaurock, Uwe (ed.) (1999): Grenzen des Wettbewerbsrechts auf deregulierten Märkten: Tagungsband Graz 1997. Baden-Baden: Nomos

Bleisteiner, Stephan (1999): Rechtliche Verantwortlichkeit im Internet – unter besonderer Berücksichtigung des Teledienstegesetzes und des Mediendienste-Staatsvertrags. Köln/München [et al.]: Heymann

Bock, Matthias (1996): Neue Medien im Bildungswesen – Erfahrungen mit Regulierung und Selbstkontrolle in den USA. Gütersloh: Bertelsmann

Bonin, Andreas von/Oliver Köster (1997): Internet im Lichte neuer Gesetze. Zeitschrift für Urheber- und Medienrecht, 41, pp. 82 passim

Bowden, C./Y. Akdeniz (1999): Cryptography and Democracy: Dilemmas of Freedom. In: Liberty (ed.): Liberating Cyberspace: Civil Liberties, Human Rights, and the Internet. London: Pluto Press, pp. 81–125

Branscomb, Anne W. (ed.) (1998): Emerging Law in the Electronic Frontier. London: Hampton Press

Branscomb, Anne W. (1994): Who Owns Information? New York, NY: Basic Books

Brisch, Klaus M. (1998): Gemeinsame Rahmenbedingungen für elektronische Signaturen: Richtlinienvorschläge der Europäischen Kommission. Computer und Recht, 14 (8), pp. 492–499

Bruno, Bonnie/Joel Comm (1997): Internet Family Fun: The Parent's Guide to Safe Surfing. San Francisco: No Starch Press

Bücking, Jens (1999): Namens- und Kennzeichenrecht im Internet (Domainrecht). Stuttgart [et al.]: Kohlhammer

Büllesbach, Alfred (ed.) (1997): Datenschutz im Telekommunikationsrecht. Deregulierung und Datensicherheit in Europa. Cologne: O. Schmidt

Bullinger, Martin/Ernst-Joachim Mestmäcker (1997): Multimediadienste. Struktur und Aufgaben nach deutschem und europäischem Recht. Baden-Baden: Nomos

Bulmer, Simon (1994): The Governance of the European Union: A New Institutionalist Approach. Journal of Public Policy, 4, pp. 351 passim

Bundesamt für Verfassungsschutz (1998): Rechtsextremistische Bestrebungen im Internet. Köln: Bundesamt für Verfassungsschutz/ Presse- und Öffentlichkeitsarbeit

Bundesprüfstelle für Jugendgefährdende Schriften (1998): Neue Medien – neue Gefahren?! Köln [et al.]: Böhlau

Burk, Dan L. Burk (1996): Federalism In Cyberspace. Conn. Law Review, 28, pp. 1095–1134

Burton, John (1997): The Competitive Order or Ordered Competition? The 'UK Model' of Utility Regulation in Theory and Practice. Public Administration, 75 (2), pp. 157–188

Calvert, Clay (1998): Regulating Cyberspace: Metaphor, Rhetoric, Reality, and the Framing of Legal Options. Comm/Ent., 20 (3), pp. 541–566

Campbell, Penny (1998): Bausteine der Informationsgesellschaft in Europa: die Entwicklung der europäischen Politik zur Förderung der Informationsgesellschaft. Düsseldorf: Europäisches Medien-institut

Carter, T. Barton/Marc A., Franklin/Jay B. Wright, (1996): The First Amendment and the Fifth Estate: Regulation of Electronic Mass Media. Westbury, NY: Foundation Press (4 ed)

Castells, Manuel (1996): The Information Age: Economy, Society and Culture. Vol. I: The Rise of the Network Society. Malden/Mass: Blackwell Publishers

Castells, Manuel (1997): The Information Age: Economy, Society and Culture. Vol. II: The Power of Identity, 1997. Malden/Mass: Blackwell Publishers

Castells, Manuel (1998): The Information Age: Economy, Society and Culture. Vol. III: End of Millennium, 1998. Malden/Mass: Blackwell Publishers

Cavazos; Edward A./Gavino Morin (1994): Cyberspace and the Law: Your Rights and Duties in the On-line World. Cambridge, Mass.: MIT

Chomsky, Noam (1999): The Umbrella of U.S. Power: The Universal Declaration of Human Rights and the Contradictions of U.S. Policy. New York: Seven Stories Press

Cleaver, Cathleen A. (1997): Cyberchaos V. Ordered Liberty: Protecting Children from Pornography on the Internet. Texan Review Law & Pol., 61 (1)

Cohen, Barbara (1996): A Proposed Regime for Copyright Protec-tion on the Internet. Brook J. International Law., 22, pp. 401 passim

Cooter, Robert D. Cooter (1994): Decentralized Law for a Complex Economy. SW. Univ. Law Rev., 23, pp. 443 passim

Cornils, Karin (1999): Der Begehungsort von Äußerungsdelikten im Internet. Juristenzeitung, 54 (8), pp. 394–398

Cragom, Patrick G. (1997): Fundamental Rights on the Infobahn: Regulating the Delivery of Internet Related Services Within the European Union. Hastings International & Comp. Law Review, 20, pp. 467–471

Crawford, Henry E. (1997): Calling: FCC Jurisdiction over Internet Telephony. CommLaw Conspectus, 43 (5)

Creech, Kenneth C. (1999): Electronic Media Law and Regulation. Boston: Focal Press (3 ed)

Cunningham, Neil/Peter Grabosky/Darren Sinclair (1998): Smart Regulation. Designing Environmental Policy. Oxford: Clarendon Press

Dammann, Ulrich/Spiros Simitis (1997): EG – Datenschutzrichtlinie. Kommentar. Baden Baden: Nomos 1997

Deas, Susanne (1998): Jazzing up the Copyright Act? Resolving the Uncertainties of the United States Anti-bootlegging Law. Comm/ Ent., 20 (3), 1998, pp. 567–640

Debatin, Bernhard (1998): Ethik und Internet. Überlegungen zur normativen Problematik von hochvernetzter Computerkommunikation. In: Beatrice Dernbach/Anna Maria Theis-Berglmair/ Manfred Rühl (eds.): Publizistik im vernetzten Zeitalter. Opladen: Westdeutscher Verlag, pp. 207–221

Der Hamburgische Datenbeauftragte (1997): Datenschutz bei Multimedia und Kommunikation. Hamburg

Derksen, Roland (1997): Strafrechtliche Verantwortung für in internationalen Computernetzen verbreitete Daten mit strafbarem Inhalt. Neue juristische Wochenschrift, 50 (29), pp. 1878–1885

Derieux, Emmanuel (1998): France: Les journalistes défendent leur droit d'auteur pour Internet. Media Lex, 4, pp. 195–196

Deutscher Bundestag (1998): Bürger und Staat in der Informationsgesellschaft. Enquête-Kommission "Zukunft der Medien in Wirtschaft und Gesellschaft – Deutschlands Weg in die Informationsgesellschaft." Bonn: Zeitungsverl.-Service

Deutscher Bundestag (1998): Kinder- und Jugendschutz im Multimediazeitalter. Enquête-Kommission "Zukunft der Medien in Wirtschaft und Gesellschaft – Deutschlands Weg in die Informationsgesellschaft." Bonn: Zeitungsverl.-Service

Deutscher Bundestag (1997): Meinungsfreiheit – Meinungsvielfalt –

Wettbewerb: Rundfunkbegriff und Regulierungsbedarf bei den neuen Medien. Enquête-Kommission "Zukunft der Medien in Wirtschaft und Gesellschaft – Deutschlands Weg in die Informationsgesellschaft." Bonn: Zeitungsverl.-Service

Deutscher Bundestag (1997): Zur Ökonomie der Informationsgesellschaft: Perspektiven – Prognosen – Visionen. Enquête-Kommission "Zukunft der Medien in Wirtschaft und Gesellschaft – Deutschlands Weg in die Informationsgesellschaft." Bonn: Zeitungsverl.-Service

Dibbell, Julian (1996): A Rape in Cyberspace; or How an Evil Clown, a Haitian Trickster Spirit, Two Wizards, And a Cast of Dozens Turned a Database Into a Society. In: Peter Ludlow (ed.): High Noon on the Electronic Frontier: Conceptual Issues in Cyberspace, pp. 375 passim

Dietz, Ingo Marco/Michael Richter (1998): Netzzugänge unter Internet Service Providern. Computer und Recht, 14 (9), pp. 528–535

Dirks, Karin (1999): Von der Theorie zur Praxis: Grenzkonflikte im Jugendmedienschutz. Baden-Baden: Nomos

Dittler, Ulrich (1997): Computerspiele und Jugendschutz. Neue Anforderungen durch Computerspiele und Internet. Baden-Baden: Nomos

Dombrow, Jennifer (1998): Electronic Communications and Law: Help or Hindrance to Telecommuting? Federal Communications Law Journal, 50 (3), pp. 685–710

Donges, Patrick/Otfried Jarren/Heribert Schatz (eds.) (1999): Globalisierung der Medien? Medienpolitik in der Informationsgesellschaft. Opladen: Westdeutscher Verlag

Doyle, C. (1997): Self-Regulation and Statutory Regulation. Business Strategy Review 8 (3), pp. 35–42

Drucker, Susan J./Gary Gumpert (eds.) (1998): Real Law @ Virtual Space. Communication Regulation In Cyberspace. London: Hampton Press

Du Castel, François (1995): Autoroutes de l'information et société de communication. Réseaux, 71, pp. 107–116

Dutton, William H. (1996): Network Rules Of Order: Regulating Speech In Public Electronic Fora. Media, Culture & Society, 18 (2), pp. 269–290

Dyson, Esther (1998): Design for Living in the Digital Age. New York: Broadway Bodes

Edwards, Lilian (1997): Law and the Internet. Regulating Cyberspace. Oxford: Hart

Egan, Patrick T. (1996): Virtual Community Standards: Should Obscenity Law Recognize the Contemporary Community Standard of Cyberspace? Suffolk U. L. Rev., 30, pp. 117 passim

Eisel, Stephan (ed.) (1998): Internet und Politik. Sankt Augustin: Konrad-Adenauer-Stiftung

Electronic Privacy Information Center (ed.) (1999): Privacy and Human Rights. An International Survey of Privacy Laws and Developments. Washington/DC: EPIC

Elkin-Koren, Niva (1996): Cyberlaw and Social Change: A Democratic Approach to Copyright Law in Cyberspace. Cardozo Arts & Ent LJ, 14, pp. 215 passim

Engel, Christoph (1998): Die Vorschriften des Telekommunikationsgesetzes über den Zugang zu wesentlichen Leistungen: eine juristisch-ökonomische Untersuchung. Baden-Baden: Nomos

Engel, Christoph (1996): Inhaltskontrolle im Internet. AfP – Zeitschrift für Medien- und Kommunikationsrecht, 27 (3), pp. 220–227

Engel-Flechsig, Stefan/Frithjof A. Maennel (1997): Das neue Informations- und Kommunikationsdienste-Gesetz. Neue juristische Wochenschrift, 50 (45), pp. 2981–2992

Engels, Stefan (1998): Das neue Recht der Telekommunikation und der Medien: ein Kurzüberblick über die Novellierungen 1996 und 1997. Regelungen des Telekommunikationsgesetzes, des Informations- und Kommunikationsdienste-Gesetzes, des Mediendien-

ste-Staatsvertrages und des Dritten Rundfunkänderungsstaats-
vertrages. Hamburg: Hans-Bredow-Institut

Entmann, Robert (1996): The Communication Devolution: Federal,
State, And Local Relations In Telecommunications Competititon
And Regulation. Washington: Aspen Institute

Epstein, Keith J./Bill Tancer (1997): Enforcement of Use Limitations
By Internet Services Providers: "How To Stop That Hacker,
Cracker, Spammer, Spoofer, Flamer, Bomber," Comm/Ent L.J.,
9, pp. 661–676

Ernst, Stefan (1998): Rechtsprobleme im Internet: urherber-, wett-
bewerbs- und markenrechtliche Sicht: Eine Nachlese zur DGRI-
Jahrestagung 1998. Kommunikation & Recht, 1 (11), pp. 536–
541

Ernst, Stefan (1997): Internet und Recht. Juristische Schulung, 37
(9), pp. 776–782

Europäisches Medien- und Telekommunikationsrecht (1998): Text-
sammlung. Baden-Baden: Nomos

European Commission (1998): Globalisation and the Information
Society. The Need for Strengthened International Co-ordination.
COM(98) 50 final, 4 February

European Commission (1997): Green Paper on Convergence of the
Telecommunications. Media and Information Technology Sectors, and the Implications for Regulation. Towards an Information Society Approach. COM (97) 623 final, Brussels, 3 December

European Parliament Report on the Communications from the
Commission (1998): Green Paper on Convergence of the Telecommunications. Media and Information Technology Sectors,
and the Implications for Regulation (COM (97) 0623 – C4 –
0664/97), Committee on Economic and Regional Affairs and
Industrial Policy, Rapporteur: Reino Paasilinna, A4 – 0328/98,
24 September

Feintuck, Mike (1999): Media Regulation, Public Interest and the
Law. Edinburgh: Edinburgh University Press

Ferguson, Karl (1998): World Information Flows and the Impact of New Technology. Is There a Need for International Communications Policy and Regulation? Social Science and Computer Review 16 (3), pp. 252–267

Filk, Christian (1998): Online, Internet und Digitalkultur. Bibliographie zur jüngsten Diskussion um die Informationsgesellschaft. Rundfunk und Geschichte, 24, pp. 287–296

Finke, Thorsten (1998): Die strafrechtiche Verantwortung von Internet-Providern. Tübingen: Medienverlag Köhler (MVK)

Fischer, Stefan/Achim Steinacker/Reinhard Bertram/Ralf Steinmetz (1998): Open Security. Berlin: Springer

Flatz, Christian (ed.) (1998): Rassismus im virtuellen Raum. Berlin/Hamburg: Argument

Flechsig, Norbert P. (1996): Haftung von Online-Dienstanbietern im Internet. AfP – Zeitschrift für Medien- und Kommunikationsrecht, 27 (4), pp. 333–346

Flichy, Patrice (1995): Dynamics of Modern Communication: the Shaping and Impact of New Communication Technologies. London/Thousand Oaks: Sage

Foerstel, Herbert N. (1998): Banned in the Media: a Reference Guide to Censorship in the Press, Motion Pictures, Broadcasting and the Internet. Westport: Greenwood Press

Foerstel, Herbert N. (1997): Free Expression and Censorship in America. Westport: Greenwood Press

Freedman, Des (1996): Political Consensus on the Information Superhighway. Communications, 21 (3), pp. 273–280

Freund, Wolfgang (1998): Die Strafbarkeit von Internetdelikten. Eine Analyse am Beispiel pornographischer Inhalte. Wien: WUV

Fries, Cornelia/Franz Büllingen (1998): Offener Zugang privater Nutzer zum Internet: Konzepte und regulatorische Implikationen unter Berücksichtigung ausländischer Erfahrungen. Bad Honnef: WIK

Furchert, Dirk/Monika Haller/Lambert Müller/Michael Huber (1998): Konflikte, Krisen und Kommunikationschancen in der Mediengesellschaft. Berlin: Vistas

Garnham, Nicholas (1996): EC Convergence Task Force Report. Telecommunications and Audiovisual Convergence: Regulatory Issues. The Computer Law and Security Report, 12, pp. 284–287

Gates, Bill (1995): The Road Ahead. New York: Viking

Gelman, Robert M./Stanton McCandlish (1998): Protecting Yourself Online: The Definitive Resource on Safety, Freedom & Privacy in Cyberspace – An Electronic Frontier Foundation Guide. New York: Harper Edge

Gershon, Richard A. (1997): The Transnational Media Corporation. Mahwah, NJ: Erlbaum

Gibbons, Llewellyn J./Joseph Gibbons (1997): No Regulation, Government Regulation, or Self-Regulation: Social Enforcement or Social Contracting for Governance in Cyberspace. Cornell Journal of Law and Public Policy, 6, p. 475 passim

Gillett, S. E./M. Kapor (1997): The Self-Governing Internet: Coordination by Design. In: B. Kahin & J. H. Keller (eds.): Coordinating the Internet. Cambridge: MIT Press, pp. 3–38

Glassner, Barry (1999): The Culture of Fear: Why Americans Are Afraid of the Wrong Things. New York: Basic Books

Godwin, Mike (1998): Cyber Rights. Defending Free Speech in the Digital Age. New York: Times Books

Goldberg, David/Anthony Prosser/Stefaan Verhulst (eds.) (1998): Regulating the Changing Media: A Comparative Study. Oxford: Clarendon Press

Goldring, John (1998): Netting the Cybershark: Consumer Protection, Cyberspace, the Nation-State, and Democracy. In: Brian Kahin/Charles Nesson (eds.): Borders in Cyberspace. Information Policy and the Global Information Infrastructure. Cambridge/Mass. [et al.]: MIT Press (2 ed.), pp. 322 passim

Gounalakis, Georgios/Lars Rhode (1998): Das Informationsdienste-Gesetz: ein Jahr im Rückblick. Rechtsrahmen für die Informationsgesellschaft. Kommunikation und Recht, 1 (8), pp. 321–331

Gottardo, David A. (1997): Commercialism and the Downfall of Internet Self-Governance: an Application of Antitrust Law. Marshall J. Computer & Info L., 16, pp. 125–132

Graack, Cornelius (1997): Telekommunikationswirtschaft in der Europäischen Union. Innovationsdynamik, Regulierungspolitik und Internationalisierungsprozesse. Heidelberg: Physica

Grewlich, Klaus W. (1997): Konflikt und Ordnung in der globalen Kommunikation. Wettstreit der Staaten und Wettbewerb der Unternehmen. Baden-Baden: Nomos

Gringras, Clive (1997): The Laws of the Internet. London [et al.]: Butterworths

Gruhler, Alexander K.A. (1998): Ein staatsfreier Raum: Freie Informationsbeschaffung und Zensur im Internet. Internationale PoPolitik und Gesellschaft, 3, pp. 310–323

Gruhler, Alexander K.A. (1998): Zensur im Internet. Der weltweite Kampf gegen unliebsame Internetinhalte. Bertelsmann-Briefe 139, pp. 40–41

Gruhler, Alexander K.A. (1998): Das Ende der "totalen" Freiheit im Internet? Die Auswirkungen inkriminierter Inhalte auf die Informationsgesellschaft. Marburg: Tectum

Haenens, Leen d'/M. Alvarez (1998): Media Dynamics & Regulatory Concerns in the Digital Age. Berlin: Quintessenz

Hadley, Michael (1998): The Gertz Doctrine and Internet Defamation, Va. L. Rev., 84 (11), pp. 477–478

Halvey, John K. (1996): The Virtual Marketplace. Emory Law Journal, 45, pp. 959 passim

Hamelink, Cees J. (1994): The Politics of World Communication. London [et al.]: Sage

Hamm, Ingrid/Jens Waltermann (eds.) (1999):Kommunikationsord

nung 2000 – Innovation und Verantwortung in der Informationsgesellschaft. Band 2: Dokumentation zu Symposium und Festakt.
Carl Bertelsmann-Preis 1998, Gütersloh: Bertelsmann Foundation

Hamm, Ingrid/Jens Waltermann (eds.) (1998): Communications
2000 – Innovation and Responsibility in the Information Society
Vol. 1: The Research. Carl Bertelsmann-Prize 1998. Gütersloh:
Bertelsmann Foundation

Hamm, Ingrid (ed.) (1996): Verantwortung im freien Medienmarkt.
Internationale Perspektiven zur Wahrung professioneller Standards. Gütersloh: Bertelsmann Foundation

Hammond, Allen S. (1998): The Telecommunications Act of 1996:
Codifying the Digital Divide. Federal Communications Law
Journal, 50 (1), pp. 179–214

Härting, Niko (1999): Internetrecht. Cologne: O. Schmidt

Hasebrink, Uwe (1998): Jugendmedienschutz im internationalen
Vergleich. Media Perspektiven, 9, pp. 454–462

Hein, Werner J. (1998): Haftung für fremde Inhalte im Internet nach
US-amerikanischem Recht. Multimedia und Recht, 1 (11), pp.
627–630

Held, Thorsten/Wolfgang Schulz (1998): Überblick über die Gesetz-
gebung für elektronische Medien von 1994 bis 1998: Aufbau auf
bestehenden Regelungsstrukturen. Rundfunk und Fernsehen, 47
(1), pp. 78–117

Heretakis, Emmanuel (1998): Regulation in the Electronic Media
Scene. AfP – Zeitschrift für Medien- und Kommunikationsrecht,
29 (4), pp. 34

Herman, Ed/Robert Waterman McChesney/Edward S. Herman
(1998): The Global Media: The New Missionaries of Global
Capitalism (Media Studies). London: Cassell Academic

Herzog, Roman (1996): Remarks on the Communication Society of
the Future. Communications, 21 (3), pp. 291–296

Hillebrand, Annette (1997): Sicherheit im Internet zwischen Selbstorganisation und Regulierung. Eine Analyse unter Berücksichtigung von Ergebnissen einer Online-Umfrage. Bad Honnef: WIK

Hinner, Kajetan (1996): Gesellschaftliche Auswirkungen moderner Kommunikationstechnologien am Beispiel des Internet. Berlin: Logos

Hoeflich, Joachim R. (1996): Technisch vermittelte interpersonelle Kommunikation. Grundlagen, organisatorische Verwendung, Konstitution "elektronischer Gemeinschaften." Opladen: Westdeutscher Verlag

Hoeren, Thomas (ed.) (1999): Rechtsfragen der Informationsgesellschaft. Berlin: Schmidt

Hoeren, Thomas (1998): Internet und Recht – neue Paradigmen des Informationsrechts. Neue juristische Wochenschrift, 39, pp. 2849–2854

Hoeren, Thomas (1998): Rechtsoasen im Internet: eine erste Einführung. Multimedia und Recht, 1 (6), pp. 297–298

Hoffmann, Ute (1997): Panic Usenet. Netzkommunikation in (Un-) Ordnung. WZB Discussion Paper FS II. Berlin: Wissenschaftszentrum, pp. 97–106

Hoffmann-Riem, Wolfgang (1998): Informationelle Selbstbestimmung in der Informationsgesellschaft. Auf dem Wege zu einem neuen Konzept des Datenschutzes. Archiv des öffentlichen Rechts, 123 (1998), pp. 513–540

Hoffmann-Riem, Wolfgang (1996): Regulating Media. The Licensing and Supervision of Broadcasting in Six Countries. New York: Guildford Press

Hoffmann-Riem, Wolfgang (1995): Multimedia-Politik vor neuen Herausforderungen. Rundfunk und Fernsehen 43 (2), pp. 125–138

Hoffmann-Riem, Wolfgang/Heide Simonis (eds.) (1995): Chancen, Risiken und Regelungsbedarf im Übergang zum Multimedia-Zeitalter. Kiel: Landesregierung

Holmes, David (ed.) (1997): Virtual Politics: Identity and Community in Cyberspace. London: Sage

Holloway, N. (1996): Caught in the Net: U.S. Sanctions Debate Moves to Cyberspace. Far Eastern Economic Review, 159 (28), pp. 28 passim

Holznagel, Bernd (1996): Regulierungsprobleme bei Online-Diensten und im Internet. Zeitschrift für Urheber- und Medienrecht, 40 (11), pp. 864–866

Holznagel, Bernd/Stefan Poth/Christoph Werthmann (eds.) (1998): Datenschutz und Multimedia. Münster: Lit

Huber, P. (1997): Law and Disorder in Cyberspace: Abolish the FCC and Let Common Law Rule the Telecoms. New York: Oxford University Press

Hudson, Heather E. (1997): Global Connections. International Telecommunications Infrastructure and Policy. New York [et al.]: Van Nostrand Reinhold

Hulsink, Willem (1999): Privatisation and Liberalisation in European Telecommunications: Comparing Britain, the Netherlands, and France. London [et al.]: Routledge

Humpert, Christian (1999): Die Regulierungsbehörde im britischen Telekommunikationsrecht. Münster: Lit

Hurley, Deborah/Brian Kahin/Hal Varian (eds.) (1999): Internet Publishing and Beyond: The Economics of Digital Information and Intellectual Property. Cambridge: MIT Press

Internationale Gesellschaft für Urheberrecht (1998): Der Schutz von Kultur und geistigem Eigentum in der Informationsgesellschaft. Baden-Baden: Nomos

Jarass, Hans (1998): Rundfunkbegriff im Zeitalter des Internet: zum Anwendungsbereich der Rundfunkfreiheit, des Rundfunkstaatsvertrags und des Mediendienste-Staatsvertrags. AfP – Zeitschrift für Medien- und Kommunikationsrecht. 29 (1), pp. 133–141

Jarren, Otfried (1999): Medienregulierung in der Informationsgesellschaft?. Über die Möglichkeiten zur Ausgestaltung der zukünftigen Medienordnung. Publizistik 44 (2), pp. 149–154

Jarren, Otfried (1998): Internet – neue Chancen für die politische

Kommunikation? Aus Politik und Zeitgeschichte, B 40, pp. 13 passim

Jochum, Manfred/Norbert Bolz (eds.) (1998): Recht, Moral und Datenhighway. Vienna: Manz

Johnson, David R./David G. Post (1996): Law And Borders – The Rise of Law in Cyberspace. Stanf. Law Rev., 48, pp. 1367 passim

Johnson, Dawn L. (1996): It's 1996: Do You Know Where Your Cyberkids Are? Captive Audiences and Content Regulation on the Internet. Marshall J. Computer & Info. L., 15, pp. 51 passim

Jones, S. G. (ed.): (1998). Cybersociety 2.0: Revisiting Computer-mediated Communication and Community. Thousand Oaks [et al.]: Sage

Jones, S. G. (ed.): (1997). Virtual Culture: Identity and Communication in Cybersociety. London [et al.]: Sage

ITU (International Telecommunication Union) (1997): Regulatory Implication of Telecommunication Convergence. Chair's Report of the Six Regulatory Colloquium 11–13 December 1996. Geneva: ITU

Kahin, Brian/Charles Nesson (eds.) (1998): Borders in Cyberspace. Information Policy and the Global Information Infrastructure. Cambridge/Mass. [et al.]: MIT Press (2 ed.)

Kahin, Brian/James Keller (eds.) (1997): Coordinating the Internet. Cambridge/Mass. [et al.]: MIT Press

Kahn, Alfred E. (1995): Déréglement des services publics: problèmes de transition et solutions. Réseaux, 72–73, pp. 19–36

Kay, Jason (1995): Sexuality, Live Without a Net: Regulating Obscenity and Indecency on the Global Network. South Cal. Interdisciplinary Law Journal, 4, pp. 355–386

Kennedy, Charles H. (1996): An Introduction to International Telecommunications Law. New York: Artech House

Kienle, Michael (1998): Internationales Strafrecht und Straftaten im Internet: zum Erfordernis der Einschränkung des Ubiquitätsprinzips des § 9 Abs. 1 Var. 3 StGB. Konstanz: Hartung-Gorre

472

Kiessling, Thomas (1998): Optimale Marktstukturregulierung in der Telekommunikation. Lehren aus den USA und anderen Ländern für die EU. Baden-Baden: Nomos

Kizza, Joseph Migga (1998): Civilizing the Internet. Global Concerns and Efforts toward Regulation. Jefferson, NC [et al.]: McFarland

Kleinsteuber, Hans (ed.) (1996): Der "Information Superhighway." Amerikanische Visionen und Erfahrungen, Opladen: Westdeutscher

Klett, Alexander (1998): Urheberrecht im Internet aus deutscher und amerikanischer Sicht. Baden-Baden: Nomos

Knauth, Michael (1998): Chancengleicher Zugang zur Informationsgesellschaft: eine Studie zur Politik der Europäischen Union im Bereich digitaler Informations- und Kommunikationstechnologien. Düsseldorf : Europäisches Medieninstitut (2 ed.)

Knieps, Günter: Zugang zu Netzen: Verselbständigung, Nutzung, Eigentumsschutz. Multimedia und Recht, 1 (6), pp. 275–280

Knoche, Manfred (1999): Zum Verhältnis von Medienpolitik und Medienökonomie in der globalen Informationsgesellschaft. In: Patrick Donges/Otfried Jarren/Heribert Schatz (eds.): Globalisierung der Medien? Medienpolitik in der Informationsgesellschaft. Opladen: Westdeutscher, pp. 89–106

Knoll, Amy (1996): Any Which Way but Loose: Nations Regulate the Internet.Tul. J. International & Comp. Law, 4, pp. 275 passim

Köhntopp, Kristian/Maritt Köhntopp (1988): Sperrung im Internet. Eine systematische Aufarbeitung der Zensurdiskussion: technische Hintergründe. Kommunikation und Recht, 1 (10), pp. 417–421

König, Christian (1998): Regulierungsoptionen für die Neuen Medien in Deutschland. Multimedia und Recht, 1 (12), pp. 1–16

König, Christian/Ernst Röder (1998): Plädoyer zur Überwindung der zersplitterten Aufsicht über neue Informations- und Kommunikationsmedien. Kommunikation und Recht, 1 (10), pp. 417–421

König, Klaus/Angelika Benz (eds.) (1997): Privatisierung und staatliche Regulierung. Bahn, Post, Telekommunikation und Rundfunk. Baden-Baden: Nomos

Kreile, Reinhold (1996): Bericht über die WIPO-Sitzungen zum möglichen Protokoll zur Berner Konvention und zum "Neuen Instrument" vom 1. – 9.2.1996. Zeitschrift für Urheber- und Medienrecht 40 (7), pp. 564–573

Kreile, Reinhold (1996): Bericht über die WIPO-Sitzungen zum möglichen Protokoll zur Berner Konvention und zum "Neuen Instrument" vom 22. – 24.5.1996. Zeitschrift für Urheber- und Medienrecht 40 (12), pp. 964–966

Kress, Carl B. (1997): The 1996 Telekommunikationsgesetz and the Telecommunication Act of 1996: toward More Competitive Markets in Telecommunications in Germany and the United States. Federal Communication Law Journal, 49 (3), pp. 551–619

Kressin, Roger (1998): Neue Medien zwischen Rundfunk- und Individualkommunikation. Frankfurt: Lang

Kubicek, Herbert/William H. Dutton/Robin Williams (eds.) (1997): The Shaping of Information Superhighways: European and American Roads to the Information Society. Frankfurt/New York: Campus/St. Martin's Press

Kushner, David (1996): The Communications Decency Act and the Indecent Indecency Spectacle. Comm/Ent. 19 (1), pp. 87–131

Kusserow, R. P. (1996): The Government Needs Computer Matching to Root Out Waste and Fraud. In: R. Kling (ed.): Computerization and Controversy. San Diego, CA: Academic Press, pp. 652–658 (2 ed.)

Ladeur, Karl-Heinz (1998): Regulierung nach dem TKG. Kommunikation & Recht, 1 (11), pp. 479–486

Ladeur, Karl-Heinz (1997): Die Regulierung von Multimedia als

Herausforderung des Rechts: Zur rechtlichen Ordnung komplexer Märkte. AfP – Zeitschrift für Medien- und Kommunikationsrecht, 28 (3), pp. 598–605

Laffont, Jean-Jacques (1995): Sur l'éconnomie politique de la règlementation. Réseaux, 72–73, pp. 11–18

Laga, Gerhard (1998): Rechtsprobleme im Internet, Vienna: Wirtschaftskammer Österreich

Lahrmann, Markus (1998): Virtuelle Wächter: Jugendschutz im Internet funktioniert nicht mit herkömmlichen Mitteln: Eine gesellschaftliche Debatte ist an der Zeit. Communicatio Socialis, 31 (3), pp. 283–295

Lang, Brian/Bill Wilson (1999): A Christian Parent's Guide to Making the Internet Family Friendly. Nashville/Tenn.: T. Nelson

Lange, Bernd-Peter (1999): Medienkompetenz im Zeitalter globaler Kommunikation. Wie läßt sich die europäische Informationsgesellschaft politisch gestalten? Bonn: Stiftung Entwicklung und Frieden

Lange, Bernd-Peter/Peter Seeger (eds.) (1997): Technisierung und Medien. Strukturwandel und Gestaltungsperspektiven, Baden-Baden: Nomos

Lange, Knut Werner (1998): Das Recht der Netzwerke. Heidelberg: Recht und Wirtschaft

Latzer, Michael (1997): Die Konvergenz von Telekommunikation, Computer und Rundfunk. Opladen: Westdeutscher Verlag

Lee, Thomas L./Preeti Sharma (1998): The Internot? Understanding the Problem of Internet Congestion. Journal of Media Economics. 11 (1), pp. 13–31

Leer, Anne C. (1997): It's a Wired World: the New Network Economy. Oslo: Scandinavian University Press

Leggewie, Claus/Christa Maar (eds.) (1998): Internet & Politik. Von der Zuschauer- zur Beteiligungsdemokratie. Köln: Bollmann

Lehmann, Michael (ed.) (1997): Internet und Multimediarecht (Cyberlaw). Stuttgart: Schäfer-Poeschel

Lessig, Lawrence (1996): Reading the Constitution in Cyberspace. Emory Law Journal, 45, pp. 869 passim

Lessig, Lawrence (1999): Code and Other Laws of Cyberspace. New York: Basic Books

Liberty Compaign (ed.) (1999): Liberating Cyberspace. Civil Liberties, Human Rights and the Internet. London: Pluto Press

Lippard, Jim/Jeff Jacobsen (1995): Scientology v. the Internet. Free Speech & Copyright Infringement on the Information Super-Highway. Skeptic, 3 (3), pp. 35–41

Lipschultz, Jeremy Harris (1996): Broadcast Indecency: F.C.C. Regulation and the First Amendment. Boston: Focal Press

Litan, Robert E./William Niskanen (1998): Going digital! A Guide to Policy in the Digital Age. Washington/D.C.: Brookings Institution Press

Lively, Donald E./Allen S. Hammond/Blake D. Morant/Russel Weaver (1997): Communications Law: Media, Entertainment, and Regulation. Cincinnati, Ohio: Anderson Pub Co.

Loader, Brian A. (ed.) (1997): The Governance of Cyberspace. Politics, Technology and Global Restructuring. London/New York: Routledge

Ludes, Peter (ed.) (1997): Multimedia-Kommunikation. Theorien, Trends und Praxis. Opladen: Westdeutscher Verlag

Mc Adams, Richard H. (1997): The Origin, Development, and Regulation of Norms. Mich. L. Rev., 96, pp. 338 passim

McChesney, Robert W. (1996). The Internet and U.S. Communication Policy-making in Historical and Critical Perspective. Journal of Communication, 46, pp. 98–124

MacKie-Mason, Jeffrey K. (ed.) (1998): Telephony, the Internet, and the Media: Selected Papers from the 1997 Telecommunications Policy Research Conference. Mahwah, NJ [et al.]: Erlbaum

McLaughlin, Margaret L./Kerry K. Osborne/Christine B. Smith (1995): Standards of Conduct on Usenet. In: Steven G. Jones (ed.): Cybersociety. Computer-mediated Communication and Community. Thousand Oaks [et al.]: Sage, pp. 90–111

McGinnis, John O. (1996): The Once and Future Property-Based Vision of the First Amendment. Univ. Chi. Law Review, 63, pp. 49 passim

McKnight, Lee W./Joseph P. Bailey (eds.) (1997): Internet Economics. Cambridge/Mass.: MIT Press

Mecklenburg, Wilhelm (1997): Internetfreiheit. Zeitschrift für Urheber- und Medienrecht, 41 (7), pp. 525–543

Michael, Douglas C. (1995): Federal Agency Use of Audited Self-Regulation as a Regulatory Technique. Admin. L. Rev., 47, pp. 171 passim

Michalis, Maria (1999): European Union Broadcasting and Telecoms. Toward a Convergent Regulatory Regime? European Journal of Communication, 14 (2), pp. 147–172

Messner, Dirk (1997): Netzwerktheorien: Die Suche nach Ursachen und Auswegen aus der Krise staatlicher Steuerungsfähigkeit. In: Elmar Altvater [et al.] (eds.): Vernetzt und Verstrickt. Nicht-Regierungs-Organisationen als gesellschaftliche Produktivkraft. Münster: Westfälisches Dampfboot

Mehta, M. D., & E. Darier (1998). Virtual Control and Disciplining on the Internet: Electronic Governmentality in the New Wired World. The Information Society, 14, pp. 107–116

Metha, Arun (1998): Media Regulation in India. Media Asia, 25 (2), pp. 109–112

Meyerson, Michael I. (1997): Ideas of the Marketplace: a Guide to the 1996 Telecommunications Act. Federal Communication Law Journal, 49 (2), pp. 251–288

Mikat, Claudia (1998): Eine Frage der Weltanschauung: Jugendschutz in Europa. Medien Concret, 1, pp. 27–29

Mohammadi, Ali (ed.) (1997): International Communication and Globalization. London: Sage

Moritz, Hans-Werner (1998): Anmerkungen zum Urteil des AG

München vom 28. Mai 1998. Computer und Recht, 14 (8), pp. 505

Müller-Hengstenberg, Claus D. (1996): Nationale und internationale Rechtsprobleme im Internet. Neue juristische Wochenschrift, 49 (28), pp. 1777–1782

Müller-Terpitz, Ralf (1998): Internet-Telefonie: eine regulatorische Betrachtung. Multimedia und Recht, 1 (1), pp. 65–69

Nahikian, James (1996): Learning To Love "The Ultimate Peripheral" – Virtual Vices Like "Cyberprostitution" Suggest A New Paradigm To Regulate Online Expression. J. Marshall J. Computer & Info. L. 779, 14, pp. 782–783

Neuman, W. Russell/Lee McKnight/Richard Jay Solomon (1997): The Gordian Knot: Political Gridlock on the Information Highway. Cambridge/Mass. [et al.]: MIT Press

Oliver, Charles M. (1998): The Information Superhighway: Trolls at Tollgate. Federal Communications Law Journal, 50 (1), pp. 53–85

Organisation for Economic Co-Operation and Development (1997): Global Information Infrastructure – Global Information Society (GII–GIS). Paris: OECD

Paraschos, Emmanuel E. (1998): Media Regulation in the European Union: National, Transnational und U.S. Perspectives. Ames: Iowa State University Press

Pelz, Christian (1998): Die strafrechtliche Verfolgung von Internet-Providern. Zeitschrift für Urheber- und Medienrecht, 42 (6), pp. 530–534

Penchina, Robert/Christopher Serbagi (1998): Publisher's Electronic Rights: Comfortable Times to Come? Kommunikation und Recht, 1 (1), pp. 23–24

Perritt, Henry H. Jr. (1996): Law and the Information Superhighway. New York: John Wiley & Sons

Pichler, Rufus (1998): Haftung des Host-Providers für Persönlichkeitsrechtsverletzungen vor und nach dem TDG. Multimedia und Recht, 1 (1), pp. 79–87

Polly, Jean Armour (1999): The Internet Kids and Family Yellow Pages. Berkeley: Osborne McGraw-Hill (3 ed.)

Post, Robert C. (ed.) (1998): Censorship and Silencing: Practices of Cultural Regulation. Los Angeles: Getty Research Institute for the History of Art and the Humanities

Post, David G. (1995): Anarchy, State, and the Internet: An Essay on Law-Making in Cyberspace. Journal of Online Law, 3, p. 29

Price, Monroe E. (ed.) (1998): The V-chip Debate: Content Filtering from Television to the Internet. Mahwah/N.J./London: Lawrence Erlbaum

Pridgen, Dee (1997): How Will Consumers Be Protected on the Information Superhighway? Land & Water L. Rev., 32, pp. 237–253

Prosser, Tony (1997): Law and the Regulators. Oxford: Clarendon Press

Rath-Glawatz, Michael/Arhur Waldenberger: Freiwillige Selbstkontrolle Multimedia-Dienstanbieter e.V.: ein Beitrag der Medienwirtschaft zum Jugendschutz im Internet. Computer und Recht, 13 (12), pp. 766–769

Recke, Martin (1998): Medienpolitik im digitalen Zeitalter. Zur Regulierung der Medien und der Telekommunikation in Deutschland. Berlin: Vistas

Rees, J. (1988): Reforming the Workplace. A Study of Self-Regulation in Occupational Safety. Philadelphia: Univ. of Philadelphia Press

Reeves, Harold Smith (1996): Property in Cyberspace. Univ. Chi. Law Review, 63, pp. 761 passim

Reinicke, Wolfgang H. (1998): Global Public Policy. Governing without Government. Washington: Brookings Institution Press

Rheingold, H. (1993): The Virtual Community: Homesteading on the Electronic Frontier. Reading/Mass.: Addison-Wesley Publishing Company

Riemann, Thomas (1997): Künftige Regelungen des grenzüberschreitenden Datenverkehrs. Computer und Recht, 13 (11), pp. 762–766

Riley, Gail Blasser (1998): Censorship. New York: Facts on File

Riley, D. M. (1996): Sex, Fear and Condescension on Campus: Cybercensorship at Carnegie Mellon. In: L. Cherny/E. R. Weise (eds.): Wired Women, Gender and New Realities in Cyberspace. Seattle: Seal Press, pp. 158–168

Ringel, Kurt (1997): Rechtsextremistische Propaganda aus dem Ausland im Internet. Computer und Recht, 13 (5), pp. 302–307

Röger, Ralf (1997): Internet und Verfassungsrecht. Zeitschrift für Rechtspolitik. 30 (5), pp. 203–211

Rogerson, Kenneth S./G. Dale Thoma (1998): Internet Regulation Process Model: the Effect of Societies, Communities, and Governments. Political Communication, 15 (4), pp. 427–444

Rosenau, James N./Ernst-Otto Czempiel (1992): Governance without Government: Order and Change in World Politics. Cambridge: Cambridge University Press

Rosenoer, Jonathan (1997): Cyberlaw: The Law of the Internet. New York [et al.]: Springer

Rosenthal, Daniel (1999): Internet: Schöne neue Welt? Der Report über die unsichtbaren Risiken. Zürich: Orell Füssli

Rosenthal, Michael (1998): Die Kompetenz der Europäischen Gemeinschaft für den rechtlichen Rahmen der Informationsgesellschaft. Berlin: Duncker & Humblot

Roßnagel, Alexander (1997): Ohnmacht des Staates – Selbstschutz der Bürger. Zeitschrift für Rechtspolitik, 30 (1), pp. 26–29

Rotenberg, Marc (ed.) (1999): The Privacy Law Sourcebook 1999: United States Law, International Law, and Recent Developments. Washington/DC: EPIC

Sardar, Ziauddin/Jerome R. Ravetz (eds.) (1996): Cyberfutures – Culture and Politics on the Information Superhighway. London: Pluto Press

Sassen, Saskia (1996): Losing Control? Sovereignty in an Age of Globalization. New York: Columbia University Press

Schäfer, Martin/Clemens Rasch (1998): Zur Verantwortlichkeit von

Online-Diensten und Zugangsvermittlern für fremde urheber-
rechtsverletzende Inhalte. Zeitschrift für Urheber- und Medienrecht, 42 (6), pp. 451–458

Scheja, Katharine (1998): Das Grünbuch der Konvergenz. Computer
und Recht. 14 (6), pp. 358–360

Schlechter, Richard (1998): Sicherheit im Internet: Grundzüge euro-
päischer Rechtspolitik. Kommunikation und Recht, 1 (4), pp.
147–152

Schmidt, Susanne K. (1998): Coordinating Technology: Studies in
the International Standardization of Telecommunications. Cambridge: MIT Press

Schneider, Volker (1999): Staat und technische Kommunikation. Die
politische Entwicklung der Telekommunikation in den USA,
Japan, Großbritannien, Deutschland, Frankreich und Italien. Opladen: Westdeutscher

Schneier, Bruce/David Banisar (eds.) (1997): The Electronic Privacy
Papers: Documents on the Battle of Privacy in the Age of Surveillance. New York: John Wiley & Sons

Schulz, Wolfgang (1998): Jugendschutz bei Tele- und Mediendien-
sten. Multimedia und Recht, 1 (4), pp. 182–187

Schulz, Wolfgang (1998): Gewährleistung kommunikativer Chan-
cengleichheit als Freiheitsverwirklichung. Baden-Baden: Nomos

Schulz, Wolfgang (1996): Jenseits der Meinungsrelevanz – Verfas-
sungsrechtliche Überlegungen zu Ausgestaltung und Gesetzge-
bungskompetenzen bei neuen Kommunikationsformen. Zeitschrift
für Urheber- und Medienrecht, 40 (6), pp. 487–497

Schwarz, Mathias (ed.) (1998): Recht im Internet. Der Rechtsberater
für Online-Anbieter und -Nutzer. Loseblattsammlung, Stand Ja-
nuar 1998. Stadtbergen: Kognos-Verl. Braun

Seaton, Jean (1998): Politics & the Media. Harlots and Prerogatives
at the Turn of the Millennium. Oxford [et al.]: Blackwell

Sefton-Green, Julian (ed.) (1998): Digital Diversions: Youth Culture
in the Age of Multimedia. London: UCL Press

Shade, Leslie Regan (1996): Is There Free Speech on the Net? Censorship in the Global Information Infrastructure. In: Rob Shields (ed.): Cultures of Internet. Virtual Spaces, Real Histories, Living Bodies. London [et al.]: Sage, pp. 11–33

Shapiro, Andrew L. (1999): The Control Revolution: How The Internet is Putting Individuals in Charge and Changing the World We Know. New York: Public Affairs

Sieber, Ulrich (1999): Die rechtliche Verantwortlichkeit im Internet. Grundlagen, Ziele und Auslegung von § 5 TDG und § 5 MDStV. München: Beck

Sieber, Ulrich (1998): Freie Datenkommunikation und Kriminalitätsbekämpfung im Internet. Bertelsmann Briefe 140, pp. 27–30

Sieber, Ulrich (1997): Kontrollmöglichkeiten zur Verhinderung rechtswidriger Inhalte in Computernetzen (I): Zur Umsetzung von §5 TDG am Beispiel der Newsgroups des Internet. Computer und Recht, 13 (10), pp. 581–598

Sieber, Ulrich (1997): Kontrollmöglichkeiten zur Verhinderung rechtswidriger Inhalte in Computernetzen (II): Zur Umsetzung von §5 TDG am Beispiel der Newsgroups des Internet. Computer und Recht, 13 (11), pp. 653–669

Sinclair, D. (1997): Self-Regulation Versus Command and Control? Beyond False Dichotomies. Law & Policy, 19 (4), pp. 529 passim

Sobel, David (1999): Filters and Freedom: Free Speech Perspectives on Internet Content Controls. Washington/DC: EPIC

Spindler, Gerald (1998): Dogmatische Strukturen der Verantwortlichkeit der Diensteanbieter nach TDG und MDStV. Multimedia und Recht, 1 (11), pp. 639–643

Spindler, Gerald (1997): Haftungsrechtliche Grundprobleme der neuen Medien. Neue juristische Wochenschrift, 50 (48), pp. 3193–3199

Spinello, Richard (1997): Case Studies in Information and Computer Ethics. Upper Saddle River, NJ: Prentice Hall

482

Spinner, Helmut F. (1998): Die Architektur der Informationsgesellschaft. Bodenheim: Philo Verlagsgesellschaft

Staiman, Ari (1997): Shielding Internet Users From Undesirable Content: The Advantages of a PICs Based Rating System. Fordham Int'l L.J., 20, pp. 866 passim

Stallings, William (1999): Cryptography and Network Security: Principles and Practice. Upper Saddler River, NJ: Prentice Hall (2 ed.)

Stone, Alan (1997): How America Got Online: Politics, Markets and the Revolution in Telecommunications. New York: Sharpe

Strossen, Nadine (1998): Zensur im Internet? Laßt die Verbraucher entscheiden. Bertelsmann Briefe 140, pp. 24–26

Street, F. Lawrence (1997): Law of the Internet. Charlottesville/Va.: Lexis Law Publ.

Strömer, Tobias H. (1999): Onlinerecht. Rechtsfragen im Internet und in Mailboxen. Heidelberg: dpunkt (2 ed.)

Swire, Peter P./Robert E. Litan (1998): None of Your Business: World Data Flows, Electronic Commerce, and the European Privacy Directive. Washington/D.C.: Brookings Institution Press

Tauss, Jörg (ed.) (1996): Deutschlands Weg in die Informationsgesellschaft: Herausforderungen und Perspektiven. Baden-Baden: Nomos

Tettenborn, Alexander (1998): Europäische Union: Rechtsrahmen für die Informationsgesellschaft. Multimedia und Recht, 1 (1), pp. 18–23

Thompson, Kenneth (ed.) (1997): Media and Cultural Regulation. The Open University. London [et al.]: Sage

Toulouse, Chris (1998): The Politics of Cyberspace: a New Political Science Reader. New York: Routledge

Trudel, Pierre (1998): Droit du cyberspace. Montreal: Les Éditions Thémis

Ukrow, J. (1999): Die Selbstkontrolle im Medienbereich in Europa. Eine rechtsvergleichende Untersuchung. Saarbrücken: EMR

Unesco (1997): World Communication Report. The media and the challenge of the new technologies. Paris: Unesco

Venturelli, Shalini (1998): Liberalizing the European Media: Politics, Regulation and the Public Sphere. Oxford/New York: Clarendon Press

Vogelsang, Waldemar/Linda Steinmetz/Thomas A. Wetzstein (1995): Öffentliche und verborgene Kommunikation in Computernetzen. Dargestellt am Beispiel der Verbreitung rechter Ideologien. Rundfunk und Fernsehen 43 (4), pp. 538–548

Voigt, Rüdiger (1998): Ende der Innenpolitik? Politik und Recht im Zeichen der Globalisierung. Aus Politik und Zeitgeschichte, B 29–30, S. 3 passim

Wacks, R. (1998): Privacy in Cyberspace. In: Peter Birks (ed.): Privacy and Loyalty. Oxford: Clarendon Press, pp. 93–112

Wagner, Michael A. (1998): Technische Konvergenz – rechtliche Ausdifferenzierung. Media Lex, 3, pp. 135–137

Webb, Peter (1997): Media Regulations for New Times. Media Asia, 24 (3), pp. 131–136

Werle, Raymund (1999): Zwischen Selbstorganisation und Steuerung. Geschichte und aktuelle Probleme des Internet. In: Jürgen Wilke (ed.): Massenmedien und Zeitgeschichte. Konstanz: UVK Medien, pp. 499–517

Werle, Raymund/Christa Lang (eds.) (1997): Modell Internet? Entwicklungsperspektiven neuer Kommunikationsnetze. Frankfurt a.M.: Campus

Wilke, Jürgen/Christiane Imhof (eds.) (1996): Multimedia. Voraussetzungen, Anwendungen, Probleme. Berlin: Vistas

Wilske, Stephan/Teresa Schiller (1997): International Jurisdiction in Cyberspace: Which States May Regulate the Internet. Federal Communications Law Journal, 50 (1), pp. 117–125

Wimmer, Norbert/Gerhard Michael (1998): Der Online-Provider im neuen Multimediarecht. Baden-Baden: Nomos

Windthorst, Kay (1998): Regulierungsansätze im deutschen und

US-amerikanischen Telekommunikationsrecht (I). Computer und Recht. 14 (5), pp. 281–285

Windthorst, Kay (1998): Regulierungsansätze im deutschen und US-amerikanischen Telekommunikationsrecht (II). Computer und Recht. 14 (6), pp. 340–345

Wright, R. George (1997): Selling Words: Free Speech in a Commercial Culture. New York/London: New York University Press

Wu, Timothy S. (1997): Cyberspace Sovereignty? – The Internet and the International System, Harvard J. Law & Tec, 10, pp. 647–649

Zielke, Jörn (1997): Meinungsfreiheit im Internet: staatlicher Eingriff und evolutionäre Entwicklung vor dem Hintergrund der US-amerikanischen Erfahrung. Computer und Recht, 13 (5), pp. 313–318

Zelger, Christian (1999): Zensur im Internet: eine Argumentationsanalyse auf Grundlage des Naturrechts und der Menschenrechte. Berlin: Verlag für Wiss. und Forschung, VWF

Zerdick, Axel [et al.] (1999): Die Internet-Ökonomie. Strategien für die digitale Wirtschaft. Berlin [et al.]: Springer

Zimmerling, J./U. Werner (1999): Schutz vor Rechtsproblemen im World Wide Web. Berlin [et al.]: Springer

Zydorek, Christoph (1998): Soziale Steuerung und Koordinatioon in der Telekommunikation. Baden-Baden: Nomos

Sources via Internet

Akdeniz, Yaman (1999): Regulation of Child Pornography on the Internet. Cases and Materials Related to Child Pornography on the Internet. The Journal of Information, Law and Technology, 1. *http://www.cyber-rights.org/reports/child.htm*; visited July 7, 1999

485

Akdeniz, Y./N. Bohm/C. Walker, C. (1999): Internet Privacy: Cy-
ber-Crimes vs Cyber-Rights. Computers & Law, (10) 1. *http://
www.scl.org/members/emagazine/vol10/iss1/vol10-iss1-akdeniz-
bohm-walker-art.htm*; visited July 7, 1999

Akdeniz, Y./N. Bohm/C. Walker, C. (1999): Cyber-Rights &
Cyber-Liberties (UK) Response to the March 1999 DTI Paper:
Building Confidence in Electronic Commerce – A Consultation
Document. The Source Public Management Journal. *http://www.
thesourcepublishing.co.uk/articles/a00227.html*; visited July 7,
1999

Ang, Peng Hwa (1997): How Countries are Regulating Internet
Content. Nanyang Technological University Singapore 1997.
*http://www.isoc.org/isoc/whatis/conferences/inet/97/proceedings/
B1/B1_3.HTM*; visited June 23, 1999

Bangemann, Martin (1997): The Need for an International Charter.
A New World Order for Global Communications. Speech at the
International Telecommunications Union on Sept. 8, 1997 in Geneva. *http://www.ispo.cec.be/infosoc/promo/speech/geneva.html*;
visited June 23, 1999

Beck, Klaus/Gerhard Vowe (1997): Markt, Staat oder Gemeinschaft: Zur Regulierung internationaler computervermittelter
Kommunikation. Telepolis. *http://www.heise.de/tp/*; visited July
7, 1999

Berlandi, Brian (1998): It's Our Way or the Highway: Americans
Ruling Cyberspace – A Look Back at Bad Policy and a Look
Ahead at New Policy, Journal of Technology Law and Policy, 3
(2). *http://journal.law.ufl.edu/~techlaw/3-2/berlandi.html*; visited
July 9, 1999

Bertelsmann-Stiftung (1997): Kommunikationsordnung 2000 –
Grundsatzpapier zu Leitlinien der zukünftigen Kommunikationsordnung. *http://www.stiftung.bertelsmann.de/publika/download/
texte/kom2000d.txt*; visited July 10, 1999

Boyle, James (1997): Foucault in Cyberspace. Surveillance, Sovereignity, and Hard-Wired Censors. *http://www.wcl.american.edu/ pub/faculty/boyle/foucault.htm*; visited July 10, 1999

Cate, Fred H. (1994): Global Information Policymaking and Domestic Law. Indiana Journal of Global Legal Studies, Vol. 1 Iss. 2 Spring 1994; *http://www.law.indiana.edu/glsj/vol1/cate.html*; visited July 10, 1999

Clarke, Roger (1998): Net-Ethiquette Mini Case Studies of Dysfunctional Human Behaviour on the Net. *http://www.anu.edu. au/people/Roger.Clarke/II/Netethiquettecases.html*; visited June 3, 1998

Cryptography (Links); *http://www.uni-siegen.de/security/policies/ export.html*; sowie *http://cwis.kub.nl/~frw/people/koops/lawsurvy. htm*; und *http://www.crypto.de/*; all visited July 10, 1999

Dearing, Mark C. (1999): Personal Jurisdiction and the Internet: Can the Traditional Principles and Landmark Cases Guide the Legal System into the 21st Century? Journal of Technology Law and Policy, 4 (1). *http://journal.law.ufl.edu/~techlaw/4/dearing. html*; visited July 09, 1999

Department of Trade & Industry and Home Office (1999): Review of the Internet Watch Foundation. London: KPMG/Denton Hall. *http://www.kpmgiwf.org/iwfrevu.pdf*; visited July 14, 1999

European Commission Legal Advisory Board (1999): Illegal and Harmful Content on the Internet. Communication to the European Parliament, the Council, the Economic and Social Committee and the Committee of the Regions. May 11, 1999. *http:// www.2.echo.lu/legal/en/internet/commumt.html*; visited July 20, 1999

European Commission (1999): Research and Technological Development Activities of the European Commission. Annual Report 1999 (Com(99)284final/2), Brussels, June 25, 1999. *http://ewopa. en.int/comm/dg12/reports/1999/index_en.html*; visited July 20, 1999

European Commission (1998): Council Recommendation of 24 September 1998 on the Development of the Competitiveness of the European Audiovisual and Information Services Industry by Promoting National Frameworks Aimed at Achieving a Comparable and Effective Level of Protection of Minors and Human Dignity Official Journal, L 270 of July 10.1998, p.48. *http:// europa.eu.int/comm/dg10/avpolicy/new_srv/recom-intro_en.html*; visited July 9, 1999

European Commission (1996): Green Paper on the Protection of Minors and Human Dignity in Audovisual and Information Services, Brussels, 16 October 1996. *http://www2.echo.lu/legal/ en/internet/content/content.html*; visited July 14, 1999

European Commission (1996): Communication to the European Parliament, The Council, The Economic and Social Committee and the Committee of the Regions: Illegal and Harmful Content on the Internet, Com (96) 487, Brussels, 16 October 1996. *http:// www2.echo.lu/legal/en/internet/content/content.html*; visited July 14, 1999

Executive Committee of ISPA – Internet Services Providers Association (1996): R3 Safety-Net Rating Reporting Responsibility For Child Pornography & Illegal Material on the Internet. An Industry proposal. Adopted and Recommended by LINX – London Internet Exchange. The Safety-Net Foundation 23 September 1996. *http://www.dti.gov.uk/safety-net/r3.htm*; visited May 6, 1998

Fair, Ray C. (1997): FAIRMODEL. New Haven, CT. *http://fairmodel .econ.yale.edu*; visited July 10, 1999

Goverment, U. S. (1998). Global Framework for Electronic Commerce. *http://www.ecommerce.gov/danc8.htm*; visited July 7, 1999

Hazlett, Thomas W./David W. Sosa (1998): "Chilling" the Internet? Lessons from FCC Regulation of Radio Broadcasting. Michigan Technology Law Review, 4. *http://www.law.umich.edu/mttlr/ html/volume_four.html*; visited July 7, 1999

Hoeren (1998): Zivilrechtliche Haftung im Internet. Humboldt Forum Recht, 2. *http://www.rewi.hu-berlin.de/ HFR/2-1998/ drucktext.html*; visited July 7, 1999

House of Lords, Select Committee on Science and Technology (1996): "Information Society: Agenda for Action in the UK," Session 1995-96, 5th Report, London: HMSO, 23 July 1996. *http://www.parliament.the-stationery-office.co.uk/pa/ld199596/ ldselect/inforsoc/inforsoc.htm*; visited July 14, 1999

Jacobs, Jeffrey A. (1996): Comparing Regulatory Models – Self-Regulation vs. Government Regulation: The Contrast Between the Regulation of Motion Pictures and Broadcasting May Have Implications for Internet Regulation. Journal of Technology Law and Policy, 1 (1); *http://journal.law.ufl.edu/~techlaw/1/jacobs.html*; visited July 9, 1999

Johnson, David R./David G Post (1996a): Law and Borders. The Rise of Law in Cyberspace. Stan. L. Rev., 48, pp. 1367 passim. *http://www.cli.org/X0025_LBFIN.html*; visited July 9, 1999

Johnson, David R./David G. Post (1996b): And How Shall the Net Be Governed? A Meditation on the Relative Virtues of Decentralized, Emergent Law. Draft. *http://www.cli.org/emdraft.html*; visited July 9, 1999

Journal of Computer-Mediated Communication (1996): Emerging law on the electronic frontier – Part 1 of a Special Issue (ed. By Anne W. Branscomb). 2 (1). *http://jcmc.huji.ac.il/vol2/issue1/*; visited July 7, 1999

Journal of Computer-Mediated Communication (1996): Emerging law on the electronic frontier – Part 2 of a Special Issue (ed. By Anne W. Branscomb). 2 (2). *http://jcmc.huji.ac.il/vol2/issue2/*: visited July 9, 1999

Kahin, Brian/James H. Keller (1997): Coordinating the Internet. *http://www.ksg.harvard.edu/iip/cai/cisupp.html*; visited July 7, 1999

Larson, Alexander (1996): Resale Issues In Telecommunications

Regulation: An Economic Perspective. *http://www.mttlr.org/ voltwo/larson.html*; visited July 9, 1999

Lessig, Lawrence (1997): Tyranny in the Cyberspace: The CDA was bad – but PICS may be worse. Cyber Rights, 5 (7). *http:// wired.com/wired/5.07/cyber_rights.html*; visited July 7, 1999

Lutterbeck, Bernd with Kei Ishii (1998): Internet Governance – ein neues Regulierungskonzept oder alter Wein in neuen Schläuchen? *http://ig.cs.tu-berlin.de/bl/035/*; visited June 23, 1999

Mayer-Schönberger, Viktor/Teree E. Fost (1997): A Regulatory Web: Free Speech and the Global Information Infrastructure. Michigan Technology Law Review, 3. *http://www.law.umich. edu/mttlr/html/volume_three.html*; visited July 9, 1999

Mefford, Aron (1998): Lex Informatica: Foundations of Law on the Internet. Updated June 98. *http://www.law.indiana.edu/glsj/vol5/ n01/mefford.html*; visited July 9, 1999

Menthe, Darrel (1998): Jurisdiction in Cyberspace: A Theory of International Spaces. Michigan Technology Law Review, 4. *http:// www.law.umich.edu/mttlr/html/volume_four.html*; visited July 9, 1999

Moore, Nick (1998): Rights and Responsibilities in an Information Society. Journal of Information, Law and Technology, 1. *http:// elj.warwick.ac.uk/jilt/infosoc/98_1moor*; visited July 7, 1999

National Conference of State Legislatures (1998): The Internet and Electronic Commerce. *http://www.usic.org/ncsl02.htm*; visited June 19, 1999

Post, David G./David R. Johnson (1998): The New Civic Virtue of the Net: Lessons from Models of Complex Systems for the Governance of Cyberspace. Firstmonday, 3 (1). *http://www. firstmonday.dk/issues/issue3_1/johnson/index.html*; visited July 9, 1999

Resnick, Paul (1997-98): PICS, Censorship, & Intellectual Freedom: FAQ. Updated January 1998. *http://www.si.umich.edu/ ~presnick/pics/intfree/FAQ.htm*: visited July 9, 1999

Siegele, Ludwig (1998): Verfassungsvater des Cyberspace. Die US-Regierung will das Internet durch Selbstkontrolle regulieren – hinter der Idee steckt Clintons Berater Ira Magaziner. Die Zeit, 34. *http://www.archiv.zeit.de/daten/pages//199834.magaziner.neu_. html:* visited July 9, 1999

Swire, Peter P. (1998): Markets, Self-Regulation, and Government Enforcement in the Protection of Personal Information. *http://www.osu.edu/units/law/swire.htm;* visited May 3 1998

Swire, Peter P. (1998): Of Elephants, Mice, and Privacy: International Choice of Law and the Internet (Draft submitted to International Lawyer, with endnotes August 23, 1998); *http://www.osu.edu/units/law/swire.htm;* visited July 14, 1999

United Nations High Commissioner for Human Rights (ed.) (1997): Seminar on the Role of Internet with Regard to the Provisions of the International Convention on the Elimination of all Forms of Racial Discrimination, Nov. 10–14, 1997. *http://193.135.156. 15/html/menu2/10/c/racism/semIRD.htm;* visited July 9, 1999

Weinberg, Jonathan (1997): Rating The Net. Comm/Ent 19, pp. 453 passim. *http://www.msen.com/~weinberg/rating.htm;* visited May 3, 1998

Some relevant Websites
(with many further links and downloads)

http://www.aclu.org/issues/cyber/hmcl.html; [American Civil Liberties Union] visited July 12, 1999

http://www.americancomm.org; [American Communication Association] visited July 12, 1999

http://www.benton.org; [Benton Foundation] visited July 12, 1999

http://www.childnet-int.org; [Childnet International] visited July 12, 1999 *http://www.cybertelecom.org/index.html;* [Internet Telecom Project – Cybertelecom] visited July 12, 1999

http://www.cdt.org [Center for Democracy and Technology]; visited July 20, 1999

http://www.dmmv.de; [Deutscher Multimedia Verband] visited July 12, 1999

http://www2.echo.lu/legal/; [Information Market Europe – European Commission Legal Advisory Board]; visited July 12, 1999

http://www.eff.org; [Electonic Frontier Foundation] visited July 12, 1999

http://www.eimf.org; [European Interactive Media Federation] visited July 12, 1999

http://www.epic.org; [Electronic Privacy Information Center] visited July 13, 1999

http://www.epn.org; [Electronic Policy Network] visited July 12, 1999

http://www.euroispa.org; [Pan-European Association of the Internet Services Providers Associations of the Countries of the European Union] visited July 13, 1999

http://www.fsm.de; [Freiwillige Selbstkontrolle Multimedia Dienstanbieter e.V.] visited July 12, 1999

http://www.ftc.org; [US-Federal Trade Commission] visited July 13, 1999

http://www.geocities.com/CapitolHill/Senate/1879; visited July 12, 1999

http://www.gilc.org; [Global Internet Liberty Campaign] visited July 12, 1999

http://www.hfac.uh.edu/media_libel; [University of Houston School of Communication] visited July 12, 1999

http://www.hatewatch.org; visited July 12, 1999

http://www.iana.org; [Internet Assigned Numbers Authority] visited July 12, 1999

http://www.icann.org; [Internet Corporation for Assigned Names and Numbers] visited July 12, 1999 *http://www.icra.org*; [Internet Content Rating Association] visited July 20, 1999

http://www.ifea.org; [Internet Free Expression Alliance] visited July 12, 1999

http://www.ifex.org; [International Freedom of Expression Exchange Clearing House] visited July 12, 1999

http://www.iitf.nist.gov/eleccomm/ecomm.htm; [Information Infrastructure Task Force – US Gov.] visited July 12, 1999

http://www.ilpf.org/selfreg/selfreg.htm; [Internet Law & Policy Forum] visited July 12, 1999

http://www.intern.de; [Internet intern] visited July 12, 1999

http://www.incore.org; [Internet Content Rating for Europe] visited July 20, 1999

http://www.iwf.org.uk; [Internet Watch Foundation] visited July 14, 1999

http://www.isoc.org; [Internet Society] visited July 12, 1999

http://www.ispo.cec.be/Convergencegp/lab.html; [Information Society Promotion Office of EC]. visited July 07, 1999

http://www.law.cornell.edu/jol; [Journal of Online Law] visited July 12, 1999

http://www.libertysearch.com/Free_Speech; visited July 12, 1999

http://www2.medienrat.de/bda/int/medienrat; [Deutscher Internet Medienrat] visited July 12, 1999

http://www.meldpunt.org; [Internet Meldpunt Kinderpornographie, NL] visited July 12, 1999

http://www.ntia.doc.gov/ntiahome/privwhitepaper.html; [PRIVACY AND THE NII: Safeguarding Telecommunications Related Personal Information]visited July 12, 1999

http://www.online.de/home/rodenberg/zensur/index.html; visited July 12, 1999

http://www.perkinscoie.com/cgi-bin/folioisa.dll/netcase.nfo? [U.S. Court Cases Related to the Internet; Updated Weekly] visited July 12, 1999 *http://www.rsac.org*/homepage.asp; [Recreational Software Advisory Council on the Internet] visited July 12, 1999

http://www.stiftung.bertelsmann.de/internetcontent/index.html; visited July 12, 1999

http://www.whitehouse.gov/WH/New/Commerce/; [White House, Framework for Global Electronic Commerce] visited July 12, 1999

http://www.wipo.org; [World Intellectual Property Organisation] visited July 12, 1999

http://www.w3.org/PICS/; [World Wide Web Consortium – Platform for Internet Content Selection] visited July 12, 1999

The Authors

Jack M. Balkin is Knight Professor of Constitutional Law and the First Amendment at Yale Law School. He teaches and writes in the areas of constitutional law (with a special emphasis on the law of freedom of speech), torts, jurisprudence, telecommunications and cyberspace law, multiculturalism, social theory, and the theory of ideology. Professor Balkin received his A.B. and J.D. degrees from Harvard University and his Ph.D in philosophy from Cambridge University. He served as a clerk for Judge Carolyn D. King of the United States Court of Appeals for the Fifth Circuit and practiced as an attorney at Cravath, Swaine, and Moore in New York City before entering the legal academy. Professor Balkin has taught at several law schools in the United States and been a visiting professor at the Buchman Faculty of Law at Tel Aviv University and Queen Mary and Westfield College at the University of London. He is the founder and director of Yale's Information Society Project, a center devoted to the study of law and the new information technologies.

- Cultural Software: A Theory of Ideology. New Haven: Yale University Press 1998.
- Media Filters, The V-Chip and the Foundations of Broadcast Regulation. 45 Duke L. J. 1133 (1996).
- Some Realism about Pluralism: Legal Realist Approaches to the First Amendment. 1990 Duke L. J. 375.

Herbert Burkert studied history, political science and law at the University of Cologne and at University College Dublin; PhD in law from the University Frankfurt am Main; Habilitation University St. Gallen. Senior Information Law & Policy Adviser, GMD German National Research Center for Information Technology, St.Augustin, Germany; Chairman, Legal Advisory Board, European Commission, DG XIII-A; Member of the Senior Experts' Group Info 2000, European Commission; teaches public law, information and communication law at the University of St. Gallen. Member of the committee accompanying the program "Diplôme en droit et gestion des technologies de l'information et de la communication (DGTIC)" Department of Law, Facultés Universitaires Notre-Dame de la Paix, Namur, Belgium; Member IFIP Working Group 9.2 (Social Accountability) and member of the editorial board of various international journals.

- Privacy Enhancing Technologies: Typpology, Critique, Vision. In: Philip E. Agre/Marc Rotenberg (eds): Technology and Privacy: The New Landscape. Cambridge: MIT-Press 1997, pp. 125–142.
- Involving the Citizens: The Normative Model of the "Information and Communication Citizen." In: Herbert Kubicek/William H. Dutton/Robin Williams (eds.): The Social Shaping of Information Superhighways. Frankfurt, New York 1997, pp. 211–220.

- Wieviel Information gebührt dem Bürger – Freedom of Information? In: Herbert Kubicek et al. (eds.): Jahrbuch Telekommunikation und Gesellschaft. Vol. 3. Heidelberg 1998, pp. 301–309.

Renate Köcher is the managing director of the Allensbach institute for opinion research. She studied political economics, journalism and sociology in Mainz and Munich. For her Ph.D. thesis, she worked on the subject of professional ethics of German and British journalists. She began her career at the Allensbach institute in 1977 as a researcher; in 1988 she became the managing director. In her research she puts particular emphasis on issues such as the acceptance of new technologies, financial research, election research and comparative analyses of former East and West Germany. Dr. Köcher writes periodically for the Frankfurter Allgemeine Zeitung. She is a member of the Future Commission of Baden-Württemberg and of the board of the Academy for Political Education, Tutzing.

Marcel Machill is the Bertelsmann Foundation's Director Media Policy. After studying journalism in Paris, France (M.A.) and media policy and media economics in Dortmund, Germany (Ph.D.), he spent two years as a McCloy Scholar in Cambridge, USA, at Harvard University. There, at the John F. Kennedy School of Government, he received a Masters Degree in Public Administration (MPA). Dr. Machill has published several books and articles on media policy and journalism culture. He served as an editor and consultant for Euronews-Television in Lyon, France, and for Radio France International in Paris. He also worked as a journalist for the Public Service Broadcasting in Germany (WDR, Deutsche Welle), for the German Television Studio in Washington, D.C., as well as for newspapers such as Die Zeit and Frankfurter Rundschau. Dr. Machill has been a

497

research fellow at the "Laboratoire Communication et Politique" of the Centre National de la Recherche Scientifique in Paris and a lecturer in media policy and European journalism at the "Journalism Institute" at the University of Dortmund.

- Frankreich Quotenreich. Nationale Medienpolitik und Europäische Kommunikationspolitik im Kontext nationaler Identität. Berlin: Vistas 1997. [France as Realm of Quotas. National Media Policy and European Communications Policy in the Context of National Identity]
- Journalistische Kultur. Rahmenbedingungen im internationalen Vergleich (ed.). Wiesbaden: Westdeutscher Verlag 1997. [Journalistic Culture. International Comparison of Settings for Journalism]
- Transatlantik. Transfer von Politik, Wirtschaft und Kultur (ed. with S. Lorenz). Wiesbaden: Westdeutscher Verlag 1999. [Transatlantic. Transfer of Politics, Economics and Culture]

Ira C. Magaziner is currently President of SJS, Inc., a business strategy consulting and investment firm. Ira C. Magaziner served as Senior Advisor to the President of the United States for Policy Development from January 1993 to December 1998. From December 1995 to December 1998, Mr. Magaziner coordinated the US Government's strategy on electronic commerce and the emerging digital economy. He supervised the development of the President's strategy paper "A Framework for Global Electronic Commerce" released in July 1997, and coordinated the interagency team to implement the strategy. This effort led to a declaration signed by 132 nations to refrain from imposing customs duties on electronic commerce; agreements supporting a market-driven approach to electronic commerce with the European Union, Japan, Australia and other nations; a law to put a three-year moratorium on new and discriminatory taxes on

498

electronic commerce; an international treaty to protect intellectual property on-line; legislation making it possible to conduct official transactions electronically; funds to challenge the nation's research community to develop the next generation Internet; a law to protect the privacy of children on-line; an effort among companies representing a large share of the Internet traffic to set privacy guidelines for the Internet; a privatization of the Internet's domain name and routing systems; and initiatives to improve the security and reliability of cyberspace.

Beth Simone Noveck is Director of International Programs of the Yale Law School Project on the Information Society and a lead expert of the initiative. She also practices telecommunications and information technologies law at the firm of Duane, Morris & Heckscher LLP in New York City. Dr. Noveck has published and lectured in the United States and Europe on legal affairs and technology in the international information society. Her research interests include comparative constitutional and regulatory issues in telecom, Internet and media law with special emphasis on free speech, privacy and democratic political theory. A graduate of Harvard University and Yale Law School, she pursued graduate work at the University of Oxford and holds a doctorate from the University of Innsbruck. Dr. Noveck is an editor of the book series, *Facetten der Medien* (Haupt Verlag) and of the *International Journal of Communications Law and Policy*. Dr. Noveck is a member of the Committee on Telecommunications Law and International Telecommunications Law Subcommittee of the Association of the Bar of the City of New York.

- The End of Sovereignty, The End of Privacy (Beth Noveck, ed., Bern: Haupt Verlag, forthcoming 2000).
- Transparency, Law & Technology: Reinvigorating Deliberative

Democracy in the Information Society. In: Catherine Kratz (ed.): Cultural Values. London: Blackwell 1999.
- Digital Television, Analogue Regulation: The Future of European Public Interest Regulation. In: Chris Marsden (ed.): Convergence in European Digital Television Regulation. London: Blackstone Press 1999.

Monroe E. Price, Professor of Law, Cardozo School of Law and co-director, Programme in Comparative Media Law and Policy, University of Oxford. Studied at Yale College, 1960, Yale Law School, 1964. Was law clerk to Associate Justice Potter Stewart, United States Supreme Court and professor of law at UCLA.

- Television, Public Sphere and National Identity. Oxford: OUP 1995.
- The V-Chip Debate: Content Filtering from Television to the Internet (ed.). Mahway, New Jersey: LEA Associates 1998.
- Cable Television and Non-Broadcast Video. New York: Boardman 1986. (Treatise, with Daniel Brenner and Michael Meyerson).

Kermit Roosevelt received a A.B. summa cum laude in philosophy from Harvard University in 1993, where he was elected to Phi Beta Kappa in his junior year. A 1997 graduate of the Yale Law School, he clerked for Judge Stephen F. Williams on the Court of Appeals for the D.C. Circuit before joining the Information Society Project as Resident Fellow in 1998–1999. He is currently clerking for Justice David H. Souter of the United States Supreme Court. He is also a member of the Human Rights Advisory Board of Harvard's Kennedy School of Government. His publications have appeared in a number of law reviews, including the Yale Law Journal, the Michigan Law Review, the Connecticut Law Review, and the Yale Journal on Regulation

Otto Schily is Federal Minister of the Interior of Germany since October 1998. He studied law in Munich, Hamburg and Berlin. As co-founder of the party "DIE GRÜNEN" he was – with interruptions – a member of the German Parliament from 1983 to 1989. In 1989 Schily joined the Social Democratic Party and has been a member of the German Parliament since 1990. He was a member of the Economics Committee, and the Committee for Environment, for Nature Conservation and Reactor Safety. From October 1993 to December 1994 Schily chaired the "Treuhand" Inquiry Committee of the Federal Government. After the Federal parliamentary Elections in 1994 he was deputy chairman of the Social Democratic party's parliamentary group and coordinated its interior and legal policy committee. Schily was also a member of the Election Committee for Constitutional Judges.

Ulrich Sieber, Professor of law, head of the department of criminal law, information law and legal informatics at the University of Munich; President of the German Association for European Criminal Law. He studied law at the Universities of Tübingen, Lausanne and Freiburg; from 1978 to 1987 he was a practising attorney and research fellow at the University of Freiburg; from 1987 to 1991, he was professor at the University of Bayreuth and from 1991 to 2000 professor at the University of Würzburg. In addition, he has been a visiting professor at the University of Tokyo (1994), a personal special advisor to two EC-Commissioners, and a legal consultant for various companies, German and foreign government posts and other international organizations (e.g. European Union, Council of Europe, OECD, UN). He is editor of the European book series "ius informationis" and "ius criminale" as well as co-editor of the series "ius europaeum" and the periodical "Multimedia und Recht."

- Verantwortlichkeit im Internet – Technische Grundlagen und medienrechtliche Regelungen. Munich: C.H. Beck 1999.
- Kinderpornographie, Jugendschutz und Verantwortlichkeit von Internet-Providern. Bonn 1999 (ed. by the German Ministry of Justice).
- Multimedia-Strafrecht. In: Hoeren/Sieber (eds.): Handbuch des Multimedia-Rechts. Munich: C.H. Beck 1999.

Stefaan G. Verhulst, co-director of the Programme in Comparative Media Law and Policy (http://pcmlp.socleg.ox.ac.uk) at the University of Oxford. He studied film production in Brussels, political and social sciences and communications sciences at the University of Ghent (Belgium). He was a lecturer on communications law and policy issues in Belgium before becoming founder and co-director of the International Media and info-comms Policy and Law studies at the School of Law, University of Glasgow. He has served and serves as consultant and researcher for numerous organisations including the Council of Europe, European Commission and Unesco. He became recently Chairholder – together with Monroe Price – of the Unesco Chair in Communications Law. He is also the UK legal correspondent for the European Audiovisual Observatory and founder and co-editor of the International Journal of Communications Law and Policy.

- Regulating the Changing Media. Oxford: OUP 1998.
- EC Media Law and Policy. London: AWL 1998 (together with D. Goldberg and T. Prosser).
- Broadcasting Reform in India. New Delhi: OUP 1998 (together with Monroe Price).

502

Jens Waltermann has been the Deputy Head of the Media Division of the Bertelsmann Foundation, Germany, until April 2000. He completed his law degree (Ass. iur.) at the Goethe-Universität Frankfurt/Main and studied international law at the Université de Genève. After working in commercial litigation and arbitration with the international law firm Baker and McKenzie in Frankfurt, Berlin and Sydney he spent two years from 1995 to 1997 as a McCloy Scholar at the Kennedy School of Government, Harvard University, where he received a Master in Public Administration (MPA). He is admitted to practice as an attorney in Frankfurt/Main. Jens Waltermann joined the Bertelsmann Foundation in 1997 as Director of Media Policy. He currently serves as Chairman of the Board of the Internet Content Rating Association (ICRA).

- Public Television in America. Gütersloh: Bertelsmann Foundation Publishers 1998 (ed. with Eli M. Noam).
- Communications 2000 – Innovation and Responsibility in the Information Society. Gütersloh: Bertelsmann Foundation Publishers 1998 (ed. with Ingrid Hamm).

Appendix

Appendix I

The lead experts prepared reports on four aspects of Internet content self-regulation, which were then discussed by the expert network. The Memorandum (Chapter I), written by the Bertelsmann Foundation, is based on the lead experts' reports and the discussions of the expert network. Needless to say, not every expert agreed with every point of the document. We nevertheless strived for an adequate representation of the rich and complex discussions.

Lead experts

Jack Balkin
> Knight Professor of Constitutional Law and the First Amendment; Director, Project on the Information Society, Yale Law School, New Haven, USA

Beth Simone Noveck
Director of International Programs, Project on the Information Society, Yale Law School, New Haven, USA

Herbert Burkert
Professor for Media and Information Law, University of St. Gallen, Switzerland

Monroe E. Price
Founder and Co-director of the Programme in Comparative Media Law and Policy, University of Oxford, Great Britain; Danciger Professor of Law, Benjamin N. Cardozo School of Law, Yeshiva University, New York, USA

Stefaan Verhulst
Co-director, Programme in Comparative Media Law and Policy (PCMLP), Centre for Socio Legal Studies, Wolfson College, University of Oxford, Great Britain

Ulrich Sieber
Professor and Head of the Chair for Criminal Law, Criminal Procedural Law, Information Law and Legal Informatics, University of Würzburg, Germany

Expert network[*]

Peng Hwa Ang
Associate Professor and Vice Dean, School of Communication Studies, Nanyang Technological University, Singapore

[*] As of September 1999.

Zoë Baird
President, John and Mary R. Markle Foundation, New York, USA

Stephen Balkam
Executive Director, Internet Content Rating Association (ICRA), Brighton, Great Britain

Albert Bischeltsrieder
Detective Director, Bavarian Criminal Investigation Department, Munich, Germany

Rainer Bührer
INTERPOL, Specialized Officer, Economic Crime Branch, Financial Crime Sub-division, Lyon, France

Josef Dietl
Head of Member Relations, W3C Worldwide, Sophia Antipolis, France

Rüdiger Dossow
Directorate of Human Rights, Media Section, Council of Europe, Strasbourg, France

Esther Dyson
Chairman, EDventure Holdings, New York, USA

Clare Gilbert
Vice President, General Counsel, AOL Europe, London, Great Britain

Gareth Grainger
> Deputy Chairman, Australian Broadcasting Authority (ABA), Sydney, Australia

Jo Groebel
> Director General, European Institute for Media, Düsseldorf, Germany

Ingrid Hamm
> Head, Media Division, Bertelsmann Foundation, Gütersloh, Germany

Marie-Thérèse Huppertz
> Microsoft Europe, European Affairs Office, Bruxelles

Ekkehart Kappler
> Head, IT-Crime Unit, Federal Bureau of Criminal Investigation, Wiesbaden, Germany

David Kerr
> Chief Executive, Internet Watch Ltd., Cambridge, Great Britain; Secretary General, Internet Content Rating Association (ICRA), London, Great Britain

Henner Kirchner
> Center for European and Middle East Studies, Federal Armed Forces University, Hamburg, Germany; Editor, Middle East Press Digest, Perleberg, Germany

Akio Kokubu
> Executive Director, Electronic Network Consortium, Tokyo, Japan

Ling Pek Ling
Director, Policy and Planning, Singapore Broadcasting Authority, Singapore

Marcel Machill
Director Media Policy, Bertelsmann Foundation, Gütersloh, Germany

Ira Magaziner
President, sjs Inc., Boston, USA

Elke Monssen-Engberding
Chair, Federal Media Examination Board for the Protection of Children from Illegal and Harmful Content, Bonn, Germany

Eli M. Noam
Director, Columbia Institute for Tele-Information, Columbia University, Columbia Business School, New York, USA

John B. Rabun
Vice President and CEO, National Center for Missing and Exploited Children, Arlington, USA

Jim Reynolds
Former Head of the Paedophilia Unit, New Scotland Yard, International Paedophilia Consultant, London, Great Britain

Michael Schneider
Chairman, Electronic Commerce Forum (eco e.V.), Hennef, Germany

Nadine Strossen
  President, American Civil Liberties Union (ACLU); Professor of Law, New York Law School, New York, USA

Richard Swetenham
  Directorate General XIII – E2 Telecommunications, Information Market and Exploration of Research, Luxembourg

Jens Waltermann
  Deputy Head, Media Division, Bertelsmann Foundation, Gütersloh, Germany

Nigel Williams
  Director, Childnet International; Founder INHOPE-Forum, London, Great Britain

Ted Woodhead
  Director, New Media and International Affairs, Canadian Radio-television and Telecommunications Commission (CRTC), Hull, Canada